MILITANT GROUPS IN SOUTH ASIA

MILITANT GROUPS IN SOUTH ASIA

Surinder Kumar Sharma
Anshuman Behera

idsa
INSTITUTE FOR DEFENCE STUDIES & ANALYSES
NEW DELHI

PENTAGON PRESS

Militant Groups in South Asia
Surinder Kumar Sharma and Anshuman Behera

First Published in 2014

ISBN 978-81-8274-754-8

Published by
PENTAGON PRESS
206, Peacock Lane, Shahpur Jat,
New Delhi-110049
Phones: 011-64706243, 26491568
Telefax: 011-26490600
email: rajan@pentagonpress.in
website: www.pentagonpress.in

In association with
Institute for Defence Studies and Analyses
No. 1, Development Enclave,
New Delhi-110010
Phone: +91-11-26717983
Website: www.idsa.in

Printed at Avantika Printers Private Limited.

Contents

II. Northeast India

III. Left-wing Extremism

IV. Islamist Groups

Part-C
PAKISTAN

Part-D
SOUTH ASIA

Foreword

South Asia has been witnessing proliferation of militant groups of all kinds for last several decades. These militant groups defy national frontiers and often indulge in acts of violence, which have both regional and international ramifications. While some of these groups operate within the territorial limits of one particular country, many of them have international linkages and are transnational in character. They can be divided into different categories on the basis of their ideological orientation as well as their socio-political and economic objectives. Their basic aim however remains the same, i.e., to paralyse the existing state structure and achieve their aim through violent means. Sri Lanka is perhaps the only state which has succeeded in its efforts to eliminate a highly motivated militant group in the region, whereas most of the other countries have been victims of violence directed against them by militant groups of one kind or other and have found it difficult to deal with them. Some of them have weathered heavy armed operations against them—waged by both national armies and international forces—and still managed to survive with new leadership and recruits. In some cases, they have changed their names, habitat, operational styles, and linkages and confused the security forces, making their tasks even more challenging.

There is thus a need to undertake an updated account of the militant groups operating in South Asia from time to time. This particular project initiated by Institute for Defence Studies and Analyses (IDSA) aims at collating information about important militant groups operating in the region. The Institute had undertaken a similar study in 2003 focussing on the militant groups operating in Jammu and Kashmir (J&K). The outcome of the study was published in the form of a book entitled "Jihadis in Jammu and Kashmir: A Portrait Gallery" subsequently. A need, therefore, was felt to update information on several of these groups and also widen the scope of the study to go beyond J&K and cover other important militant groups operating in the entire region and gather detailed information on their genesis, ideology, objectives, cadre strength, training, alliance, areas of operation, leadership, funding sources, weapons they use, their links with other militant groups and current status, etc. The study excludes militant groups, which are either dormant or inactive for a long time.

I commend the efforts of Shri S K Sharma and Dr Anshuman Behera to gather information and process them efficiently for use by wider academic and strategic community. They have collected their data mostly from open sources, taken adequate care to cross-check different data-sources and cull out the most reliable information on the groups they have included in this volume. Their work was duly refereed by two anonymous experts and revised in light of their comments. This study, as it obtains now, is quite comprehensive and provides a detailed profiling of important militant groups in South Asia. It is hoped that the efforts will be appreciated by the readers.

Arvind Gupta
Director General

Acknowledgements

We have been associated with this book project for quite some time. We have received help from a number of individuals for successful completion of this project. We owe a debt of gratitude to those individuals without whose help and contribution this book project could not have been completed.

First and foremost, we record our debt to Dr. Arvind Gupta, Director General, IDSA, for conceiving the idea of this project and for his constant support, comments and suggestions to improvise upon the book. He has been an important source of inspiration and motivation to complete this project. We sincerely owe our gratitude to him.

We take this Opportunity to thank Dr. Ashok Behuria, Research Fellow, IDSA, for his patient supervision of this project. His constant guidance, comments and suggestions has enriched the content of the book. Without his support this book project would not have been complete.

We also thank Brig. (Retd) Rumel Dahiya, Deputy Director General, IDSA and Group Captain Hemlata Lohani, Assistant Director, IDSA, for their support and help.

Few research scholars, experts in various fields, extended their unconditional academic support whenever they were requested to do so. We would like to take few names: Dr. Pushpita Das, Associate Fellow and Centre coordinator of Internal Security Centre, IDSA, Dr. Namrata Goswami, Research fellow, IDSA, Dr. P.V. Ramana, Research Fellow, IDSA, Dr. Smruti Pattanaik, Research Fellow IDSA and Dr. Wilson John, Senior Fellow, ORF. We thank all these scholars for their support and expert suggestions.

Few friends have been source of encouragement for completion of this project. They include Dr. Prashant Pradhan, Associate Fellow, IDSA, Mr. Saurabh Mishra, Researcher, IDSA and Mr. Prashant Hosur, Research Scholar at Indiana University, USA. We also thank Ms. Husanjot Chahal for her help in proof-reading the book.

This book would not have been same without critical and constructive comments from the reviewers. We thank the reviewers for their critical analysis and reviews.

The Library staffs of IDSA have been very helpful in pulling out literature for this project. We would like to thank all the Library Staff for the help they have extended. A special word of thanks to Mr. Mukesh Kumar Jha in this regard.

The maps given in this book are designed with active support of Mr. Vivek Dhankar and Ms. Asha Mallik. We thank them for patiently designing and redesigning the maps for this book.

Our special gratitude for Mr. Vivek Kaushik, Associate Editor, IDSA, for taking care of the editing and production process of the book. We also thank the copy editor who has done a good job in editing the manuscript.

Last but not the least, the right atmosphere was created at our homes and for this we thank Mrs. Kaumudi Sharma and Dr. Nibedita Priyadarshini Jena for their unconditional support. Without their encouragement and support this book could not have been successfully completed with ease.

List of Abbreviations

AHAB	Ahle Hadith Andolan Bangladesh
AJYCP	Asom Jatiyabadi Yuva Chhatra Parishad
AL	Awami League
APHC	All Party Hurriyat Conference
APLA	Assam People' Liberation Army
AQ	Al Qaeda
AQAP	Al Qaeda in Arabian Peninsula
AQIM	Al Qaeda in Islamic Magherb
ASWJ	Ahle-Sunnat-Wal-Jamaat
AuM	Al Umar Mujahideen
BdSF	Bodo Security Force
BLT	Bodo Liberation Tigers
BNP	Bangladesh Nationalist Party
CAVOW	Committee against violence against Women
CC	Central Committee
CCOMPOSA	Co-ordination Committee of Maoist Parties and Organisations in South Asia
CIA	Central Intelligence Agency
CMAS	Chasi Mulia Adivasi Sangha
CMIT	Central Military Instructors Team
CPI-M	Communist Party of India-Maoist
CRPF	Central Reserve Police Force
CTC	Central Technical Committee
DHD	Dima Halam Daogah
DSU	Democratic Students Union
FATA	Federally Administered Tribal Areas
FICN	Fake Indian currency notes
GHQ	General Headquarters

HM	Hizb-ul-Mujahideen
HuA	Harkat-ul-Ansar
HuJI	Harkat-ul-Jihad-al-Islami
HuJI-B	Harkat-ul-Jihad-al-Islami-Bangladesh
HuM	Harkat-ul-Mujahideen
HuT	Hizb-ut-Tahrir
IBRF	Indo-Burma Revolutionary Front
ICS	Islamic Chhatra Shibir
IDP	Islamic Democratic Party
IEDs	Improvised Explosive Devices
IM	Indian Mujahideen
IMU	Islamic Movement of Uzbekistan
IOJ	Islamic Oikyo Jote
ISI	Inter Services Intelligence
JAA	Jama'atul Ansar Afghani
JeI	Jamaat-e-Islami
JeM	Jaish-e-Mohammad
JKLF	Kashmir Liberation Front
JMB	Jamaat-ul-Mujahideen Bangladesh
JMJB	Jagrata Muslim Janata Bangladesh
JuD	Jamaat-ud-Dawa
JUI(F)	Jamiat Ulema-e-Islam - Fazlur Rahman
KCP	Kangleipak Communist Party
KFD	Karnataka Forum of Dignity
KIA	Kachin Independence Army
KNF	Kuki National Front
KP	Khyber Pakhtunkhwa
KYKL	Kanglei Yawol Kanna Lup
LeI	Lashkar-e-Islam
LeJ	Lashkar-e-Jhangvi
LeO	Lashkar-e-Omar
LeT	Lashkar-e-Taiba
LTTE	Liberation Tigers of Tamil Eelam
LWE	Leftwing Extremism
MASS	Manab Adhikar Sangram Samiti

MCCI	Maoist Communist Centre of India
MJC	Muttahida Jihad Council
MPA	Manipur People's Army
MPLF	Manipur People's Liberation Front
MQM	Muttahida Quami Movement
MULFA	Muslim United Liberation Front of Assam
MULTA	Muslim United Liberation Tigers of Assam
NATO	North Atlantic Treaty Organisation
NDFB	National Democratic Front of Bodoland
NIA	National Investigation Agency
NLFT	National Liberation Front of Tripura
NNC	Naga National Council
NSCN-IM	National Socialist Council of Nagalim-Isak-Muivah
NSCN-K	National Socialist Council of Nagalim-Khaplang
PAN	People's Army of Nagaland
PB	Politburo
PBCP	Purbo Banglar Communist Party
PCPA	People's Committee against Police Atrocities
PDFI	People's Democratic Front of India
PFI	Popular Front of India
PLA	People's Liberation Army
PLGA	People's Liberation Guerilla Army
PML(N)	Pakistan Muslim League (Nawaz)
PoK	Pakistan Occupied Kashmir
POTA	Prevention of Terrorism Act
PREPAK	People's Revolutionary Party of Kangleipak
PSS	Peoples Security Service
PWG	People's War Group
RDF	Revolutionary Democratic Front
RIM	Revolutionary Internationalist Movement
RPF	Revolutionary People's Front
RSO	Rohingya Solidarity Organisation
SGPC	Salafist Group for Preaching and Combat
SIMI	Students Islamic Movement of India
SMP	Sipah-e-Mohammad

SSP	Sipah-e-Sahaba Pakistan
ST	Sunni Tehrik
SUF	Strategic United Front
TCOC	Tactical Counter-offensive Campaign
TeJ	Tehrik-e-Jihad
TJP	Tehrik-e-Jafariya
TNSM	Tehrik-e-Nifaz-e-Shariat-Mohammadi
TRAM	Technical Research and Arms Manufacturing
TTP	Tehrik-e-Taliban Pakistan
TuF	Tactical United Front
TuM	Tehrik-ul-Mujahideen
UAPA	Unlawful Activities Prevention Act
UCPN-M	Unified Communist Party of Nepal-Maoist
UJC	United Jihad Council
ULFA	United Liberation Front of Asom
UNLF	United National Liberation Front

1
Introduction

South Asia has been home to terror outfits of all kinds, often called 'Militant Groups', for a long time. It is natural, therefore, that it has become the principal theatre of the war on terror at the international level. It is quite distressing to note that during the last more than 12 years of prolonged efforts (since 9/11) to root out terror in the region, the international community has clearly developed a sense of fatigue, while the terror outfits have proliferated and grown from strength to strength. The decision of the United States (US) to talk to the Taliban before final withdrawal of its forces clearly indicates that the forces of terror are back in the reckoning in the region.

To say that the rise of the militant groups has challenged not only the security of various states but also the international security system, will be hardly any exaggeration. These outfits not only pose serious challenge to the peace and security of a state but also adversely affect the state-building process and relations with other nations. The number of the militant groups has been on a constant rise. According to a database, there are more than 200 militant groups in the South Asia region alone.[1]

While the phenomenon of terror has come to stay, the states in the region are not expected to surrender tamely. It is true that the legitimate coercive power of the state has suffered a setback with the proliferation of militant groups all over South Asia. In some cases, these groups are in total control of the areas they operate in and threaten to expand their influence in the neighbouring region. Even if the state machineries have managed to eliminate the top leaderships of different outfits, they have recovered quite remarkably from such temporary setbacks and reasserted their strength. The situation is quite alarming. In fact, terrorism has become a flourishing industry funded and patronised by many sources. Because of money, power and clandestine official patronage, the number of terrorist groups has been on the rise in the past few years.

Thus, there is a need to undertake periodic review of the ground situation detailing the militant groups: their mission, leadership, strength, areas of operation, support base, domestic and international linkages, sources of funding, publications, etc. The *Institute for Defence Studies and Analyses* (IDSA) had undertaken a similar study in the year 2003 focussing mainly on jihadi groups operating then in Jammu and Kashmir. It was considered necessary to revisit the problem after a decade and compile credible data from various sources on militant groups operating not only in Jammu and Kashmir but also in the entire region. The main aim of the exercise was to make available a ready reference source for scholars, analysts and policymakers. The present volume is thus an updated account of the militant groups operating in different countries of South Asia.

Any discussion on terrorism in South Asia is usually focused on terrorism which has global ramifications. The main focus of this study is terrorist outfits which operate both at the domestic and transnational levels. There are militant groups like Harkat-ul-Jihadi-al-Islami (HuJI), Harkat-ul-Mujahideen (HuM), Lashkar-e-Taiba (LeT), Jaish-e-Mohammad (JeM) in Pakistan, *Liberation Tigers of Tamil Eelam* (LTTE) in Sri Lanka (until 2009), HuJI in Bangladesh, Maoists in Nepal, Left Wing Extremism (LWE) and small reactive Hindu groups in India, majority of which operate within the region; however, some of them do have linkages with groups outside the region and spawn international terrorism.

The Pakistan–Afghanistan Factor

Any study of terrorism in South Asia has to start with a critical examination of the socio-political environment in Pakistan which, since the 1980s, has been the epicentre or fountainhead of terrorism in the region as well as the world. It radiates terrorism to other countries in the region, i.e., Afghanistan, India, Bangladesh and Nepal. A number of outfits covered in this study have their primary bases in Pakistan where they receive active or passive help from the agencies embedded within the military and security establishment of Pakistan. Pakistan has sought to use many of these groups as extended arms of the military to destabilise India on the one hand, and to enhance its influence in Afghanistan on the other. Pakistani mindset vis-à-vis India helps sustain this suicidal strategy. For the security establishment of Pakistan, India is a sworn enemy eternally conspiring to either absorb or destroy Pakistan. Moreover, the desire to avenge the defeat of 1971 is carefully drilled into the psyche of the average Pakistani soldier over the years. Therefore, the use of terror as an instrument of the state policy, especially towards India, looks quite logical and legitimate to the Pakistani strategists.

Unfortunately, despite the recognition at very top levels that the blow-back effect of nurturing non-state terror outfits has been disastrous for Pakistan, there has not been any significant revision of this policy of nurturing terror groups for use against India. The adverse consequence of the Afghan war of the 1980s has made the situation more complex. During this time, Pakistan became the hub of jihadi activities and radical elements from all over the world descended on Pakistan to participate in the jihad in Afghanistan against the Soviet forces. Ever since, Pakistan has become a laboratory of Islamic radicalism and a hotbed of terror. In the post-9/11 period—in the presence of international forces in Afghanistan who were regarded as an illegitimate occupying force—the call for jihad became popular again and Pakistan became the nerve centre of terror.

The history of promoting cross-border terrorism in India by Pakistan began immediately after the state came into being. In October 1947, Pakistan armed the tribal *lashkars* and sent them to Kashmir to take it by force. That was the beginning of the use of non-state actors by the state of Pakistan vis-à-vis a neighbouring principality or state. With Kashmir's accession to the Indian Union, the *lashkar* invasion of Kashmir turned into an inter-state war between India and Pakistan. Despite the United Nations (UN)-mediated ceasefire of 1 January 1949, during the 1960s, General Ayub Khan reverted to stories of jihad and pushed army men, disguised as Kashmiris jihadis, into Kashmir to kick off insurgency in Kashmir which led to the 1965 war.

The Impact of Afghan Jihad

The pre-Al Qaeda and pre-Taliban groups, like HuA, HuM, HM, HuJI, LeT and JeM, were created by state agencies in Pakistan for specific objectives, that is, to launch a protracted proxy war in Kashmir and also to help the Americans in their efforts to drive out the Soviet forces from Afghanistan through guerilla tactics. These groups largely depended on state patronage and funds generously provided by the US and other Western nations, and also West Asian countries like Saudi Arabia, through a network of newly created banking organisations like the Bank of Credit and Commerce International (BCCI). In certain cases, even innovative methods were adopted to fly in currency chests into Pakistan, besides guns and ammunition shipped and airlifted in tonnes from different parts of the world. In 1986, the then *Central Intelligence Agency* (CIA) chief, William Cassey, was able to persuade the US Congress to provide the Mujahideen in Afghanistan with stringer missiles and also post US advisers in Afghanistan to train the insurgents.

The jihadi groups in the Afghanistan–Pakistan (Af-Pak) region largely drew their cadres from madrassas and extremist religious groups in Pakistan which were amply supported by the Inter Services Intelligence (ISI) directorate and the Pakistan Army. They relied primarily on the sentiments of religious "brotherhood", both within Pakistan and outside, and their association with the ISI to create a chain of madrassas and training grounds for recruiting, indoctrinating and training the so-called "freedom fighters" (Mujahideen). Their area of operation was predetermined and they worked strictly under the control of the ISI (and CIA) in Afghanistan. The ISI also started training Kashmiri militants in the camps in Afghanistan.

The Afghan war of the 1980s strengthened the Pakistani Army's penchant to use terrorism as a weapon to enforce its foreign policy. Soon after the end of the Afghan war in 1988–89 in Afghanistan, Pakistan took full advantage of the unstable political situation in Kashmir and launched its subversive war against India. It continued for a decade, until the people of Kashmir disassociated from the militant struggle and took to democracy. To reinject militancy in Kashmir, the military, under the leadership of General Pervez Musharraf, started a mini-war along the Kargil sector on the line of control (LoC) in direct violation of the trust being built with India by the civilian government of Nawaz Sharif courtesy the Lahore agreement of February 1999. In May 1999, Pakistani generals used the jihadi itch to invade Kargil by violating the LoC. Pakistan told the world that Kashmiri insurgents had captured the heights of Kargil, whereas in reality, the so-called "Kashmiri jihadis" were none other than disguised Pakistani Army men.

Terrorism underwent dramatic changes in the Indian subcontinent after the disintegration of Soviet Union and more so, after 9/11. Funds, resources and support for the jihadi groups dried up rapidly. Pakistani agencies found it difficult to provide open support to many of these groups. Many of these groups were asked to scale down their activities and lie low. As a result, a large number of the cadres from these jihadi organisations either joined rabid Sunni groups like Sipah-e-Sahaba of Pakistan (SSP) and Lashkar-e-Jhangvi (LeJ), or shifted to the tribal areas to join Afghan Taliban and its affiliate groups. Most of these groups indulged in criminal activities like carjacking, extortion, kidnapping for ransom and smuggling.

There is a clear distinction between the groups which operated during the Afghan jihad and those that exist today. There are marked differences in their composition, objectives, modus operandi, networks, finances and reach. In Kashmir, the agenda and tactics employed by groups like HM and various off-shoots of it—like HuM and Al Faran—were different. These groups operated in Kashmir more as an instrument of Pakistan's foreign policy than for any "religious" objectives as it was made out to be. The first stated objective of Pakistan's foreign policy was to free Kashmir from India. Groups like HuA, HuM and JeM were tasked to fuel secession within the Kashmiri Muslim community, engage Indian security forces in an internal conflict and launch an ethnic cleansing of the areas dominated by Muslim communities in Kashmir. These groups took to kidnapping, mass murders, assassinations, arson and sabotage to achieve these objectives. As counter-insurgency measures grew in strength and scope, the groups turned against security forces through suicide missions and improvised explosive device (IED) blasts.

Massive funding from the Islamic countries, especially from the Saudi Arabia and other Gulf countries, lack of governance and inability of the government to control the militant activities have strengthened these groups in Pakistan. Groups like the LeT, Haqqani Network and Tehrik-e-Taliban Pakistan (TTP) are growing in strength every year. The state of Pakistan uses LeT and other such groups against India and therefore, these groups receive encouragement from ISI/ Pakistan Army. The transnational groups like the Al Qaeda and Muslim Brotherhood have become models for many radical Islamic groups in the subcontinent.

The Emerging Patterns

In Pakistan, after the decimation of the Taliban in 2001, new alliances have been established among jihadi outfits. Sectarian extremist groups like SSP and LeJ have joined the fray. Drawing upon the resources of the ISI, these groups established sleeper cells in different parts of India and in other parts of the world. Already preparations are on in Afghanistan where the ISI seems determined to bolster the Taliban to capture power in Afghanistan after the US exit. In a testimony before the Senate Foreign Relations Committee, the then Assistant Secretary of Defence, Peter Rodman, had said, "There are elements in the Pakistan government who we suspect are sympathetic to the old policy of before 9/11", adding that there still exists in north-western Pakistan, a radical Islamic infrastructure that "spews out fighters that go to Kashmir as well as into Afghanistan".[2] Still 42 camps including 25 in PoK are active in Pakistan where about 2500 militants are undergoing training. They belong to LeT, JeM, HuJI and HM. In its *Country Report on Terrorism 2011*, US State Department said that Afghanistan has experienced more aggressive and coordinated attacks by the Taliban, Haqqani Network and other AQ-affiliated insurgent elements in anticipation of the 2014 withdrawal of coalition forces.[3]

With cumulative bans imposed on their activities by the US State Department, the UN and various governments, including that of Pakistan, these groups, particularly LeT, established new networks of finances, tapping into Pakistani diaspora in the United Kingdom (UK), West Asia, the US, Australia and Europe. These groups began relying on transnational smuggling and hawala syndicates to transfer funds and arms. There has been a decisive shift in targets, both in terms of location and character, and modus operandi. The targets today range from political leaders to mass transit systems to nuclear stations, with the clear objective of instigating communal violence in India and inflicting heavy damage to the economy.

The pattern of terror attacks in India has also shifted from isolated attacks to bombings of public transport systems and market and religious places to spread panic and fear. Kashmir is no longer the operational ground, nor the sole target. The groups today have a pan-India, and at times a pan-global, agenda of establishing the caliphate. In fact, in recent years, inspired by radical Islamic groups in the neighbourhood, and encouraged by ISI, a new radical Islamist group called Indian Mujahideen (IM) has made its presence felt in India with a resolve to take up arms against, what it calls, injustice done to the Muslims in India and against the domination of the Hindus over the Muslims. In this process, this group also has an objective to establish Islamic rule in India.

India's Concerns

India has been a target of terror activities for a long time. It is only in recent years, especially after the 9/11, that the international community recognised the threat posed by various terror outfits to India and the region. However, increased international effort in the region in the name of war on terror, for the last one decade, has neither been able to root out the phenomenon nor made it any easier for India to handle the issue. On the contrary, it has aggravated the regional security situation and the challenge faced by India is much graver now. Indian strategic analysts and policymakers have been particularly alive to the issue of changing pattern of terror in the region. It is in this context that Ambassador Jayant Prasad summed up:

> Nature of terrorism has changed. A quarter of century ago, it was regarded as a law and order problem, but now it is posing the biggest security threat to nation states. Almost all the countries of the world have been affected by terrorism. Today, terrorist groups are operating beyond the natural boundaries and are drawing support from many sources including the States in many cases. They have global networking with potential allies, other terrorist groups, arms suppliers and have financial support from different sources.[4]

Factors leading to the rise of a particular militant group vary from outfit to outfit. These groups vary from each other in ideological motivations as well as power structure. Factor like deprivation, ethnicity, religious and cultural assertion are some of the important factors that lead to the rise of a militant/terror group. These groups pose a critical challenge to the state when they come together and coordinate their activities. These groups often come together to fight a common enemy. For example, the outfits operating in the north-eastern part of India perceive the state of India as their common enemy; hence the alliances and links between various groups. Similarly, radical Islamic groups often come together in the name of waging jihad against perceived enemies and aim at establishing an Islamic caliphate through violent means. In many instances, the Militant Groups are supported by one state against the other, perceived as an "enemy". For example, the ISI of Pakistan has been instrumental in funding militant groups against India in Kashmir for a long time. Not long ago, the Bangladesh Nationalist Party (BNP)-led coalition government, headed by Khaleda Zia, provided safe heavens to Indian insurgent groups in the North-East India with a view to keeping India internally engaged.

So far as South Asia is concerned, there have been number of issues that have given rise to terror groups in the region. Afghanistan continues to be one of the important theatres of such outfits. The involvement of foreign powers like the former Union of Soviet Socialist Republic (USSR), the US and other Western countries in Afghanistan has not only led to the rise of indigenous armed groups but also attracted transnational Militant Groups like the Al Qaeda to the region.

In case of India, there has been a combination of factors responsible for the rise of various armed insurgent groups. The left-wing extremism fuelled by the Communist Party of India-Maoist (Maoists in short) has been regarded by the Indian government as the single largest threat to the internal security of India. Obsessed with capturing the political power by force, the Maoists are involved in armed activities in the name of fighting for the interests of the downtrodden against all sorts of exploitation, deprivation and domination. The Maoists have spread into almost 21 states and pose a serious threat to the Indian state.

In the north-eastern theatre of India, the issue of ethnicity and culture has played a major role in the rise of various armed groups. The groups like the National Socialist Council of Nagalim-Isak-Muivah (NSCN-IM) have taken up arms against the state of India demanding a separate state for the ethnic Nagas. Same has been the case with the United Liberation Front of Asom (ULFA), National Democratic Front of Bodoland (NDFB) and People's Liberation Army (PLA) of Manipur. Most of these armed groups operating from the North-East are engaged in dialogue with the Union government. At the same time, there have been factions unwilling to shun violence and join the dialogue process. The north-eastern states such as Tripura, Meghalaya and Mizoram have witnessed peace to a great extent since the militant groups in these states have either laid down their arms or have become dormant. Yet, the region continues to be affected by the activities of many armed groups.

The Case of Bangladesh

During the Cold War, due to internal dissent as well as external manipulations, various hues of extremist sentiments came to the fore in various South Asian states. Quite a few insurgent groups, especially in India and Sri Lanka, emerged for political reasons, with the demand for creation new nation-states on religious, ethnic and linguistic basis. South Asia, by a quirk of fate and history, happens to be both the battleground and home for many radical groups, threatening to destabilise political structures and social fabric of the region by acts of terror directed against specific religious and ethnic communities.

Unlike Pakistan where religious extremist groups have remained on the fringe of the political spectrum, in Bangladesh, such groups have had a decisive role to play. One such group is Jamaat-e-Islami (JeI) which owes much of its growth to the Islamisation of the country's political institutions initiated by President Zia-ur Rahman in 1977. Both the Awami League, led by Sheikh Hasina, and the BNP, led by Khaleda Zia, have been courting JeI to gain electoral/political advantage over each other. The JeI, as a result, has emerged as the third-largest political party in Bangladesh.

The rise of radical political and religious parties like JeI has promoted the growth of madrassas in the country, mostly funded by West Asian countries. These madrassas have played host to various terrorist groups anxious to recruit and train young students. One of the more prominent ones is HuJI-Bangladesh (HuJI-B), widely regarded as the operating arm of Al Qaeda in South Asia. The HuJI has been consolidating its position in Bangladesh where it boasts a membership of more than 15,000 activists, of whom at least 2,000 are regarded as hardcore. Earlier in the 1980s, about 3,500 Bangladeshis had reportedly gone to Pakistan and Afghanistan to take part in jihad. Barring 34 who died, a large number of them returned home; of these, about 500 battle-hardened militants form the backbone of HuJI-B, a group which is today emerging as a partner of terrorist groups in South Asia.

The Islamist armed groups in Bangladesh, Jamaat-ul-Mujahideen Bangladesh (JMB) and HuJI-B, like many of the like-minded groups in Pakistan, aim at establishing Islamic rule in Bangladesh. What makes these groups different is the kind of patronage they get from the constituencies like the JeI Bangladesh and the BNP. The JeI Bangladesh, which played a major role in killing millions of innocent individuals during the Liberation war in 1971, continues to be major supporter of all these groups. For last few years, Bangladesh has also been witnessing the involvement of Hizb-ut-Tahrir (HuT), a pan-Islamic radical group, in radicalising the youth and intellectuals. It is being suspected that this group has engineered several mutinies against the Sheikh Hasina government in Bangladesh. The HuT has its presence in more than 50 countries the world over and has been active in Pakistan and Bangladesh for the last few years.

Other Countries

In Nepal, almost all the armed groups have become dormant. Some of the important armed groups such as the Unified Communist Party of Nepal-Maoist (UCPN) and the Madheshi Janadhikar Forum (MJF) have laid down their arms and have joined the mainstream political process. Few other armed groups such as Janatantrik Terai Mukti Morcha (JTMM) have become inactive in last few years. But the ongoing political instability in Nepal has all the potential to spark the rise of armed groups again.

Sri Lanka has witnessed peace and tranquility after the elimination of the notorious LTTE in 2009 by the state security forces. However, the issue of political reconciliation (based on the demand for meaningful devolution of power to the Tamils) remains unaddressed. Many observers from Sri Lanka have held that if the issue is allowed to fester, it could lead to the rise of Tamil insurgency again.

Design of the Book

In the present volume, an attempt has been made to profile various terror outfits presently active in South Asian countries. As has been mentioned earlier, more than 200 groups are operating in the region today. However, in this book, only select important outfits have been chosen for rigorous study. Many groups which have either merged into some larger groups or have been inactive for some years have been deliberately left out. Nevertheless, the book does cover some inactive groups given their potential to regroup and get into action. Groups like the HuT and Popular Front of India (PFI), which are not necessarily armed groups, have also been covered because of the kind of radical activities they have been involved in. The information related to these outfits has been culled from open sources and due care has been taken to gather information in a standardised format along the following heads, to make it as reader friendly as possible:

History and genesis of the group to make the reader aware of the socio-political conditions as well as the ideological motivation that gave rise to the group.

Objectives and agenda of a group to help understand the purpose and goals of the group.

Ideology plays an important role in setting up of an organisation. Therefore, ideological orientation and affiliation of each group has been dealt with carefully for proper analysis and assessment.

Organisational structure and leadership of an organisation determines the success and failure of the same. Hence, the organisational structure and leadership of each group has been covered in detail.

Cadre strength, recruitment and training of the groups have been given due consideration.

Area of operation and influence is another important aspect of each group which has been covered in the profiles.

Network, local, regional and global, plays an important part for all the armed groups. This critical dimension has been analysed for each group in this study.

Alliances among the armed groups usually make the task of the security agencies difficult in understanding these groups. This study does not intend to compare the armed groups with one another, but it certainly tries to analyse the links and alliances of the groups.

Finance and funding sources are the lifeblood of the armed groups. It is the flow of the funding that keeps the movement going.

Weapon in possession and procurement by the armed groups is the most important task. The number and types of weapons each group possesses and the source of procurement of these weapons have been covered in this study.

The current status of each group covers the present capacity as well as future threat perception coming out of each of the groups taken up for study.

NOTES

1. For details, see South Asia Terrorism Portal, available at www.sapt.org.
2. See K. Alan Kronstadt, "International Terrorism in South Asia", CRS Report for Congress, 3 November, 2003, p. 4

3. For details see "Country Reports on Terrorism 2011", available at http://www.state.gov/j/ct/rls/crt/2011/195545.htm, accessed on 19 September 2013.
4. Address by Ambassador Jayant Prasad, Special Secretary, Ministry of External Affairs (MEA), 4th South Asian Conference, New Delhi, 2–3 November 2010, available at http://www.idsa.in/sac/2010/Report_SessionV.html, accessed on July 10, 2013

PART-A
BANGLADESH

2

Jamaat-ul-Mujahideen
(Assembly of Holy Warriors)

Introduction

The Jamaat-ul-Mujahideen Bangladesh (JMB), a militant organisation, continues to remain a threat to the state of Bangladesh. The JMB, the Assembly of Holy Warriors in Bangladesh, was formed in the year 1998. It came to prominence as a terrorist/ militant group after it engineered a serial attack across the country on 17 August 2005. It is, however, important to mention that the JMB was proscribed by the Bangladeshi government led by Begum Khalida Zia of Bangladesh Nationalist Party (BNP) on 23 February 2005, under the pressure from Awami League (AL) and secularists in Bangladesh. Since the serial blasts by JMB, the law enforcement agencies of Bangladesh have arrested hundreds of JMB cadres. A number of kingpins of JMB, including its founding members like Sheikh Abdur Rahman and Bangla Bhai, have been executed. According to the government sources, the JMB as a militant group has been weakened by the measures taken by the Sheikh Hasina-led government. However, there are reports suggesting that more number of cadres belonging to the JMB have been arrested by the law enforcement agents and huge amount of arms and explosive materials have been recovered from ex-JMB hubs. Such reports certainly demonstrate that though the JMB has been weakened with the arrest and execution of its cadre and some of the kingpins, it is still trying to regroup, recruit and raise funds for more spectacular strikes.

Genesis

The JMB was founded as a militant jihadi organisation in Bangladesh in the year 1998 by Sheikh Abdur Rahman. The founder of the JMB himself has gone on the record to say that JMB as an organisation was born in the British colonial era.[1] The JMB is also believed to be the youth front organisation of Al Mujahideen. Al Mujahideen was believed to have existed during 1990s and remains obscure even today. A number of organisations were believed to have

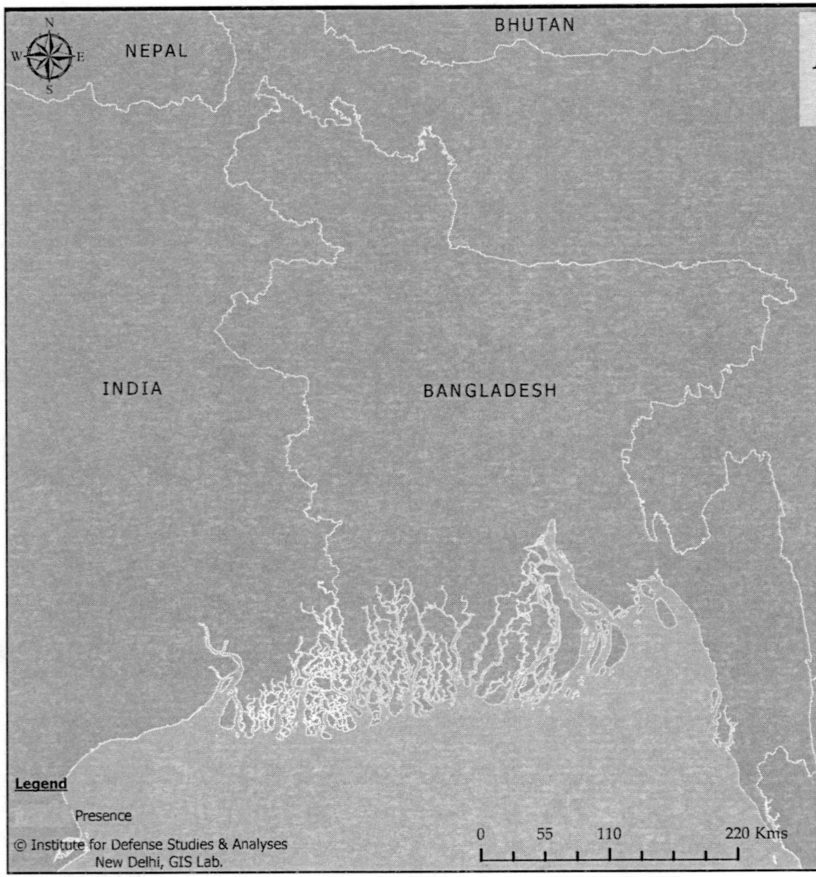

Jamaat-ul-Mujahideen Bangladesh

Formation: The Jamaat-ul-Mujahideen Bangladesh was formed in 1998 by Sheikh Abdur Rahman. This group came to prominence for its role in engineering bomb blasts across 63 districts in Bangladesh in August 2005.

Leadership: Important leaders of this group used to be Sheikh Abdur Rahman, Siddiqur Rahman alias Bangla Bhai. At present important leaders of the group are Saidur Rahman (arrested), Sohel Mahfuzahd (acting chief) and Nazmul Anwar Alam alias Bhagina Shahid (military wing commander).

Presence: Though this group has been less active for some years now, yet it has its presence all over Bangladesh.

Links: The JMB has its links with groups like HuJI-B, JeI of Bangladesh, Al Qaeda, ICS, JMJB, and RSO.

Funding Sources: The JMB got financial support from the JeI of Bangladesh. It also received financial help from Al Qaeda and from charitable organisations such as Al Fuziara and Khairul Ansar al Khairia Foundation in Saudi Arabia, Daulatul Kuwait in Kuwait and Daullatul Bahrain and Al Harmain Foundation.

Current Status: Not Active.

affiliation with Al Mujahideen. They were/are Jama'at-ul-Jihad, JMB, Ahle Hadith Andolan Bangladesh (AHAB), Ahle Hadith Jubo Shangha, Harkat-ul-Jihadi-al-Islami (HuJI), Hizb-ut-Tawhidi Janata, Islami Jubo Shangha, Islami Shangha, Al Falah A'am Unnayan Shastha and Shahadat-e al Hiqma.[2] The JMB as a militant organisation was deeply associated and influenced by the ideas and practices of Salafist[3] movement in Bangladesh known as the AHAB.[4]

As a militant organisation, the JMB continued to grow unnoticed by the security forces and the government till 2005. There were a number of instances indicating the covert expansion of the organisation both militarily and ideologically. Initially, Abdur Rahman followed a two-pronged action to strengthen the organisation. The JMB cadres were sent to various parts of the country, first, for extensive *da'wah* (religious preaching outreach) and second, for garnering support from the politically influential people and supporters of jihad for his agenda. In a way, he was successful to a great extent as the then government, led by the BNP in alliance with the Jamaat-e-Islami Bangladesh (JeI), did not acknowledge or accept the existence of JMB. Such covert backing from the government is evident from a couple of incidents. In 1999, the Chittagong police arrested 41 suspected militants with arms. It was also reported that they confessed to the police to being members of the Abdur Rahman's group. However, the matter was not investigated further, thereby giving JMB a chance to rise. Similarly, in 2000, some cadres of the JMB were arrested in Parbatipur with petrol bombs. They were released after a local court thought them to be ordinary criminals. So, the two-pronged action plan of Abdur Rahman to garner the support of radical Islamic constituencies in face of the apathy of the government was successful to a great extent. Finally, JMB as a militant organisation came to the prominence in 17 August 2005, when it carried out serial blasts across the country.

Objective and Ideology

As far as the ideological underpinning of the JMB is concerned, to a great extent, it is influenced by the ideological orientation of the AHAB. The reason has been the family lineage and socialisation of Abdur Rahman. Abdur Rahman was educated in a madrassa run by his father who was an Ahle Hadith scholar. Rahman's family was also closely associated with AHAB. His AHAB experienced was mixed with the ideological input he gained from his association with the HuJI-Bangladesh (HuJI-B). In the year 1997, when he was blamed for the conviction of some 41 cadres of HuJI-B, he deserted HuJI-B citing ideological disagreements.

Unlike many Islamic militant groups worldwide, Rahman never wanted to raise a global jihad. Rather, the primary aim of JMB was to establish Islamic rule in Bangladesh. For Rahman, the near enemy–supporters of democracy and secularism in Bangladesh were more important than the global enemies of Islam like the United States (US) and its Western allies. Capitalising on the discontent among the various Islamic groups in Bangladesh, the JMB grew from strength to strength. Such rapid growth of JMB did not go without criticism by various Islamic groups like Islamic Oikyo Jote (IOJ). The JMB wanted to implement the Islamic rule, it had thought of, on its own. A member of the IOJ is reported to have said that, "we told them that the time has not come for such a revolution. But they did not listen to us."[5]

It is, however, important to mention that the serial blast it engineered was, in fact, an attempt to show its strength and disseminate its ideology and objectives. The bomb-disseminated pamphlet of JMB, titled "Call to implement Islamic Law in Bangladesh", read:

> The Jamaat ul Mujahideen Bangladesh, keeping in mind the laws of Allah, does not recognize the prevalent system. In addition to the constitution under which the state is functioning is contradictory to and does not confirm to Allah's system. The JMB calls all those who are cognizant to shape the country as per Allah's order and the prophet's way and to reject the rule of law and the so-called electoral system and functions. Otherwise the JMB has resolved to implement Allah's law in Allah's land through comprehensive realisation of Allah's directed *Kital* (armed struggle) method...[6]

The JMB was very clear on its targets, that is, who it considered as enemies of Islam. The prime enemies of Islam in Bangladesh, according to the JMB, are the democrats and secularists. For JMB, democrats and the secularists, like the leftists and cultural organisations, are the instruments promoting un-Islamic values. Therefore, they have been attacked many a time by JMB. Various attacks on cultural programmes like *jatra*, communist rallies, cinema hall and religious shrines in Bangladesh are testimonies of the mindset of the JMB. So, the main targets of JMB can be categorised as:

- democratic institutions like judiciary, legislative assemblies and their members;
- intellectuals and public figures necessarily supporting secularism;
- the leftists;
- non-Muslims and the minorities like the Hindus and the Ahmediya communities; and
- cultural function halls, cinema halls, etc.

Though the JMB does not a wage a global jihad, it follows the same ideological orientation as most of the other radical Islamic groups. For example, in one of its handwritten leaflets recovered from the blast site, it goes on to say: "we do not want Taguti (non-Islamic) law, let Quranic law be introduced. Law framed by humans can not be continued and only the laws of Allah will prevail."[7]

Organisation Structure and Leadership

So far the organisational structure of the JMB is concerned, it is designed in accordance with a manual titled, *Shamorik Shakhar Obhijan Nirdeshika* (Operational Manual of Military Branch). Accordingly, the JMB has a four-tier structure:

- "Majlis-e-Shura" is mainly a consultative decision-making body that works under the leadership of an amir (chief).
- "Ehsar" consists of the full-time members of the organisation. The main responsibility given to these full-time members is to engage in the activities like military operations and *da'wah.* These members are also engaged in recruiting new members to the organisation.
- "Gayeri Ehsar" consists of the part-time members of the organisation. Though not involved with the military and preaching-related activities, they are supposed to give the due donations and also undergo a low level of military training. One of the most important responsibility that these members are supposed to discharge is to give shelter to the full-time militants of the organisation.
- "Sudhi", or "Saathi", are primarily the sympathisers and well-wishers of JMB. They help raise funds for the organisations and provide shelter to the militants as and when needed.

The highest structure of the JMB, Majlis-e-Shura, divides the members of the organisation into military and non-military wings. According to the above-mentioned manual, JMB will ideally have six divisions and each division will be guided by a chief and his deputy. Similarly, the military wing of JMB divides Bangladesh into regional operational commands. By 2005, it had nine regional operational units.[8] They are Dhaka North, Dhaka South, Chittagong, Sylhet, Khulna and Barisal and three units in Rajshahi.

The decision-making power of the JMB has always been with the Majlis-e-Shura, and it continues to be highly centralised in nature. Till the execution of Abdur Rahman, the decision-making power of the JMB remained in the hands of Abdur Rahman, his sons and family members. After his death, according to the available sources, some new shura members like Saidur Rahman were appointed. As far as the military wing of JMB is concerned, it used to be headed by Bangla Bhai. The JMB is believed to have a suicide squad known as Shahid Nasirullah Arafat Brigade. It is also believed to be in the process of organising a women's wing to act as intelligence operatives.[9]

Recruitment

A group of dedicated full-timers of JMB, mainly the Ehsars, have been given the responsibility of recruiting new people for JMB. These Ehsars use multiple platforms for recruiting new cadres. The most important platform for targeting people for recruitment is from the madrassas run by the Ahle Hadith groups. In its initial stage, JMB depended heavily on the Ahle Hadith madrassas, mostly in the north-western part of Bangladesh, for the recruitment of *Imam* and Islamic teachers. In the course of time, these imams and teachers helped JMB to recruit other entrants. According to the report, by 2000, the JMB was able to establish four of its own madrassas in four different parts of Bangladesh.[10] These four madrassas cater to the needs of the JMB as far as recruitment is concerned.

Apart from the madrassas, the JMB also targets other Islamic organisations like JeI and Islamic Chhatra Shibir (ICS) for recruitment. Many JeI and ICS members who were having disagreements with the functioning of their organisations joined JMB. The likes of Saidur Rahman, Bangla Bhai, former shura members—Hafez Mahmud and Salahuddin—and former military wing head, Ataur Rahman Sunny, had past linkages with JeI and ICS. People who joined JMB from organisations like ICS and JeI were the link persons for JMB to penetrate into these organisations for further recruitment.

The third source of recruitment for the JMB is believed to be the family network. The influential members of JMB like Abdur Rahman, Bangla Bhai and Saidur Rahman often recruited from their family. The sons, brothers and son-in-laws of these leaders and other members of the JMB became part of the JMB in the course of time. As the security concerns mounted, JMB leaders married within the group. Those who were already married were sometimes asked to go in for a second marriage to a person from the trusted JMB family.[11]

The strength of the JMB can be divided into pre- and post-2005 period. According to the available sources, at its peak in 2005, it had 10,000 Ehsars, hundred thousand part-timers and one million sympathisers/supporters.[12] It is believed that after the crackdown on them by the Bangladesh government, the strength of JMB has gone down drastically. Though the strength has gone down drastically, yet the capability of the JMB to strike cannot be underestimated. There have been reports claiming that the former JMB cadres are moving around the country changing their affiliation to other organisations like Tablighi Jamaat (supposed to be peaceful Islamic organisation). According to the confession report of Saidur Rahman, at present, the JMB has 400 full-timers across the country and a military wing capable of launching major attacks. He also said that the hardliners who had taken over the leadership of JMB would be more destructive in his absence.[13]

The JMB is also believed to have had women wings. Each women wing consisted of 10–12 members. The main responsibility given to them was confined to the *da'wah*, to read Quran, persuade people to perform namaz regularly and encourage their husbands and other family members for jihad.[14] The existence of such wings was also spelt out during an interrogation of one of the senior leaders of JMB, Abu Bakkr Siddique alias Shiblu. He said to the security forces that the JMB had trained some female cadres in using grenades and they have been making preparations to carry out a series of grenade attacks in Dhaka on a small scale.[15]

Network and Alliances

The JMB has a very strong network both at the domestic and international level. At the domestic level, it has connections with the like-minded militant groups like the HuJI-B. Similarly, it has also links with the Islamic groups like JeI, ICS and the AHAB. The strong connection of JMB with JeI was officially established in a face-to-face interview of the former chief of the JMB, Saidur Rahman, and the senior leaders of JeI, Motiur Rahman Nizami, Ali Ahsan Mojahid and Delwar Hossain Sayeedi, on 13 July 2010. During the interrogation, according to the security forces, Motiur Rahman Nizami threatened Saidur Rahman with regard to disclosing anything about the links between JeI and JMB.[16] It is also a fact that both the important leaders of the JMB, Abdur Rahaman and Bangla Bhai (already executed), were active members of the JeI. Similarly, Saidur Rahman was the chief of JeI's Habibganj unit in 1983. Saidur Rahman also revealed that at least 25 JeI *rokans* (high-ranking field operatives) were directly involved with the JMB and that the JeI provided arms training to them.

Apart from the Islamic organisations in the Bangladesh, the JMB was able to garner support from political parties like the BNP and from some of the police officers till 2005. This is evident from the fact that the intelligence wing had cautioned the government in 2003 about the threat potential of the JMB.[17] Despite this, it took two years for the government to ban the organisation in February 2005. The reason for such delayed action was very simple. The government, led by the BNP, depended on the JeI's support. Any action against the JMB would have put the JeI in trouble as many of the JMB leaders had connections with the JeI.

The JMB was also supported covertly by the BNP-led government that came to power in 2001. One of the most important factors that cemented the links between the government and the JMB was the common aim of suppressing the communist movement in Bangladesh. The communist movement, mainly led by the Sarbahara Party and the Purbo Banglar Communist Party (PBCP), was a major threat to the government. In the year 2004, with support of the government, the JMB, with its front organisation—Jagrata Muslim Janata Bangladesh (JMJB)—launched the programme, "annihilate the *Sarbahara*".[18] Though there was a constant pressure from the AL to crackdown on the JMB, the BNP-led government instead blamed the AL for manufacturing militancy to tarnish the government. Similarly, the police also played an important role in helping the JMB leaders and the members by not arresting them in many cases.[19]

As far as the international linkages of the JMB are concerned, it is believed to have a strong connection with the Al Qaeda. The reason is that some of the important leaders of the JMB are believed to have fought in Afghanistan with the Al Qaeda. Similarly, it also has a strong connection with HuJI-B and the Rohingya Solidarity Organisation (RSO). The JMB has also has links with the front organisations that promote the cause of radical Islam and jihad. Some of the charitable organisations like the Al Fuziara and Khairul Ansar al Khairia Foundation in Saudi Arabia, Daulatul Kuwait in Kuwait and Daullatul Bahrain are also linked to the JMB. The JMB is also believed to be connected to the Al Harmain Foundation, a front organisation of Al Qaeda, which is banned in many countries.

Finance and Funding

The JMB raises funds both from domestic and external sources. In the initial days of its existence, it used to be dependent on its members like Ehsars, shura members and Gayeri Ehsars for donations. In the course of time, it started collecting donations from its supporters in terms of *zakat* (alam). During its peak time, at the domestic level, the outfit depended a lot on criminal activities of its members for funds, and to some extent, it invested in the local markets to generate some money. As one report suggested, JMB invested in several small and medium enterprises like rickshaws, auto rickshaws and taxis in the capital to raise funds locally.[20] An interrogation of Saidur Rahman revealed that the JMB gets cash around Taka (Bangladesh currency) 50–60 lakh during Ramadan. Another report states that the highest earning by a unit (several villages) is 10,000–12,000 taka; by a subdistrict unit, it is up to 50,000 taka; by district unit, it is up to 200,000 taka; and it goes up to 500,000–600,000 taka at the divisional level.[21]

At the domestic level, JMB also gets some assistance from the Ahle Hadith community. Similarly, some top businessmen in Bangladesh are also believed to be funding JMB. Though many of the members of the JMB are behind bars, it is believed that the flow of fund from the supporters in terms of monthly contribution, zakat and donations remains uninterrupted.

So far the external funding of the JMB is concerned, as mentioned earlier, it receives fund from the so-called charitable organisations in countries like Saudi Arabia, Kuwait and Bahrian. Apart from that, every month, around Taka 600,000 is being sent by around 3,000 JMB supporters staying in Australia, England, Italy, Canada, Malaysia and the Middle East countries.[22] The system of *hundi* (an informal banking sector that operates mostly illegally) continues to be one of the most important sources of funding for JMB. The Bangladeshi workers employed in the Middle East and other parts of the world send money to their families through human couriers, and a portion of that amount goes to the JMB fund.

The involvement of JMB cadres in the fake Indian currency note (FICN) is another source of funding for JMB. Solaiman alias Majumdar, kingpin of Pakistan-based FICN racket, disclosed in one of the interrogations that at the behest of Pakistani intelligence agency, Inter Services Intelligence (ISI), he entrusted two Bangladeshi militant organisations, JMB and HuJI-B, with smuggling of FICN.[23] According to the Detective Branch of Bangladesh Police, many JMB cadres are involved in marketing the FICN. Out of the money earned in this process, Taka 50,000 is deposited in JMB account every month. Some reports also indicate that JMB is also well involved in the armed struggle across the Indian border.

State Response to JMB

The response of the Bangladesh government towards JMB remained rather favourable till 2009, when Sheikh Hasina-led AL took over power. From the beginning, JMB continued to garner support from the radical Islamic constituencies like the JeI and the ICS. The JeI's alliance with the BNP-led government was a major factor for the growth of JMB. As mentioned earlier, the BNP-led government, supported by the JeI, continued to refuse the existence of JMB till February 2005 when it was banned. Rather, it went on to say that the AL was trying to get political mileage by highlighting these false security issues. There were instances where the politicians in power in those days asked the police not arrest certain JMB members after the 2005 serial blast by the JMB.

The caretaker government of the Bangladesh by the army (which took over in 2007 and ruled for almost two years) did a little to bring the JMB under control. According to the available sources, the caretaker government arrested some 226 militants belonging to the JMB, of whom 57 have been put behind bar, 30 were charge sheeted, six were hanged to death and one killed in encounter.[24] The caretaker government never showed any interest in seriously investigating JMB's financial linkages.

Meanwhile, Sheikh Hasina's government has taken some drastic steps to crackdown on the JMB. The government of the day has invested significant resources for the counter-terrorism programme and continues to be committed to the same. The Sheikh Hasina government remains committed not only to crackdown on the JMB but it also has been trying to punish the war criminals of the 1971 liberation war. Sheikh Hasina's good intentions against the radical and terrorist elements in the country have been under constant threat. The JeI has been constantly criticising and trying to cause disturbances by organising strikes and protests against the government. At the same time, the poor infrastructure of the security forces has been a major hindrance in the counter-terrorism initiative.

According to the media sources, since the August 2005 blast by the JMB, the security forces have so far have been able to arrest some 985 leaders. According to the Bangladesh Police sources, a total of 322 cases were filed with different police stations since the blast. Of these cases, the police have submitted charge sheets in 289 cases and final reports in 25 cases and 18 cases are under investigation. Similarly, trials of 115 cases have been completed, in which 51 persons got death sentence, 131 life imprisonment and 184 different terms. There have been 318 people acquitted and 174 cases are under trail.[25]

Though the government has shown interest in cracking down on the extremist elements, still there are some lacunae from the government's side. There is need to seize the bank accounts of the so-called NGOs and charitable organisations. There is also a need for better inter-agency coordination.

Current Status

Though many of the leaders of the JMB have been arrested and punished, it will not be prudent to think that the JMB is out of the scene in Bangladesh. Some of the interrogation reports and continuous arrests of the JMB cadres are indicators of the fact that the JMB is capable of reorganising and carrying out some major attacks. As far as the present structure of the JMB as an organisation is concerned, it continues to garner support from a considerable number of Islamic constituencies. After the executions in 2007, there was a change in the leadership of the JMB. Maulana Saidur Rahman alias Abu Zafar was made the amir of the JMB till his arrest in May 2010. According to the confession note of Saidur Rahman, it was revealed that after his arrest, Sohel Mahfuzahd has become the acting chief of the JMB and Nazmul Anwar Alam alias Bhagina Shahid has been recruited as the military wing commander.

There have been reports highlighting various splits inside JMB. In 2007, there emerged a breakaway faction from JMB which planned to form another radical organisation named Jadid Al-Qaeda (New Al-Qaeda). This was the result of the JMB's decision to refrain from military attacks for some time. Many also believe that such a faction emerged because of disagreement among the shura members over a number of issues relating to funding and leadership.[26] There was another split in the organisation when two senior members of JMB—Selim alias Saifullah and Shahadat alias Abdur Rahim—formed another organisation named Islam-o-Muslim (Islam and Muslim). Islam-o-Muslim wanted to take a hardliner approach against the JMB's decision to lie low for some time. However, the entire leadership of this organisation was arrested in July 2009.[27]

As mentioned earlier, the flow of funds from the locals in terms of donations is indicative of the fact that JMB as a militant organisation is not out of the scene. According to some locals, a lot of JMB cadres were seen working for BNP and JeI during the 2008 elections.[28] There are also reports suggesting that the JMB has a hit list of some 12 politicians from the ruling party. Also, it is tasking female operatives to carry out operations. The security forces and the law enforcement agencies are not very sure of the arms that JMB possesses. While some leaders of JMB claim that they have destroyed them all, some other leaders are of the opinion that they have been shifted to a safer place. It is, however, important to mention that the JMB retains a strong cadre base and residual capacities to create havoc in the country.

NOTES

1. For details of Sheikh Abdur Rahman's confession on the background of the JMB, see "The Threat from Jamaat-Ul Mujahideen Bangladesh", International Crisis Group, Asia Report No. 187, 1 March 2010, p. 3.
2. See Anwar Ali, "Jama'at-ul Tentacles Spread in Five and Half Years", *The Daily Star*, Vol. 5, No. 438, 19 August 2005, available at http://www.thedailystar.net/2005/08/19/d5081901033.htm (accessed on 1 December 2011).
3. Salafis subscribe to Sunni Islam but form a separate sect. Salafis call for return to Islam practices of the first generation of Muslims and adherence to original text believing that Islamic practices have since drifted away from its root through various interpretations. Salafis are also known as Ahle Hadith. The difference between the Sunnis and the Salafis is that the former believe that Prophet Mohammad was "Nur" or enlightened soul to guide the Muslims, while the latter believe that he was a normal human being. Available at http://www.differencesbetween.net/miscellaneous/difference-between-Sunni-Salafi/.
4. The AHAB is led by Asadullah Ghalib and was founded in 1994. This is believed to be a breakaway faction of the Ahle Hadith movement. Under Asadullah Ghalib's leadership, the AHAB made significant progress by constructing mosques, madrassas, women and children networks and non-governmental organisations (NGOs) through which it received funds from various Islamic organisations worldwide.
5. Smruti Pattanaik, "Radical Islamic Groups in Bangladesh: The Case of Jama'atul Mujahideen Bangladesh", in Arpita Anant (ed.), *Non-State Armed Groups in South Asia*, New Delhi: Pentagon Security International, 2011, p. 282.
6. Ibid.
7. See "JMB Suicide Bomber Kills 2 Judges", *The Daily Star*, Vol. 5, No. 522, 15 November 2005, available at http://archive.thedailystar.net/2005/11/15/d5111501011.htm, (accessed on 1 January 2012)
8. For details, see "The Threat from Jamaat-ul Mujahideen Bangladesh", pp. 4–5.
9. See Pattanaik, "Radical Islamic Groups in Bangladesh", pp. 283–84.
10. One of the four madrassas is established in the Jatrabari area of Dhaka region. The second one is established in Naogaon district's Atari, named as Agram Dakhali. The third one is in Khulna district and the fourth one is in Jamalpur.
11. For details, see "The Threat from Jamaat-ul Mujahideen Bangladesh", p. 5.
12. See Zayadul Ahsan, "Trained in Foreign Lands, they Spread Inland", *The Daily Star*, Vol. 5, No. 440, 21 August 2005, available at http://www.thedailystar.net/2005/08/21/d5082101044.htm (accessed on 10 January 2012).
13. See Anshuman Behera, "Islamist Vestiges", *South Asia Intelligence Review*, Vol. 9, No. 3, 26 July 2010, available at http://www.satp.org/satporgtp/sair/Archives/sair9/

9_3.htm#assessment2 (accessed on 2 January 2012).
14. For details, see Pattanaik, "Radical Islamic Groups in Bangladesh", p. 284.
15. See Behera, "Islamist Vestiges".
16. Ibid.
17. See Zayadul Ahsan, "They go free too easily", *The Daily Star*, 24 August 2005, available at http://archive.thedailystar.net/2005/08/24/d5082401033.htm (accessed on 3 January 2012).
18. For details, see Julfikar Ali Manik, "Trading in Death under Shadow of Govt", *The Daily Star*, Vol. 5, No. 1086, 21 June 2007, available at http://www.thedailystar.net/2007/06/21/d7062101011.htm (accessed on 2 January 2012).
19. For details of police support for the JMB, see "The Threat from Jamaat-ul Mujahideen Bangladesh", p. 11. Also, see "Tales of Horror: Cops Help Bangla Bhai Free from Naogaon", *The Daily Star*, 29 May 2004, available at http://archive.thedailystar.net/2004/05/29/d4052901033.htm (accessed on 2 January 2012).
20. For details of domestic fund raising of the JMB, see "The Threat from Jamaat-ul Mujahideen Bangladesh", p. 19.
21. See "JMB still getting plenty of funds: Flow of money from local, foreign sources remains intact despite arrest of top brass" *The Daily Star*, 15 September 2010, available at http://www.thedailystar.net/newDesign/news-details.php?nid=154489, (accessed on 2 January 2012)
22. Ibid.
23. See Rajeev Sharma, "Fake Indian Currency Note Racket in Bangladesh", South Asia Analysis Group, 13 September 2011, available at http://www.southasiaanalysis.org/%5Cpapers47%5Cpaper4695.html (accessed on 3 January 2012).
24. See Pattanaik, "Radical Islamic Groups in Bangladesh", p. 287.
25. For details, see "JMB Active despite Arrest of Top Brass", *The Daily Star*, 17 August 2010, available at http://www.thedailystar.net/newDesign/news-details.php?nid=151076 (accessed on 19 August 2010).
26. See "The Threat from Jamaat-ul Mujahideen Bangladesh", p. 15.
27. Ibid.
28. For details, see "Bangladesh: Elections and Beyond", International Crisis Group, Asia Briefing Paper No. 84, 11 December 2008.

3

Harkat-ul-Jihad-al-Islami-Bangladesh

The Harkat-ul-Jihad-al-Islami-Bangladesh (HuJI-B) is a militant organisation active mostly in Bangladesh since 1992. The HuJI-B can be called as the Bangladesh chapter of the Harkat-ul-Jihad-al-Islami (HuJI), which is believed to have been formed in 1980s by the Islamists of Pakistan, who fought against the Union of Soviet Socialist Republics (USSR) in Afghanistan. Initially, the HuJI operated as a group of supporters of the Afghanistan's fight against the Soviet forces. Those days, it used to work under the umbrella of an organisation called as the Jama'atul Ansar Afghani (JAA) (group of helpers). It is also believed that in the later stage, with the active support of the Pakistan's Inter Services Intelligence (ISI), the JAA was rechristened as the HuJI in 1988. According to the available sources, by the year 1988, when the Soviet forces left Afghanistan, the HuJI was believed to have the strength of about 4,000 cadres. In the 1980s, the HuJI mostly restricted its activities in Afghanistan only. In the later stage, it tried to expand its base and activities in different parts of the South Asian region. The HuJI-B is the result of the expansion project of the HuJI which was guided by an ideological orientation towards the belief in waging a war for the Muslims in the non-Muslim countries.

The HuJI-B, however, came to the notice only in the year 1992, and got prominence in 1999 when it engineered a plot to kill one of the renowned secularist poets of Bangladesh, Shamsur Rahman. Again, the group's presence was felt in a big way when it plotted to kill the then Prime Minister, Sheikh Hasina, by planting a bomb on 20 July 1999.

Genesis of HuJI-B

The formation of HuJI-B is an outcome of the expansionist project of the HuJI. The HuJI-B formally declared its existence in 1992 when a group of Bangladeshi Islamist fighters in the Afghan war declared it at a press conference in Dhaka on 30 April 1992. Such a declaration was made immediately a week after the mujahideens in Afghanistan emerged victorious against the Soviet force. The group of people who were present in this meeting were: Abdus Salam, president

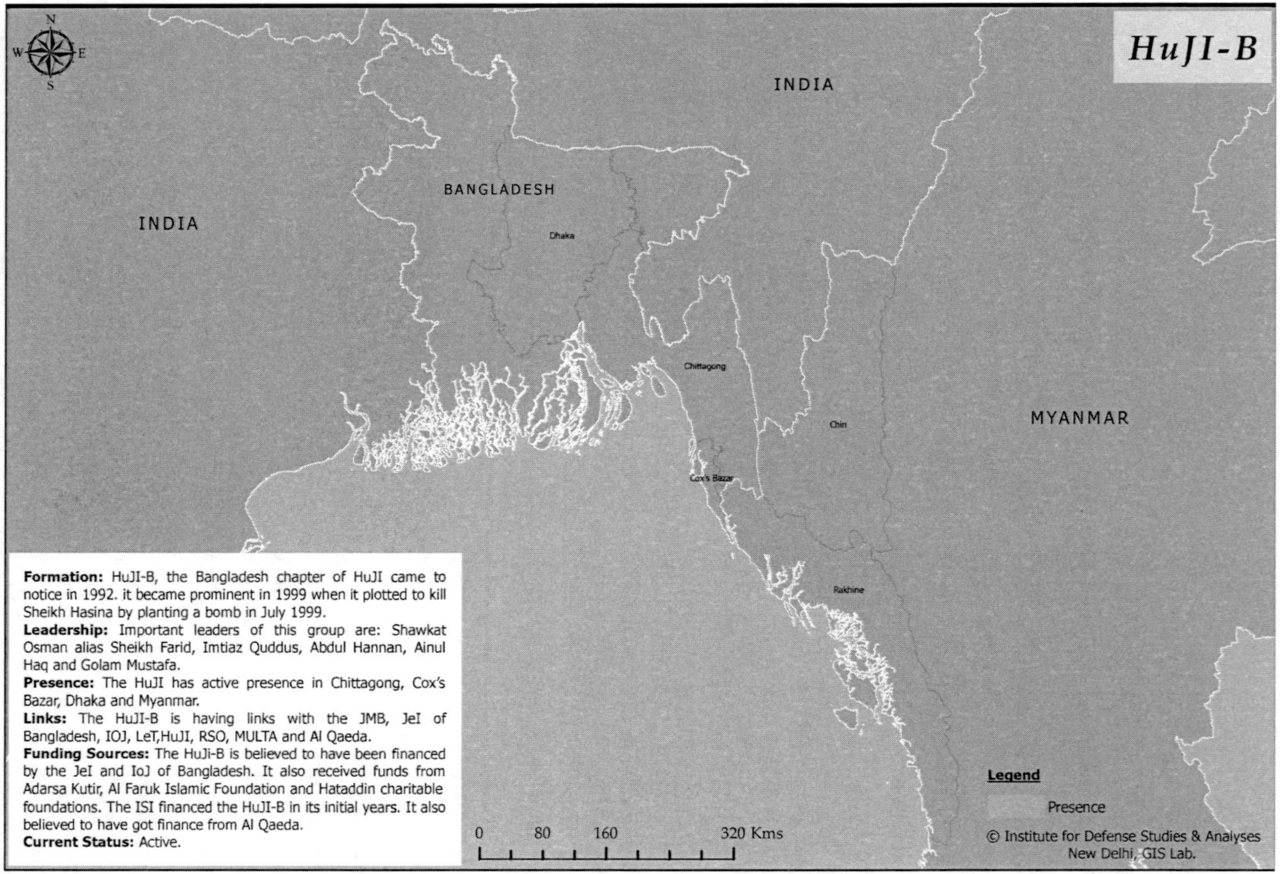

Formation: HuJI-B, the Bangladesh chapter of HuJI came to notice in 1992. it became prominent in 1999 when it plotted to kill Sheikh Hasina by planting a bomb in July 1999.
Leadership: Important leaders of this group are: Shawkat Osman alias Sheikh Farid, Imtiaz Quddus, Abdul Hannan, Ainul Haq and Golam Mustafa.
Presence: The HuJI has active presence in Chittagong, Cox's Bazar, Dhaka and Myanmar.
Links: The HuJI-B is having links with the JMB, JeI of Bangladesh, IOJ, LeT,HuJI, RSO, MULTA and Al Qaeda.
Funding Sources: The HuJi-B is believed to have been financed by the JeI and IoJ of Bangladesh. It also received funds from Adarsa Kutir, Al Faruk Islamic Foundation and Hataddin charitable foundations. The ISI financed the HuJI-B in its initial years. It also believed to have got finance from Al Qaeda.
Current Status: Active.

of HuJI-B; field commander, Manzur Hasan; Dhaka city unit president, Maulana Delwar Hossain; publicity secretary, Mufti Shafiqur Rahman; and Maulana Mufti Abdul Hye.[1] It was in this meeting that the HuJI-B declared that the first-ever Bangladesh mujahideen group was formed by Abdur Rahman with the help of the HuJI in 1984. He, however, died in 1989 in the Afghan war. Similarly, the meeting also identified the members of the HuJI-B and demanded from the then government, led by the Bangladesh Nationalist Party (BNP), to recognise the mujahideen government in Afghanistan and show proper respect to the Bangladesh "martyrs"[2] in Afghan war and establish a complete Islamic state in Bangladesh.

Objective and Ideology of HuJI-B

There is a very little ideological difference between the HuJI and the HuJI-B. The HuJI aims to be seen as the main patron by all the Muslims in the Indian subcontinent, and possibly elsewhere in the world.[3] Moreover, the HuJI also has an ambition to take over of the state of Pakistan, the eastern provinces of India and the western neighbours in Central Asia.[4] The (in)famous slogan of the HuJI-B that read "amar sobai hobo Taliban, Bangla hobe Afghanistan" (We will all turn to be Talibans and the state of Bangladesh will be Afghanistan), indicated that it was motivated by the ideology of Osama bin Laden and the Taliban rule of Afghanistan. According to the reports from the United States (US) government, the HuJI-B signed the February 1998 fatwa of Osama bin Laden which termed the American citizens are legitimate targets of Islam.

The HuJI-B has both a military and non-military wing for carrying out its operations. The military wing is meant for waging an armed jihad, whereas the non-military wing is engaged in the propaganda business. The non-military wing, again, has two sections: *dawat* (inviting someone to Islam) and *irshad* (religious preaching). The HuJI-B, like any other Islamic radical/militant group, believes that the ideas of secularism, composite culture and democracy are un-Islamic. Hence, it has targeted a number of scholars, politicians and cultural celebrations.

Leadership and Strength

Among the leaders of the HuJI-B, Fazlur Rahman was the most important one under whose leadership HuJI-B worked during the initial years. Some of the founding members of the HuJI-B were: Shaikhul Hadith Allama Azizul Haq, who was also associated with the Islami Oikyo Jote (IOJ) and a member of the former ruling coalition led by the BNP; Muhammad Habibur Rahman of Sylhet; Ataur Rahman Khan of Kishoreganj; Sultan Jaok of Chittagong; Abdul Mannan of Faridpur; and Habibullah of Noakhali.[5] It is also important to mention that it was under the leadership of Fazlur Rahman that the HuJI-B signed the official document of Osama bin Laden of armed jihad against the US on 23 February 1998.

According to the available sources, in the subsequent years, Shawkat Osman alias Sheikh Farid was appointed as its leader and Imtiaz Quddus was appointed as the general secretary. Sheikh Farid was arrested by the Rapid Action Battalion (RAB) of Bangladesh on 26 April 2011 from Ghazipur district. Similarly, another colleague of Sheikh Farid, Abdul Hannan, and the recruitment and secret training coordinator, Ainul Haq, was arrested on 25 April 2011 from Dhaka. Golam Mustafa was also an important leader of the HuJI-B and the chief of the United Kingdom (UK) unit. He, was arrested on 15 April 2010. The counter-terrorism initiatives by the Sheikh Hasina-led Awami League (AL) government have forced the leadership of the HuJI-B to go underground. However, according to the intelligence sources of Bangladesh, Maulana Yahiya has been given the charge of the HuJI-B. He received training in Pakistan in 1998 and on returning home, joined HuJI-B. He is also believed to have gone to Afghanistan and taken part in Afghan war against the Soviet Union along with Mufti Hannan and Sheikh Farid.[6]

According to the HuJI-B militants, arrested on various occasions, the organisation has about 15,000 members. However, this number cannot be verified. The arrest of 41 HuJI-B operatives with a huge arms cache at Cox's Bazar on 19 January 1996 and the recovery of some 76 kg bomb from Gopalganj on 20 July 2000 are indicative of the fact that the HuJI-B has a huge amount of explosives capable of causing major damage to Bangladesh. So far as the armed cadres of the HuJI-B are concerned, they are expected to be 700 in number. These 700 armed cadres are mainly Bangladeshis, Rohingya Muslims from the Arakan area of Myanmar and Pattani Muslims from southern Thailand.[7] There are some estimates which say that out of the strength of 15,000 cadres, 2,000 can be described as hardcore.[8]

Area of Operation

The HuJI-B is believed to have its main operational bases in the coastal areas stretching from Chittagong to Cox's Bazar to Myanmar.[9] Reportedly, the HuJI-B has six training camps in the hills of Chittagong and six more in and around Cox's Bazar area. Moreover, HuJI-B has a very strong network in various madrassas and non-governmental organisations (NGOs). According to a Bengali daily newspaper, *Prothom Alo*, the HuJI-B had its camps in Bandarban, Naikhangchari, Ukhia, Dailpara, Chandgaon and Khatunganj.[10]

Abul Kalam Azad alias Bulbul, who was believed to be the "chief trainer" of the HuJI-B till 2005, revealed to the Criminal Investigation Department (CID) that his activities were based in Borodah Dakhil madrassa in Shailakupa subdistrict of Jhenidah district and gave training to some 65 cadres at the bank of Kumar river. He also revealed to have trained at Balidapara Quami madrassa in Kaliganj subdistrict, Bhabanipur in Harinakundu subdistrict and some students' messes in Pabahati, Chaklapara, Dhol-Somudrer-Pukur and Bhuttiargati areas of Jhenidah district.[11]

Network and Funding

The HuJI-B has a very strong network at the national level and outside Bangladesh as well. At the national level, it has been successful in garnering support from like-minded militant groups and the politic groups which, in a way, supported the activities of the outfit by ignoring them. So far the links with the militant groups are concerned, the HuJI-B maintains a very strong link with the Jamaat-ul-Mujahideen Bangladesh (JMB). Since its emergence as a militant organisation, the HuJI-B has been getting support from the Rohingya Solidarity Organisation (RSO). Reportedly, the cadres of the HuJI-B have merged with other militant organisations after a ban being imposed on them.

At the political level, the HuJI-B got support from political parties like the Jamaat-e-Islami (JeI) and IOJ, when both the parties were part of the BNP-led government. There have been a number of instances where these two parties tried their best to cover up the activities of the HuJI-B. The HuJI-B carried out an attack on a rally of the AL on 21 August 2004 which killed 23 individuals and injured more than 150. In this case, the investigation under the direct supervision of the then state minister for home arrested some individuals, including two of AL members. Ironically, another investigation agency found out "foreign hand" behind the attack. There have been instances where the political leaders belonging to JeI have gone on record to say that "Bangla Bhai was the creation of the media". On 11 September 2005, the JeI lawmaker, Riasat Ali Biswas, said in the Parliament that "Reports of militant training of JMB and HuJI-B to turn Bangladesh into an Islamic State is nothing but Propaganda".[12] Moreover, some of the HuJI-B leaders were also leaders of the BNP-led four-party alliance. Prominent among them were IOJ leader, Shaikhul Hadith Allama Azziul Haq; Bangladesh Khelafat Majlish (Bangladesh Caliphate Council) second-in-command, Muhammad Habibur Rahman; Ataur Rahman Khan; Sultan Jaok; Abdul Mannan; and Habibullah.[13]

Outside Bangladesh, the HuJI-B has a strong link with the HuJI Pakistan, which is quite obvious. At the same time, HuJI-B is also believed to have support from the ISI Pakistan. An investigation report by the CID of Bangladesh has revealed that of the 32 Arges grenades sent to HuJI-B by Pakistan-based militant outfit, Lashkar-e-Taiba (LeT), most were used in at least seven major terror attacks in 2004–05. Investigators unearthed this while trying to get to the source of the grenade used in the killing of AL leader and former Finance Minister, S.A.M.S. Kibria.[14] This report provides credible evidence of the link between HuJI-B and the LeT.

The arrest of one LeT leader in October 2009 in Dhaka and a subsequent statement from the LeT militant revealed that it had links with the HuJI-B and they were planning for a terror network in the region.[15] Similarly, there have been reports suggesting HuJI-B having links with militant groups in South Asia in general, and India in particular. In May 2002, some nine radical Islamist groups, including HuJI-B, formed Bangladesh Islamic Manch. This newly formed radical association was believed to have included a group representing the Rohingyas of Myanmar and the Muslim United Liberation Tigers of Assam (MULTA).[16]

So far the funding of the HuJI-B is concerned, reportedly, it receives financial assistance from Pakistan, Saudi Arabia and Afghanistan through some NGOs like Adarsa Kutir, Al Faruk Islamic Foundation and Hataddin. There are also reports suggesting financial help from the ISI for the HuJI-B. In the initial years of HuJI-B's existence, it was believed that the funding came from different organisations supported by Osama bin Laden via NGOs to construct madrassas and training camps. A Pakistani citizen, Mohammad Sajid, who was arrested for attacking poet Shamsur Rahman on 18 January 1999, told police that he received Taka 2 crore and gave it to someone called Bakhtiar. Bakhtiar, when arrested in Sirajganj the same year, confessed to police that he distributed the money among 421 madrassas for training cadres of HuJI-B.[17]

Apart from that, the HuJI-B has demanded Taka 400 million as extortion from Asha University located at Dhaka.[18] According to this report, two men claiming to be the cadres of the HuJI-B set a deadline of 17 October 2011 for the money and threatened to blow up the university if the university authorities failed to comply with such a demand. Besides extortion, HuJI-B also gets donations from its supporters and various madrassas. It is also involved in criminal activities like piracy, smuggling and small arms running in many parts of Bangladesh to raise funds.

Government Response

As mentioned earlier, the threat of HuJI-B was first felt in January 1999 when it attempted to kill a poet. Similarly, in the year 2000 also, it attempted to kill the then Prime Minister, Sheikh Hasina. A number of terror activities were undertaken by the HuJI-B from 1999 to 2005. Ironically, the US blacklisted the HuJI as an international terrorist group in 2002. Again, the Bangladesh chapter of the HuJI, HuJI-B, was blacklisted by the US in 2003. But the Bangladesh government outlawed the organisation only in the year 2005 after growing pressure from political opponents of the BNP and international actors.

The HuJI-B garnered support from the Islamic parties like the JeI and the IOJ and to some extent, the BNP. For example, the then Foreign Minister of Bangladesh, M. Morshed Khan, once said in 26 February 2005 "There maybe some local goons, working in the name of religion, who are being hunted down. There is a difference between international terrorists and local goons.There are no international terrorists in the country".[19] There are many instances where it was found that political persons in the BNP-led government, mostly from the JeI and the IOJ, had links with the HuJI-B. The BNP-led government in Bangladesh banned the HuJI-B in 2005 following a countrywide blast on 17

August 2005, terming it as a "self-confessed militant organisation". There are reports which claim that the Prime Minister, Khalida Zia, had held a meeting with the HuJI-B leaders who had called on her, after the ban. Further, a number of HuJI-B leaders, under a different banner, held a meeting in Dhaka with the government approval.

It is, however, important to mention that the law enforcement agencies have arrested a number of key leaders of the HuJI-B despite the support of the BNP-led government. Some of the important leaders who have been arrested by the law enforcement agencies are: the operations commander, Mufti Abdul Hannan, in 2005; a key accomplice of Hannan, Abu Zandal, in 2008; one of the founding members of the HuJI-B, Abdus Salam, in 2009; and many others. The AL-led government has been committed towards counter-terrorism activities which are proving to be positive in controlling the activities of the HuJI-B. On 29 June 2011, Prime Minister Sheikh Hasina said that apart from banning five organisations (Jagrata Muslim Janata Bangladesh [JMJB], JMB, Shahadat-e al Hiqma, HuJI-B and Hizb-ut-Tahrir [HuT]) for militant activities, the government is closely watching some other suspected organisations. She stated, "acts of militancy and terrorism will not be allowed on the soil of the country".[20]

In this connection, on 14 July 2011, a Dhaka court issued arrest warrants against BNP Senior Vice Chairman, Tarique Rahman, and 11 others in the 21 August 2004 grenade attack. The law enforcement agencies produced former State Minister for Home, Lutfozzaman Babar, JeI secretary general, Ali Ahsan Mohammad Mojaheed, former BNP Deputy Minister, Abdus Salam Pintu, HuJI-B chief, Mufti Abdul Hannan, and 25 others before the court in this connection.

Current Status

The HuJI-B has not been involved in major acts of militancy in last few years. Soon after the ban imposed by the government, many of the cadres and leaders of the HuJI-B are believed to have joined other militant groups like JMB or are at large. The HuJI-B is suspected to have opened up a number of sleeper cells in Bangladesh which may pose serious security threats to Bangladesh. Though the law enforcement agencies have arrested many of the key leaders of the outfit, they are facing difficulties in catching more cadres of the HuJI-B as they do not come out openly.

Some of the former leaders of the HuJI-B have gone on to float a new political party, Islamic Democratic Party (IDP). Maulana Sheikh Abdus Salam, who was instrumental in floating the party, has been charge sheeted by Bangladesh court over 21 August 2004 grenade attack. A number of HuJI-B cadres and leaders who have been arrested by the law enforcement agencies have been punished. On 13 October 2011, a special tribunal in Brahmanbaria district sentenced six militants of HuJI-B to various terms of imprisonment in four separate cases. The convicts were identified as Shamsul Islam Mollah, Musa Miah, Maulana Hedayatullah, Saiful Islam Sajib alias Saifullah, Jamal Miah and Mizanur Rahman.

Though the militant activities of the HuJI-B have gone down drastically in Bangladesh, but still, HuJI-B maintains a full-fledged military wing and has spread into India for its activities. There have been in a number of occasions where HuJI-B's hand has been suspected by the security agencies. The Intelligence Bureau of India suspects that the HuJI-B is on a recruitment spree. Allegedly, some 150 youths of West Bengal have gone missing and they are suspected to have been trained by the HuJI-B for its anti-India activities.[21]

In Bangladesh, the government, under the leadership of Sheikh Hasina, has taken strong and positive steps to crack down on the terrorist organisations. But very little attempt has been made to investigate the roles of madrassas and NGOs in supporting and promoting groups like HuJI-B. With continuous support from the NGOs and the madrassas, HuJI-B has not ceased to be a terrorist organisation and continues to be a threat to the security of Bangladesh and its neighbouring countries, especially India.

NOTES

1. See Zayadul Ahsan, "HuJI Men Holed Up in Other Militant Groups", *The Daily Star*, Vol. 5, No. 498, 19 October 2005, available at http://www.thedailystar.net/2005/10/19/d5101901011.htm (accessed on 15 April 2012).
2. For the list of Bangladeshi mujahideens killed in Afghan war, see ibid.
3. See Sundeep Waslekar, *The Final Settlement: Restructuring India–Pakistan Relations*, Bombay: Strategic Foresight Group, 2005, available at http://www.strategicforesight.com/finalsettlement/extremists2.pdf (accessed on 2 April 2012).
4. Ibid.
5. See B. Raman, "US Designates HuJI-B as a Foreign Terrorist Organisation", South Asia Analysis Group, 10 March 2008, available at http://www.southasiaanalysis.org/%5Cpapers27%5Cpaper2613.html (accessed on 10 April 2012).
6. See "Attack Plan of Huji", available at http://203.202.240.242/component/news/task-show/id-48699 (accessed on 10 April 2012).
7. See Raman, "US Designates HuJI-B as a Foreign Terrorist Organisation".
8. See Bertil Lintner, "Extremist Islamist Consolidation", available at http://www.satp.org/satporgtp/publication/faultlines/volume14/Article1.htm (accessed on 20 March 2012).
9. See Raman, "US Designates HuJI-B as a Foreign Terrorist Organisation".
10. See "Bangladeshi Group Training Indian Extremists", *The Times of India*, New Delhi, 2 September 2004, available at http://articles.timesofindia.indiatimes.com/2004-09-02/india/27145773_1_arms-training-outfit-media-report (accessed on 20 March 2012).
11. For details, see Hossain Seraj and Azibor Rahman, "65 HuJI Cadres Trained in Jhenidah Camps till 2005", *The Daily Star*, 18 November 2007, available at http://www.thedailystar.net/newDesign/news-details.php?nid=12055 (accessed on 15 March 2012).
12. See "Harkatul Jihad banned at last: Govt terms it a terrorist outfit," *The Daily Star*, 18 October 2005, available at http://archive.thedailystar.net/2005/10/18/d5101801033.htm (accessed on 16 March 2012).
13. See Sarwar Alam, "The Genesis of Islamic Extremism in Bangladesh", Unpublished thesis, Emory University, Georgia, September 2008, available at http://www.humiliationstudies.org/

documents/AlamNY08meeting.pdf (accessed on 15 June 2012).

14. See Julfikar Ali Manik, "32 LeT Grenades Let Terror Loose", *The Daily Star*, 28 January 2011, available at http://www.thedailystar.net/newDesign/news-details.php?nid=171859 (accessed on 20 March 2012).
15. "Extremists are Regrouping", *The Daily Star*, 3 October 2009, available at http://archive.thedailystar.net/newDesign/news-details.php?nid=107971 (accessed on 15 June 2012).
16. See Lintner, "Extremist Islamist Consolidation".
17. See Zayadul Ahsan, "Foreign Funding, Local Business Keep them Going", *The Daily Star*, 22 August 2005, available at http://www.thedailystar.net/2005/08/22/d5082201044.htm (accessed on 10 January 2012).
18. For details, see "HuJI Demands Extortion from Private University", *Weekly Blitz*, 15 October 2011, available at http://www.weeklyblitz.net/1889/huji-demands-extortion-from-private-university (accessed on 12 October 2012).
19. See B Raman, "Terrorists? yes, but Al Qaeda? No", 7 March 2005, available at http://orfonline.org/cms/sites/orfonline/modules/analysis/AnalysisDetail.html?cmaid=2633&mmacmaid=956 (accessed on 4 September, 2013)
20. See "Suspected militant outfits under watch", 29 June 2011, available at http://ns.bdnews24.com/details.php?id=199698&cid=3 (accessed on 4 September 2013)
21. See "HuJI on recruitment spree against India: IB", 12 July 2011, available at http://www.rediff.com/news/report/huji-on-recruitment-spree-against-india-ib/20110712.htm (accessed on 4 September 2013)

PART-B
INDIA

I. Jammu and Kashmir

4

Hizb-ul-Mujahideen
(Party of Holy Warriors)

Introduction

The Hizb-ul-Mujahideen (HM) is claimed to be one of the largest militant outfits operating in Jammu and Kashmir (J&K). It is also one of the most dangerous outfits in terms of its effectiveness in perpetrating violence in J&K. The HM was founded by one Master Ahsan Dar of Patan in North Kashmir in September 1989. The group was formed to marginalise the pro-independence Jammu and Kashmir Liberation Front (JKLF). The group is basically a pro-Pakistani group and is a militant outfit of Jamaat-e-Islami in Kashmir (JeIK). Ashan Dhar continued to be the chief of the HM till 1991 when he was charged with misappropriation of funds. Supported by the JeIK, the former Amir-e-Zila (chief of the district) of Srinagar, Mohammad Yusuf Shah alias Syed Salahuddin, took over as the supreme commander of the HM on 11 November 1991. The takeover by Salahuddin saw increased activities of the JeIK cadres as the over ground force of the HM. However, the difference between the JeIK supporters and the non-supporters led to a split in the HM. One faction was led by Salahuddin, whereas the other was led by Hilal Ahmed Mir. Hilal Ahmed Mir was killed in 1993.

The Pakistani intelligence agency, the Inter Services Intelligence (ISI), played a vital role as far as the militant activities of the HM are concerned in its initial years. As reported, a number of HM militants hailing from Rajouri and Poonch had joined the ISI to carry out sabotage activities in Jammu.[1] It was also revealed that the HM, along with the ISI, carried out explosion in the Maulana Azad Memorial (MAM) stadium in Jammu on 26 January 1995.

Objectives

The HM's prime objective is the integration of the J&K with Pakistan. The integration process, it believes, can be achieved through Islamisation of J&K and jihad. The commander of the HM, Salahuddin, declared during a rally in March 2010 in Pakistan that "the only way to liberate Kashmir is jihad". It is

Hizb-ul-Mujahideen

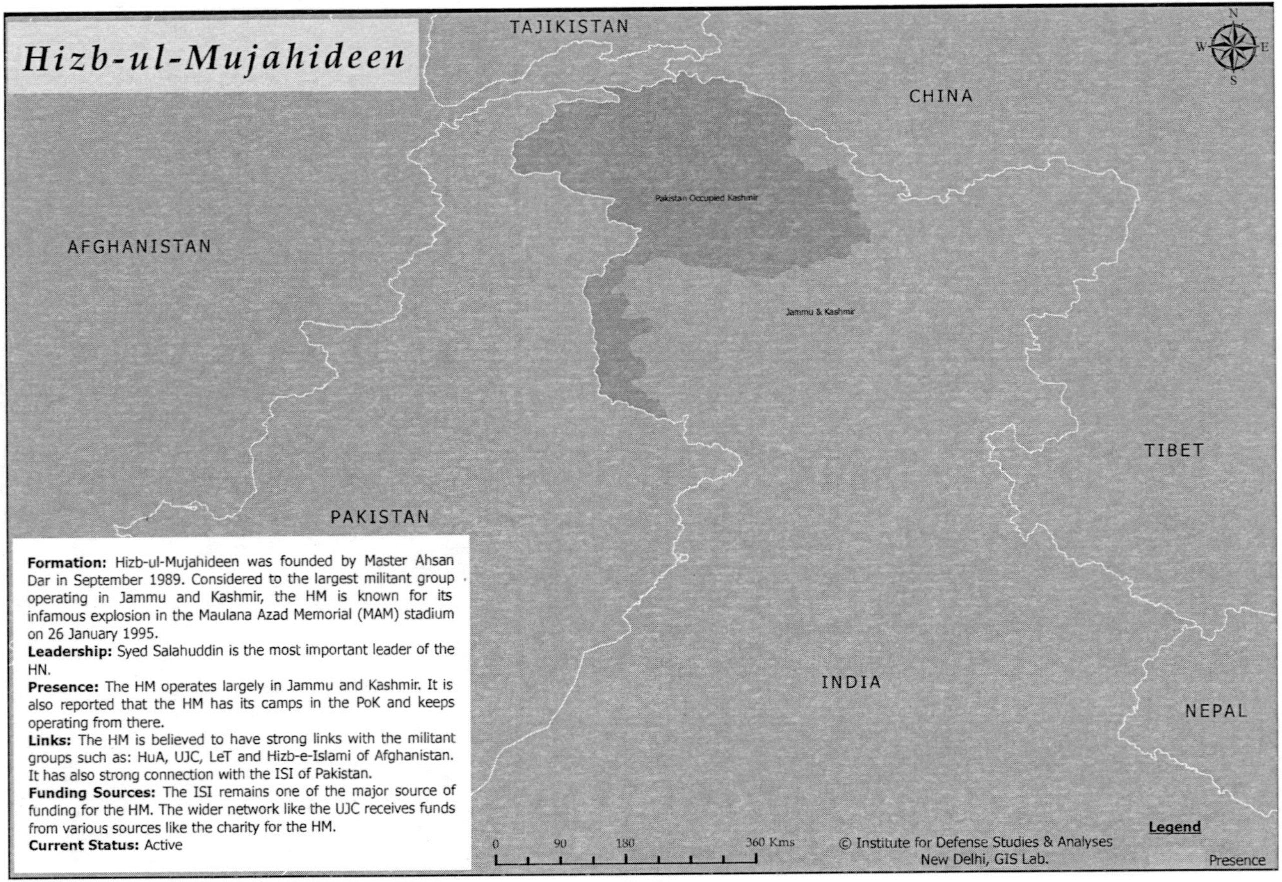

Formation: Hizb-ul-Mujahideen was founded by Master Ahsan Dar in September 1989. Considered to the largest militant group operating in Jammu and Kashmir, the HM is known for its infamous explosion in the Maulana Azad Memorial (MAM) stadium on 26 January 1995.

Leadership: Syed Salahuddin is the most important leader of the HN.

Presence: The HM operates largely in Jammu and Kashmir. It is also reported that the HM has its camps in the PoK and keeps operating from there.

Links: The HM is believed to have strong links with the militant groups such as: HuA, UJC, LeT and Hizb-e-Islami of Afghanistan. It has also strong connection with the ISI of Pakistan.

Funding Sources: The ISI remains one of the major source of funding for the HM. The wider network like the UJC receives funds from various sources like the charity for the HM.

Current Status: Active

important to mention that the rally was also attended by some key leaders of the Jamaat-ud-Dawa, a front for the Lashkar-e-Taiba (LeT).[2] The HM is against those who stand for independence as the third option. In a hand written statement issued on July 30, 1991, it described the JKLF stand as "childish and highly irresponsible".[3]

Organisation and Leadership

According to the constitutional norms of the HM, the organisation would have a central command led by the amir (chief) and commander-in-chief. There will also be district-level and local-level commanders.

For better geographical operations, the HM has been divided into five divisions. The central division controls Srinagar; the northern division controls the districts of Kupwara–Bandipora–Baramulla; Anantnag and Pulwama come under the control of southern division; Chenab division controls Doda and Udhampur districts; and Pir Pinjal division controls the Rajouri and Poonch districts.

The command structure of the HM is highly centralised. The supreme commander of the HM is Syed Salahuddin who operates from Muzaffarabad in POK. Some of the important leaders of the HM are: Ahsan Dar who became first commander chief; Al Badr commander, Bakht Zameen; founder of Hizb-e-Islami, Masood Sarfaraz, Nasir-ul-Islam, Abdul Majeed Dar, Saif-ul-Islam, Ghazi Nasiruddin, Ghazi Shahab-ud-din, Latif Dar, Nasir Ahmad Dar, Talib Lali etc. Factions and divisions among the leaders of the HM have been a common phenomenon. The HM was in a rude shock on July 24, 2000, when its Salar-e-Ala i.e. commander-in-chief in J&K Abdul Majid Dar announced a conditional ceasefire to the Indian government at a press conference at Srinagar. The offer was promptly endorsed by Syed Salahuddin but he backed out on August 8, 2000 presumably under pressure from ISI. This led to the suspension of Majid Dar and clashes between Salahuddin and Majid Dar supporters. Majid Dar was subsequently killed on March 23, 2003 in Sopore in north Kashmir. Saif ul Islam who was appointed as chief commander of J&K by Salahuddin following suspension of Majid Dar was also killed in Srinagar on April 2, 2003. Saif ul Islam was replaced by Ghazi Nasirudin as its commander in chief in J&K. Ghazi Nasirudin whose real name was Ghulam Rasool Dar was also killed by security forces on January 16, 2004. Following this, HM appointed Ghazi Shahab-ud-Din as new chief operational commander and Mohammad Ghazavi as chief military adviser.[4]

The HM has also a media department based ar Muree Road, Rawalpindi. It runs a news agency, the Kashmir Press International and a research centre, the Kashmir Information Centre based in Muzaffarabad in Pakistan-occupied Kashmir (PoK). The militant group has also appointed Saleem Hashmi as its spokesman. It had also set up a women's wing, the Binat-ul-Islam led by Umi-Arifa. Its main aim is to convince women to send their youth to join jihad and look after the families of slain militants.[5]

Areas of Operation

The HM reportedly has a substantial support base in the Kashmir Valley and in the Doda, Rajouri, Poonch districts and parts of Udhampur district in the Jammu region. The HM operates from Muzaffarabad in PoK. It has regularly been targeting Indian security forces stationed in Jammu & Kashmir. Besides, it also killed many prominent political, bureaucrats, moderate religious and secular leaders. In its bid to enforce islamisation in Kashmir, the militant group has proclaimed bans on cinema, advertisement hoardings, entertainment cable television channels, liquor shops and beauty parlours for women.[6] It was also responsible for setting on fire the shrine of Charar-e-Sharif on 11 May 1995.[7] The HM has also lost hundreds of its armed cadres during insurgency operations by Indian security forces. The Ikhwan comprising of its surrendered militants also gave a support to security forces by killing nearly 2,000 HM militants and commanders. Led by Kukka Parrey, this counter-insurgency force was active in Sonawari-Bandipora, Sareer Khan in Pattan, Nabi Azad in rural Anantnag and Hilal Hider in Anantnag town.[8] It is estimated that half of the 11,000 militants killed in the first 11 years of militancy in Kashmir belonged to the HM. The HM suffered another set back in 2007 when the Indian security forces eliminated about 350 militants including 33 senior commanders and its chief operational commander Ijaz Ahmed Chopan.[9] Thus with the large scale arrests, killings and surrenders of HM militants and its commanders, the organization has weakened considerably. During the last one year also, security forces have arrested number of its commanders. They included, Lateef Dar alias Lateef Kachru, Talib Ali and Nisar Ahmad Dar alias Usman.

Cadre Strength, Recruitment and Training

The exact cadre strength of the HM is difficult to know. Different sources cite different figures. Within one year of its formation, the HM had around 10,000 armed cadres mostly trained in Pakistan or PoK. However, the cadre strength of the HM can be now around 1,000–2,000.[10] The cadres recruited by the HM are mostly local Kashmiris and from the PoK. Syed Salahuddin has also mentioned that there had been cadres from Pakistan at some point of time in HM.[11] The chief of the HM has also gone on the record to say that there has been full support of the Pakistan Army in allowing the HM cadres to move free in PoK and undergo the training programme. He said, "And we have hundreds of training camps in the state where we recruit and train the mujahideen".[12] Initially a vast training complex for HM known as Badr I and Badr II was established at Jihadwal on the southeast of Zhawara near Khost in Afghanistan. Here thousands of HM militants were trained which were resourced by the Haqqani Network.[13]

Training of the HM cadres usually takes place in the PoK region. According to one source,[14] in the 1990s, the HM had its training camps in Punjab, Khyber Pakhtunkhwa (KP) and Islamabad. The ISI played a major role in allowing the newcomers for training, mainly in Kotli and Muzaffarabad. So far the training of the cadres is concerned, physical, ideological and military training has been given. Its recruits were given training to handle weapons such as AK-47s, RPGs, hand grenades and light machine guns. Some of the main training camps of the HM were: Kotli training camp (in PoK's Kotli district); the Gujar Khan Training Centre in Rawalpindi; Mangla Dam camp (for training in swimming-related activities), located on the banks of the Mangla Lake in PoK; Kot Jamial camp (located on the outskirts of Kot Jamial in PoK's Bhimber district); Bhimber camp (situated on Gujrat Road in PoK's town of Bhimber); Samani camp (located on Mirpur Road); and the Al Markaz camp (located in the basement of a mosque which is three kilometers from central Mirpur).[15] After 9/11, most of these camps were closed following mounting international pressure. The militant group is currently operating two training camps – Garhi Habibullah Camp in Mansehra in KP and Sensa in Kotli (PoK).

The HM has been successful through its propaganda and social work initiatives. The initiatives like the rescue-and-relief work during the 2005 earthquake and "save the forest" work in Doda district are some of the measures that have helped the HM in recruiting individuals.

Networks

The HM's link and association with the ISI is very strong. At the same time, the HM also enjoys support of all the groups that are members of the United Jihad Council (UJC), and Syed Salahuddin is heading the UJC. In the initial years, the HM established links with the Afghan militant group; the Hizb-e-Islami headed by Gulbuddin Hekmtiyar and sent some of its cadres to Afghanistan for training with Hizb-i-Islami militants. The HM is also reported to have links with the militant groups such as LeT and Harkat-ul-Ansar /Harkat ul Mujahideen and have been providing logistical support to them in carrying out militant activities in Kashmir.[16] The HM's link with the LeT was made clear when Syed Salahuddin was photographed with Zaki-ur-Rehman Lakhvi after the 26 November 2008 attack on Mumbai by the latter. HM is also supported by Washington based Kashmir American Council and London based World Kashmir Freedom Movement.

Weapons

The cadres of the HM are believed to possess weapons such as AK-47s, RPG-7s, hand grenades and light machine guns.

Finance and Funding

In its initial years of formation, the HM was mostly supported by the ISI for carrying out its militant activities. These days, the HM has a wider network through which it generates its finance. On 3 March 2012, a Delhi court framed charges against a close aide of Hurriyat leader (hardline), Syed Ali Shah Geelani, and three others for allegedly running hawala rackets to finance the militant organisations in the valley.[17] The National Investigation Agency (NIA) accused these men for helping the HM to raise funds. According to the NIA sources, the network goes to Saudi Arabia.[18] Apart from this, the HM also raises funds through charity and during religious festivals. Extortion is another important source of fund raising for the HM.

Current Status

Despite the arrest and killing of its top commanders and militants, the HM still remains the biggest indigenous militant outfit. On 13 December 2012, the Union Home Minister, Sushil Kumar Shinde, said that both the LeT and the HM continue to be a serious threat to the security situation of India despite the improved security situation. He also added that the HM is mostly operating in the areas of Baramulla, Kupwara and Bandipora, Anantnag and Pulwama districts in Kashmir and Poonch, Ramban and Rajouri in Jammu region.[19]

The HM has also been active in threatening the *sarpanch*es at the local level to resign and raise voice against the democratic systems of India. The HM has so far killed three *sarpanch*es since the panchayat election of 2011. According to intelligence reports, HM and Al Badr militants carried out fidayeen attacks at a police station in Harinagar town in Kathua district and an Army camp in adjoining Sambha district in Jammu region on 26 September 2013.[20] 12 people, including four policemen and six army personnel were killed in the twin attacks. It also claimed responsibility of attack on CRPF picket killing two of its jawans in Awantipora in south Kashmir on November 7, 2013. Such militant activities of the HM will keep on posing a serious threat to the security in J&K.

NOTES

1. See K. Santhanam, Sreedhar, Sudhir Saxsena and Manish, *Jihadis in Jammu and Kashmir*, New Delhi: Sage, 2003, p. 126.
2. See Bill Roggio, "Hizbul Mujahideen Chief: Pakistan Allows Terror Group to Run 'Hundreds of Training Camps'", *The Long War Journal*, 27 May 2011, available at http://www.longwarjournal.org/archives/2011/05/hizbul_mujahideen_ch.php#ixzz2Ar0Yqaa1 (accessed on 21 July 2012).
3. Sati Sahni, "The birth of the Hizbul Mujahideen", *redif.com*, 31 July 2000 available at http://www.rediff.com/news/2000/jul/31hizb.htm (accessed on 11 September 2012.
4. See Naveed Ahmad, "Under Fire," *The Newsline*, February 2004, pp. 37-38.
5. See Muzamil Jaleel, "Spawning Militancy: The Rise of Hizbul", *The Indian Express*, 22 May

2003, available at http;//www.jammu-kashmir.com/archives2003/kashmir20030522d.html (accessed in 27 July 2013).

6. Jane's World Insurgency and Terrorism, Hizbul Mujahideen, available at http://articles.janes.com/articles/Janes-World-Insurgency-and-Terrorism/Hizb-ul-Mujahide... (accessed on 11 September 2012.
7. See Hizbul Mujahideen: A profile, *Times of India*, 20 May 2003, available at http://articles.timesofindia.indiatimes.com/2003-05-20/pakistan/27287499_1_jammu-and...(accessed on 25 October 2012.
8. See Muzamil Jaleel, "The Spawnining Militancy:The Rise of Hizbul".
9. See Frank Hyland & Animesh Roul, Hizb-ul-Mujahideen:Reaching beyond Kashmir available at http://counterterrorismblog.org/2008/01/hizbulmujahideen_reaching_beyo.php (accessed on 31 October 2012.
10. See Sati Sahni, n.3.
11. For details, see Aditya Raj Kaul, "Dialogue is Useless, Armed Struggle will Continue", an interview with Syed Salahuddin, 15 July 2012, available at http://www.thesundayindian.com/en/story/dialogue-is-useless-armed-struggle-will-continue/24/37202/ (accessed on 1 January 2013).
12. See "Pak Supports Militants in Kashmir: Hizbul Mujahideen Chief", *The Times of India*, 27 May 2011, available at http://articles.timesofindia.indiatimes.com/2011-05-27/pakistan/29590513_1_kashmir-issue-militants-terror-links (accessed on 1 January 2013).
13. See Vahid Brown & Don Rassler, Fountainhead of Jihad: The Haqqani Nexus 1973-2012, Hachette India, 2013, p.70.
14. See Nikhil Raymond Puri, "Inside the Camps that Foment Terror", *The Hindu*, 3 February 2012, available at http://www.thehindu.com/opinion/op-ed/article2854401.ece (accessed on 1 January 2013).
15. Ibid.
16. See Hizbul Mujahideen: A profile, *Times of India*, 20 May 2003.
17. For details, see "4 on Trial for Funding Hizbul Mujahideen in Valley", *The Times of India*, 4 March 2012, available at http://articles.timesofindia.indiatimes.com/2012-03-04/delhi/31121203_1_hawala-charge-sheet-nia (accessed on 1 January 2013).
18. Ibid.
19. See "Hizbul, LeT Continue to be Dominant in J&K: Shinde", *The Times of India*, 14 December 2012, available at http://articles.timesofindia.indiatimes.com/2012-12-14/india/35818959_1_hizbul-mujahideen-counter-terrorism-issues-terror-outfits (accessed on 1 January 2013).
20. Yatish Yadiv, "Al Badr, Hizbul behind Jammu attack", *The New Indian Express*, 27 September 2013, available at http://newindianexpress.com/nation/Al-Badr-Hizbul-behind-Jammu-attack/2013/09/27/ar (accessed on 29 Sept 2013).

5

Jammu and Kashmir Liberation Front

Introduction

The Jammu and Kashmir Liberation Front (JKLF) advocates independent Jammu and Kashmir (J&K) comprising all Kashmir territory that is presently under the control of India, Pakistan and China. It was founded by Amanullah Khan, a native of Gilgit in the Northern Areas (now Gilgit–Baltistan) of Pakistan, and Maqbool Bhat, who hailed from Trehgam village of Kupwara district, in Birmingham (the United Kingdom [UK]) on 29 May 1977. It was Maqbool Bhat who had first formed the Kashmir Independent Committee, which was merged into Sheikh Abdullah's Plebiscite Front, and then, in 1965, he formed the National Liberation Front. Ever since its formation in 1977, till 1994, JKLF remained an active terrorist organisation with branches in the UK, Europe, the United States (US) and the Middle East. In the 1980s, it also opened branches in Pakistan-occupied Kashmir (PoK) and J&K. Its major terrorist acts include the hijacking of Indian Airlines plane to Lahore in 1971, and again in 1976, and the killing of Indian diplomat, Ravindra Mhatre, in Birmingham in 1984.

There were violent acts in the Valley too. On 31 July 1988 Srinagar was rocked with twin blasts at Central Telegraph office and Gulf Club making the beginning of militancy in Kashmir. Thereafter, JKLF militants unleashed a reign of terror in Kashmir by killing many bureaucrats, politicians, teachers, Kashmir Pundits and security forces. The JKLF militants kidnapped, in 1989, Rubaiya Sayeed, daughter of the then Indian Home Minister, Mufti Mohammad Sayeed, who was released in the exchange of five JKLF militants. In 1990, they also kidnapped and killed the Kashmir University vice chancellor and his secretary. In the UK, Amanullah Khan was charge sheeted but he was acquitted by the British court. However, he was deported to Pakistan by the British authorities, where he re-established contacts with the Inter Services Intelligence (ISI) of Pakistan to internationalise and intensify militancy in J&K by setting up training camps in PoK and encouraging Kashmir youth to cross over and receive training at these camps. Emboldened by these steps, Amanullah Khan went a step further and announced the formation of provisional government of the independent state

JKLF

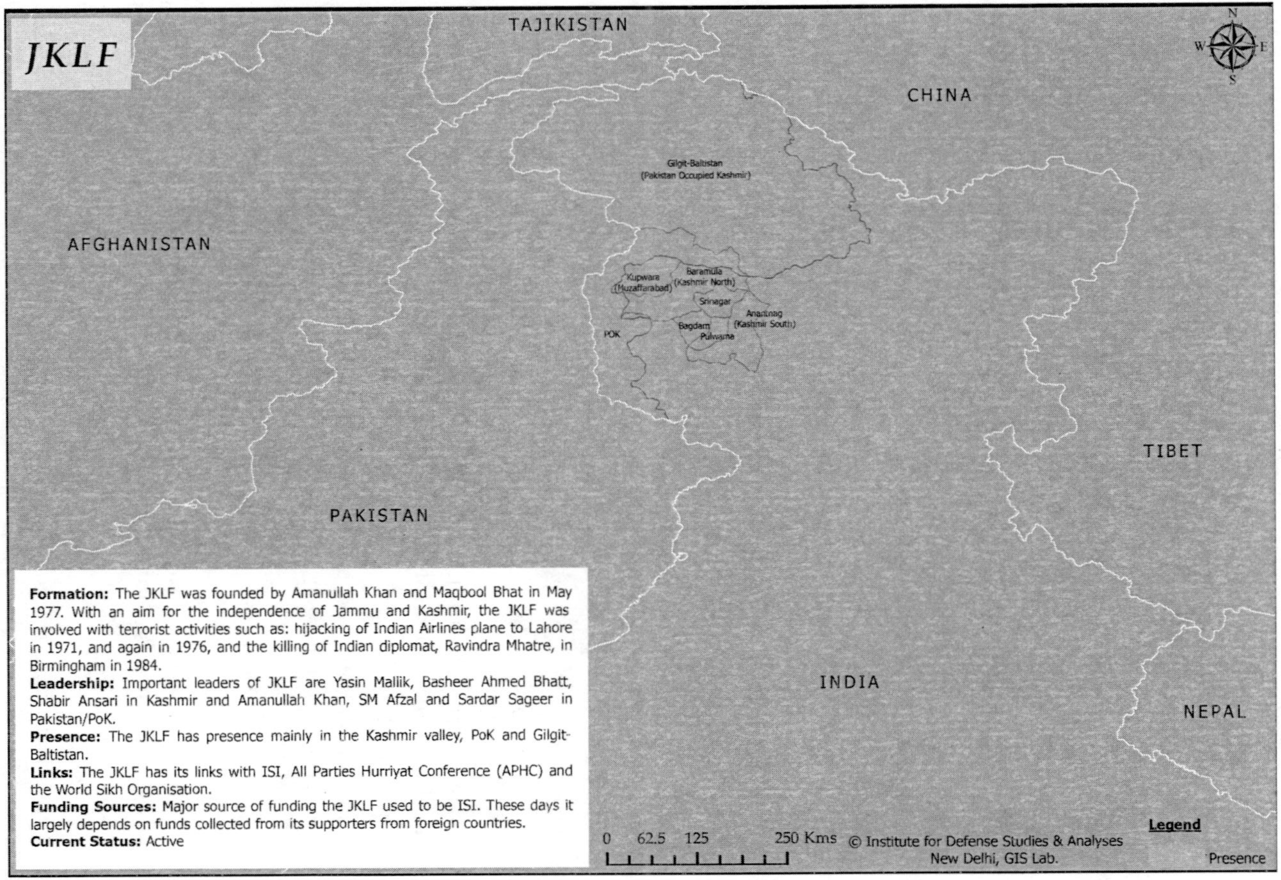

Formation: The JKLF was founded by Amanullah Khan and Maqbool Bhat in May 1977. With an aim for the independence of Jammu and Kashmir, the JKLF was involved with terrorist activities such as: hijacking of Indian Airlines plane to Lahore in 1971, and again in 1976, and the killing of Indian diplomat, Ravindra Mhatre, in Birmingham in 1984.

Leadership: Important leaders of JKLF are Yasin Mallik, Basheer Ahmed Bhatt, Shabir Ansari in Kashmir and Amanullah Khan, SM Afzal and Sardar Sageer in Pakistan/PoK.

Presence: The JKLF has presence mainly in the Kashmir valley, PoK and Gilgit-Baltistan.

Links: The JKLF has its links with ISI, All Parties Hurriyat Conference (APHC) and the World Sikh Organisation.

Funding Sources: Major source of funding the JKLF used to be ISI. These days it largely depends on funds collected from its supporters from foreign countries.

Current Status: Active

of J&K in 1990. Meanwhile, Farooq Haider emerged as a centre of power in the group. This led to Amanullah Khan retaliating by expelling him from JKLF, which led to a vertical split in the group.'. In the efforts to widen the support base in PoK and internationalise the Kashmir issue, JKLF, led by Amanullah Khan, made three attempts to cross the Line of Control (LoC) in the 1990s. Alarmed by the public support for independence, the ISI cut down its assistance to the JKLF and propped up the Hizb-ul-Mujahideen (HM) and in some instances provided intelligence to security forces against JKLF. It is estimated that about 600 militants of JKLF were killed and many of its senior leaders including Mohammad Yasin Malik, Abdul Hamid Shikh and Kaka Hussain were arrested. It was then Yasin Mallik announced unilateral ceasefire in 1994 and pursued political agenda under the APHC. Faction led by Ammanullah Khan also made similar decision in 1997.

Similar crisis was faced by the JKLF in J&K also, where Indian security forces arrested almost all the senior leaders, including Mohammad Yasin Malik, Abdul Hamid Sheikh and Kaka Hussain. In September 1995, Yasin Malik and some his associates revolted against Amanullah Khan, who retaliated by expelling Yasin Malik from the outfit. Hence, two factions of the JKLF were formed, one led by Amanullah Khan and the other, by Yasin Malik. However, both the leaders agreed, in principle, to work together to strengthen the movement to achieve the objective. This development took place in August 2011.[1] It is important to mention that in 1995, Yasin Malik had decided to renounce violence, which had led to the split.

Objectives

Politically, the organisation strives for an independent and sovereign J&K. As mentioned in the official website of the JKLF, the organisation believes that

> all citizens of the entire State should enjoy equal political, economic and social rights and freedom of expression and faith, irrespective of their race, religion, region, culture and sex. The sole objective of JKLF is to struggle, by all means allowed to the subjugated peoples by the United Nations (UN) under its General Assembly Resolution No. 2621, to enable Jammu Kashmir State to obtain a respectable place in the comity of free nations.[2]

Further, the outfit claims that "the best solution of the issue is to re-unite the divided Jammu Kashmir State and make it a fully independent and truly democratic sovereign State".[3] Though the JKLF, in many ways, was responsible for the expulsion of the Kashmiri Pundits, its chairman, Yasin Malik, has appealed a number of times to the Kashmiri Pundits to return to the Valley. However, the sincerity of Yasin Malik on this issue has been questioned by the Pundits.

Organisation and Leadership

The organisational structure of the JKLF includes central office bearers, central executive committee (CEC), standing committee, policy and planning committee and subcommittees. The central office bearers of the JKLF include a chairman, a senior vice chairman and three vice chairmen. Similarly, the CEC includes all the central office bearers, chairman and the secretary general of Jammu Kashmir Students' Liberation Front (JKSLF), the student wing of the JKLF, and 15 other members. The CEC is the chief decision-making body of the organisation. The policy and planning committee includes heads of all the subcommittees, the senior vice chairman and secretary general. The JKLF also has many subcommittees and auxiliary committees.[4]

Key leaders of the JKLF, led by Yasin Malik, are Basheer Ahmed Bhat, Sabir Ansari, Parveiz Iqbal, Mohammad Rafiq Dar, Shiekh Abdul Rashid, Basheer Ahmed Kashmiri, Baker Ahmed Rather (Boya), Mohammad Latif, Noor Muhammad Kalwal, Showkat Ahmad Bakshi, Muhammad Siddique and Gayasuddin. Amanullah Khan also has a team of leaders, namely, S.M. Afzal, Sardar Sageer, Hafeez Anwar Samwai, Amnzoor Ahmed Khan and Rafiq Ahmed Dar.

Network and Area of Operation

The JKLF is active in Srinagar city and some other district headquarters of Kashmir Valley. The head office of JKLF is located at Yasin Malik's residence in Maisuma in Srinagar. Amanullah Khan has set up his network in almost all the districts of PoK and in Gilgit, Diamer and Skardu districts of Gilgit and Baltistan and in some cities in Pakistan. The JKLF has its branches in foreign countries like Holland, Belgium, France, Germany, Denmark, Norway and Sweden. It has also a base in the US. In New York, it organises demonstrations in front of United Nations Headquarters demanding plebiscite in Kashmir and protesting against violation of human rights by the Indian security forces in Kashmir.

Funding and Arms Sources

As JKLF was the first militant outfit to start a violent movement in Kashmir against India, according to the available sources, the ISI of Pakistan is believed to have supported the organisation both financially and in terms of providing arms and weapons in the initial days.[5] However, the ISI's financial support declined in the course of time as the popular support of the JKLF escalated. In the past, one of the major sources of financial support for the JKLF used to be from its branches in the UK. It also received funds from Saudi Arabia. Didar Singh, who used to fund the World Sikh Organisation, was also suspected to have funded the JKLF. Recently, it is believed that the funding sources for the JKLF have declined as the organisation has decided to renounce violence, which ultimately goes against the desired objective of the ISI and the fundamentalist groups in India.

A local court of Srinagar, on 24 February 2012, charged Yasin Malik under the Prevention of Terrorism Act (POTA) for allegedly raising funds to strengthen his militant outfit. According to the media report, Malik allegedly deputed two people—Mushtaq Ahmad Dar and Shameema—to collect $100,000 from Kathmandu in 2002.[6] Such an incident indicates JKLF's involvement in hawala transactions to raise money for violent activities.

Current Status

After the visit of Yasin Malik to Pakistan last year, where both the factions decided to work together, Yasin Malik has intensified his movement by regularly visiting various towns of J&K where he has been raising the issue of "custodial killings" by Indian security forces, release of prisoners and repeal of AFSPA in Kashmir. Yasin Malik and his associates were arrested on 1 September 2012 for protesting against the forthcoming talks between Pakistan and India. The JKLF leadership is of the opinion that both India and Pakistan have been ignoring Kashmiris in all their talks. In this regard, Yasin Malik stated that in the upcoming talks between India and Pakistan, the issue of Kashmir should be the central point of discussion.

The last few years have witnessed a change in approach of the JKLF. The JKLF has turned towards non-violence. Its leaders like Yasin Malik have been vocal against the role of Pakistan in Kashmir. According to a media report, Yasin Malik said that the Kashmir issue can be solved without the help of Pakistan.[7]

Recently, the JKLF has suffered a further split. The JKLF (Haqeeqi) was formed on 3 January 2012 in Islamabad, Pakistan. Javed Ahmad Mir, a senior separatist, has been appointed as its chairman.

Despite the many splits and divisions within the organisation, the JKLF continues to be one of the popular groups in Kashmir. Though it has been weakened a bit because of lack of support from the ISI and heavy crackdown on it by the Indian security forces, it continues to be the group which can attract the youth and motivate them against India.

NOTES

1. For details, see Nisar Ahmed Thokar, "Amanullah Khan, Yasin Malik Join Hands", *Greater Kashmir*, 14 August 2011, available at http://www.greaterkashmir.com/news/2011/Aug/14/amanullah-khan-yasin-malik-join-hands-48.asp (accessed on 20 May 2012).
2. The official objectives of the JKLF are available at http://jklf.info/jklfhistory.html.
3. Ibid.
4. For details of the organisation structure, see http://jklf.info/.
5. See B. Raman, "Transnational Security Threats in India", South Asia Analysis Group, Paper No. 2927, November 2008.
6. See "Yasin Malik Charged under POTA", *The Times of India*, 25 February 2012, available at http://articles.timesofindia.indiatimes.com/2012-02-25/india/31100342_1_yasin-malik-jammu-srinagar-national-highway-mushtaq-ahmad-dar (accessed on 20 May 2012).
7. See "Kashmir Issue will be Resolved without Help of Pakistan: Yasin Malik", *The Economic Times*, 23 April 2012, available at http://articles.economictimes.indiatimes.com/2012-04-23/news/31386833_1_kashmir-issue-yasin-malik-kashmiris (accessed on 20 May 2012).

6

Jamiat-ul-Mujahideen
(Party of Holy Warriors)

A breakaway group of the Hizb-ul-Mujahideen (HM), the Jamiat-ul-Mujahideen (JuM) was formed in 1991. The initiative to form the group was taken by Hilal Ahmed Mir alias Nasirul Islam. He developed differences with Master Ahsan Dar, commander-in-chief of the HM, who wanted to turn the new group into the armed wing of the Jamaat-e-Islami (JeI) Pakistan.[1] The Inter Services Intelligence (ISI) of Pakistan supported Ahsan Dar with the result that Nasirul Islam left HM along with some supporters like Ghulam Rasool Shah and Manzoor Ahmed Shah and formed HM-Nasirul Islam group. This group was later renamed as JuM in 1991.

Objective

Like many other jihadi organisations, the JuM initially worked with the aim of using violence to separate Jammu and Kashmir (J&K) from India and merge it with Pakistan. The outfit is opposed to any negotiations on the Kashmir issue. This is one of the major factors for its opposition to All Party Hurriyat Conference (APHC), which held talks with Government of India on the Kashmir issue. The outfit feels that the APHC would create impediments in establishing Islam rule in Kashmir after it achieves freedom. The JuM rejects APHC's claim of being the sole representative of the Kashmiris. The outfit has also strongly opposed the peace initiatives in the talks between India and Pakistan.

Organisation and Leadership

The organisational structure of the JuM is on the similar lines of the HM. There is a political wing which is headed by an amir. The political wing amir looks after the political affairs and management of the organisation. The military wing is headed by a commander-in-chief, supported by four divisional commanders, area commanders and district commanders. The military wing has also specialised wings such as Al Jabbar squad. The Al Jabbar squad is reported to have been trained in carrying out deadly attacks.

Jamiat-ul-Mujahideen

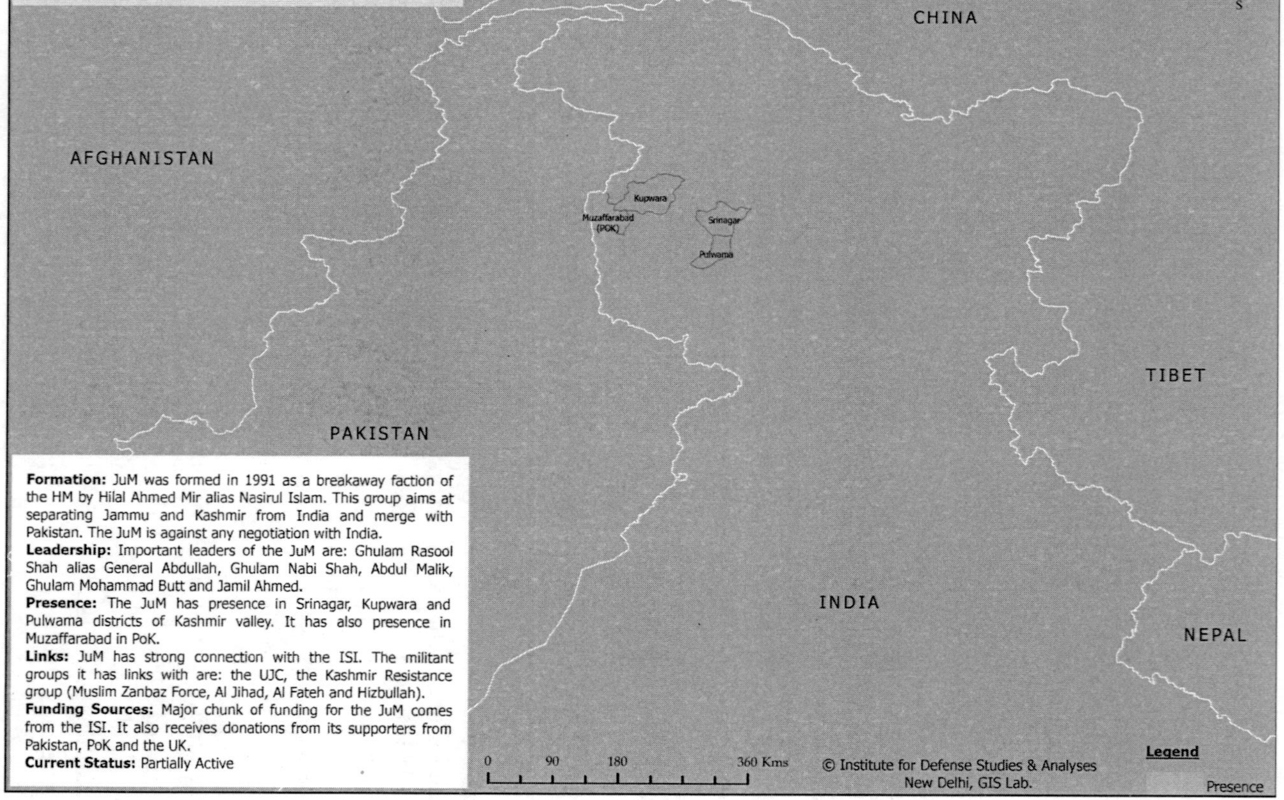

Formation: JuM was formed in 1991 as a breakaway faction of the HM by Hilal Ahmed Mir alias Nasirul Islam. This group aims at separating Jammu and Kashmir from India and merge with Pakistan. The JuM is against any negotiation with India.

Leadership: Important leaders of the JuM are: Ghulam Rasool Shah alias General Abdullah, Ghulam Nabi Shah, Abdul Malik, Ghulam Mohammad Butt and Jamil Ahmed.

Presence: The JuM has presence in Srinagar, Kupwara and Pulwama districts of Kashmir valley. It has also presence in Muzaffarabad in PoK.

Links: JuM has strong connection with the ISI. The militant groups it has links with are: the UJC, the Kashmir Resistance group (Muslim Zanbaz Force, Al Jihad, Al Fateh and Hizbullah).

Funding Sources: Major chunk of funding for the JuM comes from the ISI. It also receives donations from its supporters from Pakistan, PoK and the UK.

Current Status: Partially Active

With the formation of the JuM, Nasirul Islam continued as the chief of the outfit. With his death, Ghulam Rasool Shah alias General Abdullah became the amir. It may be mentioned that in February 2000, Ghulam Rasool Shah escaped from Srinagar jail and crossed over to Pakistan-occupied Kashmir (PoK). He is believed to be directing militant operations in Kashmir from there.

Other important leaders of the outfit are Ghulam Nabi Shah, general secretary, Abdul Malik, commander-in-chief, Ghulam Mohammad Butt, launching chief, and Jamil Ahmed, spokesman of the outfit.

Cadre Strength and Training

At the time of the formation, it was decided to have its cadres from among the local Kashmir youths. With the killing and arrest of its leaders, the outfit was forced to recruit Pakistanis into the group.[2] The present strength of the JuM is less than 100. The JuM mostly conducts operations in Srinagar, Kupwara and Pulwama districts of J&K. Although it has a base camp in Muzaffarabad, its real strength lies in J&K where its cadres are stationed.

So far the training of the JuM cadres is concerned, it is believed that most of the training camps are located in the Kashmir Valley. Reports indicate that the JuM runs training camps near Muzaffarabad in PoK.

Network/Alliances

The JuM is a member of the United Jihad Council (UJC). Its amir, Ghulam Rasool Shah, is head of the Kashmir Resistance Group comprising four other members of the UJC. The four other members are Muslim Janbaz Force, Al Jihad, Al Fateh and Hizbullah. After joining the UJC, it has established close links with the ISI of Pakistan. The JuM had also reported to have operated with the ISI in Kathmandu in Pakistan Embassy. It had opened a shop in Kathmandu in 1996 where a satellite communication centre was set up to facilitate conducting operations in Kashmir.[3]

Finance and Funding

Besides ISI, JuM has been getting substantial amount of funds from expatriate Kashmiris, such as World Kashmir Freedom Movement, United Kingdom, and from Kashmiris and Pakistanis in PoK, Rawalpindi and Islamabad. It was also involved in extortion in the Kashmir Valley to raise its financial capacities.

Current Status

In the initial years of its formation, the JuM was in the forefront in the jihadi activities in J&K. But with the killing of large number of its cadres and commanders—such as Assadullah, battalion commander; Billal Ahmed, district commander; Mirazuddin alias Faizal; and Manjoor ul Islam alias Manzoor Ahmed

Bhat, chief commander—the outfit was weakened. Moreover, it also faced competition from other jihadi outfits. It remained dormant for years and showed its muscles on 11 December 2011 when its specialised squad, Al Jabbar, made an abortive attempt to kill a J&K state minister, Ali Mohammad Sagar, in Srinagar. It alleged that the attack was in retaliation to National Conference President Farooq Abdullah's advocacy for reopening liquor shops in the Valley.[4] Similarly, the JuM also claimed responsibility on an attack in Lal Chowk, Srinagar, in January 2010. The JuM claimed that the attack in Lal Chowk was to assert that the militancy in Kashmir was not over.[5] These terror attacks are indicative of the fact that though the JuM has become weak, it has certainly not been out of the scene totally. The mouthpiece of the outfit, *Mahaz-e-Kashmir*, is being published on a regular basis and through this magazine, the JuM has been trying to influence the youth to join the outfit.

NOTES

1. See Muhammad Amir Rana, *Gateway to Terrorism*, London: New Millennium Publications, 2003, p. 530.
2. See "Jamiat ul-Mujahideen", available at http://www.start.umd.edu/start/data_collections/tops/terrorist_organization_profile.asp?id=3617 (accessed on 20 September 2012).
3. For details, see K. Santhanam, Sreedhar, Sudhir Saxsena and Manish, *Jihadis in Jammu and Kashmir*, New Delhi: Sage Publications, 2003, p. 206.
4. See "Jamiat-ul-Mujahideen Claims Responsibility for Attack on J&K Minister", 12 December 2011, available at http://www.dnaindia.com/india/report_jamiat-ul-mujahideen-claims-responsibility-for-attack-on-j-and-k-minister_1624849 (accessed on 16 September 2012).
5. See "Jamiat-ul-Mujahideen Claims Responsibility for Lal Chowk Attack", 6 January 2010, available at http://www.dnaindia.com/india/report_jamiat-ul-mujahideen-claims-responsibility-for-lal-chowk-attack_1331664 (accessed on 16 September 2012).

7

Al Badr

(Aliases: Al Badar, Al-Badr Mujahideen—The full moon)

Formation

Al Badr, also known as the Al-Badr Mujahideen, is an Afghan-trained militant wing of the Jamaat-e-Islami (JeI) Pakistan. It is reported to have been formed in June 1998. Although the Al Badr was a creation of the JeI Pakistan, the relation between the two was strained in the course of time as the Al Badr allegedly violated the code of conduct prescribed by the Jamaat. So far the historical evolution of the Al Badr goes, it operated under the supervision of the Hizb-ul-Mujahideen (HM), beginning in 1971, and later, under Hizb-e-Islami supremo, Gulbuddin Hekmatyar.[1] Like its strained relationship with the Jamaat, the Al Badr also distanced itself from the HM as it focused on Kashmir as its main area of operation. However, Al Badr was also reported to be pitched against indigenous militant groups in Kashmir by the Inter Services Intelligence (ISI) to marginalise them and to carry out Pakistan's Kashmir jihad agenda.

Interestingly, the name Al Badr has been used by other militant groups in the past. The groups' namesake reportedly traces its origins to 1971 when a group carrying same name attacked the Bengalis in the then East Pakistan. Al Badr as a militant group was banned in India on 1 April 2002, and it has also been designated as a foreign terrorist organisation (FTO) in the United States (US).

Objectives

So far the main objective of the Al Badr goes, it aims for an independent and sovereign Kashmir. But at the same time, it is also critical of the indigenous Kashmir militant groups such as Jammu and Kashmir Liberation Front (JKLF). The Al Badr follows hardline ideas as it does not believe in allowing women enrolling in the colleges and opting for jobs. There are a number of instances when the Al Badr has killed women for not complying with its diktats. In the similar fashion, it sought to enforce 'Islamist' lifestyle in the areas of its presence. The Al Badr also advocates unity among the Islamist forces against the supremacy of the US, Israel and the regime in Saudi Arabia.

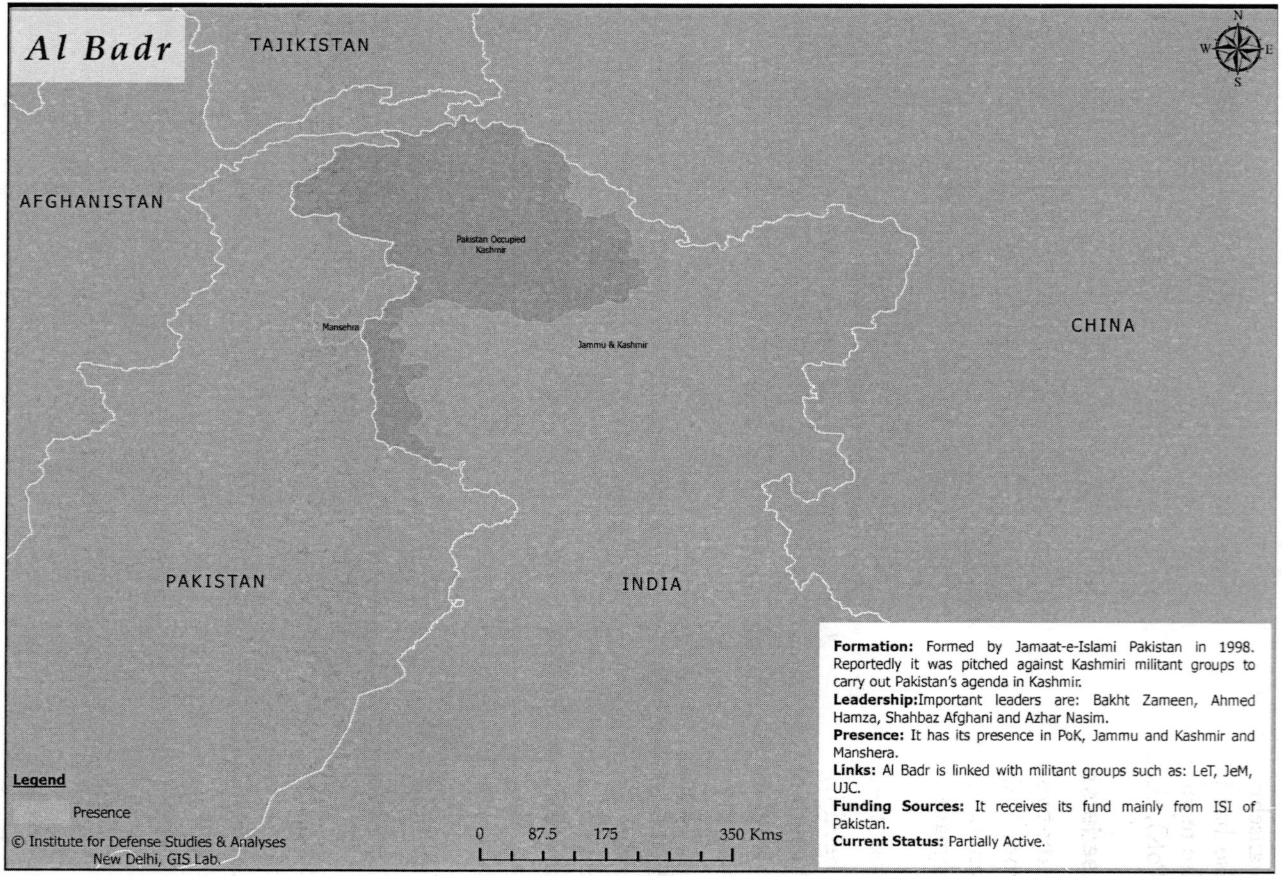
Al Badr
TAJIKISTAN
AFGHANISTAN
CHINA
PAKISTAN
INDIA
Pakistan Occupied Kashmir
Mansehra
Jammu & Kashmir
N
W
E
S
Legend
Presence
© Institute for Defense Studies & Analyses
New Delhi, GIS Lab.
0 87.5 175 350 Kms
Formation: Formed by Jamaat-e-Islami Pakistan in 1998. Reportedly it was pitched against Kashmiri militant groups to carry out Pakistan's agenda in Kashmir.
Leadership: Important leaders are: Bakht Zameen, Ahmed Hamza, Shahbaz Afghani and Azhar Nasim.
Presence: It has its presence in PoK, Jammu and Kashmir and Manshera.
Links: Al Badr is linked with militant groups such as: LeT, JeM, UJC.
Funding Sources: It receives its fund mainly from ISI of Pakistan.
Current Status: Partially Active.

Area of Operation

According to the available sources, the headquarters of the Al Badr is located at Mansehra in Khyber Pakhtunkhwa province of Pakistan. In India, the outfit also has its presence in some parts of Jammu and Kashmir (J&K). There are also reports which suggest that in Muzaffarabad area of Pakstan-occupied Kasmir (PoK), the Al Badr runs a training camp.

Leadership

Sixty-two years old Bakht Zameen is the current chief of the Al Badr. He hails from Peshawar. Its deputy head is Ahmed Hamza. Rizwan Bhai is the chief commander of its training wing. The other key leaders of the outfit are Shahbaz Afghani and Azhar Nasim.

Cadre—Strength, Recruitment and Training

The Al Badr is believed to be a small organisation. The outfit is believed to have strength of 300 cadres, with about one-third being of foreign origin. According to another source, the Al Badr has cadre strength of less than 50 operatives estimated to be active in J&K at any given time.[2]

Though Al Badr is a small outfit in terms of its cadre strength, yet, it is capable of carrying out major attacks against the Indian security forces. It is one of the first militant groups which has used suicide squads for their targets. Off late, the Al Badr's suicide squad has increased its capacity to carry out devastating terrorist attacks. The available sources suggest that the Al Badr, in the recent past, has lost many of its important operatives as the Indian security forces have cracked down on them.[3]

Financial Resources

The Al Badr receives funds from JeI and the ISI. It also collects donations with its "jihad fund campaign". So far the jihad fund campaign of the Al Badr goes, according to one of the reports, Al Badr has been collecting donations openly in some places like Rawalpindi in Pakistan.[4] In its two-day conference, "Shuada Conference", in the Swan Adda area of Rawalpindi, 8–9 July 2012, Al Badr sought to recruit and raise funds for its jihad project of independent Kashmir. Similar fund-raising drives have also been made by its cadres in major cities and towns in Pakistan. One of the sources available indicates that Al Badr is finding it difficult to raise funds and many of its training camps have been closed.[5]

Networks

As already mentioned, the Al Badr had its links, rather its original affiliations, with the militant outfits such as HM and Hizb-e-Islami. There are reports suggesting its link with groups like the Lashkar-e-Taiba (LeT), Jaish-e-

Mohammad (JeM) and the Muttahida (United) Jihad Council (MJC).[6] The Al Badr's links with the LeT have been prominent on many occasions. According to one report, the LeT had announced to work closely with the Al Badr because of the nature of its cadres.[7]

Though it has not been established but some of the statements by the key operatives of the Al Badr indicate that it has some connection with the All Party Hurriyat Conference (APHC) of the Kashmir Valley. On 25 April 2001, the senior commander of the Al Badr said that they would definitely give a befitting reply to the attempt on the life of the APHC leaders in Kashmir.[8] This statement was made in the context of an alleged attack on the APHC office by the Indian security forces. He said, "if any damage is done to the APHC leaders including Ali Gilani, Al-Badr terrorists would eliminate the top brass of the Indian Army, Advani and Vajpayee".[9]

Current Status

From the security point of view, the Al Badr is of great concern for India. It is against any sort of negotiation and peace deal with Indian authorities with regard to independence of Kashmir. Such a stand was prominent when it helped the militants in the Kargil war in 1999 and opposed vehemently against the peace deal signed between India and Pakistan. Currently, the group is not very active as many of its key leaders have been neutralised or put behind bars. Yet, the capability of its cadres to strike major terrorist attacks cannot be ruled out.

NOTES

1. For details, see "Al Badr Mujahideen", available at http://vkb.isvg.org/Wiki/Groups/Al_Badr_Mujahideen (accessed on 10 April 2012).
2. See Praveen Swami, "The Tanzeems and their Leaders", *Frontline*, Vol. 17, No. 17, 19 August–1 September 2000, available at http://www.frontlineonnet.com/fl1717/17170200.htm (accessed on 20 April 2012).
3. See "Kashmir's al-Badr Mujahideen Hard Hit by Indian Offensive", *James Town Report*, Vol. 6, No. 2, 21 January 2001, available at http://www.jamestown.org/programs/gta/single/?tx_ttnews[tt_news]=34385&tx_ttnews[backPid]=458&no_cache=1 (accessed on 20 April 2012).
4. See Tahir Khan, "Jihadists Recruit and Raise Funds Openly in Rawalpindi", *The Express Tribune*, 9 July 2012, available at http://tribune.com.pk/story/405671/jihadists-recruit-and-raise-funds-openly-in-rawalpindi/, (accessed on 10 December 2012)
5. See "Al-Badr", available at http://www.start.umd.edu/start/data_collections/tops/terrorist_organisatio_profile.asp? (accessed on 20 April 2012).
6. The MJC was formed in 1994 and is headed by Syed Salahuddin of Hizb-ul-Mujahideen. Originally, there were 15 terrorist organisations in this group but now only six outfits are its important members. They are LeT, JeM, Hizb-ul-Mujahideen, Harkat-ul-Mujahideen, Al Badr and Tehrik-i-Jihad. The details of its functioning are given later.
7. See Swami, "The Tanzeems and their Leaders".
8. See *Nawa-E-Waqt*, Pakistani Urdu Daily, 26 April 2001.
9. Ibid.

8

Muslim Janbaz Force

Introduction

The Muslim Janbaz Force (MJF) was formed in 1980 in Srinagar by Firdous Ahmed Baba alias Babbar Badr. The MJF is supposed to be the military wing of the People's Democratic Front (earlier known as People's League) led by senior Kashmir leader, Shabir Ahmed Shah. Following the formation, the MJF sent Babbar Badr to Pakistan to seek Inter Services Intelligence's (ISI) financial assistance and arm supply for the outfit. The ISI agreed to provide assistance to the outfit by directing it to widen its base. The outfit earned prominence in the world media when two Swedish engineers were abducted by the militants at the Uri Hydel Project area in 1991. The outfit also claimed responsibility of kidnapping Shabnam Lone, daughter of Abdul Gani Lone of People's Conference, along with her friend, in January 1991.

Objectives

The main objective of the MJF is to wage armed movement against the Indian state to achieve secession of Jammu and Kashmir (J&K).

Organisation Structure and Leadership

As far the organisational hierarchy of the MJF goes, it is headed by an amir who is supported by a commander-in-chief, deputy chief, finance chief, military advisor and commanders. The first amir of the outfit was Babbar Badr. But due to differences with Shabbir Shah, Babbar Badr left the outfit. Badr was one among the four outfit leaders who was invited by the Government of India to hold dialogues on the Kashmir issue.

Other important leaders of the MJF were: Mohammad Iqbal Kotwal, commander-in-chief; Mastrat Rafiqie, deputy chief; Bashir Ahmed Shah, finance chief; and Yonus Tak, military advisor. The MJF had also appointed Mohammad Usman as its amir in Pakistan-occupied Kashmir (PoK). He was also, temporarily, chairman of the United Jihad Council (UJC).

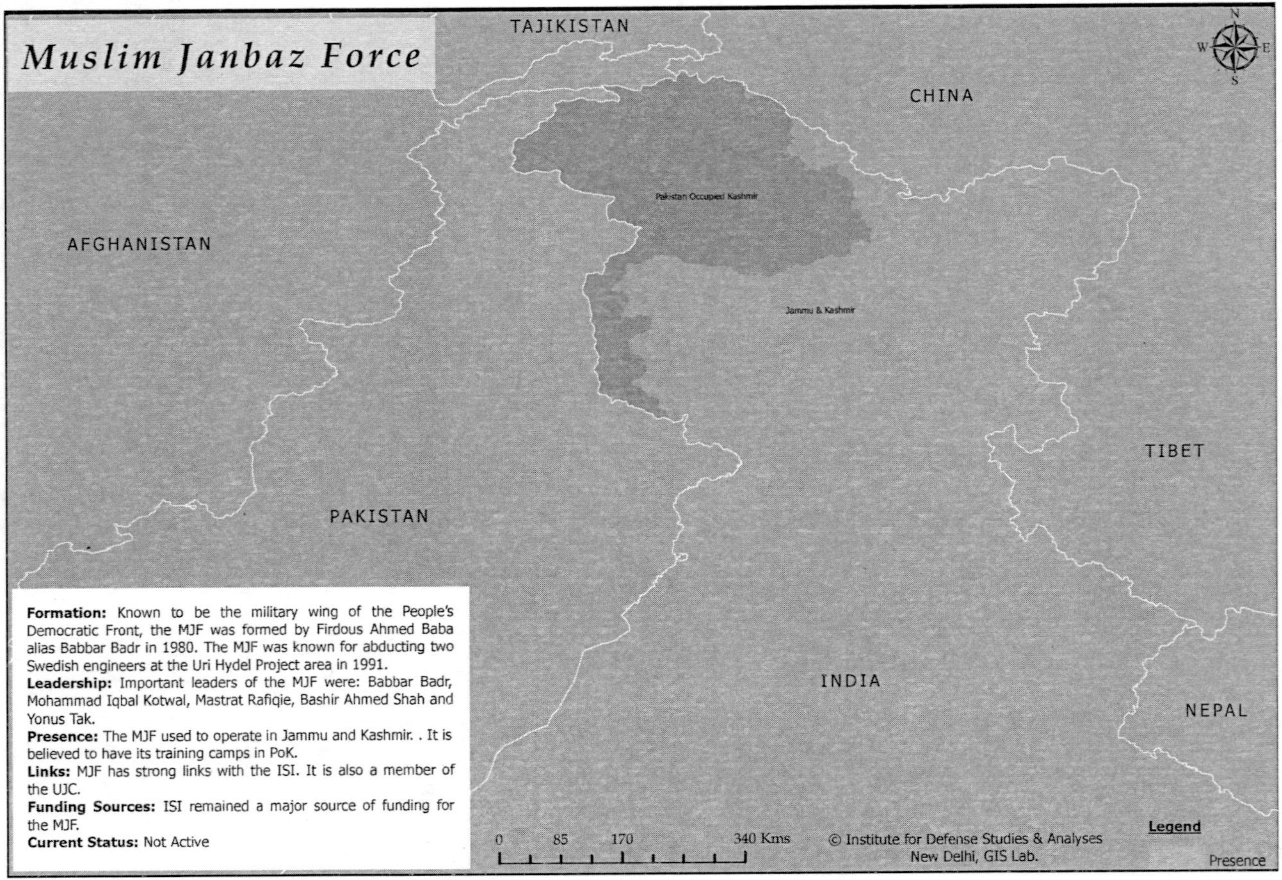

Muslim Janbaz Force

Formation: Known to be the military wing of the People's Democratic Front, the MJF was formed by Firdous Ahmed Baba alias Babbar Badr in 1980. The MJF was known for abducting two Swedish engineers at the Uri Hydel Project area in 1991.
Leadership: Important leaders of the MJF were: Babbar Badr, Mohammad Iqbal Kotwal, Mastrat Rafiqie, Bashir Ahmed Shah and Yonus Tak.
Presence: The MJF used to operate in Jammu and Kashmir. . It is believed to have its training camps in PoK.
Links: MJF has strong links with the ISI. It is also a member of the UJC.
Funding Sources: ISI remained a major source of funding for the MJF.
Current Status: Not Active

Cadre Strength

In the initial years of its formation, the MJF was believed to have strength of around 100 militants. However, the figure has been contested and contradicted by many. Majority of the militants in the MJF were local Kashmiris. Some of the militants were believed to have been recruited from PoK. However, the MJF has claimed that it carried out about 300 missions in which it lost more than 300 of its cadres.[1] Its cadre strength weakened when Shabbir Shah declared ceasefire and agreed to join talks with the Government of India.

Area of Operation

The MJF has its headquarters in Muzaffarabad which used to be headed by Mohammad Usman, amir of PoK. Training was imparted to its cadres near Afghanistan border. The MJF was highly active in the Kashmir Valley and Rajouri, Poonch and Doda districts of Jammu till 1997.

Alliances and Network

Besides its close association with the ISI, the MJF is a member of the UJC. The MJF was also suspected to be coordinating with various militant groups in J&K and rest of India.[2]

Funding and Finance

The major source of funding for the MJF comes from the ISI. The ISI had deputed Col Assad to arrange funding and arms supply. This assignment of the ISI was carried out with the help of Abdul Hamid Wani who had earlier visited Pakistan along with Mohammad Akbar Lone, a lecturer.

Current Status

With the arrest/killing of its cadres and release of Shabbir Shah who opted for a political dialogue, the organisation has not come to notice for carrying out military activities in the last few years.

NOTES

1. For details see Muhammad Amir Rana, "A to Z of Jehadi Organisations in Pakistan", Lahore, Mashal Books, 2004, p. 489.
2. See K. Santhanam, Sreedhar, Sudhir Saxsena and Manish, *Jihadis in Jammu and Kashmir*, New Delhi: Sage Publication, 2003, p. 240.

9

Al Barq
(The Lightening)

Introduction

Al Barq (The Lightening) is a jihadi militant outfit. It was formed in March 1990 in Srinagar. It is the militant wing of the People's Conference led by Abdul Gani Lone who was killed by some militants in May 2002. The decision to form the Al Barq was supported by the Inter Services intelligence (ISI) of Pakistan as it wanted to win the support of Gujjar community settled in Kupwara and Baramulla districts to facilitate the infiltration/exfiltration of militants.

Objective/Agenda

Initially, the outfit aimed for the liberation of Kashmir through armed struggle. In the mid-1990s, it adopted a moderate stance as it participated in the talks between Kashmiri militants and the Government of India on the Kashmiri issue. Moreover, after its alignment with the United Jihad Council (UJC) in 2000, it kept itself away from the People's Conference and intensified attacks against the Indian security forces and politicians.

Organisation Structure and Leadership

The outfit is headed by a supreme council which has a patron, commander-in-chief, amir, intelligence chief, military advisor and publicity head. For operational purposes, the Valley is divided into three divisions headed by divisional commanders. Prominent leaders of the outfit are Muhammad Yusuf Shah, Amir-e-Ala (chief amir), Advocate Zahid (amir) and Bilal Rahi (commander-in-chief).

Cadre Strength and Training

The exact strength of the outfit is not known. Majority of its cadres were drawn from the Gujjars residing in Kupwara and Baramulla districts and the party workers of the People's Conference. Number of Kashmiri refugees settled in Pakistan-occupied Kashmir (PoK) have also joined the outfit.

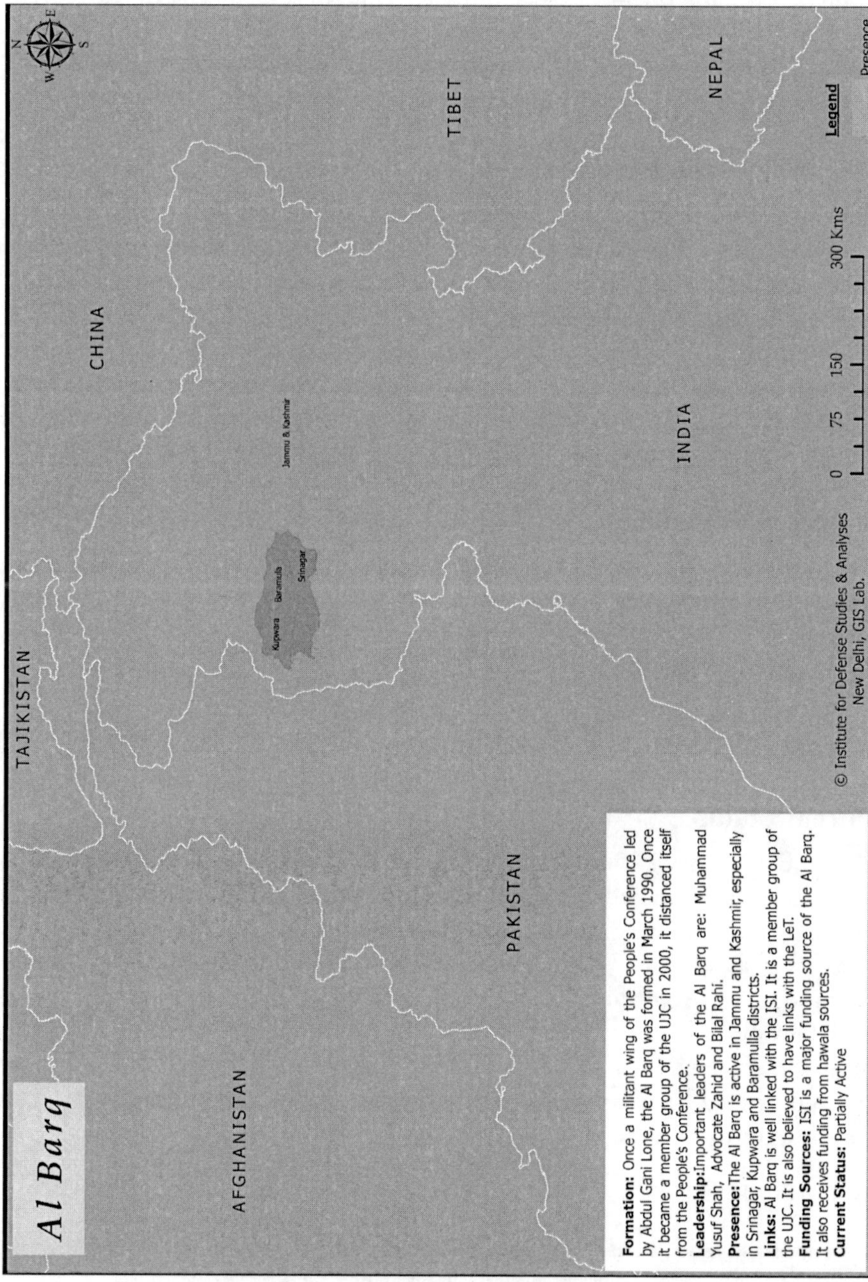
Al Barq
TAJIKISTAN
CHINA
TIBET
NEPAL
AFGHANISTAN
PAKISTAN
INDIA
Jammu & Kashmir
Kupwara
Baramulla
Srinagar
N
E
S
W
© Institute for Defense Studies & Analyses
New Delhi, GIS Lab.
0 75 150 300 Kms
Legend
Presence
Formation: Once a militant wing of the People's Conference led by Abdul Gani Lone, the Al Barq was formed in March 1990. Once it became a member group of the UJC in 2000, it distanced itself from the People's Conference.
Leadership: Important leaders of the Al Barq are: Muhammad Yusuf Shah, Advocate Zahid and Bilal Rahi.
Presence: The Al Barq is active in Jammu and Kashmir, especially in Srinagar, Kupwara and Baramulla districts.
Links: Al Barq is well linked with the ISI. It is a member group of the UJC. It is also believed to have links with the LeT.
Funding Sources: ISI is a major funding source of the Al Barq. It also receives funding from hawala sources.
Current Status: Partially Active

The training was given at the training camps in Chelabandi near Muzaffarabad and Mansehra in Khyber Pakhtunkhwa. To keep these jihadi organisations under its full control, the ISI also inducted foreign militants, including Afghan veterans, in the Al Barq. Besides, the Markaz-e-Dawa-wal-Irshad (MDI), the parent body of the Lashkar-e-Taiba (LeT), also agreed to provide foreign militants. The expenditure on the foreign militants was born by the ISI.[1]

Area of Operation/Influence

The outfit used to be active in Srinagar, Kupwara and Baramulla districts. It was involved in a number of attacks against the Indian security forces and politicians. It earned prominence with the setting ablaze of a bridge at Beeru in Budgam district; attacking the security forces convoy at Ganderbal in Srinagar, in November 1990; attack on security forces in Srinagar in May 1996; attack on police posts at Beeru, Budgam, in October 1997; destruction of police vehicles at Keran sector in August 1998; and claiming responsibility for the assassination of J&K state law minister in 2002.

Finance and Funding

The outfit has been regularly getting assistance from the ISI and other foreign sources through hawala.

Arms and Weapons

Al Barq is suspected to have possessed weapons like AK-47 series rifles, grenades and modern communication system devices.

Current Status

The Al Barq is now working under the Kashmir Freedom Force formed by the UJC. Al Barq as an independent outfit operating in Kashmir Valley has been almost inactive in its militant activities. However, many of its militants are believed to have joined other militant groups like Harkat-ul-Mujahideen and Tehrik-e-Jihad. According to the available sources, it has been established that there have been traces of role of Al Barq in planning and executing the series of bombings in London in 2005. Such incidents are indicative of the fact that the cadres of the Al Barq are active through other outfits in training, planning and executing terror strikes.

NOTES

1. For details, see K. Santhanam, Sreedhar, Sudhir Saxsena and Manish (et), *Jihadis in Jammu and Kashmir*, New Delhi: Sage Publications, 2003, pp. 58–59.

10
Tehrik-ul-Mujahideen

Introduction

Tehrik-ul-Mujahideen (TuM) was one of the front-ranking local jihadi outfits in Jammu and Kashmir (J&K). It was formed in June 1990 by Yunus Khan, a close confident of Mohammad Abdullah Tairi, ex-president of the J&K Jamiat Ahle Hadith.

Objective

Like other jihadi organisations, the TuM also stands for merger of J&K with Pakistan. The outfit also claims to be the only organisation in the Kashmir Valley that is working as a Salafist group besides getting involved in jihadi activities. The TuM, apart from its jihadi activities, is also engaged in propagation of its version of Islam. According to some reports, the TuM, has been relying on the Ahle Hadith members for safe heaven. It may be noted that for last few years the Ahle Hadith has grown strength to strength in the valley and reportedly, it has built 700 mosques and funded 150 schools.[1]

Leadership/ Organisation Structure

The organisation structure of the TuM is composed of management and military wings. The management wing is headed by an amir (chief) and his team, consisting of *naib* amir, operational chief, military advisor and intelligence chief. Under the military wing are the divisional commanders and regimental commanders who are based in the field.

The amir of the TuM was Maulana Abdul Gazali who hailed from Srinagar. Gazali, reportedly, was involved in the sectarian clashes in the Valley. Gazali was succeeded by Sheikh Jamilur Rahman as the amir of the TuM. Jamilur Rahman was believed to have spent a number of years in Pakistan where he played an important part in setting up the Pakistan chapter of TuM. Jamilur Rahman, who is a resident of Srinagar, is also the general secretary of the United Jihad Council (UJC) based in Muzaffarabad in Pakistan-occupied Kashmir (PoK).

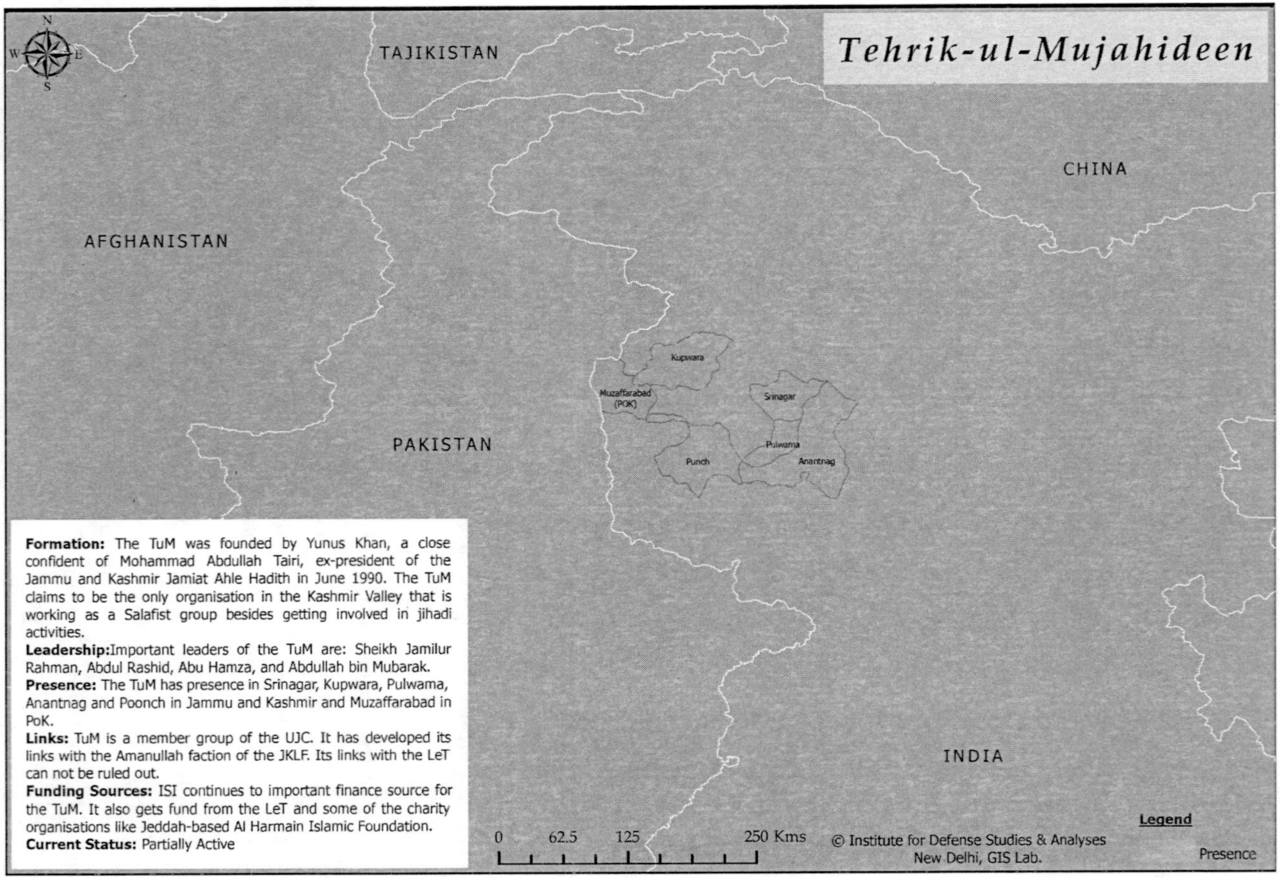

Formation: The TuM was founded by Yunus Khan, a close confident of Mohammad Abdullah Tairi, ex-president of the Jammu and Kashmir Jamiat Ahle Hadith in June 1990. The TuM claims to be the only organisation in the Kashmir Valley that is working as a Salafist group besides getting involved in jihadi activities.

Leadership: Important leaders of the TuM are: Sheikh Jamilur Rahman, Abdul Rashid, Abu Hamza, and Abdullah bin Mubarak.

Presence: The TuM has presence in Srinagar, Kupwara, Pulwama, Anantnag and Poonch in Jammu and Kashmir and Muzaffarabad in PoK.

Links: TuM is a member group of the UJC. It has developed its links with the Amanullah faction of the JKLF. Its links with the LeT can not be ruled out.

Funding Sources: ISI continues to important finance source for the TuM. It also gets fund from the LeT and some of the charity organisations like Jeddah-based Al Harmain Islamic Foundation.

Current Status: Partially Active

Other important members of the TuM are Abdul Rashid, chief commander, and Abu Hamza, launching commander-cum-secretary of Abdullah bin Mubarak camp in Muzaffarabad. The TuM has also named Basheer Ahmed as its representative in Saudi Arabia. He is a leading businessman from Kashmir.

Area of Operation/Influence/Network

The group mostly operates in and around Srinagar, Kupwara, Pulwama, Anantnag and Poonch. It is linked with the TuM Pakistan which has a training camp called Abdullah bin Mubarak in Muzaffarabad where arms training is imparted to its cadres. The arms training is given under the supervision of Abu Hamza, an expert in military training. In addition to military training, the trainees are also imparted eight days Tablighi[2] course.

Since its inception, the TuM has suffered major setbacks as its founder, Yunus Khan, was killed in 1990. But it continued its militant activities as it was able to tie up with like-minded groups in Kashmir and Pakistan. One of the sources claimed that the TuM has been working through a social organisation called the Welfare Organisation for Kashmiri Muslims. It is, however, important to mention that the Welfare Organisation for Kashmiri Muslims has been instrumental in collecting funds from foreign sources.[3]

The TuM was able to set up an operation base in Kathmandu from where it used to infiltrate its cadres into India through its open border with Nepal. In addition, Kathmandu was also used as the base for hawala transactions. This link was closed following the arrest of Mohammad Safi, First Secretary in Pakistan Embassy in Kathmandu, who was reportedly engaged in providing funds to visiting Kashmiris.[4]

So far its alliances with other groups are concerned, the TuM, being an Ahle Hadith Tanzeem, is close to Lashkar-e-Taiba (LeT) and has been conducting joint operations against the Indian security forces. It is also a member of UJC and has also been associated with the Amanullah faction of the Jammu and Kashmir Liberation Front (JKLF). In the mid-1990s, the TuM established links with youth wing of the Ahle Hadith Bangladesh to carry out trans-border operations. In this connection, the outfit was able to recruit quite a few youths from the border districts of West Bengal.[5]

Funding and Finance

Besides the Inter Services Intelligence (ISI) which has been funding the outfit through LeT, the outfit is also getting financial help from many countries in the Gulf, as well as Pakistan and Bangladesh, and also from Muslims settled in the United Kingdom (UK) and the United States (US). The Jeddah-based Al Harmain Islamic Foundation, which is engaged in missionary and welfare activities, has also been providing funds to the outfit. The general secretary of the foundation visited Pakistan in 2000. In an interview with *Sahadat*, the mouthpiece of the TuM, he gave the following reasons for giving financial help to the TuM. He said:

> As for the Kashmir problem, I am glad to say that we have been in touch with different institutes and groups there from the beginning, especially those groups like Tehrik-ul-Mujahideen that are following the footsteps of Salafi reformers. In occupied Kashmir, this organisation is known as Ahl-e-Hadith or Tehrik-ul-Mujahideen. They are involved in missionary and Jihadi activities which are very close to our heart...Anyway, we are offering our services in Occupied Kashmir through Jamiat Ahl-e-hadith and Tehrik-ul-Mujahideen.[6]

Weapons

The organisation is in possession of a number of small arms, including AK-series rifles, pistols, grenades, etc. Major source for the procurement of weapons is believed to be the ISI and terrorist outfits like the LeT. Since it is one of the members of the UJC, one can always suspect TuM getting help in terms of weapons from fellow terrorist outfits.

Current Status

At present, in terms of militant activities, the TuM is not very active. So far the present organisational strength of the TuM is concerned, it has weakened over the period of time. One of the major reasons for the weakening of the TuM is the infighting among the leaders. At the same time, the arrest and killing of top leaders of the TuM after 1996 has further weakened it. The top leaders who have been killed or arrested are: finance chief, Ahmadullah Nathani, in New Delhi in February 1997; commander-in-chief, Abdul Rahman, and operational commander, Bilal Ahmed, in Srinagar on 23 March 1997; Shoukat Hussain Wani in Srinagar on 24 March 1997; military advisor, Nazir Ahmed, in December 1997; Commander Wasim Salafi in 1999; Maulana Abdul Gazali in Febraury 2002; and finance chief, Maulvi Farooq Anwar, on June 2003, to name a few.

The TuM received another jolt on 8 April 2011, when president of its parent organisation, Jamiat Ahle Hadith, Shaukat Ahmed Shahwas, was killed in a bomb blast. Earlier, its president, Abdul Gani Dar, was seriously injured in a murderous attempt.[7]

NOTES

1. See Asit Jolly, "The Wahhabi Invasion", The India Today, 23 December 2011, available at http://indiatoday.intoday.in/story/saudi-charities-pump-in-funds-through-hawala-channels-to-radicalise-kashmir-valley/1/165660.html, (accessed on 23 October 2012)
2. Tabligh is an Arabic word, which means "to deliver". In other words, "to make Islam's message known to people". The Tabligh Jamaat is known as a proselytising or conveying group that works with the objective of making people aware of the primary duties of Muslims

based on Quran and Sunnah (the traditions of the Prophet). The Tablighi course is aimed at making the trainees aware of the duties of the Muslims.

3. See Muhammad Amir Rana, *Gateway to Terrorism*, London: New Millennium Publications, 2003, p. 321.
4. See See K. Santhanam, Sreedhar, Sudhir Saxsena and Manish, *Jihadis in Jammu and Kashmir*, New Delhi: Sage Publication, 2003, p. 266.
5. Ibid., p. 265.
6. See Rana, *Gateway to Terrorism*.
7. For details, see "Bill Papa Denies Involvement", *Greater Kashmir*, 29 August 2011, available at http://www.greatkashmir.com/news/2011/Aug/30/bill-papa-denies-involvement-26.asp (accessed on 23 October 2012). Also, see "Tehrik-ul-Mujahideen Releases Probe Report in Moulana Showkat Killing", 29 August 2011, available at http://kashmirwatch.com/news.php/2011/08/29/Tehrik-ul-mujahideen-releases-probe report (accessed on 23 October 2012).

11

Lashkar-e-Jabbar
(The Army of the Omnipotent Almighty)

Introduction

There is no available information about the origin or nature of Lashkar-e-Jabbar (LeJ). Its existence came to notice when media in Jammu and Kashmir (J&K) highlighted two attacks on women in Srinagar in August 2001. The first attack occurred on 7 August, when two unidentified youths poured diluted acid on two teachers. Following day, an armed militant entered into a girls' school and threatened violence unless they adopted "Islamic dress code". After creating panic in the Kashmiri society, an unidentified person informed the media that his outfit, LeJ, is behind these attacks by adding that the organisation meant "business in implementing the dress code in Kashmir". He further added that as such, the Muslim women must always wear burqa in public, and set 1 September 2001 as deadline. This gave an opportunity to Dukhtaran-e-Millat (DeM), led by Asiya Andrabi, which had already started a campaign in 1993 exhorting Muslim women to observe purdah and desist from watching television, video and movies, to join the movement. However, the DeM appealed to LeJ to postpone the deadline which the latter readily accepted. This led to a suspicion that LeJ might be a creation of DeM which could not force the Kashmiri women to comply with its diktat. The outfit issued separate instructions on 8 September 2001 to non-Muslim women to wear clothing or jewellery that identified them as non-Muslims by putting bindis on their forehead or yellow clothes.

Objective/Agenda

The main aim was to enforce the Islamic dress code and strict Islamist practice in Kashmir. The LeJ also drew a line of demarcation by asking men and women to sit separately in the buses. The group also issued another set of instructions on 25 December 2002 by circulating posters in which Kashmiri Muslims were directed to follow a set of guidelines on the lines of Taliban in Afghanistan which directed woman to wear burqas and men to wear caps and grow beards, in keeping with the "Islamic traditions". It asked women to desist from going to school

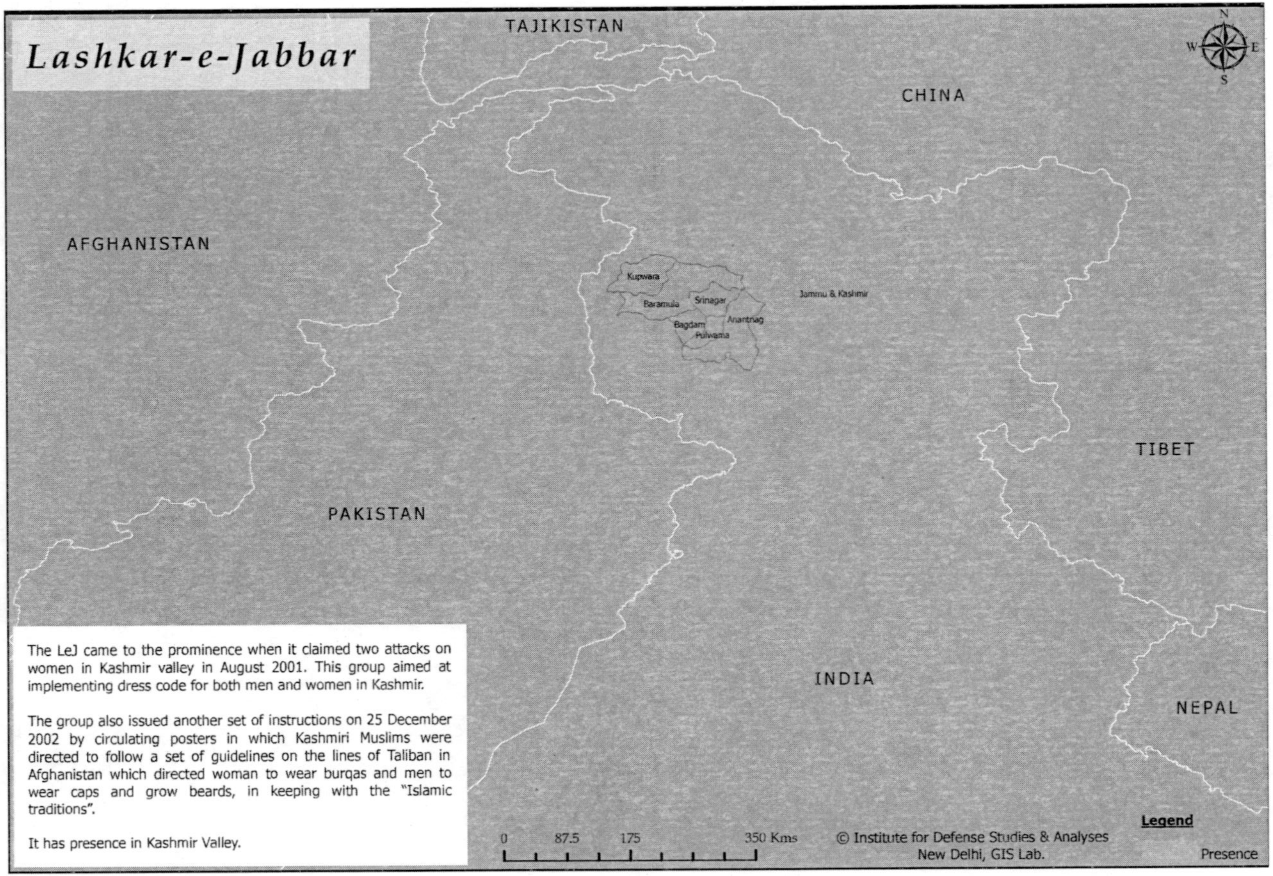
Lashkar-e-Jabbar
TAJIKISTAN
CHINA
AFGHANISTAN
Kupwara
Baramula
Srinagar
Bagdam
Anantnag
Pulwama
Jammu & Kashmir
TIBET
PAKISTAN
INDIA
NEPAL
The LeJ came to the prominence when it claimed two attacks on women in Kashmir valley in August 2001. This group aimed at implementing dress code for both men and women in Kashmir.
The group also issued another set of instructions on 25 December 2002 by circulating posters in which Kashmiri Muslims were directed to follow a set of guidelines on the lines of Taliban in Afghanistan which directed woman to wear burqas and men to wear caps and grow beards, in keeping with the "Islamic traditions".
It has presence in Kashmir Valley.
0 87.5 175 350 Kms
© Institute for Defense Studies & Analyses
New Delhi, GIS Lab.
Legend
Presence

and went a step further by asking them to have a male escort while going out of the house. It also asked all non-Muslim doctors working in J&K to leave the state within 10 days by circulating another poster on 14 January 2012.

The diktats issued by the LeJ were condemned by the Hurriyat Conference, the Hizb-ul-Mujahideen (HuM), the Lashkar-e-Taiba (LeT) and the Jaish-e-Mohammad (JeM). The LeT claimed that the aim of those involved in such activities is to turn public opinion against separatist groups. The LeJ, however, got the support of Jamait-ul-Mujahideen (JuM). Two prominent Indian Muslim organisations, the Jamiat-ul-Ulema-e-Hind and the Jamaat-e-Islami Hind, said the activities of the elements represented by LeJ are bringing a bad name to Islam and Muslims.

Due to the terror created by LeJ, a large number of women initially started wearing burqas. However, the movement did not get the support of Kashmiris who desisted from enforcing strict Islamic laws to the secular culture of Kashmir.

The LeJ has not disclosed the names of its leaders and strength of its cadres. Information about its office and finances is also not available. Its actions have been supported by DeM and JuM.

12

Al Umar Mujahideen

Introduction

The Al Umar Mujahideen (AuM) was formed in 1989 by Mushtaq Ahmed Zargar alias Latrum. He is believed to have acted at the behest of Mirwaiz, Maulvi Farooq of Srinagar, who was shot dead, reportedly, by the Hizb-ul-Mujahideen (HM) on 21 May 1990.

There appear to be two reasons which led to the formation of AuM. First, Zargar had developed differences with the Jammu and Kashmir Liberation Front (JKLF) over the release of five militants in exchange for the release of Rubaiya Sayeed, daughter of Mufti Mohammad Sayeed, who was then India's Home Minister. And second, a need was felt to check the activities of HM and the like, which did not bother to acknowledge the religious authority of the Mirwaiz.

It is also said that Zargar was supported by the former President of Pakistan, Pervez Musharraf, in order to make a point that not only Pakistan-based militants groups but others like the AuM also were disrupting peace in Kashmir.[1]

Under the leadership of Zargar, the outfit was able to build a small cadre in Srinagar. It suffered a setback when Zargar was captured by the security forces on 14 May 1992. It may be mentioned that Zargar was one of the three hardcore terrorists swapped at Kandahar to secure the release of the passengers of hijacked Indian Airlines flight, IC 814.

Objective

The AuM stands for liberation of Jammu and Kashmir (J&K) through armed struggle and merger of Kashmir with Pakistan. In an interview, Zargar said: "The stand taken by our organisation is corroborated by the Quran and the Sunnah. We stand by jihad that can never be subordinated to the conventional politics. We will obtain Occupied Kashmir through jihad, and then it will be annexed to Pakistan."[2]

The AUM as a militant Islamist group believes in armed jihad. It claims legitimacy for its jihad quoting the Quran and Sunnah.

Al Umar Mujahideen

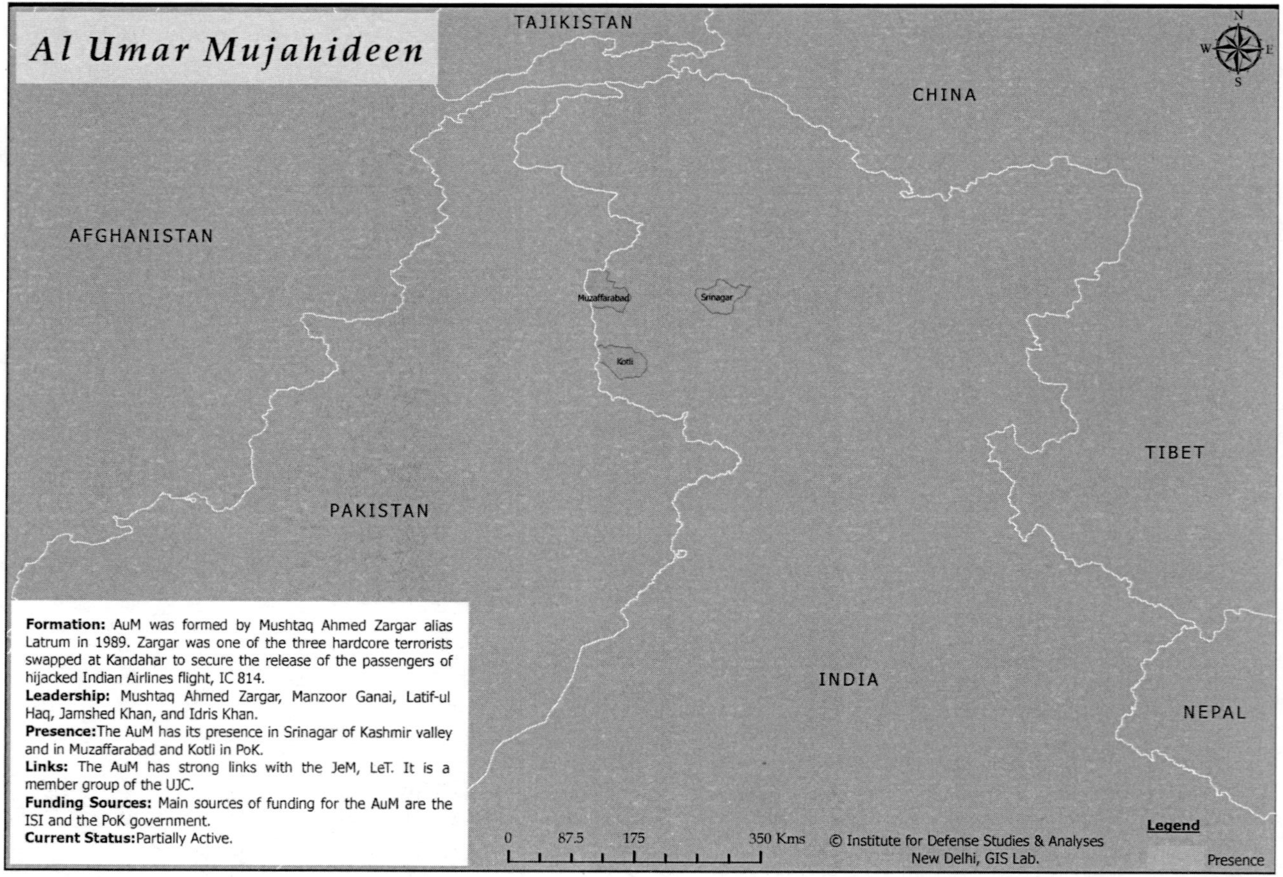

Formation: AuM was formed by Mushtaq Ahmed Zargar alias Latrum in 1989. Zargar was one of the three hardcore terrorists swapped at Kandahar to secure the release of the passengers of hijacked Indian Airlines flight, IC 814.

Leadership: Mushtaq Ahmed Zargar, Manzoor Ganai, Latif-ul Haq, Jamshed Khan, and Idris Khan.

Presence: The AuM has its presence in Srinagar of Kashmir valley and in Muzaffarabad and Kotli in PoK.

Links: The AuM has strong links with the JeM, LeT. It is a member group of the UJC.

Funding Sources: Main sources of funding for the AuM are the ISI and the PoK government.

Current Status: Partially Active.

Leadership

The AUM has a centralised command structure so far the operational activities are concerned. The outfit is controlled by a supreme command headed by chairman and chief commander, two deputy chief commanders, military advisors and intelligence chief as its members.

Mushtaq Ahmed Zargar is the chairman and supreme commander, while Manzoor Ganai was appointed as the chief commander and training organiser of the AuM following the arrest of Zargar in 1992. Other leaders of the outfit are Latif-ul Haq, acting chief commander, Jamshed Khan, deputy chief commander, and Idris Khan, deputy chief.

Cadre Strength

In spite of the stiff opposition from HM and its mentors, Jamaat-e-Islami and JKLF, Zargar was able to raise a cadre of 700 militants. Most of them hail from Srinagar and surrounding areas and are Kashmiri youth who had crossed over to Pakistan-occupied Kashmir (PoK). Due to infighting, as also the arrest and killing of many of its commanders, the outfit became weak in the last part of the 1990s.

When the outfit was shrinking in terms of cadre strength, Mast Gul along with 150 supporters joined the AuM in July 2000.[3] Mast Gul was earlier associated with HM. His association with the AuM lasted for a short period of time and he returned to Pakistan and organised a number of anti-Indian rallies and demonstrations. At present, the outfit seems to be very weak and it has been almost inactive for a long time.

Areas of Operation/Network

The AuM's offices are located in Muzaffarabad and Kotli in PoK but its activities are mainly focused on areas in Srinagar. It has also influence over the Kashmiri refugees in Muzaffarabad.

The AuM has mainly targeted Kashmiri Pundits, businessmen and senior government functionaries, besides security personnel. In 1994, it chief commander and organiser of training, Manzoor Ahmed Ganai, visited Pakistan and met Inter Services Intelligence (ISI) officials

During J&K assembly elections in the year 2000, Zargar was given the task by the ISI to carry out attacks on candidates and political parties.[4]

On many platforms, the AuM leadership confirmed links with terrorist outfits like Lashkar-e-Taiba (LeT) and Jaish-e-Mohammad (JeM). It has been reported that the AuM, along with the LeT, carried out many joint suicide attacks.[5] The AuM is also a member of United Jihad Council (UJC). There are reports that the AuM has established links with Khalistan Liberation Force (KLF) and various other terrorist organisations.

Infrastructure/Training Camps

The AUM has a training centre in Keel sector in PoK where its cadres are given arms training. Zargar visited Pakistan a couple of times during 1989–90, where he acquired military training.

Finance and Funding

The AUM is suspected to have been funded by the ISI and PoK government. It has also been collecting large amount of money through extortion and kidnappings in Kashmir.

Current Status

With the killing of many of its commanders and the arrest of chief operation commander, Farroq Ahmed Sofi alias Javid Junaid, the AUM has become weak. There is hardly any report on its militant activities in recent years. Since the outfit is weak, there is a possibility that the cadres of AuM will join other militant groups.

NOTES

1. See Wilson John, "Terror Factory's New Trojan Horse", *The Kashmir Herald*, Vol. 2, No. 3, August 2002, available at http://www.kashmirherald.com/profiles/zargar.html (accessed on 12 September 2012).
2. See the interview of Mushtaq Zargar, as cited in Muhammad Amir Rana, *Gateway to Terrorism*, London: New Millennium Publication, 2003, pp. 560–61.
3. See Yusuf Jameel, "Mast Gul in New Outfit AL-Omar, Returning to Valley to Fight 'Jihad'", *The Asian Age*, New Delhi, 3 July 2000.
4. See "Al-Umar Mujahideen", available at http://start.umd.edu/start/data_collections/tops/terrorist_organization_profile.asp?id=3557 (accessed on 12 September 2012).
5. See Rana, *Gateway to Terrorism*, p. 561.

II. Northeast India

13
United Liberation Front of Asom

The United Liberation Front of Asom (ULFA) has been waging an armed struggle against the state of India for the last three decades. It has been one of the major militant groups which has challenged the sovereignty of India over Assam. In the process of the armed struggle, approximately 20,000 people have lost their lives and many have lost their home. Since its ban by the Union Government of India, the armed forces of India have been deployed in aid of civil authorities to deal with the ULFA. It has been banned by Government of India under the Unlawful Activities Prevention Act (UAPA) of 1967 as a terrorist organisation. In the recent past, there have been some positive changes in Assam in relation to the ULFA so far the violent activities of ULFA are concerned. There has been a vertical split in ULFA as a group. The Pro-Talk Faction of ULFA (ULFA-PTF), led by its chairman, Arabinda Rajkhowa, is engaged with peace talks with both the Assamese government and the central government. At the same time, the ULFA Anti-Talk Faction (ULFA-ATF), led by its commander-in-chief, Paresh Baruah, is believed to be a more radical kind of group that is committed to continue with the armed struggle for the "independence" of the "Assamese" people. On the one hand, there is positive hope that the peace talks between the ULFA-PTF and the government will bring about some settlement, and on the other hand, Paresh Baruah and its faction remain a matter of concern.

History of ULFA

The ULFA as a militant organisation was founded on 7 April 1979 at Rang Ghar of Sibsagar (now Sivasagar) district of Assam. The people who laid the foundation of the ULFA were Bhimakanta Buragohain, Rajiv Rajkonwar alias Arabinda Rajkhowa, Golap Baruah alias Anup Chetia, Samiran Gogoi alias Pradip Gogoi, Bhadreshwar Gohain and Paresh Baruah. The main objective was to establish a "sovereign socialist Assam" through an armed struggle.

Looking into the history of Assam, one would find that the ULFA was not the only organisation that came into existence for the separate sovereignty for Assamese people. There were many organisations that emerged for the similar

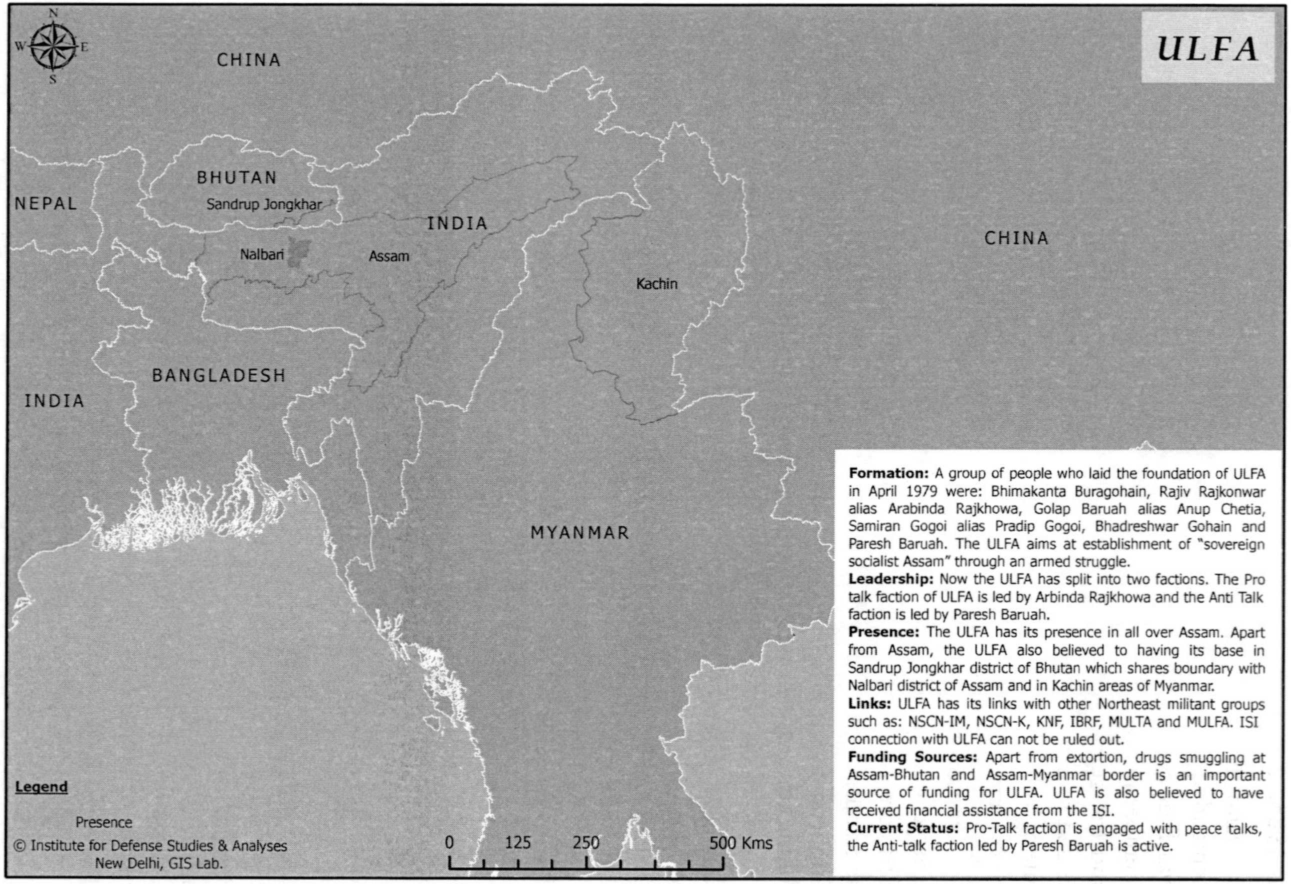
ULFA
N
W
E
S
CHINA
NEPAL
BHUTAN
Sandrup Jongkhar
Nalbari
Assam
INDIA
CHINA
Kachin
INDIA
BANGLADESH
MYANMAR
Legend
Presence
© Institute for Defense Studies & Analyses
New Delhi, GIS Lab.
0 125 250 500 Kms
Formation: A group of people who laid the foundation of ULFA in April 1979 were: Bhimakanta Buragohain, Rajiv Rajkonwar alias Arabinda Rajkhowa, Golap Baruah alias Anup Chetia, Samiran Gogoi alias Pradip Gogoi, Bhadreshwar Gohain and Paresh Baruah. The ULFA aims at establishment of "sovereign socialist Assam" through an armed struggle.
Leadership: Now the ULFA has split into two factions. The Pro talk faction of ULFA is led by Arbinda Rajkhowa and the Anti Talk faction is led by Paresh Baruah.
Presence: The ULFA has its presence in all over Assam. Apart from Assam, the ULFA also believed to having its base in Sandrup Jongkhar district of Bhutan which shares boundary with Nalbari district of Assam and in Kachin areas of Myanmar.
Links: ULFA has its links with other Northeast militant groups such as: NSCN-IM, NSCN-K, KNF, IBRF, MULTA and MULFA. ISI connection with ULFA can not be ruled out.
Funding Sources: Apart from extortion, drugs smuggling at Assam-Bhutan and Assam-Myanmar border is an important source of funding for ULFA. ULFA is also believed to have received financial assistance from the ISI.
Current Status: Pro-Talk faction is engaged with peace talks, the Anti-talk faction led by Paresh Baruah is active.

cause. One of them was the Assam Movement. It was one of the most popular movements of independent India in Assam. But with the signing of Assam Accord in 1985, the Assam Movement came to an end.

Another movement which advocated for independence of Assam and demanded secession from India was Assam People' Liberation Army (APLA). It was founded in 1980 in Tezpur. This organisation was believed to have more membership than the ULFA and other groups in Assam. With many of its activists and the general secretary, Arpan Bezbaruah, surrendering in 1986, the group ceased to exist. It is important to mention that many of its activists, including one of its leaders, Sunil Nath (presently, publicity secretary of ULFA), and Munin Nobis and Salien Konwar, joined the ULFA in the later stage.

One of the important groups in Assam which contributed a lot to the emergence of the ULFA was the Asom Jatiyabadi Yuva Chhatra Parishad (AJYCP). The core demands of AJYCP were: larger political power to Assam, control over its resources and also, they pressurised for introduction of dual citizenship. It is important to mention that some of the key leaders of ULFA like Arabinda Rajkhowa, Pradip Gogoi and Anup Chetia have had membership in AJYCP.

Though ULFA was established in 1979 it remained inactive till 1986. It is only after it established its contact with the Kachin Independence Army (KIA) of Myanmar and the Nationalist Socialist Council of Nagaland (NSCN) that ULFA emerged as a militant organisation and got into serious business of extortion and training.

Ideology and Objective

So far the ideology of ULFA is concerned, it believes in armed struggle for establishment of a separate Assam. For ULFA, Assam as a state was never part of India. According to this organisation, "independent Assam" was occupied by India and the Assamese have been oppressed and prosecuted by India in many ways. According to one leaflet of ULFA, one of the basic reasons of the armed struggle is the issue of national identity.[1] Another factor for the armed struggle is the influx of the Bangladeshi migrants to Assam in large numbers after the creation of Bangladesh in 1971. For ULFA, the large-scale influx of the Bangladeshis is a threat to the demography of Assam and it has been supported by the Government of India for its political future. This act, according to ULFA, is nothing but the colonial aspect of Indian state. In the economic sphere, ULFA alleges that despite its huge natural resources, Assam continues to remain one of the backward states in the country.

The salient objective of ULFA, therefore, is: to liberate Assam from the illegal occupation of India and to establish "scientific socialism in an independent Assam" by waging an armed struggle.

Organisational Structure and Strength

The ULFA is supposed to be one of the better organised militant groups in Assam. So far the organisational structure of the ULFA is concerned, it has a three-tier structure consisting of central unit, district units and the *anchalik* units (local units). The central unit is controlled by the central executive council. The members of the central executive council of ULFA (undivided) are:

1. Arabinda Rajkhowa (chairman);
2. Pradip Gogoi (vice chairman);
3. Anup Chetia (general secretary);
4. Paresh Baruah (commander-in-chief);
5. Chitrabon Hazarika (finance secretary);
6. Asanta Bagphukan (organising secretary);
7. Robin Neog;
8. Jiban Moran (chief of foreign relations);
9. Benning Rava;
10. Sasadhar Chowdhary (foreign secretary);
11. Mithinga Daimary (publicity secretary);
12. Raju Baruah (military spokesperson);
13. Pranati Deka (cultural secretary);
14. B.K. Buragohian;
15. Robin Handique; and
16. Ramu Mech.

The district units are controlled by the district presidents. The *anchal* units are the lowest units of the ULFA which are clusters of villages controlled by the *anchalik* presidents.

For better operation, the ULFA has divided the whole of Assam into four zones. They are: EAST ZONE (Purba Mandal districts), West Zone (Paschim Mandal districts), Central Zone (Madhya Mandal districts) and the South Zone (Dakshin Mandal districts). Each zone is further divided into sub-zones, and sub-zones into *anchals* and *anchals* into *sakhas* (wings). The ULFA has both civil/political wing and military wing. The civil wing of ULFA is headed by its chairman, Arabinda Rajkhowa, and the military wing is headed by Paresh Baruah.

So far the membership of ULFA is concerned, it is open to all the permanent residents of Assam who are committed to the idea of achieving independence of Assam through an armed struggle. Like many other militant groups, ULFA also has active women cadres. One of the high-ranking women cadres of ULFA is Pranati Deka. The main tasks given to the women cadres are mostly related to gathering intelligence, providing medical support to the cadres, networking, etc.

The military wing of the ULFA is one of the best organised one. Of many battalions, four main battalions of ULFA are: the 28 Battalion, the 27 Battalion, the 109 Battalion and the 709 Battalion.

Area of Operation and Network

The area of operation of the ULFA is evident from its division of Assam into four zones. One can say that the ULFA has a presence in almost all the districts of Assam. As mentioned earlier, the four zones of ULFA are East Zone, West Zone, Central Zone and the South Zone. The East Zone consists of the districts like Lakhmipur, Jorhat, Sibsagar, Tinsukia, Dibrugarh, Bokajan division of Karbi Anglong, Golaghat and parts of Sonitpur. The districts coming under the West Zone are Dhubri, Kokrajhar, Bongaigaon, Golpara, Barpeta, Nalbari and South Kamrup. In the Central Zone, the ULFA covers the districts like Darrang, Karbi Anglong, Nagaon, Morigaon, Dhemaji, parts of Sonitpur and North Kamrup. The South Zone consists of the districts like Hailakandi, North Cachar Hills and Karimganj.[2]

So far the network and alliance of ULFA with other groups and actors is concerned, it has strong network and alliances with groups and actors at local regional and international level.

In its initial years, ULFA got support from the locals of Assam. The media, including the political actors, also did not label ULFA as a terrorist organisation outright. In February 1992, the Assamese magazine, *Aamee*, wrote: "ULFA did not drop from the sky, nor is ULFA a wild animal. ULFA is our child. [The members of] ULFA are our brothers, they are our kins. [We must understand] why they have chosen the path of the jungle?"[3] Similarly, the then chief minister of Assam, in one of his television speeches, spoke of ULFA's surrender as "the return home of boys".[4] In this way, ULFA garnered local support in its initial years, though the public perception towards ULFA slowly changed in the course of time. Apart from the general public support, the ULFA has been able to operate through its social groups or fronts. One of the important fronts of ULFA is Manab Adhikar Sangram Samiti (MASS). The active support of MASS for ULFA was evident with arrest of one Mridul Rahman on 1 June 2005 from Jorhat district. Similarly, on 16 July 2005, four ULFA militants, including a member of MASS, were killed by police in Dibrugarh district.[5]

In the North East region, the ULFA has substantial linkages with the militant groups like the NSCN. It was NSCN which provided training and other logistic help to the ULFA to make it active in 1986. Moreover, the NSCN helped the ULFA in establishing its links with the Kachins of Myanmar. Through the Indo-Burma Revolutionary Front (IBRF), the ULFA developed linkages with a number of north-eastern militant groups. The IBRF was set up by militant groups like NSCN-Khaplang (NSCN-K), ULFA, United Liberation Front of Bodoland, Kuki National Front (KNF) and Chin National Front of Myanmar in 1989.[6] In the recent past, there have been reports suggesting growing ties between the Maoists and the ULFA. In this regard, the chief minister of Assam has said that "Maoist activities are increasing in Assam. We are not denying it. They are increasing their activities in some districts. There is no doubt that they have established relations with the ULFA and other insurgency groups."[7]

Outside India, the ULFA has links with like-minded groups in Bhutan, Myanmar and Bangladesh. In many cases, there have been records suggesting that the governments of these countries had provided safe havens to the ULFA camps. Till 2003, the ULFA operated from the Indo-Bhutan border. The ULFA established good rapport with the Royal Bhutan Army (RBA) and other government officials of Bhutan. It operated with more than 2,000 cadres from Bhutan. Most of the ULFA's camps were in the Sandrup Jongkhar district of Bhutan that shares boundary with Nalbari district of Assam. In 2003, the RBA destroyed all the camps of ULFA in a military operation. Once the camps were destroyed in Bhutan, Bangladesh turned into a safe haven for ULFA till 2009. It was Sheikh Hasina's government which cracked down on the ULFA camps and arrested many ULFA leaders and handed them over to India. The ULFA's links with the militant groups like the KIA in Myanmar have already been mentioned. The leader of the ULFA-ATF, Paresh Baruah, is believed to be in Myanmar these days. There are also reliable reports of Pakistan's Inter Services Intelligence (ISI) supporting ULFA.

Weapon: Possession and Procurement

As mentioned earlier, in its initial years of existence, ULFA used to procure arms and weapons from the KIA and the NSCN. With the formation of the IBRF with many other militant groups, ULFA started procuring arms from China through Myanmar. Myanmar remained a major gateway for ULFA's procurement of arms. The first ever consignment for the ULFA was believed to be brought from Thailand through the Kachins.[8]

The Chinese grey arms market has been a major source for the procurement of arms for ULFA. According to a media report in 2011, Paresh Baruah received a massive arms consignment worth $2.5 million from China in May 2011. The report also revealed that the consignment included 1,600 pieces of arms and ammunition, including AK-47s, rocket launchers, light machine guns and 8 lakh rounds of ammunition.[9] Similarly, ULFA also procured arms from Pakistan in a substantial manner. In an interview, Arabinda Rajkhowa revealed that some fundamentalist organisations in Pakistan supplied arms to ULFA. He also went ahead to say that sophisticated weapons were being brought in ships to Bangladesh and then transported inland in trucks. He further said, "One big consignment was caught in Chittagong, many ships were captured and in one case an entire shipload of arms was dumped into the sea to evade seizure. But many made it through."[10] In this interview, he also said that ULFA was the chief procurer of arms from Pakistan.

Apart from this, the Muslim United Liberation Tigers of Assam (MULTA) and Muslim United Liberation Front of Assam (MULFA) are the chief suppliers of arms to the ULFA through Bangladesh.[11]

Source of Finance/Funding

The main source of finance is through the act of extortion. The ULFA cadres extort money largely from the businessmen, tea estate owners and the landowners of Assam. In number of cases, ULFA cadres have been engaged in the acts of robbery and loot. Apart from this, cadres of ULFA are also engaged in drug smuggling in the border areas of Assam–Myanmar and Assam–Bhutan. The ULFA has also got financial help from the ISI of Pakistan and the militant groups in Bangladesh. There is a media report that suggest that Paresh Baruah, the leader of the ULFA-ATF, is trying to transfer a huge amount of money stashed somewhere outside Burma.[12]

State Response

So far the state response towards ULFA is concerned, a two-way strategy of dialogue and security measures has been followed throughout. There are also instances where ULFA had been used by some of the political parties to achieve their own narrow objectives. For instance, in 1991, the Congress Party was reported to have bribed ULFA to help it in the election. It is through ULFA's help that the Congress Party, led by Hiteshwar Saikia, returned to power in 1991. Both the state government of Assam and the Union Government of India have also taken a number of measures to bring the ULFA leadership to the negotiation table. The governments have been successful in convincing the major faction of the ULFA, led by Arabinda Rajkhowa, to resolve the problem through talks.

Current Status

The current status of ULFA is both a positive sign and a matter of concern as well. As mentioned already, the ULFA-PTF is engaged with peace talks with both state and union governments. The latest development in the peace talks between the ULFA-PTF and Union of India is that it entered into the fourth round of talks on 29 June 2012. All these talks between the government and ULFA-PTF revolve around latter's 12-point charter of demands. Some of the core demands of the ULFA-PTF are: grant of greater autonomy to the state of Assam; constitutional amendment to safeguard the rights of the "indigenous people of Assam"; status report regarding the 50 or so missing ULFA cadres since the 2003 operations by RBA; the issue of illegal Bangladeshi immigration; and rehabilitation of ULFA cadres.[13]

At the same time, the ULFA-ATF is not willing to give up its arms and join the negotiations. Moreover the ULFA-ATF has constituted a new central committee consisting of commander-in-chief, Paresh Barua, assistant general secretary, Jibon Moran, and deputy commander-in-chief, Drishti Rajkhowa. The other members are: "Major" Michael Deka Phukon (assistant finance secretary); "Captain" Partha Gogoi (assistant finance secretary); assistant organising secretaries—"Captain" Mantu Saikia, "Captain" Nayan Medhi, "Lieutenant" Salim, "Lieutenant" Ajahar Ali; assistant cultural secretaries—"Lieutenant" Samiran Bhuyan, "Lieutenant" Sagar Topno, "Lieutenant" Jyotirmoy Bharali; assistant information and publicity secretary, "Lieutenant" Orunudoy Dahotia; and assistant finance secretary, Dr Pranmoy Asom.[14] There are reports suggesting Paresh Baruah's attempt to motivate the lower rank ULFA-PTF cadres to join his gang and to derail the peace process.

While the peace talks with one faction of ULFA is a positive sign, continuation of violent activities by Paresh Baruah and his gang remains a matter of concern. The peace process with the ULFA-PTF has to be carefully handled and pushed forward by the state authorities. Any wrong move during the peace talks would attract a number of cadres from the "Pro-Talk Faction" to join Paresh Baruah faction. At the same time, an appropriate response to Paresh Baruah faction's violent activities is needed as this faction has the strength and capacity to go in for some strike in the future.

NOTES

1. See a leaflet of ULFA, "Ulfar Raijor Uchurat Nibedon", 1985.
2. For details, see http://www.satp.org/satporgtp/countries/india/states/assam/terrorist_outfits/ulfa.htm.
3. See Sanjib Baruah, "The State and Separatist Militancy in Assam: Winning a Battle and Losing the War?", *Asian Survey*, Vol. 34, No. 10, October 1994, p. 866.
4. Ibid.
5. See Bibhu Raoutray, "Assam: ULFA's Sleepers", available at http://www.satp.org/satporgtp/sair/Archives/3_51.htm#Assessment2 (accessed on 21 May 2012).
6. See "United Liberation Front of Asom (ULFA)—Terrorist Group of Assam", available at http://www.satp.org/satporgtp/countries/india/states/assam/terrorist_outfits/ulfa.htm, (accessed on 21 May 2012).
7. See "Maoists, ISI Backing Anti Talk ULFA Faction: Gogoi", 24 February 2012, available at http://in.news.yahoo.com/maoists-isi-backing-anti-talk-ulfa-faction-gogoi-124058910.html (accessed on 21 May 2012).
8. "United Liberation Front of Asom (ULFA)—Terrorist Group of Assam".
9. See Rajnish Sharma, "Ulfa Gets Weapons from China: Intelligence Report", *The Asian Age*, 26 September 2011, available at http://www.asianage.com/india/ulfa-gets-weapons-china-intelligence-report-280 (accessed on 22 May 2012).
10. See "Pakistani Weapons made Us Weak, Says ULFA Chief", *Hindustan Times*, 7 August 2011, available at http://www.hindustantimes.com/India-news/NortheastIndia/Pakistani-weapons-made-us-weak-says-Ulfa-chief/Article1-730339.aspx (accessed on 22 May 2012).
11. For details, see http://www.satp.org/satporgtp/countries/india/states/assam/terrorist_outfits/ulfa.htm.

12. See "Ulfa Chief Trying to Shift Stashed Funds", available at http://www.deccanchronicle.com/channels/nation/northeast/ulfa-chief-trying-shift-stashed-funds-815 (accessed on 22 May 2012).
13. For a detailed analysis of talks between the ULFA-PTF and the government, see Namrata Goswami, "ULFA Talks: Focusing the Dialogue on Resolvables", *Institute for Defence Studies and Analyses*, 3 July 2012, available at http://www.idsa.in/idsacomments/ULFATalksFocusingtheDialogueonResolvables_ngoswami_030712, (accessed on 5 July 2012).
14. See "Anti-Talks ULFA Faction Forms New Command", 23 November 2011, available at http://www.rediff.com/news/report/anti-talks-ulfa-faction-forms-new-command/20111123.htm (accessed on 22 May 2012).

14

National Socialist Council of Nagalim-Isak-Muivah

The National Socialist Council of Nagalim-Isak-Muivah (NSCN-IM) is one of the most lethal ethnic militant groups of the north-east of India in general, and Nagaland in particular. For more than three decades, the NSCN (initially, undivided outfit and later, its two factions) has been a threat to the internal security of the country. Due to its massive cadre strength, popular support, possession of sophisticated weapons and, moreover, running a parallel government outside India, it has been important for the Indian government and Nagaland government to control this militant group. However, the NSCN-IM is into a peace talk with the central government and Nagaland government. There are reports that suggest that the Nagaland government is ready to resign and go for an interim government that would comprise representatives from all the militant factions of Nagaland. Such an offer by any state government is unique. But the problem of the NSCN-IM still persists as the militants have not laid down their arms.

History

The state of Nagaland has witnessed armed groups like the Naga National Council (NNC), led by Angami Zapu Phizo, long before the NSCN emerged. The period from 1950 to 1975 was a turbulent time for the Nagas. There were violent fights between the state forces and the NNC militants which resulted in massive loss of life and property. With the signing of the Shillong Accord in 1975, the NNC laid down its arms and signed a peace agreement with the Government of India.

The Shillong Accord, however, was not acceptable to some of the Naga leaders like Thuingaleng Muivah, Isak Swu and S.S. Khaplang. Agitated with the signing of the Shillong Accord by the NNC leadership, these three, along with like-minded people, formed the National Socialist Council of Nagaland (NSCN) on 31 January 1980 in Myanmar. However, later, there emerged serious differences among the leaders of the NSCN on the issue of holding talks with Government

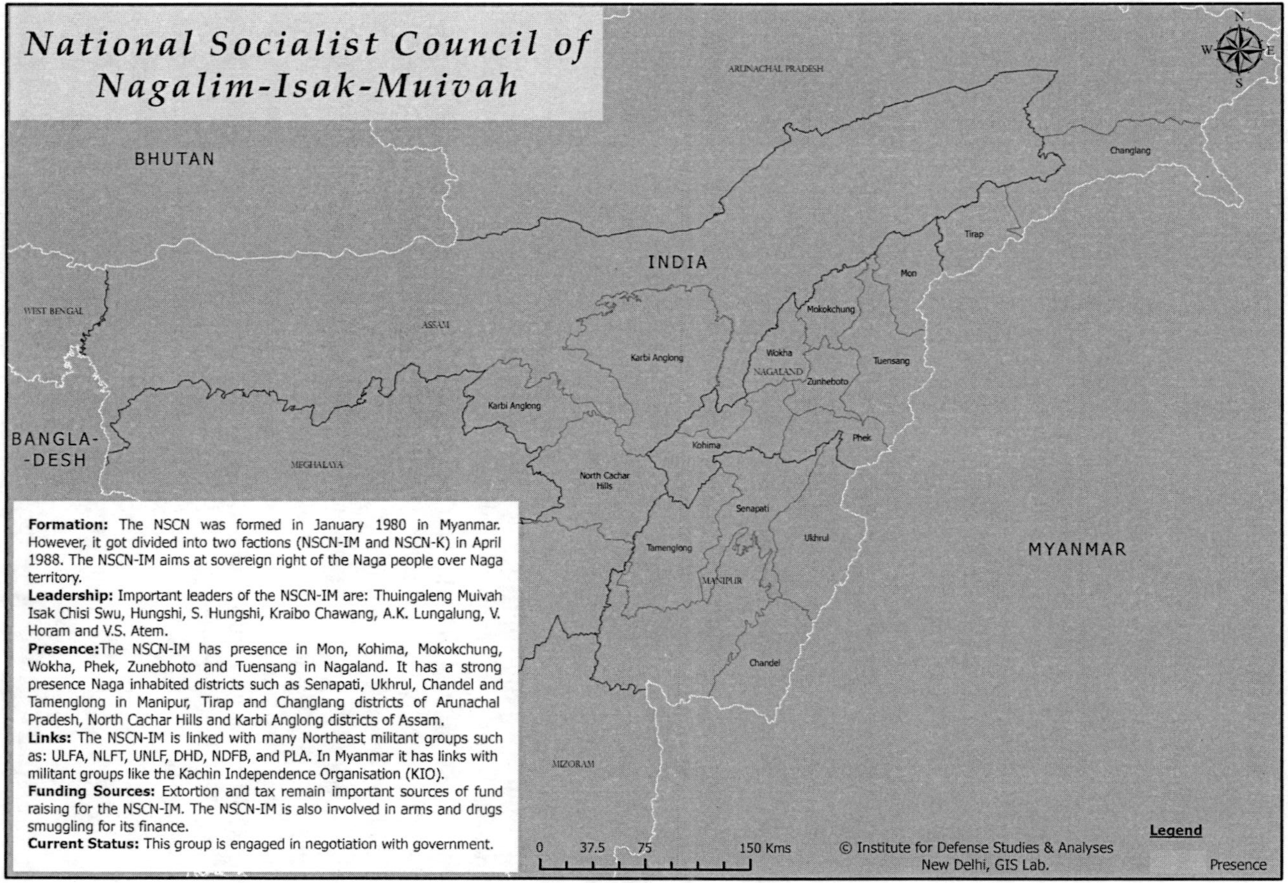
National Socialist Council of Nagalim-Isak-Muivah
BHUTAN
ARUNACHAL PRADESH
INDIA
WEST BENGAL
ASSAM
BANGLA-
-DESH
MEGHALAYA
MIZORAM
MYANMAR
Changlang
Tirap
Mon
Mokokchung
Wokha
NAGALAND
Zunheboto
Tuensang
Phek
Kohima
Karbi Anglong
Karbi Anglong
North Cachar Hills
Senapati
Ukhrul
Tamenglong
MANIPUR
Chandel
N
W
E
S
Formation: The NSCN was formed in January 1980 in Myanmar. However, it got divided into two factions (NSCN-IM and NSCN-K) in April 1988. The NSCN-IM aims at sovereign right of the Naga people over Naga territory.
Leadership: Important leaders of the NSCN-IM are: Thuingaleng Muivah Isak Chisi Swu, Hungshi, S. Hungshi, Kraibo Chawang, A.K. Lungalung, V. Horam and V.S. Atem.
Presence: The NSCN-IM has presence in Mon, Kohima, Mokokchung, Wokha, Phek, Zunebhoto and Tuensang in Nagaland. It has a strong presence Naga inhabited districts such as Senapati, Ukhrul, Chandel and Tamenglong in Manipur, Tirap and Changlang districts of Arunachal Pradesh, North Cachar Hills and Karbi Anglong districts of Assam.
Links: The NSCN-IM is linked with many Northeast militant groups such as: ULFA, NLFT, UNLF, DHD, NDFB, and PLA. In Myanmar it has links with militant groups like the Kachin Independence Organisation (KIO).
Funding Sources: Extortion and tax remain important sources of fund raising for the NSCN-IM. The NSCN-IM is also involved in arms and drugs smuggling for its finance.
Current Status: This group is engaged in negotiation with government.
0 37.5 75 150 Kms
© Institute for Defense Studies & Analyses
New Delhi, GIS Lab.
Legend
Presence

of India and this led to a split in NSCN. The NSCN split into two militant groups on 30 April 1988: one led by S.S. Khaplang, called the NSCN-Khaplang (NSCN-K), and the other led by Isak Swu and Thuingaleng Muivah, called the NSCN-Isak-Muivah (NSCN-IM).

Ideology and Objective

The ideological orientation and the objective of the NSCN-IM can be derived from the "Solemn Declaration of the Existence of the National Socialist Council of Nagaland (NSCN)".[1] Accordingly, the NSCN-IM aims at sovereign right of the Naga people over Naga territory. It believes in socialism to do away with any sort of exploitation and deprivation in Naga society. One can say that the NSCN-IM is a Christian militant group as the group itself tries to unite the Nagas with a slogan that says "Nagaland for Christ". The NSCN-IM does not believe in a peaceful means to "achieve freedom" for the Nagas; rather, it says, "it is arms and only arms again that save our nation and ensure freedom to the people".[2]

Organisation Structure and Leadership

So far the NSCN-IM as a militant group is concerned, it has two wings: the military wing and the political wing. The military wing of the NSCN-IM is termed as the People's Army of Nagaland (PAG). The structure of the PAG is like this: there is the chairman who is supposed to be "supreme commander", followed by the defence minister and the chief of army staff. The army wing is divided into five regional commands. They are: eastern, western, central, northern and southern commands. Each command comprises one division having two brigades consisting of four battalions.[3]

The political wing of the NSCN-IM is called the Government of the People's Republic of Nagaland (GPRN). The GPRN comprises of the president, vice president, prime minister and the *kilonser*s (ministers). Each Naga tribe (32 in all) elects a *kilonser*.[4] These *kilonser*s run various departments of the NSCN-IM. They include the departments of defence, education, finance, public relations, war victims, welfare and health, etc. The head office of the "parliament" of the GPRN is at Camp Hebron near Dimapur. The members of the central leadership of the NSCN-IM are:

1. Thuingaleng Muivah (general secretary);
2. Isak Chisi Swu (chairman);
3. Hungshi (press and publicity secretary);
4. S. Hungshi (commander-in-chief);
5. Kraibo Chawang (deputy *kilonser*, Ministry of Information and Publicity [MIP]);
6. A.K. Lungalung (home minister [Kilo-Kilonser]);

7. V. Horam (deputy home minister); and
8. V.S. Atem (convener, steering committee).

According to the available sources, the NSCN-IM has an armed cadre base of 4,500.[5] The leadership of the NSCN-IM recruits the cadres from various tribes of Nagaland such as the Tangkhuls, Semas, Aos, Angamis, Lothas and the Konyaks.

Area of Operation

In Nagaland, the NSCN-IM has operation bases in districts like Mon, Kohima, Mokokchung, Wokha, Phek, Zunebhoto and Tuensang. Since the Tangkhuls are represented in substantial numbers in the organisation, it also has operation bases in Naga-inhabited areas of Manipur. They are: Senapati, Ukhrul, Chandel and Tamenglong. In Arunachal Pradesh, the NSCN-IM also has a presence in Tirap and Changlang districts. Similarly, in the North Cachar Hills and Karbi Anglong districts of Assam, it has a presence.

Outside India, it has its camps in Myanmar. Also, the top leaders like Isak and Muivah used to run the exile government from Thailand.

Network and Alliances

The NSCN-IM is well linked with many groups in the north-east region of India. The militant groups like the People's Liberation Army (PLA) and United National Liberation Front (UNLF) of Manipur, National Democratic Front of Bodoland (NDFB) and United Liberation Front of Asom (ULFA) and the National Liberation Front of Tripura (NLFT) are well connected with the NSCN-IM. It is also instrumental in setting up of insurgent groups like the Dima Halam Daogah (DHD) in Assam.

At the local level, the NSCN-IM wins the support of the people. As mentioned earlier, the NSCN-IM tries to win the support of the local people through the use of religion. Similarly, it virtually runs the government and collect taxes from the people to claim legitimacy.

Outside India, the NSCN-IM has links with governments and militant groups of the neighbouring countries. As mentioned earlier, the NSCN was formed in Myanmar in 1980. It is also believed that it had its training camps in Bangladesh until they were dismantled by Sheikh Hasina government in 2009. In Myanmar, the NSCN-IM is reported to have links with the militant groups like the Kachin Independence Organisation (KIO). The presence of the top leadership of the NSCN-IM and running the exile government from Thailand was clearly established with the arrest of Muivah on 22 January 2000 in Bangkok. The arrest also led to the disclosure of Muivah's visit to Karachi[6] earlier and this, in turn, provided a credible evidence of the outfit's links with the ISI and Pakistani establishment.

Weapons: Possession and Procurement

So far the weapon procurement by the NSCN-IM is concerned, it not only procures arms from the KIO in Myanmar, but has also introduced the militant groups like NDFB and ULFA to this source for the procurement of arms.[7] Some sources also indicate that NSCN-IM is procuring arms from the Thai–Cambodian border.[8] Reports also reveal that the Pakistani Embassy officials in Thailand provided assistance to the NSCN-IM in procuring weapons.

The NSCN-IM possesses sophisticated arms and weapons. They include AK-series of rifles, M-12, 16 and 20, carbine assault rifles, light machine guns, RPG-2, -5 and -7, 40 and 60 mm mortars, self-loading rifles, Luger 9 mm (Chinese made), TNT and RDX.[9] Apart from this, the cadres of the NSCN-IM are well trained in using improvised explosive devices (IEDs). The use of modern technologies like the mobile phones and Internet add up to the military capacity of the NSCN-IM.

Finance and Funding

One of the major sources of funding for the NSCN-IM is extortion and "tax" collection from the local people. Apart from these sources, the NSCN-IM also trains various militant groups in the north-east region to generate funds.[10] Smuggling of arms and drugs is another source of income for the NSCN-IM. According to some reports, the NSCN-IM runs clandestine arms and drugs network stretching across north-east of India and South and South East Asia.[11] Along with many other militant groups in north-east of India, the NSCN-IM is also involved in weapon trafficking through Myanmar.[12]

Government Response

The central and concerned state governments have adopted a twofold strategy to deal with NSCN-IM. First, there are deployments of security forces to check and neutralise the violent activities of the militants. Second, simultaneously, the governments are also carrying out a number of developmental projects in the state of Nagaland to uplift the living conditions of the neglected section of the population. In addition, governments are also carrying on peace talks and negotiations with militant groups in Nagaland.

The first-ever peace talk offer was made by the then Prime Minister of India, P.V. Narasimha Rao, on 23 February 1996. The Union Government of India agreed to hold unconditional talks with the NSCN-IM. The NSCN-IM responded on 31 July 1996 by placing three preconditions for talks:

1. negotiations should focus on sovereignty;
2. talks would be held in a third country; and
3. a third-party mediator would be included.[13]

However, the first agreement of ceasefire between the Government of India and the NSCN-IM was signed on 25 July 1997 and came into effect on 1 August 1997. After almost a decade, on 31 July 2007, the ceasefire between the two was extended indefinitely. Since then, the government has been engaged in the peace talk process with the NSCN-IM. It is during the celebration of the 33rd "Republic Day" of the NSCN-IM in Camp Hebron that the chief of the group, Isak Swu, showed some positive signs towards peace talks. He hoped that the problems of the Nagas would be solved soon. To quote him, "I believe the day is not far off".[14] At the same time, the Nagaland government has also shown interest in solving the problem as soon as possible. In a note to the union government, it has agreed to step down to form an interim government where there will be representations from all the militant groups in Nagaland.

Current Status

Though the NSCN-IM is engaged in serious peace talks where there are positive signals of resolving the conflict, the ground situation in Nagaland may not allow for such a scenario. There are factions among the NSCN-K group. There has emerged a new group called the NSCN (Khole and Kitovi) which demands that the government must engage it in its peace process, which is vehemently opposed by the NSCN-K.

The worrisome dimension of the problem is that the outfit continues to indulge in violence and extortion activities while holding peace talks with the Government of India. While the continued violence, extortion and smuggling of arms/drugs by the NSCN-IM do not generate optimism, the continuance of peace talks gives some hope of the possibility of resolution of the Naga problem in future. The situation demands that the Government of India and the state governments of Nagaland and Manipur should make assiduous efforts to win over the Nagas and to change the perception of the NSCN-IM and NSCN-K on the use of violence to achieve their objective. It must be understood that intermittent factional clashes are working against all peace initiatives.

NOTES

1. See "Solemn Declaration of the Existence of the National Socialist Council of Nagaland (NSCN)", 31 January 1980, signed by Isak Swu, S.S. Khaplang and T.H. Muivah.
2. Ibid.
3. See Namrata Goswami, "In Guerrilla Zone: The National Socialist Council of Nagalim-Isak-Muivah", in Arpita Anant (ed.), *Non-State Armed Groups in South Asia*, New Delhi: Pentagon Security Press, 2011, p. 92.
4. Ibid.
5. See "National Socialist Council of Nagaland-Isak-Muivah", available at http://www.satp.org/satporgtp/countries/india/states/nagaland/terrorist_outfits/nscn_im.htm (accessed on 1 June 2012).
6. See "Probe into Naga Leader's 'ISI Links'", *The Hindu*, 24 February 2000, available at http:/

/www.hindu.com/2000/02/24/stories/02240002.htm (accessed on 2 June 2012).

7. See Gurmeet Kanwal and Monika Chansoria, "Small Arms Proliferation in South Asia: A Major Challenge for National Security", *CLAWS Issue Brief*, No. 18, May 2010, available at www.claws.in/download.php?action=1274853671IB-18.pdf (accessed on 2 June 2012).
8. See "National Socialist Council of Nagaland-Isak-Muivah".
9. For details, see Goswami, "In Guerrilla Zone", p. 97.
10. See "For Raising Funds, NSCN (I-M) Plans to Train Militant Groups", *The Indian Express*, 18 March 2006, available at http://www.indianexpress.com/news/for-raising-funds-nscnim-plans-to-train-militant-groups/674/0 (accessed on 3 June 2012).
11. For details, see Shelby Tucker, cited in Goswami, "In Guerrilla Zone", p. 96.
12. See "Weapons Trafficking Endangers Mizo Peace", *The Times of India*, 11 December 2005, available at http://articles.timesofindia.indiatimes.com/2005-12-11/india/27855377_1_gun-runners-mizoram-myanmar-mizo-national-front (accessed on 3 June 2012).
13. Goswami, "In Guerrilla Zone", p. 99.
14. See Namrata Goswami, "The Changing Discourse of NSCN (IM)", Institute for Defence Studies and Analyses, 31 March 2012, available at http://www.idsa.in/idsacomments/TheChangingDiscourseofNSCNIM_NamrataGoswami_300312 (accessed on 3 June 2012).

15

United National Liberation Front

History

The United National Liberation Front (UNLF) of Manipur was formed under the leadership of Arambam Samarendra Singh on 24 September 1964. The UNLF is supposed to be the oldest Meitei militant group that was formed with an aim to achieve "independence" and to establish a socialist society in Manipur. The rise of this militant organisation was a culmination of various fringe movements in Manipur that struggled for "independence". Within few years of its formation, ideological differences emerged among the leaders of the group on the strategy to be followed for achieving independence. A leader like Samarendra Singh was for ideological propaganda before resorting to an armed struggle, whereas some radical leaders like Oniam Sudhir Kumar differed from Samarendra Singh, and desired initiation of armed struggle immediately. Oniam Sudhir Kumar went ahead and established a radical organisation known as the Revolutionary Government of Manipur (RGM) in December 1968.

Going back to the evolution of the UNLF as a militant group, one would find that it remained as a pressure group spreading the ideas of free and independent Manipur. Simultaneously, the group, in the 1970s and the 1980s, concentrated on recruiting cadres. In 1990, the UNLF formed its armed wing called the Manipur People's Army (MPA), and it was in the same year that it decided to launch an armed struggle against the "illegal occupation" of Manipur by India and to make it free. The first major attack by the UNLF after the formation of the MPA was on the Central Reserve Police Force (CRPF) at Loktak Hydel Project area in December 1991. In this violent attack, five security force personnel were killed by the UNLF.

There have been factions within the UNLF and the major one was the faction led by Namoijam Oken. Oken left UNLF and formed the UNLF (Oken group). Later, UNLF (Oken group) merged with splinter groups of the Kangleipak Communist Party (KCP) and the People's Revolutionary Party of Kangleipak (PREPAK) and formed the Kanglei Yawol Kanna Lup (KYKL).

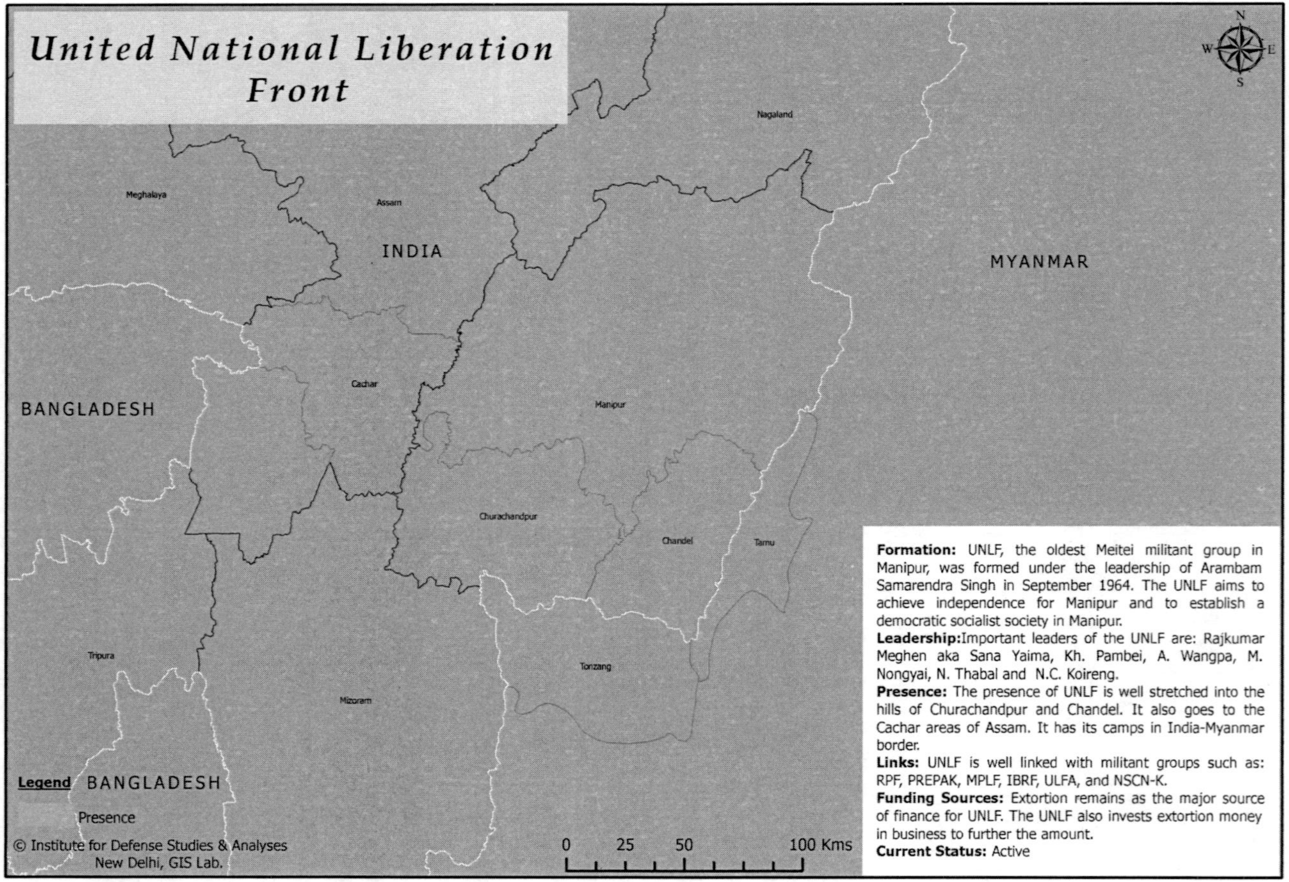
United National Liberation Front
Nagaland
Meghalaya
Assam
INDIA
MYANMAR
BANGLADESH
Cachar
Manipur
Churachandpur
Chandel
Tamu
Tonzang
Tripura
Mizoram
Legend BANGLADESH
Presence
© Institute for Defense Studies & Analyses New Delhi, GIS Lab.
0 25 50 100 Kms
N W E S
Formation: UNLF, the oldest Meitei militant group in Manipur, was formed under the leadership of Arambam Samarendra Singh in September 1964. The UNLF aims to achieve independence for Manipur and to establish a democratic socialist society in Manipur.
Leadership: Important leaders of the UNLF are: Rajkumar Meghen aka Sana Yaima, Kh. Pambei, A. Wangpa, M. Nongyai, N. Thabal and N.C. Koireng.
Presence: The presence of UNLF is well stretched into the hills of Churachandpur and Chandel. It also goes to the Cachar areas of Assam. It has its camps in India-Myanmar border.
Links: UNLF is well linked with militant groups such as: RPF, PREPAK, MPLF, IBRF, ULFA, and NSCN-K.
Funding Sources: Extortion remains as the major source of finance for UNLF. The UNLF also invests extortion money in business to further the amount.
Current Status: Active

Ideology and Objective

The primary objective of the UNLF is to achieve independence for Manipur and to establish a democratic socialist society in Manipur. Ideologically, it believes in socialism and equality for all. The "Annual Statement 2006" of the UNLF clearly underlines the objective of UNLF. It says:

> In the wake of the forcible annexation of Manipur by the Dominion of India in 1949, patriotic individuals grouped together to establish the UNLF on 24 November 1964 with the objective of restoring Manipur's sovereign independence by waging a national liberation struggle against India. The social goal of UNLF is to build a socialist society wherein all the ethnic nationalities of Manipur shall live in harmonious coexistence and co-development in a new, united, sovereign and independent "Manipur".
>
> The UNLF has also a regional outlook that believes in the basic unity of the Region inhabited by many ethnic nationalities and that this reality compels the Region to fight together to overthrow Indian rule for a common future of peace, progress and development.[1]

The UNLF believes in peaceful coexistence of all the ethnic groups in Manipur. It believes in "coexistence and co-development" of all ethnic compatriots in Manipur.

Leadership and Organisation Structure

According to the "Annual Statement 2006", the founding leaders of the UNLF were: late Oja Kalan-lung Kamei (founder president), late Oja Thongkho-pao Singsit (founder vice president), late "Tamohal" Arambam Samarendra (founder general secretary), late Dr Longjam Manimohan (hills organisation), late veteran Laishram Kanhai (central committee member), late "Tamo" Nongmeikapam Sanajaoba (youth organisation and founder editor of *Lamyanba* monthly journal) and recently departed singer, late "Tamo" Nongmaithem Pahari (first chief of army staff).[2]

So far the organisational structure of the UNLF is concerned, it has a hierarchical structure. The highest decision-making body of the UNLF is the central committee (CC). The CC is headed by the chairman. In the 2003 general assembly, there were some changes in the CC of the UNLF. The structure of the new CC is as follows: chairman, Rajkumar Meghen aka Sana Yaima; general secretary, Kh. Pambei; secretary of defence, A. Wangpa; secretary of organisation, M. Nongyai; secretary of publicity, N. Thabal; and associate member, N.C. Koireng.

As mentioned earlier, the armed wing of the UNLF is called as the MPA and it is controlled by a military affairs committee. The MPA is believed to have five battalions. There are district-level command structures to supervise the district-level affairs of the MPA. The MPA has three types of mobile task forces—Wangbran Task Force, Siroy Task Force and Maril Task Force. Department of

Publicity and Propaganda is the publicity wing of the front. The UNLF is believed to have active cadre strength of about 2,000–2,500. Apart from this, the UNLF has its overground supporters and sympathisers. The UNLF leadership targets the youth from poor and destitute background for its recruitment.

Area of Operation

Initially, the UNLF operated in the central plain areas of Manipur. By early 1990, it stretched its operation bases into the hills of Churachandpur and Chandel. Presently, its operation base is well stretched up to the Cachar areas of Assam. Like many other militant groups in north-east of India, the UNLF has its training camps on the India–Myanmar border. Similarly, it is believed to have its camps in the Myanmar territories.

Network and Alliances

At the local level, the UNLF wins support of the general public. Among the local people, the UNLF is considered to be very social in its activities. The UNLF carries out some development and social programmes to win the support of the people. Some of its programmes like National Economic Policy, National Cultural Policy and development of small and medium enterprise are aimed at development of local people in economic, cultural and social spheres.

At the regional level, it has good links with the militant groups like Revolutionary People's Front (RPF) and the PREPAK. In 1999, the UNLF, along with PREPAK and RPF, formed Manipur People's Liberation Front (MPLF). The idea of Indo-Burma Revolutionary Front (IBRF) was floated by UNLF with groups like United Liberation Front of Asom (ULFA) and Nationalist Socialist Council of Nagaland (NSCN). However, UNLF has a good relation with the National Democratic Front of Bodoland (NDFB) as well. It has a good working relation with the NSCS-Khaplang (NSCN-K) but has been against the National Socialist Council of Nagalim-Isak-Muivah (NSCN-IM) for a very long time.

Outside India, the UNLF is believed to have good relations with the military officials of Myanmar. The UNLF used to enjoy safe haven in Bangladesh till 2009. According to one source, the UNLF leaders supported Pakistan during the 1971 Bangladesh liberation war.[3] The same source also claims that on 14 June 1975, UNLF leader, N. Bisheswar Singh, and 16 other Meitei rebels proceeded to Lhasa to seek Chinese assistance.

Weapons Possession and Procurement

As mentioned earlier, some of the UNLF leaders had moved to Lhasa to procure arms from China, reflecting that the Chinese sources are supplying arms to the outfit. Recently, the National Investigation Agency (NIA) of India has revealed the source of Chinese arms procurement by the UNLF.[4] The UNLF has most of the highly developed weapons that include AK-47 and AK-56, M-16 rifles, self-loading rifles (SLRs), etc. The cadres of the UNLF are also trained in the use of improvised explosive devices (IEDs).

Finance and Funding

Like many of the militant groups in the north-east of India, the main source of income is extortion. The UNLF also has a strong support base from which it receives donations. There are also reports which indicate that the UNLF is using microfinance schemes like the women's cooperatives to win the support of the local people.[5]

The UNLF is also reported to have invested in business. The NIA has registered a complaint against 19 militants of the UNLF, including its chairman, Meghen. Investigations conducted by NIA have established that the Association of Extensive Growers Innovative Service (AEGIS) factory is the financial asset of proscribed terrorist organisation (UNLF). The market value of the said property is more than Rs 2 crore.[6] This revelation of the NIA indicates that the UNLF invests its extortion money in business to enhance its income.

Response of Government

The central and state governments are following a two-pronged strategy towards the UNLF. On the one hand, security forces have been deployed to crack down on the militants of the UNLF. The security forces have neutralised and arrested a number of UNLF militants. On the other hand, the governments have extended an offer for peace talks and negotiation with the UNLF.

The outline for peace talks was offered by the Union Government of India in 2001. However, on 13 February 2001, the chairman of the UNLF put conditions for the negotiations. He said that issues such as independence of Manipur, right to self-determination and demilitarisation must be brought under the ambit of the negotiations. In 2004, the Government of India made one more attempt for negotiation. This time around, the UNLF put four major demands for negotiation before the government. They were:

1. To hold a plebiscite under the United Nations (UN) aegis so that the people of Manipur can exercise their democratic right to decide on the core issue of the conflict—the restoration of Manipur's sovereignty and independence.
2. To deploy a UN peacekeeping force in Manipur to ensure free and fair conduct of the plebiscite.
3. The UNLF to deposit all its arms to the UN peacekeeping force and India to withdraw all its regular and paramilitary forces from Manipur before a deadline prior to the plebiscite date to be decided by the UN. Also, the UN peacekeeping force to call upon all other armed opposition groups in Manipur to follow suit.

4. The UN to hand over political power in accordance with the result of the plebiscite.[7]

Again, on 15 July 2005, the Government of Manipur adopted a resolution urging the union government to hold peace talks with militant outfits operating in the state. During discussion on the resolution, Chief Minister Okram Ibobi Singh ruled out the UNLF's demand for a plebiscite under the aegis of the UN on question of Manipur's sovereignty. Despite many such attempts from the government's side, there has not been any positive signal from the UNLF for negotiations.

Current Status

The UNLF continues to be a militant group even though some of its kingpins, including its chairman, have been arrested and put behind bars. The Government of India has requested the Bangladesh government to track financial assets belonging to the UNLF. The NIA has been empowered to track the financial sources of the UNLF and freeze the accounts that the UNLF has in Manipur and in the neighbouring countries.

In the meantime, the UNLF seems to be insistent over some of its demands before coming to the negotiation table. On 21 February 2011, the arrested chairman of the UNLF, Rajkumar Meghen, once again renewed the offer made to the union government by UNLF that the outfit would lay down arms before UN authorities if the centre allowed a plebiscite in Manipur in the presence of UN representatives and arranged for the deployment of UN peacekeeping forces in the state. He also insisted that before the plebiscite, the Government of India must withdraw its security forces from Manipur.

NOTES

1. See "UNLF Celebrates 42nd B'day, CC Greets People, Issues Annual Statement-I", *The Sangai Express*, 24 November 2006, available at http://thesangaiexpress.manipur.us/2006/11/24/News_pages/Local_page-06.htm (accessed on 28 May 2012).
2. Ibid.
3. See "United National Liberation Front", available at http://www.satp.org/satporgtp/countries/india/states/manipur/terrorist_outfits/Unlf.htm (accessed on 28 May 2012).
4. See "Chinese Links to Arms Procured by Manipur Terror Group?", *The Economic Times*, 15 February 2011, available at http://articles.economictimes.indiatimes.com/2011-02-15/news/28540581_1_unlf-united-national-liberation-front-manipur (accessed on 28 May 2012).
5. See "UNLF in Manipur Regaining Support by Microfinacing", 13 November 2010, available at http://www.northeastblog.in/manipur/unlf-in-manipur-regaining-support-by-microfinacing/ (accessed on 28 May 2012).
6. For details, see http://www.nia.gov.in/writereaddata/press_13012012.pdf.
7. See "UNLF Response to Manipur Governor's Appeal for Dialogue", available at http://www.satp.org/satporgtp/countries/india/states/manipur/documents/papers/unlf2005.htm (accessed on 29 May 2012).

16

People's Liberation Army (Manipur)

The arrest of militants of People's Liberation Army (PLA) from New Delhi in 2011, and from Odisha in 2012, has raised the concern of the security forces over the growing reach of the outfit. The most worrisome aspect has been the revelation of PLA's links with Communist Party of India-Maoists (CPI-Maoist). The National Investigation Agency (NIA) has revealed that the PLA is engaged in imparting training to the Maoist cadres. The NIA also revealed that the PLA, Maoists and the militant groups from Kashmir are tying up to have a strategic front to fight against India. The PLA, as its founding philosophy suggests, aims at uniting all the militant groups in the north-east region of India and claims to be a trans-tribal group. Its links with the militant groups like the CPI-Maoist and the Kashmiri militant groups will add up to the internal security concerns for India.

History

The PLA was formed on 25 September 1978 under the leadership of N. Bisheswar Singh. Like many other militant groups in Manipur, the founding aim of the PLA was to liberate the state of Manipur from the "illegal occupation" of India.

Ideology and Objective

The main objective of the PLA is to achieve independence for Manipur from the "illegal occupation of India" by waging an armed struggle. Strategically, it strives to have a revolutionary front of all the dissenting ethnic groups in the north-east of India to fight against India. As the name suggests, the PLA believes in the socialist ideology.

Leadership and Organisation Structure

So far the organisational structure of the PLA is concerned, it is hierarchical in nature. The PLA has two wings: the political wing and the military wing. The political wing of PLA is known as the Revolutionary People's Front (RPF). It was formed in 1979. The RPF has several departments like publicity, finance,

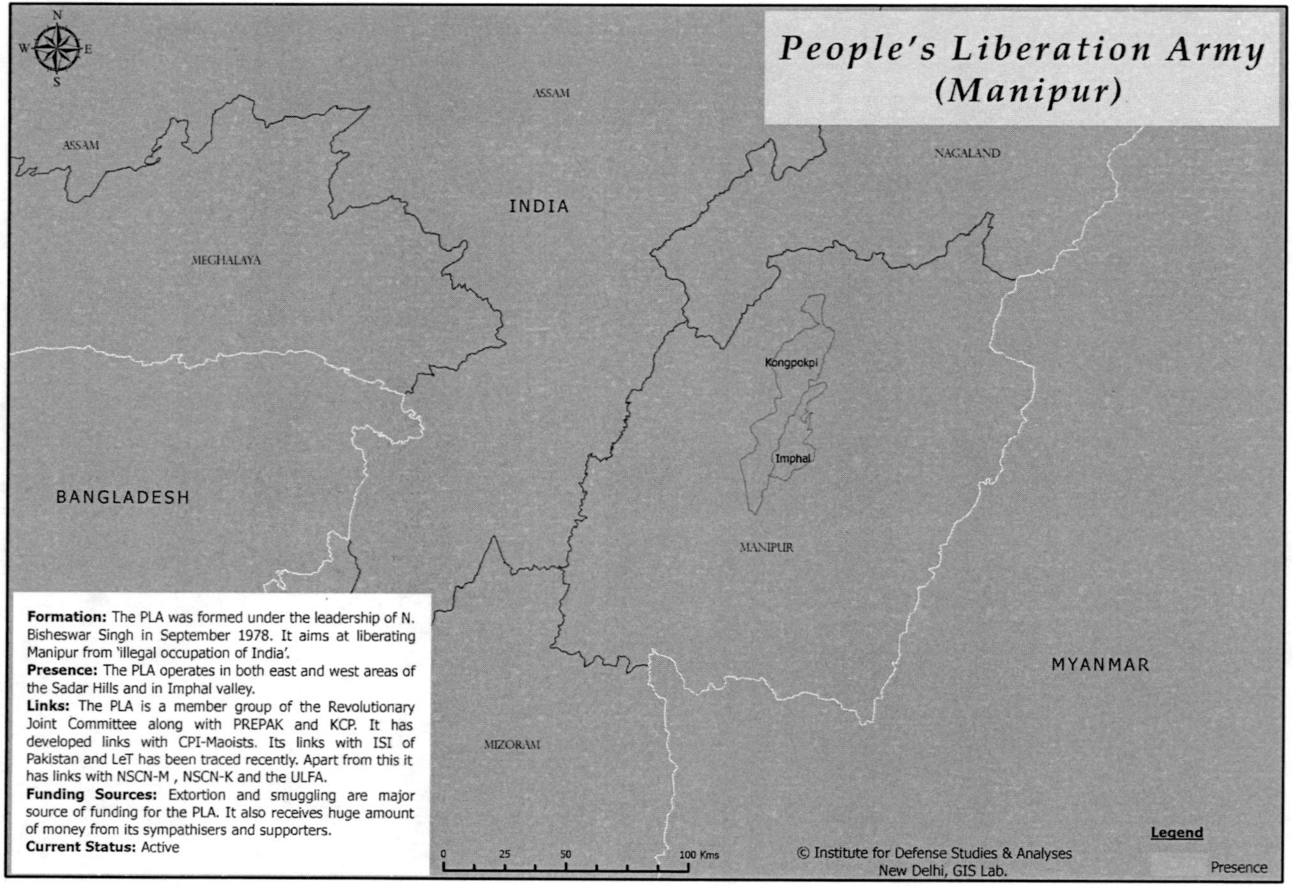

Formation: The PLA was formed under the leadership of N. Bisheswar Singh in September 1978. It aims at liberating Manipur from 'illegal occupation of India'.
Presence: The PLA operates in both east and west areas of the Sadar Hills and in Imphal valley.
Links: The PLA is a member group of the Revolutionary Joint Committee along with PREPAK and KCP. It has developed links with CPI-Maoists. Its links with ISI of Pakistan and LeT has been traced recently. Apart from this it has links with NSCN-M , NSCN-K and the ULFA.
Funding Sources: Extortion and smuggling are major source of funding for the PLA. It also receives huge amount of money from its sympathisers and supporters.
Current Status: Active

social welfare and foreign affairs. It is headed by Irengbam Chaoren, the president of PLA.

The military wing of the PLA has four divisions for its operation. They are: the Sadar Hills West Areas, the Sadar Hills East Areas, Hills in Manipur and the Imphal Valley Area division. Like other military groups, each military division of PLA has a command structure such as commander, lieutenants, sergeant and the lance corporals in its ranks. So far the strength of the PLA is concerned, it has an active strength of 1,500 cadres.

Area of Operation and Linkages

The PLA has its operation bases in both east and west areas of the Sadar Hills. It has also a presence in Imphal Valley. The hill areas of Manipur are also affected by the activities of the PLA militants. Once the RPF, the political wing of the PLA, was outlawed by the Union Government of India, it is believed to have been running a parallel government in exile somewhere in Bangladesh. There are also reports suggesting that PLA militants are using Myanmar and Bhutan territory for their safe haven.

In the recent past, there have been reports which revealed the nexus between the Maoists and the PLA. In this regard, the NIA has arrested the "external affairs secretary" of the PLA, Asem Ibotombi alias Angou, from Ganjam district of Odisha,[1] on 28 May 2012. The NIA also registered a case against three militants of the PLA, namely, N. Dilip Singh alias Wangba, Sonja Dhiren Singh alias Raghu and Kh Arnold Singh alias Becon. The NIA has confirmed that the PLA has formed an alliance with the Maoists and the militant groups in Kashmir to fight against India. According to the NIA, the PLA militants imparted military training to the Maoist cadres in Saranda forest on Jharkhand–Odisha border in 2010.[2]

The political wing of the PLA, RPF, has good links with many militant groups in the north-east region. In 1991, the RPF joined the Revolutionary Joint Committee (RJC), an umbrella group of militant groups, along with the People's Revolutionary Party of Kangleipak (PREPAK) and the Kangleipak Communist Party (KCP).[3] The PLA, in its initial years of struggle, had a good connection with the Nationalist Socialist Council of Nagaland (NSCN).

According to one source, the PLA is believed to have links with the Inter Services Intelligence (ISI) of Pakistan. Such a nexus was evident when a report was recovered from the finance secretary of the RPF, Biran Singh alias German, in January 1991.[4] According to the same report, the PLA is believed to have set up a number of bases in the Sylhet district of Bangladesh.

Weapons in Possession

The PLA is believed to have possessed sophisticated weapons. Since PLA has been linked with the ISI of Pakistan, it can be suspected that the PLA might have procured arms from Pakistan. Similarly, procurement of weapons from Bangladesh has also been reported. Apart from these, the PLA is reported to be procuring arms from other militant groups in the north-east of India. There are also reports which suggest the PLA is procuring arms from Chinese arm dealers too.[5]

Finance and Funding

The major sources of funding for the PLA are extortion and arms smuggling. The PLA, in order to win the support of the local people, is engaged in a number of social development activities. It is engaged in campaigns like enforcing restriction on sale of alcohol and drugs and control of corruption by the political leaders. Such activities by the PLA have gained it a number of supporters and sympathisers. The PLA gets good amount of money in terms of donations from these supporters and sympathisers.

Government Response

Both the Government of India and the Government of Manipur have adopted a twofold strategy to deal with the PLA. Once the PLA emerged as a violent group in 1978, the government deployed security forces to curb its violent activities. In the course of security forces' operations, a number of PLA militants were killed and a number of them were arrested. However, the remaining cadres were able to sneak into the neighbouring countries, where they have safe havens.

The second plank of the strategy is the offer of negotiations with the PLA leadership. However, it has not been accepted by the PLA. Reacting to the negotiation offer by the Union Government of India, the president of the RPF and PLA, Irengbam Chaoren, said on 24 February 2011 that "the invitation of Indian Government to the revolutionary groups for holding peace talks is not about sovereignty of Manipur but it is for consolidating integrity of India at the cost of Manipur's sovereignty".[6] Similarly, on 24 February 2008, he also said, "The more than 30-year-long battle aims to win back the lost freedom of the Manipuris. India's Army is killing the Manipuris. No Indian leader takes the issue of Manipur's freedom seriously. Under these circumstances, how can we enter into peace talks?"[7]

Current Status

As already mentioned, the PLA is not in a mood to engage itself in a peace talk with the Government of India. The PLA has already entered into negotiations with the Maoists and the militants in Kashmir to have a strategic front to fight against India. The PLA is also planning to train the Maoists and the militants from Kashmir in some of its camps in Myanmar. Though the security forces have been successful in containing the PLA militants from violent activities to a large extent, yet, the safe haven in countries like Myanmar is definitely a matter of concern for India's internal security. The governments, at both central and state levels, need to win the support of the local people to cut the public support that gives legitimacy to the groups like PLA. There is also a need for the Government of India to persuade countries like Myanmar to deny safe havens to militant groups like the PLA.

NOTES

1. For details of the arrest, see http://www.nia.gov.in/writereaddata/press_29052012.pdf.
2. Ibid.
3. See "Terrorist Organization Profile: People's Liberation Army (PLA)", available at http://www.start.umd.edu/start/data_collections/tops/terrorist_organization_profile.asp?id=4590 (accessed on 28 May 2012).
4. See "People's Liberation Army", available at http://www.satp.org/satporgtp/countries/india/states/manipur/terrorist_outfits/Pla.htm (accessed on 28 May 2012).
5. See R. Dutta Choudhury, "NE Ultras Forging Ties, Chinese Arms Posing Threat", *The Assam Tribune*, 29 January 2012, available at http://www.assamtribune.com/scripts/detailsnew.asp?id=jan3012/at05 (accessed on 28 May 2012).
6. See "Peace Talks Consolidate India's Integrity at the Cost of Manipur's Sovereignty: RPF", 24 February 2011, available at http://kanglaonline.com/2011/02/peace-talks-consolidate-indias-integrity-at-the-cost-of-manipurs-sovereignty-rpf/ (accessed on 28 May 2012).
7. See "Manipur Outfit Shuns Talks Offer", *The Telegraph*, 25 February 2008, available at http://www.telegraphindia.com/1080225/jsp/northeast/story_8945015.jsp (accessed on 28 May 2012).

17

National Democratic Front of Bodoland

Repeated violence in the Bodo-inhabited districts of Assam is a cause of concern for the Government of Assam and for the Union Government of India. The tension between the two communities, the Bodos and the immigrant Muslims from Bangladesh, is mainly because of the ownership of land that the Bodos have been complaining to have been illegally occupied by the immigrant Muslims. In addition, the demands of the Bodos to have special status as a community, and the alleged exploitation of them, have fuelled many armed groups in the Bodo heartland of Assam. Groups like the Bodo Liberation Tigers (BLT) and the National Democratic Front of Bodoland (NDFB) took up arms against all these alleged deprivations and exploitation of the Bodos. There have been signs of progress as far as the peace talks are concerned. The BLT has been successfully brought into the mainstream with the signing of an accord in 2003. The 2003 accord led to the formation of the Bodoland Territorial Council (BTC) which has been empowered with the powers to function as an autonomous administrative body within the state of Assam. However, this accord has not been able, as alleged by the NDFB, to solve the problems of the Bodos. The NDFB continued to be an armed group and caused some spectacular violent activities in the succeeding years, for example, the attacks in October 2008 and November 2010, to name a few. Presently, both the factions of the NDFB (NDFB pro-talk faction and the NDFB anti-talk faction) have declared ceasefire with the government and are confined to the designated camps. However, the inter-community clashes, like the one on 24 July 2012, may again instigate these militants to get back to violent activities.

History

The NDFB was formed as Bodo Security Force (BdSF) on 3 October 1986 at Udalgiri under the leadership of Ranjan Daimary alias D.R. Nabla. The BdSF was re-christened as the NDFB on 18 April 1993.[1] The main aim of this group was to "liberate the Bodoland and the Bodos from the colonial exploitation through an armed struggle and to establish a democratic socialist society in Bodoland".

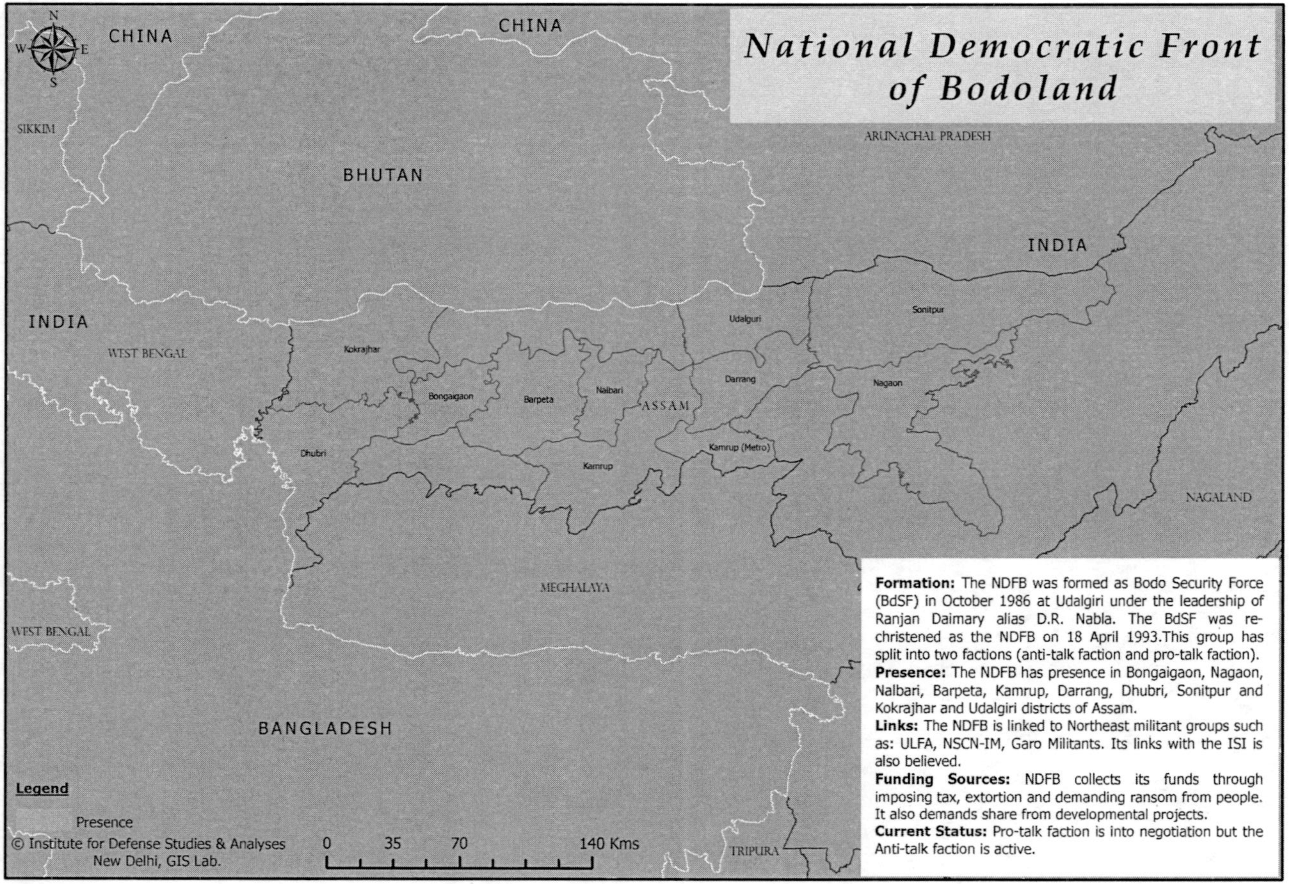
National Democratic Front of Bodoland
CHINA
CHINA
SIKKIM
BHUTAN
ARUNACHAL PRADESH
INDIA
INDIA
WEST BENGAL
WEST BENGAL
Kokrajhar
Bongaigaon
Barpeta
Nalbari
ASSAM
Udalguri
Darrang
Sonitpur
Nagaon
Dhubri
Kamrup
Kamrup (Metro)
NAGALAND
MEGHALAYA
BANGLADESH
TRIPURA
Legend
Presence
© Institute for Defense Studies & Analyses
New Delhi, GIS Lab.
0 35 70 140 Kms
Formation: The NDFB was formed as Bodo Security Force (BdSF) in October 1986 at Udalgiri under the leadership of Ranjan Daimary alias D.R. Nabla. The BdSF was re-christened as the NDFB on 18 April 1993.This group has split into two factions (anti-talk faction and pro-talk faction).
Presence: The NDFB has presence in Bongaigaon, Nagaon, Nalbari, Barpeta, Kamrup, Darrang, Dhubri, Sonitpur and Kokrajhar and Udalgiri districts of Assam.
Links: The NDFB is linked to Northeast militant groups such as: ULFA, NSCN-IM, Garo Militants. Its links with the ISI is also believed.
Funding Sources: NDFB collects its funds through imposing tax, extortion and demanding ransom from people. It also demands share from developmental projects.
Current Status: Pro-talk faction is into negotiation but the Anti-talk faction is active.

Objective and Ideology

According to the constitution of the NDFB, which was reported to have been accepted on 10 March 1998, there are four main ideological orientations of the group. According to Article 4[2] of the NDFB constitution, they are:

1. liberate Bodoland from Indian expansionism and occupation;
2. free the Bodo nation from the colonialist exploitation, expression and domination;
3. establish a democratic socialist society to promote liberty, equality and fraternity; and
4. uphold the integrity and sovereignty of Bodoland.

The constitution of NDFB goes ahead in defining the concept and idea of Bodoland. According to Article 8 of its constitution, Bodoland shall comprise the ancestral land and territories inhabited by the Bodo people.

Organisation Structure, Leadership and Membership

Article 8 of the NDFB constitution details the criteria for the members. It says, "sons and daughters with revolutionary and nationalist spirit who declare allegiance to the constitution of NDFB shall be eligible to become members of the NDFB. He/She shall have to serve and sacrifice for the nation for a maximum of 12 and 8 years respectively."[3]

So far the organisational structure of NDFB is concerned, it is controlled by the president, vice president and the general secretary. Originally, NDFB as a group was formed under the presidentship of Ranjan Daimary. Dhiren Boro was elected as the vice president and B. Swmkhwr alias Govinda Basumatary was elected as the general secretary. The president, vice president and the general secretary are elected by the members of the national council of the NDFB. The members of the national council are elected by the general assembly, which is regarded as the highest decision-making body of the NDFB.

As far as the military front of the NDFB is concerned, it is guided by the principles outlined in a manual, which was published as *Bodoland Army Number 1/1995*, dated 7 February 1995. The date given for the formal establishment of the Bodoland Army was 10 February 1995.[4] As outlined in the pamphlet, the Bodoland Army is divided under four regional commands. They are eastern, western, northern and southern commands and all of these four commands are directly regulated under a general headquarters. The general headquarters is directly under the command of the "army chief". Further, the Bodoland Army has been divided into divisions, brigades, battalions, companies, platoons and sections. The cadres of the Bodoland Army undergo a three month training period after recruitment. The pamphlet also says that the cadres once recruited can marry after a minimum service of five years. The Bodoland Army gives stress on the primary instructions of central command and discipline among the cadres.

Area of Operation

The NDFB has substantial influence in the heartland of the Bodo-inhabited areas. This covers the districts like Bongaigaon, Nagaon, Nalbari, Barpeta, Kamrup, Darrang, Dhubri, Sonitpur and Kokrajhar. As it has been mentioned, the NDFB was formed in the Udalgiri district; hence, it is one of the most traditional bases of the NDFB. The NDFB is also believed to have its presence in the Garo Hills region of Meghalaya, close to Assam–Meghalaya border. The Manas National Park, which falls in five districts of Assam (Kokrajhar, Chirang, Baksa, Udalguri and Darrang) and straddles Bhutan border, is NDFB's sanctuary.

Apart from its bases in Assam and Meghalaya, NDFB used to have safe havens in Bhutan and Bangladesh. In Bangladesh, the NDFB used to have its camps at Alikadam in Chittagong district. The operation by the Royal Bhutan Army (RBA) in 2003 and Sheikh Hasina's counter-terrorism measures in 2009 destroyed the camps of NDFB in Bhutan and Bangladesh respectively.

Weapon Possession and Procurement

The NDFB is believed to have sophisticated weapons like the AK-47s, self-loading rifles (SLRs), rocket launchers and night vision cameras. It has also trained its cadres to use the improvised explosive devices (IEDs). The north-eastern insurgent groups like the National Socialist Council of Nagalim-Isak-Muivah (NSCN-IM) and United Liberation Front of Asom (ULFA) are suspected to be the main supplier of arms and weapons to the NDFB. One report in this regard says that the military commander of the NDFB, Sonit Ingti, has procured some 50 AK-47 and AK-56 rifles from the ULFA-Anti-Talk Faction (ULFA-ATF) chief, Paresh Baruah, in order to strengthen the outfit.[5] Quoting the security forces, the same report reveals that the security forces had recovered some latest developed firearms from an NDFB sympathiser, who the security forces believe to be the courier. The vice president of the NDFB, who was arrested on 1 January 2003, revealed that the president of the outfit, Ranjan Daimary, along with its publicity secretary, B. Erakdao, visited Pakistan and Bangladesh in 1998. He also revealed that Ranjan Daimary arranged the training of the NDFB cadres along with the Naga outfits in Pakistan in 1999.[6] In this revelation, it was clear that Pakistan was using Bangladesh territory for encouraging the north-eastern insurgent groups for subversive activities.

Finance and Funding

The main source of fund raising for the NDFB is extortion. The NDFB carries out extortion drives mainly in the Bhutan–Assam border. According to a media report, the traders and businessmen of Bhalukpong, Seppa and Semma areas of Arunachal Pradesh, adjoining Sonitpur district of Assam, have been served extortion notices by the NDFB militants.[7] Besides this, the NDFB also demands its share from all the developmental projects carried out in the Bodoland territory. The NDFB is also involved in abduction activities. It demands ransoms for the release of abducted persons. Apart from these activities, the NDFB cadres collect "tax" from the tea estate owners and similarly, from every truck and goods carriage that passes through Assam–West Bengal border.

Network

The NDFB has a very strong support base at the local level. Through its effective propaganda, it wins support of the people and claims that it is fighting for the cause of the Bodos.

At the regional level, it has links with the militant groups like the NSCN-IM and the ULFA. Similarly, the NDFB has its presence at the Garo Hills region, suggesting its links with Garo militants as well.

Outside India, till 2003, the NDFB had its camps in Bhutan and enjoyed the support of some the Bhutanese officials and the RBA. Similarly, till 2009, Bangladesh was a safe haven for the NDFB. Also, constituencies like the Jamaat-e-Islami (JeI) supported the presence of the NDFB as it matched with its anti-India sentiment. The support and the links of the ISI with the NDFB have already been mentioned.

Government Response

The response of the government to the problem of the Bodos has been confusing. The government has signed two Bodo accords with the various groups demanding autonomy for the Bodos. The first one was signed in 1993 and the second in 2003. There has been a perception among the people in general, and the NDFB in particular, that these two accords have not been able to satisfy the demands of the people. Rather it has divided the Bodos. The 2003 accord gave birth to the BTC with 40 departments. But the state government has not delegated powers to these departments yet. Presenting a memorandum to the government, the NDFB-Progressive (NDFB-P) demanded:

> These accords are full of loopholes which rather have threatened the land rights of the Bodos and other indigenous people, nullifying the provisions of Tribal Belts and Blocks. The BTAD has attracted swarms of infiltration of undeserving elements. So the Bodo and other indigenous tribal people of the region want to have a separate state as they have every right to it on the basis of the unique history and distinct identity with rich cultural heritage.[8]

There have been several lacunae in government's response towards the NDFB. Though the NDFB first declared unilateral ceasefire on 4 October 2004, it was not reciprocated by the government. The NDFB again extended the ceasefire on 15 April 2005. Finally, a tripartite ceasefire agreement (with the NDFB, Government of India and Government of Assam) was signed on 25 May 2005 at New Delhi. Since then, the ceasefire agreement has been periodically extended. But substantive development on the peace talks has not taken place.

The Union Government of India's interlocutor, P.C. Haldar, has been entrusted to facilitate the peace talks with the two factions of the NDFB.

Current Status

The NDFB is a divided militant group. The group headed by the former president of the NDFB, Ranjan Daimary, is known as the NDFB-Ranjan Daimary faction (NDFB-RD). This group split from the original NDFB when the general assembly of the NDFB elected Dhiren Boro (former vice-president of NDFB), on 15 December 2008, as the president. This decision was taken by the general assembly because it suspected Ranjan Daimary's hand in the 30 October 2008 bomb blast in Assam. Such an activity by the president went against the ceasefire agreement with the government. The NDFB-RD opposed the peace talks and operated from Bangladesh and the neighbouring states till the Bangladesh government arrested Ranjan Daimary in 2009, and later handed over to India. Later, Ranjan Daimary agreed for peace talks with the government. There are demands from the cadres of NDFB-RD for the release of Ranjan Daimary. One report suggests that Ranjan Daimary may be released soon.[9] The report also goes on to say that the commander of the NDFB-RD, I.K. Songbijit, operating from Myanmar, and his deputy, Onthao, operating from Bangladesh, have agreed to Daimary's decision for holding peace talks.

On the other hand, the NDFB-P led by Dhiren Boro is holding peace talks with the government. As mentioned earlier, there has hardly been any progress on the peace talks. In this regard, on 15 February 2012, a delegation of the NDFB-P, led by its general secretary, Govinda Basumatary, met Joint Secretary (Northeast) Shambhu Singh to request him for speeding up the peace talks. Now the NDFB-P is pressing the Government of India to form a separate state for the Bodos, insisting that such a step is within the constitutional framework of India.

NOTES

1. According to some other sources like the South Asian Terrorism Portal, it was re-christened on 25 November 1994.
2. See the constitution of NDFB, cited in Subhrajeet Konwer's "National Democratic Front of Bodoland (NDFB): Continuing Stalemate", in Arpita Anant (ed.), *Non-State Armed Groups in South Asia*, New Delhi: Pentagon Security Press, 2011, pp. 118–19.
3. Ibid., p. 120.
4. *The Formation of Bodoland Army*, a manual signed by D.R. Nabla, cited by Vivek Chadha, *Low Intensity Conflicts in India*, New Delhi: Sage, 2004, p. 269.
5. See "NDFB Extortion Bids Intensify", *The Asian Age*, 5 July 2012, available at http://www.asianage.com/india/ndfb-extortion-bids-intensify-093 (accessed on 23 May 2012).
6. See "Militant Reveals ISI–Bangla Links to Militancy in NE", *The Times of India*, 12 January 2003, available at http://articles.timesofindia.indiatimes.com/2003-01-12/india/27269218_1_arms-and-ammunition-pakistan-s-isi-chittagong (accessed on 23 May 2012).
7. See "NDFB Extortion Bids Intensify".
8. See "NDFB-P Outlines Bodoland Area", *The Telegraph*, 4 March 2012, available at http://www.telegraphindia.com/1120304/jsp/northeast/story_15209487.jsp (accessed on 23 May 2012).
9. See "NDFB Chief may be freed from Jail Soon", available at http://www.deccanchronicle.com/channels/nation/others/ndfb-chief-may-be-freed-jail-soon-930 (accessed on 23 May 2012).

III. Left-wing Extremism

18

Communist Party of India-Maoist

The Communist Party of India-Maoist (CPI-Maoist), known as the Naxalites or the Maoists, has emerged as the biggest internal security challenge in India in recent years. The violent activities of this group against the state of India took momentum after 2004, when the People's War Group (PWG) and the Maoist Communist Center of India (MCCI), along with other splinter violent leftist groups, joined together and formed the CPI-Maoist. They have taken up arms against the state machinery to capture political power and to give justice to the downtrodden and the tribal population—who they think have been denied social, economic and political justice for ages. According to the Maoists, the "genuine" cause of their fight has led to their influence rising from 53 districts in nine states in 2001 to more than 200 districts by the end of 2011 in over 20 states. However, violent activities are concentrated in about 90 districts in 14 states.[1] The prime minister of India has gone on the record to say that the Left Wing Extremism (LWE) is the single largest internal security threat for India. The Maoists, with an estimated strength of 15,000 underground armed cadres, have been fighting through, what they call, a protracted people's war motivated by the political thought of Mao Tse-tung. Given next is a detailed profile of the CPI-Maoist.

Evolution

The CPI-Maoist (Maoist in short) is an amalgamation of two major left wing armed groups. They are the PWG and the MCCI. Both groups derived their ideological basis from the Naxalbari movement organised by Charu Majumdar in West Bengal in the 1960s. The merger of the MCCI and the PWG is the result of more than two decades of initiatives from both sides to merge and fight the common enemies that are "the bureaucrat comprador bourgeois, big land lords and the political elite who control the state power". Despite serious initiatives from both the sides, there were a number of issues which did not allow for a smooth merger of both the groups. In spite of ideological similarities, issues like leadership and territorial supremacy created obstacles for the merger. One of the major factors that was a stepping stone for the merger was the creation of

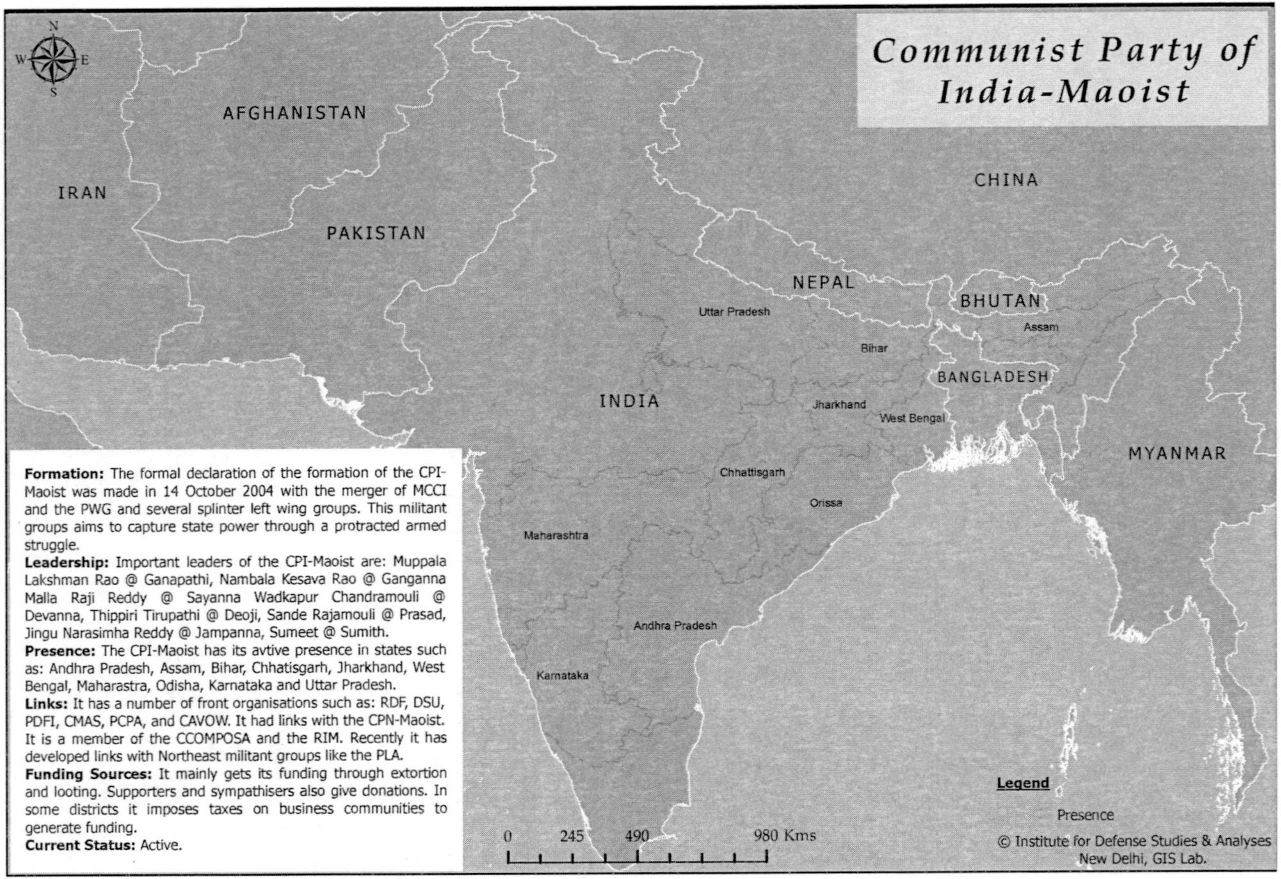

Formation: The formal declaration of the formation of the CPI-Maoist was made in 14 October 2004 with the merger of MCCI and the PWG and several splinter left wing groups. This militant groups aims to capture state power through a protracted armed struggle.

Leadership: Important leaders of the CPI-Maoist are: Muppala Lakshman Rao @ Ganapathi, Nambala Kesava Rao @ Ganganna Malla Raji Reddy @ Sayanna Wadkapur Chandramouli @ Devanna, Thippiri Tirupathi @ Deoji, Sande Rajamouli @ Prasad, Jingu Narasimha Reddy @ Jampanna, Sumeet @ Sumith.

Presence: The CPI-Maoist has its avtive presence in states such as: Andhra Pradesh, Assam, Bihar, Chhatisgarh, Jharkhand, West Bengal, Maharastra, Odisha, Karnataka and Uttar Pradesh.

Links: It has a number of front organisations such as: RDF, DSU, PDFI, CMAS, PCPA, and CAVOW. It had links with the CPN-Maoist. It is a member of the CCOMPOSA and the RIM. Recently it has developed links with Northeast militant groups like the PLA.

Funding Sources: It mainly gets its funding through extortion and looting. Supporters and sympathisers also give donations. In some districts it imposes taxes on business communities to generate funding.

Current Status: Active.

Jharkhand state in the year 2000. The MCCI and the PWG were forced to work in close cooperation against the anti-Maoist operation by the state.

However, the dialogue between the MCCI and the PWG started, for the first time, in a formal way on 21 August 2001. It was in this meeting that a joint assault against the state was planned for the Bihar/Jharkhand cadres and in 2002, for the first time, a joint statement was issued by both the parties against the use of Prevention of Terrorism Act (POTA). Number of peace dialogues and meetings between both the parties were held to finalise the concrete steps for the merger. A sincere decision was taken to not fight with class friends, and various clashes between the MCCI and the PWG were declared as "Black Chapter" of the Maoist movement in India. It was on 21 September 2004 that both the parties merged and documents relating to the establishment of a central committee were passed. However, the formal declaration of the formation of the CPI-Maoist was made on 14 October 2004 by the PWG state secretary, Ramakrishna, in Hyderabad. The CPI-Maoist group also consists of many splinter groups.[2]

Objectives and Ideological Orientation

For the Maoists, India is a backward, semi-colonial and semi-feudal country. There are four major contradictions in the Indian society. They are: (a) the contradiction between imperialism and the Indian people; (b) the contradiction between feudalism and the broad masses; (c) the contradiction between capital and the labour; and (d) the internal contradictions among the ruling classes. According to the Maoists, out of these contradictions, what matters the most to them are the fundamental contradictions of feudalism against the broad masses.

In order to overcome these contradictions, the Maoists' objective is to wage a protracted people's war to capture or seize the political power of the state to establish a new democratic order on the political lines propounded by Mao Tse-tung. The aspired new democracy will be under the leadership of the agrarian class and will be conducted through guerilla warfare methods. As Mao propounded, the Maoists of India plan to establish base areas in the rural areas, thereby encircling the towns and cities, before the final march to seize political power. The strategy appears to have been slightly modified as the Maoists have now simultaneously started penetrating into urban areas and are forming support groups who would help in achieving the objective of capturing the political power.

The Maoists adhere to the ideological thoughts of Marxism–Leninism and Maoism. In a press statement at the time of founding of the new party, it was announced that a revolution will be carried out and completed with the help of an armed agrarian revolutionary war to seize the political power of the Indian state. The above-mentioned revolutionary war will be protracted in nature. This protracted war will be directed against feudalism, imperialism and comprador bureaucratic capitalism. Elements like support for struggle for nationalities for self-determination, including the right to secession, and fight against social oppression, untouchability and casteism, also figure in the ideological orientation of the Maoists. Fight against American hegemony also gets a place in their ideology.

The Maoists have a five-phase strategy to achieve their objective: (a) survey stage: to identify regions where some segments of population suffer from a sense of deprivation and to form groups/fronts of local sympathisers; (b) struggle stage: in which groups of local sympathisers carry out effective propaganda to project the apathy of the administration; (c) resistance stage: in which protests are organised; (d) guerilla stage: in which armed groups challenge the state through violent attacks; and (e) liberated stage: in which the Maoists hope to form their own governance system.[3]

Organisational Structure

According to the constitution of the CPI-Maoist, released on 21 September 2004, Article 29(a) suggests that the party organisation shall be formed according to the geographical divisions and spheres of production. According to Article 30, the party structure shall be as follows.

The highest body of the party is the central committee (CC). Below the CC, there are special area committees/special zonal committees/state committees; regional committees; zonal committees/district/divisional committees; sub-zonal/ sub-divisional committees; area committees; and local-level committees such as village/basti/factory/college party. The primary unit of the party will be cell.[4] To be more precise, the central-level party structure consists of the politburo (PB), the CC and the central military commission (CMC). The following structures are under the direct control of the CMC: the central technical committees (CTC); regional commands (RCs); special action teams (SATs); military intelligence (MI); publications and editorial board of *Jung*; central military instructors team (CMIT); communications; tactical counter-offensive campaign (TCOC); and People's Liberation Guerilla Army (PLGA).

Following are the state committees and special zonal committees: Dandakaranya Special Zonal Committee (DKSZC); North Telangana Special Zonal Committee (NTSZC); Andhra–Odisha Border Special Zonal Committee (AOBSZC); Andhra Pradesh State Committee (APSC); Tamil Nadu State Committee (TNSC); Karnataka State Committee (KASC); Maharashtra State Committee (MRSC); Bihar–Jharkhand Special Area Committee; West Bengal State Committee; Haryana State Committee; Orissa State Committee; Kerala State Organising Committee; Punjab State Committee; Chhattisgarh State Committee; and Uttaranchal–Uttar Bihar and Uttar Pradesh Special Area Committee. The intelligence wing of the Maoists is called as Peoples Security Service (PSS). And, as mentioned earlier, CC is the highest decision-making body of the Maoists.

The eligibility for membership of the Maoist party is given in Article 6 of the CPI-Maoist constitution. It says,

> any resident of India, who has reached the age of 16 years, who belongs to worker, peasant, toiling masses petty-bourgeoisie classes or any other revolutionaries, accepts Marxism–Leninism–Maoism as his/her guiding ideology in day to day activities, accepts Party Programme and Constitutions, actively participates in party activities under any one of the party unit observing discipline, prepare to face the danger encountered in that course and agree to pay regularly membership fees and levies that are decided by the party unit may become a party member.[5]

The cadre strength of the Maoist party is about 15,000 cadres. This strength consists of both men and women from different caste and economic background, from different states of India where there is presence of the Maoists. According to one source, the women comprise 40 per cent of the total cadre strength of the Maoists.[6] The Maoists adopt various means of propaganda to attract and motivate the youth who are against the state to join the party.

Areas of Operation and Network

Answering a question raised in the Lok Sabha (Lower House of the Indian Parliament) on 22 November 2011, the Minister of State for Home Affairs, Jitendra Singh, said that the total numbers of districts in India in which some form of Maoists' activities have been noticed in 2011 is 182. He also added that 83 districts included under the Security Related Expenditure scheme are considered to be seriously affected by the Maoists.[7] The 182 districts affected by the Maoists are from Andhra Pradesh, Chhattisgarh, Jharkhand, Bihar, Odisha, Uttar Pradesh, Madhya Pradesh, Maharashtra, West Bengal, Karnataka, Tamil Nadu, Uttarakhand and Kerala. Apart from these states, there have been constant efforts from the Maoists to expand their presence in states like Gujarat, Haryana, Himachal Pradesh, Delhi and Rajasthan. There have been stray instances of Maoist activities in these states as well.

The Maoists have identified seven strategic areas to fight the Indian state. They are: Bihar–Jharkhand–Chhattisgarh–Andhra Pradesh; Chhattisgarh–Odisha; Bihar–Jharkhand–West Bengal; West Bengal–Assam; Manipur–Tripura; Jammu and Kashmir–Uttarakhand–Punjab–Haryana–Delhi; and the Golden Corridor area consisting of the industrial belt of Gujarat and Maharashtra.[8] The Maoists have been able to develop a north–south corridor, also called Red Corridor, for their activities and have been trying hard to develop an east–west corridor as well. In tribal regions, at some places, the Maoists have formed parallel governance system. In such areas, *jan adalat*s (people's court) are quite popular.

The Maoists have a strong network at local, national and global level. At the local level, the Maoists try to influence the poor and unemployed youth through the "civil societies" which consider the state not doing enough for the development of the backward masses, and hence are against the state. At the national level, the Maoists have been successful in creating Tactical United Fronts (TUF). According to the Maoist literature, the TUF is one of the most important weapons to take the revolutionary agenda to a logical end. Through TUF, the Maoists try to have coalitions with individuals and groups that are against the state and its policies, on one issue or the other, and the Maoists seek to fight the state through "peaceful" means, as well as broaden their presence.

Similarly, the Maoists also envisage penetrating the urban areas through working-class movements in industrial areas. Such penetrations in the urban areas are mostly done by the front organisations. The front organisations are those which carry out the propaganda for the party and disinformation regarding the state. They also help generate funds for the party to fight legal battles and provide safe havens to the underground cadres. According to the Ministry of Home Affairs (MHA), the front organisations for the Maoists exist in 20 states of India.[9] Some of the front organisations of the Maoists are: Revolutionary Democratic Front (RDF), People's Democratic Front of India (PDFI), Democratic Students Union (DSU), Committee against Violence on Women (CAVOW), People's Committee against Police Atrocities (PCPA), Chasi Mulia Adivasi Samiti (CMAS), etc.

According to the MHA reports, the Maoists have close links with the insurgents groups in the north-east of India. In the recent past, a few cadres of the People's Liberation Army (PLA) of Manipur had been arrested by the Delhi Police and it was revealed that the PLA and the Maoists have close links. Similarly, on a number of occasions, the Maoists have expressed their solidarity with the militant groups in Jammu and Kashmir. As the Maoist literature suggests, these ties are part of their Strategic United Front (SUF) against India.

At the global level, the Maoists have strong links with the Maoist parties in South Asia, especially with Unified Communist Party of Nepal-Maoist (UCPN-M). The Maoists of India are also a member of the Coordination Committee of Maoist Parties and Organisations of South Asia (CCOMPOSA). The CCOMPOSA aims at waving red flag in all the South Asian countries. The Maoists of India also have ideological linkages with the Maoist groups in Turkey, Philippines and Peru and also, are a member of the Revolutionary Internationalist Movement (RIM).

Finance and Funding

There are various reports regarding the sources of funds and financial strength of the Maoists of India. A report citing the director general of police of Chhattisgarh mentions that the Maoists of India are able to extort some 2,000 crore rupees every year.[10] Such a figure remains contested. The home minister of Maharashtra has gone on the record to say that some of the mining companies are also funding the Maoists.[11] However, extortion continues to be one of the main sources of fund raising for the Maoists. The Maoists targets for extortion are landlords, government officials in the Maoist-affected areas, businessmen and mining companies. Apart from extortion, the Maoist party members and the sympathisers also contribute substantially. However, the quantum of income generated through this source remains speculative.

The Maoists are also involved in the criminal activities like robbery to raise funds. The robbing of ICICI Bank in Jharkhand in May 2007 by the Maoists is a case in point. Levies from the contractors and illegal mining mafias are major sources of fund raising for the Maoists.

Weapons in Possession and Procurement

In the initial days of the Maoist movement, the Maoists used to fight the state with sickles, sticks and country-made guns. In the course of time, there has been a sea change as far as the modernisation of the Maoists' weapons is concerned. The Maoist arsenal includes weapons like AK-47, Uber Machine Guns (UMG), medium machine guns (MMGs), light machine guns (LMGs), sniper rifles, Indian Small Arms System (INSAS), carbines and locally made rocket launchers. The purchase of arms and weapons from the grey arms markets is a very common way of procuring arms for the Maoists. The Maoists have also acquired a substantial number of modern weapons through their raids on different security establishments. As the union home minister stated, the Maoists are also taking advantage of the porous boundary between India and Bangladesh, Nepal and Myanmar in procuring arms from international market.[12] The Maoists also maintain production units in selected areas of their operations and a technically trained team of Maoist cadres undertakes the repair and fabrication of the weapons.[13]

A numbers of facts about the weapons and arms of the Maoists were revealed when the Andhra Pradesh Police and the Special Task Force of West Bengal arrested Sadanala Ramakrishna, chief of the technical research and arms manufacturing (TRAM) of the Maoists, along with four other Maoist cadres on 29 February 2012. The interrogation of the arrested Maoists cadres revealed that Sadanala Ramakrishna has been stationed at Kolkata and had been procuring material for the manufacture of rocket launchers and rocket-propelled grenades. It was also revealed that some of the spare parts pertaining to 2,000–3,000 rockets had already reached DKSZC. The security forces of India believe that the Maoists might have spent Rs 4 crore to Rs 5 crore in last two to three years for the manufacture of rocket launchers and rocket-propelled grenades. So far the usage of the various modern weapons is concerned, the Maoists have developed proficiency in handling a wide range of improvised explosive devices (IEDs). These include bucket bombs, tiffin bombs, claymore mines, etc.

Reports that the Maoists had procured arms from militant groups like the *Liberation Tigers of Tamil Eelam* (LTTE) also exist. The arrest of the PLA militants in Delhi in 2011 also revealed the growing ties between the Maoists and the north-east militant groups in India. Such ties may boost the weapon procurement by the Maoists from these groups as well.

State Response

The Union State Minister for Home Affairs, Jitendra Singh, announced in the Lok Sabha on 15 May 2012 that the Government of India believes in a two-pronged strategy of security and development measures to yield the desired results against the Maoists in the long run. He went on to add that the Government of India is implementing the Integrated Action Plan in 88 selected tribal and backward districts in nine Maoists-affected states for providing public infrastructure and services. So far the security measures of the government are concerned, at present, 90 battalions of *Central Armed Police Forces* (CAPFs) and a number of Commando Battalion for Resolute Action (CoBRA) teams have been deployed in the Maoist-affected areas. The union government is considering deploying more security forces in these areas.[14] In addition to this, the affected states have also deployed their forces.

Apart from development and security measures, the Union Government of India and the concerned state governments are encouraging the Maoist cadres to lay down their arms and surrender. Some state governments like the Andhra Pradesh government have well-laid out surrender and rehabilitation policies for the Maoists who surrender. Recently, the states also have taken up the crucial aspect of the public perception management (PPM) seriously. Through PPM, the states aim at delegitimising the ideology of the Maoists and try educating the public about the horrors of the Maoist violence, and also project the positive aspects of the efforts of the states.

Current Status

The killing of Mallojula Koteswara Rao alias Kishanji in a gun battle with security forces on 24 November 2011, the arrest of Sadanala Ramakrishana, chief of TRAM, in Kolkata on 29 February 2012, the neutralisation of 19 suspected Maoists in Chhattisgarh in July 2012 and a number of arrests of the Maoists by the security forces are setbacks to the Maoists. At the same time, one can say these incidents may keep the Maoists down for a short period of time but they continue to be a threat to the state. The Maoists have been successful in targeting the security forces in the places like Dantewada, Narayanpur, Gadchiroli and Lalgarh. Such incidents definitely indicate the strength of the Maoists in their operation areas. The abductions of the politicians and public servants by the Maoists have forced the state machinery to discontinue talks for peaceful resolution of the issue. Both overt and covert support of the civil societies and front organisations of the Maoists has been helping the Maoists in legitimising their ideological stand and garnering support from many constituencies. Failure of the state in reaching the people and winning hearts and minds of the people is also one of the major factors for the growth of the Maoists in many parts of the country. Effective and efficient land reform legislations, development initiatives, PPM projects and security measures can be substantially helpful in tackling the Maoist problem.

NOTES

1. See S.D. Pradhan, "Causes and Cures of Left Wing Extremism in India", in Satish Kumar (ed.), *National Security: Annual Review*, 2011, Routledge, 2012, New Delhi p. 426.
2. For details of the evolution of the CPI-Maoist, see P.V. Raman, "Measures to Deal with Left-wing Extremism/Naxalism", IDSA Occasional Paper No.20, New Delhi, October 2011.
3. See Pradhan, "Causes and Cures of Left Wing Extremism in India", pp. 430–31.
4. See "Party Constitution", Central Committee (P), CPI (Maoist), available at http://www.satp.org/satporgtp/countries/india/maoist/documents/papers/partyconstitution.htm (accessed on 20 May 2012).
5. Ibid.
6. See P.V. Ramana, "Profiling India's Maoists: An Overview", in Arpita Anant (ed.), *Non-State Armed Groups in South Asia*, New Delhi: Pentagon Security Press, 2011, p. 152.
7. For details see Starred Question No 1, answered on 22 November 2011, Lok Sabha
8. For details, see P.V. Ramana, "Maoists in 'Golden Corridor Area'", 19 December 2011, available at http://www.idsa.in/idsacomments/MaoistsinGoldenCorridorArea_pvramana_191211 (accessed on 20 May 2012).
9. See http://mha.nic.in/pdfs/NM-FAQs-140212.pdf.
10. For details, see "Maoists Annually Extort Rs 2,000 Crore in India: Chhattisgarh DGP", *The Times of India*, 28 November 2011, available at http://timesofindia.indiatimes.com/india/Maoists-annually-extort-Rs-2000- crore-in-India-Chhattisgarh-DGP (accessed on 21 May 2012).
11. See "Mining Industry Funding Naxal Movement, says Patil", *The Times of India*, 21 May 2010, available at http://articles.timesofindia.indiatimes.com/2010-05-21/india/28312413_1_naxal-affected-areas-naxal-movement-naxal-hit (accessed on 21 May 2012).
12. See "Maoists Get Arms from Abroad: Chidambaram", 24 October 2009, available at http://news.rediff.com/report/2009/oct/24/maoist-getting-arms-from-abroad-chidambaram1.htm (accessed on 20 May 2012).
13. See Ramana, "Profiling India's Maoists: An Overview", p. 156.
14. See http://mha.nic.in/pdfs/NM-FAQs-140212.pdf.

IV. Islamist Groups

19
Indian Mujahideen

The Indian Mujahideen (IM) has been held responsible for many terrorist strikes that India has suffered in the recent years. The security agencies, media and the security experts have been alleging the involvement of IM for the terrorist strikes, like the 13 May 2008 Jaipur bombing, 26 July 2008 Ahmedabad bombing, the Delhi bombing of 13 September 2008 and the German Bakery blast in December 2010 in Pune, which have killed many innocent civilians and damaged property. It is also suspected to have been involved in February 2013 Hyderabad blasts. The United States (US) has added the IM to the list of foreign terrorist organisations as well as to the list of specially designated global terrorist entities.[1] Moreover, the security agencies, like the National Investigation Agency (NIA) of India, have filed complaints against a number of alleged IM cadres and leaders. Several e-mails by the alleged IM claiming responsibility for many of these attacks also exist. A published document by the IM, entitled "The Rise of Jihad, Revenge of Gujarat", has been there in the public domain.

Growth of IM

The growth of IM is reported to be a reaction to the alleged neglect of the Muslims in India in general, and the killing of Muslims in Godhra riot in Gujarat in 2002 in particular. One of the reasons attributed to the rise of the IM was the proscription of the Students Islamic Movement of India (SIMI). The SIMI was banned in September 2001. Many of the leaders of the SIMI are believed to have either formed the IM or have joined the group. In this regard, one report reveals that some of the former SIMI members like Qayamuddin Kapadia, Usman Agarbattiwala and Sajid Mansuri supported the formation of IM as early as 2007 with 50 SIMI cadres participating in a jihadi training camp in Aluva, Kerala.[2] This group has links with "Karachi Project"—a joint venture of Inter Services Intelligence (ISI) and Lashkar-e-Taiba (LeT) combine—planned with a view to use Indian Muslims to launch terrorist attacks at a higher level in India to maintain deniability of involvement of Pakistan's ISI. The former Home Secretary, G.K. Pillai, had stated that the links between LeT and IM as part of Karachi

Indian Mujahideen

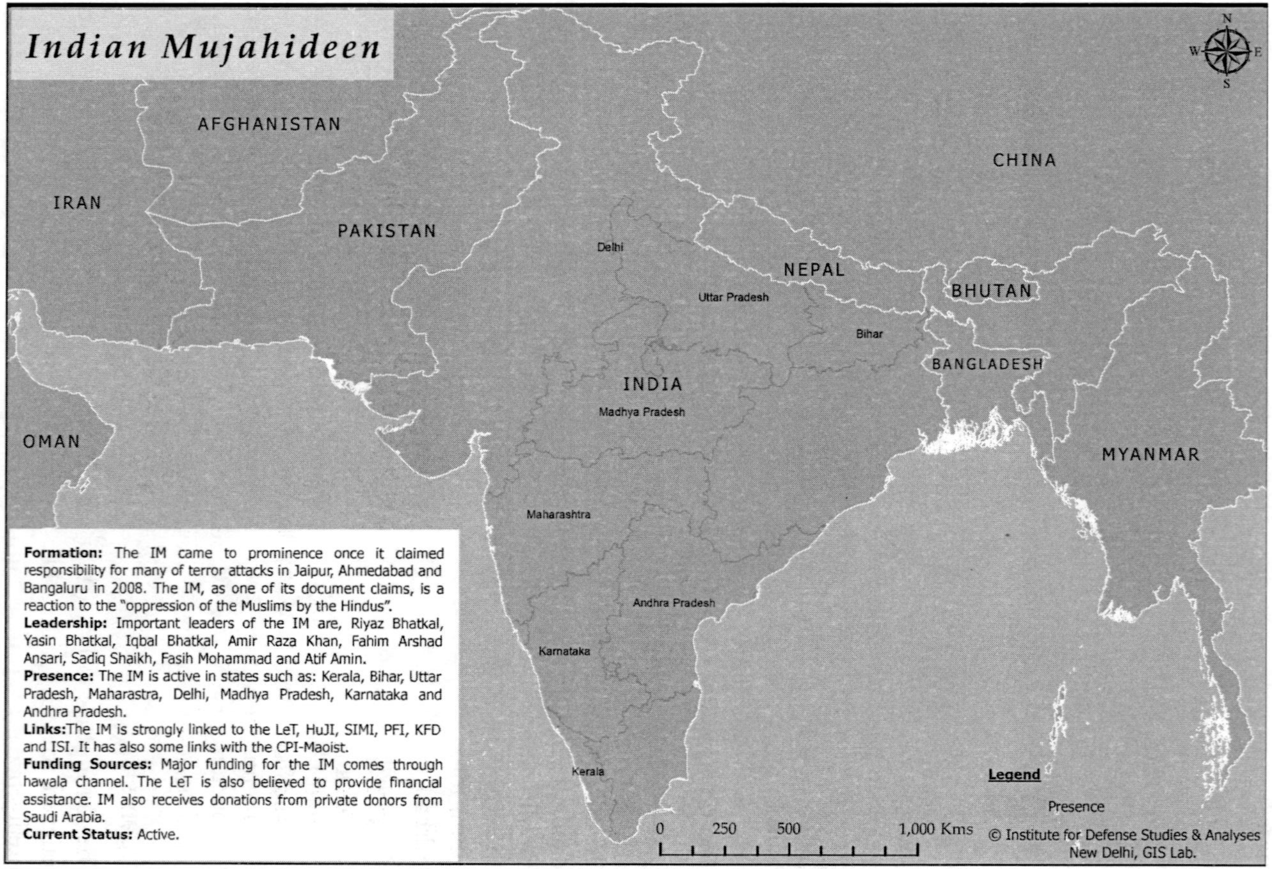

Formation: The IM came to prominence once it claimed responsibility for many of terror attacks in Jaipur, Ahmedabad and Bangaluru in 2008. The IM, as one of its document claims, is a reaction to the "oppression of the Muslims by the Hindus".

Leadership: Important leaders of the IM are, Riyaz Bhatkal, Yasin Bhatkal, Iqbal Bhatkal, Amir Raza Khan, Fahim Arshad Ansari, Sadiq Shaikh, Fasih Mohammad and Atif Amin.

Presence: The IM is active in states such as: Kerala, Bihar, Uttar Pradesh, Maharastra, Delhi, Madhya Pradesh, Karnataka and Andhra Pradesh.

Links: The IM is strongly linked to the LeT, HuJI, SIMI, PFI, KFD and ISI. It has also some links with the CPI-Maoist.

Funding Sources: Major funding for the IM comes through hawala channel. The LeT is also believed to provide financial assistance. IM also receives donations from private donors from Saudi Arabia.

Current Status: Active.

project had been established.[3] So far the document of the IM is concerned, the rise of IM is a reaction to the "oppression of the Muslims by the Hindus". To quote:

> Here we begin the answer to your tyranny and oppression, raising the illustrious banner of Jihad against the Hindus and all those who fight and resist us, and here we begin our revenge with the Help and Permission of Allah—A terrifying revenge of our blood, our lives, and our honor that will Insha-Allah terminate your survival on this land.
>
> Remember, O you Gujarati Hindus! O you filthy, shameless and foul creatures! O you Gujarati Hindus, most immoral and the most gutless cowards! Remember whom you have fought against! You have fought against the inheritors of a Messenger of Allah, of a Prophet of Allah whose terror was cast on the enemy from a distance of a month's journey.[4]

An important factor responsible for growth of the IM is the support of the terrorist groups like the LeT and Harkat-ul-Jihad-al-Islami (HuJI), as also Pakistan's intelligence agencies, and flow of money for its activities from outside India.

Ideology and Objective

Some scholars also believe that the SIMI and the IM are one and the same organisation.[5] However, there are differences in their ideological orientations. The SIMI believed and derived its ideological orientations from Maulana Maududi, the founder of Jamaat-e-Islami (JeI). The SIMI believes that the capture of political power is the main point of the struggle of the Islamic mission. However, an important document of the IM suggests that it targets mainly the Hindu forces like the Rashtriya Swayamsevak Sangh (RSS) and Vishwa Hindu Parishad (VHP). The document says:

> O You sick criminals of the Hindu Parishad! You nasty dogs of the RSS! Yes! We know you, we identify you by your ugly faces! We will not be satisfied until we make each and every criminal pay for every drop of blood you spilled and for each and every cry of the oppressed women and children. Our swords are ready to cut off your veins and to push you into the Hell Fire. This is our assurance to you, a promise to you, a pledge to you, which Allah Alone, The Most Exalted with His Will shall fulfill.[6]

Organisation and Leadership

The IM is not structured in a traditional way like other terrorist groups. It is believed to be an organisation which operates on a strong network basis. Intelligence reports suggest that it operates through a number of modules. In this system, each module is tasked to do a specific job. The modules are not privy to the tasks assigned to other modules. This system reduces the risk of exposure of the entire plan or whereabouts of other modules in case one module gets caught. Its members are believed to be computer savvy and most of the information is shared through the use of Internet. The interrogation report of Mohammad Saif, who was arrested in Delhi in September 2008, highlights different wings of the IM.[7] It says that the IM has four wings for specific responsibilities. They are:

1. Shahabuddin Ghouri Brigade: Headed by Amir Raza. The prime responsibility of this wing is to plan and execute attacks in south India, headquartered someplace in Kerala.
2. Muhammad Ghaznavi Brigade: Responsible for planning and executing attacks in northern India.
3. Shaheed-al-Zarqawi Brigade: Given the task of targeting political and important personalities and organising suicide attacks.
4. Media wing; based in Pune. It is responsible for sending e-mails, media release and manifestos after attacks.

Exact leadership of the IM is not known. One can link various names on the basis of various cases registered against the IM cadres and through the e-mails sent from the IM account citing names. One such name which has been frequently used in the e-mails is Abdul Subhan Usman Qureshi. Similarly, another name which has been associated with the IM and is suspected to be the mastermind in executing most of the blasts is Yasin Bhatkal, who also calls himself Shah Rukh and Imran. Yasin Bhatkal and his brother, Riyaz Bhatkal, are the most important militants. Safdar Nagori, who has been arrested by the security agency and hails from Ujjain of Madhya Pradesh, is believed to one of the main IM leaders. Safdar Nagori broke away from the SIMI and exhorted many SIMI cadres to join the IM. Some other important members of the IM are Fahim Arshad Ansari from Maharastra, Anwar Ali Bagwan, a doctor from Hyderabad, Sadiq Shaikh from Uttar Pradesh and Atif Amin from Uttar Pradesh.

The IM is believed to have its presence in states like Uttar Pradesh, Madhya Pradesh, Andhra Pradesh, West Bengal, Kerala, Karnataka and Maharashtra. The leaders of IM target the Muslim youths and indoctrinate them with radical ideology before they are recruited. The arrest of many IM cadres from different parts of India exhibits the geographical spread of the organisation.

Alliance and Network

The arrest of Abu Jundal and Fasih Mohammad from Saudi Arabia has revealed the IM connection with the Pakistan-based terrorist group, LeT.[8] The HuJI and the HuJI-Bangladesh are also suspected to have links with the IM. In India, the IM is suspected to have links with many of the sleeper cells of the SIMI, like Popular Front of India (PFI), the Karnataka Forum for Dignity (KFD) and Al Ummah in Tamil Nadu.

Weapon in Possession

The possession of sophisticated weapons and access to the improvised explosive device (IED) by the IM is evident from the number of attacks by IM. A report citing the Ministry of Home Affairs (MHA) revealed the unearthing of arms factory of IM by the Delhi Police.[9] According to the report, the Delhi Police recovered two AK-47 rifles, 50 cartridges, one 9 mm pistol, 14 live cartridges, 1.4 kg of explosives, five detonators and fake Indian currency notes worth Rs 2 lakh, and incriminating material.

Finance and Funding

So far the source of funding of the IM is concerned, it generates its funds through the hawala channels. The IM is also suspected to have received financial support from terrorist groups like the LeT and also, the ISI. The arrest of Fasih Mohammad in Saudi Arabia suggests that the IM may be getting financial support from some of the sources in Saudi Arabia.

Current Status

The arrest of many of the IM cadres and their revelation about the IM has raised concerns of the security agencies. The MHA report on the IM has revealed that an IM module has been busted recently and 10 persons have been arrested since November 2011 from Delhi, Bihar, Uttar Pradesh and Tamil Nadu. One of the key leaders of IM, Yasin Bhatkal has been arrested by the security forces on August 28, 2013. As per intelligence reports, IM cadres are being recruited from across the country, particularly Uttar Pradesh, Bihar, Karnataka, Delhi and Maharashtra.[10] There are also reports which suggest that the IM cadres surveyed many parts of Delhi for their future terror strike.[11]

NOTES

1. See Bill Roggio, "US State Department Adds Indian Mujahideen to List of Terror Groups", *The Long War Journal*, 15 September 2011, available at http://www.longwarjournal.org/archives/2011/09/us_state_department_2.php (accessed on 5 June 2012).
2. See Praveen Swami, "New Insights into Indian Mujahideen Network", *The Hindu*, available at http://www.hindu.com/2008/10/02/stories/2008100256021200.htm (accessed on 5 June 2012).
3. See Sandeep Unnithan, "The Karachi Project", *India Today*, 18 February 2010, available at http://www.intoday.in/story/The_Karachi+project/1/84662 (accessed on 25 March 2013).
4. See "The Rise of Jihad, Revenge of Gujarat", document released by IM.
5. See C. Christine Fair, "Students Islamic Movement of India and the Indian Mujahideen: An Assessment", *Asia Policy*, No. 9, January 2010, pp. 101–19.
6. See "The Rise of Jihad, Revenge of Gujarat".
7. See Mohammed Saif "18-yr-old IM Man Spilled the Beans on Terror Outfit", Mumbai Mirror, 18 February 2009, available at http://www.mumbaimirror.com/index.aspx?page=article&sectid=15&contentid=2009021820090218031615268b90eeff4 (accessed on 5 June 2012).

8. See Dwaipayan Ghosh, "Fasih May be Key Indian Mujahideen Hand; Bihar Module is the Oldest", *The Times of India*, 4 July 2012, available at http://timesofindia.indiatimes.com/city/delhi/Fasih-may-be-key-Indian-Mujahideen-hand-Bihar-module-is-the-oldest/articleshow/14658587.cms (accessed on 20 July 2012).
9. See "Indian Mujahideen Arms Factory Unearthed in Delhi: Minister", *The Times of India*, available at http://timesofindia.indiatimes.com/city/delhi/Indian-Mujahideen-arms-factory-unearthed-in-Delhi-Minister/articleshow/11181089.cms (accessed on 5 June 2012).
10. See "Inter State Indian Mujahideen Module Busted", MHA, 14 March 2012, available at http://pib.nic.in/newsite/erelease.aspx?relid=80966 (accessed on 3 June 2012).
11. See Neeraj Chauhan, "Indian Mujahideen Surveyed Paharganj, Dilli Haat for Strike", *The Times of India*, 3 December 2011, available at http://timesofindia.indiatimes.com/city/delhi/Indian-Mujahideen-surveyed-Paharganj-Dilli-Haat-for-strike/articleshow/10964894.cms (accessed on 5 June 2012).

20

Popular Front of India

The Popular Front of India (PFI), a radical Islamist organisation, came to the limelight for its infamous violent act when its members chopped off a hand of T.J. Joseph, a lecturer from Ernakulam district of Kerala on 4 July 2010. Joseph's hand was hacked by the members of the PFI for preparing a question paper which, according to the PFI, insulted Prophet Mohammad and hurt the sentiments of Muslims. A month later, it was reported that the PFI has taken firm roots in the state of Uttar Pradesh (UP).[1] In a similar fashion, citing the Intelligence Bureau (IB), the CNN-IBN, one of the leading television channels, reported on 2 November 2010 that the PFI had links with the banned Students Islamic Movement of India (SIMI). The report went on to state that the PFI has been operating along with some of its front organisations like the Citizen's Forum in Goa, Nagarik Adhikar Suraksha Samiti in West Bengal, Community Social and Educational Society of Rajasthan, Karnataka Forum of Dignity (KFD) in Karnataka, Liong Social Forum in Manipur and the Association of Social Justice in Andhra Pradesh (AP). However, the general Secretary of the PFI, K.M. Shareef, has denied PFI's link with any of the banned organisations, including the SIMI, and blamed the Sangh Parivar and Hindu radical forces for their supposed infiltration of the IB.

Though there has been no evidence against the PFI for its involvement in militant activities and links with any of the banned outfits, yet, some of the activities of the organisation have raised suspicion about the group. The concerned suspicion was substantiated when the former Chief Minister of Kerala, V.S. Achuthanandan, declared on 24 July 2010 that the PFI and its allies were plotting to Islamise the state of Kerala within 20 years. He went on to say that the PFI is pouring money to attract the youth from other religions and encouraging them to marry Muslims.[2] Reacting on the increasing activities of the PFI, the former Education Minister of Kerala, M.A. Baby, declared that the state government should ban the "freedom parade"[3] of the PFI.

Popular Front of India

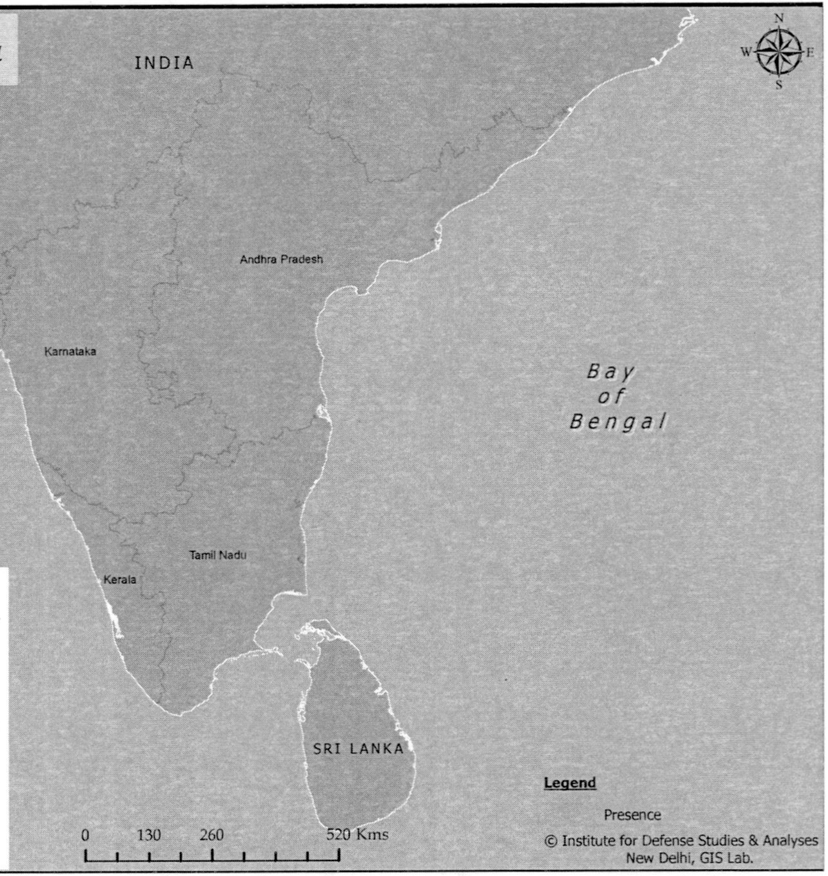

Formation: The PFI was formed with the combination of three Islamic groups-KFD, NDF and MNP in November 2006 at Calicut. The PFI, according to some, is a reincarnation of the Islamic Sevak Sangh which was banned in 1993.
Leadership: Important leaders of the PFI are: E.M. Abdul Rahiman and Professor P. Koya.
Presence: The PFI claims to have its presence in 17 states. It is active in Kerala, Karnataka, Andhra Pradesh and Tamil Nadu.
Links: It has links with banned organisations like SIMI. It is associated with JeI-Hind. Its links with the HuJI, LeT, Al Qaeda and ISI has been claimed by the government officials of Kerala.
Funding Sources: The PFI receives its funding mainly from private donors from Saudi Arabia, and UAE. The ISI of Pakistan is also believed to be financing the PFI.
Current Status: Active.

Formation

So far the official document of the PFI is concerned, the PFI was formed on 22 November 2006 when three important like-minded groups—Karnataka Forum for Dignity KFD (Karnataka), National Development Front (NDF) (Kerala) and Manitha Neethi Pasarai (MNP) (Tamil Nadu)—decided, at Calicut, to launch the PFI. Such a decision was preceded by a series of discussion by members of these groups under a platform called South India Council.[4]

There goes an altogether different historical background of the PFI. The PFI is an incarnation of the NDF. The NDF emerged in Kerala in 1993 when the Islamic Sevak Sangh (ISS)[5] was banned following its violent activities and connection with other radical groups. Once the ISS was banned, there was a space for the former members of the ISS and the members of the SIMI who had crossed the age of 30 to float a group. At its initiation, the NDF announced to adhere to missionary work, *dawa* and propagate Islam among other religious communities. Some of the important members of the NDF such as Professor P. Koya, editor of the NDF's mouthpiece, *Thejas*, and the chairman, E.M. Abdul Rahiman, encouraged aggressive propagation of Islam among other communities. It is, however, important to mention that both Professor P. Koya and E.M. Rahiman retain the same position even in the PFI.

Since its formation in 1993, till its merger as PFI, the NDF was involved in a number of violent cases, killings and alleged links with anti-India forces outside India. Some of the important violent incidents in which the NDF was involved were:

1. The Marad Massacre of January and May 2002. The NDF was responsible in instigating and killing over a dozen Hindus in a communal violence in Marad in which three Muslims were also killed by the Hindus.
2. The NDF was also accused of attacking the Kottakkal Police Station in Malapuram district on 23 March 2007. This attack injured three policemen and 27 members of the group were arrested by the police.[6]
3. There were also reports produced by the Kerala Police (Kozhikode Special Branch) that the Inter Services Intelligence (ISI) of Pakistan and Iran funded the NDF.[7]

Charged with such allegations, the NDF was defamed to a great extent. It was desperate to come out of such allegations; hence, it decided to change its name to PFI along with the groups mentioned earlier. Another reason to operate under a different banner was to avoid a possible imposition of ban by the government.

Objective

The official aim of the PFI is to work for justice and upliftment of the Dalits, the tribals, the religious, linguistic and cultural minorities, the backward classes and the women. It seeks to establish an egalitarian society in which freedom, justice and security are enjoyed by all.

Otherwise, the group believes in *dawa*. It is involved in propagating Islam among the non-Muslim communities. It holds the Hindutva forces as its enemy and enemy of the Muslims. Since 2004, under the banner of NDF, the PFI has been organising "freedom parade" every year on 15 August, Independence Day of India. During these parades—organised in Kerala, Tamil Nadu and Karanataka—the members of the PFI, with uniforms similar to the paramilitary forces, carry out marches in the streets. However, recently, such parades on the Independence Day have been banned by the government. Such parades are a symbol of show of strength.

Organisation and Leadership

The PFI has been registered as an organisation under the Societies Registration Act of 1860 on 6 November 2010. It is important to mention that though the group was formed in 2006, it took almost four years to register. The PFI as an organisation has layers of sub-organisations and units. It functions through the units starting from central level to local level. It is believed that a number of former SIMI cadres are part of the PFI. However, such allegations have been repeatedly denied by the PFI leadership. Former NDF members such as E.M. Abdul Rahiman and Professor P. Koya continue to be the leaders of the PFI.

Area of Operation and Alliance

The PFI is believed to be active in 15 states of India. The PFI operates through its front organisations in various states. They are Citizen's Forum in Goa, Nagarik Adhikar Suraksha Samiti in West Bengal, Community Social and Educational Society of Rajasthan, KFD in Karnataka, Liong Social Forum in Manipur, the Association of Social Justice in AP and MNP in Tamil Nadu. Here, it is important to mention that the PFI has been successful in gaining sympathy from political constituencies in various states. The Asom United Democratic Front (AUDF) from Assam, the Milli Ettehad Parishad in West Bengal and Tamil Nadu Muslim Munnetra Kazagham (TMMK) have shown their solidarity with the PFI.

In a report submitted to the High Court of Kerala by the Deputy Secretary (Home), R. Rajashekharan Nair, on 6 September 2010, it was stated that the Government of Kerala had obtained evidence regarding PFI's connection with terrorist outfits such as Hizb-ul-Mujahideen, Lashkar-e-Taiba and the Al Qaeda.[8] The report also states that the investigation teams had seized Talibanic material, videos and "highly communal" and subversive literature in raids conducted across Kerala. However, such allegations have not been proved.

Finance Sources and Weapons in Possession

Major source of funding for the PFI is the Middle East countries. The PFI also receives donations from its members and sympathisers. Hawala transaction from foreign countries is one of the major sources of finance for the PFI. On the issue of hawala transactions in Kerala, the former Union Home Secretary of India, G.K. Pillai, said that "the funding (for Muslim organisations) seems to be more from outside than from locals". He further stated that:

> These funds are then apportioned by World Assembly of Muslim Youth (WAMY) and Muslim World League's (MWL) local representatives to mosques and local Muslim community organisations for religious propagation, relief activities and education. More often than not these funds are used for religious indoctrination and radicalisation.[9]

So far the possession of weapons is concerned, the Kerala Police arrested 21 members of the PFI and seized three country-made bombs and a sword from them in Kannuar district on 23 April 2013.[10] Such incident is an indication of the fact that the PFI is in possession of some weapons. But the details are not known.

Current Status

The PFI as a radical outfit is a well-organised and thought-out group. Though it aims at aggressive propagation of Islam among the non-Muslims, yet at the propaganda level, it showcases itself as a group working for the upliftment of the less privileged in the society. Unlike other Islamic radical groups, it does not rule out the supremacy of Indian constitution, but at the same time, it aims at establishment of Islamic supremacy. The PFI, in itself, and its front organisations do not use any Islamic terminology in their organisational titles in order to attract individuals from other communities. According to various sources, the PFI is actively operating in 15 states of India. There are also reports indicating that the PFI is working under different names in order to avoid a ban from the government. Though it claims to be a group which adheres to non-violent means, its role in chopping off a lecturer's hand and in the communal riot in Adoni of Karnool district of AP in September 2011, as well as seizure of arms from its members, indicates the potential militant capabilities of the group. The PFI has been successful in attracting number of students across the country through its students' organisation, Campus Front of India. The PFI also has a women wing called the Women Front of India. The Social Democratic Party of India (SDPI) is the political wing of PFI. The SDPI is fighting in the elections mainly in states such as Kerala, Karnataka and Tamil Nadu. Reports also indicate that the PFI has shown its solidarity with the Welfare Party of India (WPI), a political party floated by Jamaat-e-Islam Hind in 2010.

NOTES

1. See "Popular Front Takes Firm Roots in UP", *The Indian Express*, 29 August 2010, available at http://newindianexpress.com/nation/article209625.ece?service=print (accessed on 12 January 2011).
2. See "PFI Trying to Make Kerala a 'Muslim Country', Says VS", *The Indian Express*, 25 July 2010, available at http://www.indianexpress.com/news/pfi-trying-to-make-kerala-a—muslim-country—says-vs/651344/ (accessed on 13 January 2011).
3. See "New Kerala outfit on terror radar", Times of India, 5 August, 2010, available at http://articles.timesofindia.indiatimes.com/2010-08-05/india/28322763_1_pfi-activists-outfit-muslim, (accessed on 21 March 2013).
4. For details, see PFI's website http://www.popularfrontindia.org/pp/page/about-us.
5. The ISS was formed by Abdul Nasser Madani in 1990 to counter growing influence of Rashtriya Swayamsevak Sangh (RSS), a Hindu radical outfit, in Kerala. Madani became a firebrand leader for the radical Muslims as the ISS developed into a pan-Islamic militant group. The ISS, as it had links with militant outfits such as Al Ummah, All India Jihad Committee and Islamic Defence Force, was involved in a number of terror activities. The ISS was banned in 1992 by the Ministry of Home Affairs for its role in violent activities after the demolition of Babri Mosque in 1992. Once the ISS was banned, Madani floated a political party with same agenda, named People's Democratic Party (PDP). The PDP continued to be a popular party till Madani was arrested and found guilty of Coimbatore blast in 2007 and Bangalore blast in 2008.
6. For details, see "NDF Activists Attack Kottakkal Police Station; 27 Arrested", *The Hindu*, 23 March 2007, available at http://www.hindu.com/2007/03/23/stories/2007032314290400.htm (accessed on 23 April 2013).
7. For details, see "ISI, Iran Funded NDF: Rawat", *The Hindu*, 14 May 2005, available at http://www.hindu.com/2005/05/14/stories/2005051402780700.htm (accessed on 23 April 2013).
8. See "Radical Outfit PFI Linked to LeT, Hizb: Kerala", *The Indian Express*, 6 September 2010, available at http://www.indianexpress.com/news/radical-outfit-pfi-linked-to-let-hizb-kerala/677945/ (accessed on 23 April 2013).
9. See G.K. Pillai, quoted in V.K. Shashikumar, "Here Comes Pious", *Tehelka*, Vol. 7, No. 40, 9 October 2010, available at http://archive.tehelka.com/story_main47.asp?filename=Ne091010Coverstory.asp (accessed on 23 April 2013).
10. See "Bombs Seized, 21 Popular Front of India Cadres Arrested in Kerala", *The Times of India*, 23 April 2013, available at http://articles.timesofindia.indiatimes.com/2013-04-23/india/38762524_1_kannur-pfi-two-persons (accessed on 10 May 2013).

21

Al Ummah

(Followers of the Prophet)

Formation

Officially, the Al Ummah was formed in 1993 by S.A. Basha. According to one report, the roots of Al Ummah go back to the early 1980s as it was involved in a number of violent activities. In the early 1990s, three individuals, Ahmed Pasha, S.A. Basha and M.H. Jawahirullah, came together to fight those who abuse Islam.[1] According to Pasha, Al Ummah was formed in reaction to the abuses by Hindu Munnani, a Hindu radical outfit, for leaders for Islam. When it was founded, it decided to fight democratically against those who abuse Islam.

Before the official formation of the Al Ummah, the leader of the outfit, S.A. Basha, engineered a number of attacks, especially on the "Hindu rivals". One of the major attacks in which Basha was the mastermind was the attack on Tamil Nadu state Bharatiya Janata Party (BJP) President, Jana Krishnamurthy, in 1984 at Coimbatore. Similarly, Basha was also the mastermind behind an attack on Hindu Munnani leader, Ram Gopalan, at the Madurai railway station in 1987.

Basha continued to polarise the society and radicalise the Muslim youth against the "Hindu domination". He was acquitted by the court because of lack of evidence of his involvement in the violent cases which he was alleged to have engineered.

Objective

As mentioned earlier, the Al Ummah was formed to fight against those who abuse Islam. Starting from early 1980s, it targeted Hindu radical groups such as Hindu Munnani and Rashtriya Swayamsevak Sangh (RSS). After the demolition of the Babri Mosque by Hindu fundamentalist forces, it also targeted the BJP. The prime objectives of the Al Ummah are to fight the enemies of Islam and the establishment of Islamic supremacy in India.

Al Ummah

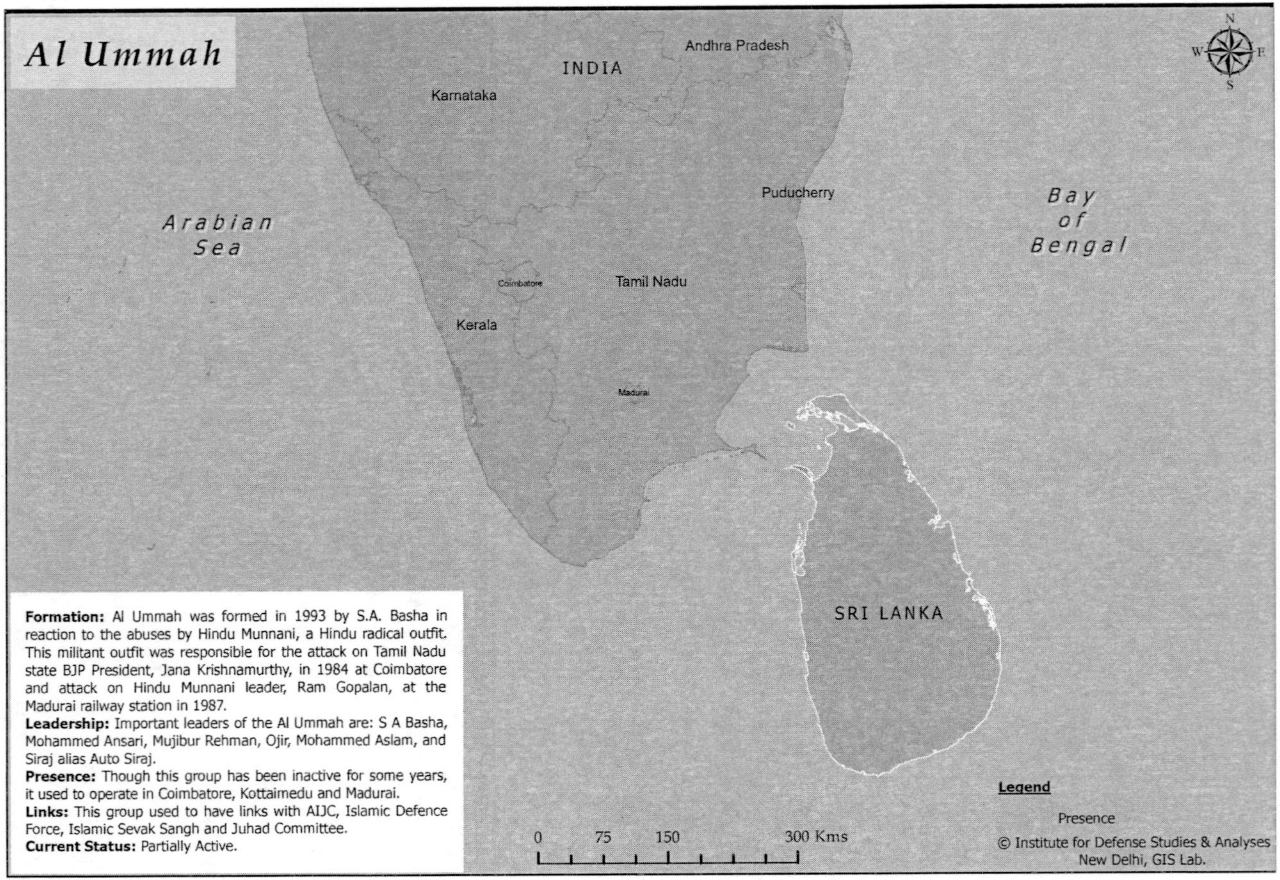

Formation: Al Ummah was formed in 1993 by S.A. Basha in reaction to the abuses by Hindu Munnani, a Hindu radical outfit. This militant outfit was responsible for the attack on Tamil Nadu state BJP President, Jana Krishnamurthy, in 1984 at Coimbatore and attack on Hindu Munnani leader, Ram Gopalan, at the Madurai railway station in 1987.
Leadership: Important leaders of the Al Ummah are: S A Basha, Mohammed Ansari, Mujibur Rehman, Ojir, Mohammed Aslam, and Siraj alias Auto Siraj.
Presence: Though this group has been inactive for some years, it used to operate in Coimbatore, Kottaimedu and Madurai.
Links: This group used to have links with AIJC, Islamic Defence Force, Islamic Sevak Sangh and Juhad Committee.
Current Status: Partially Active.

Organisation and Leadership

As mentioned earlier, Al Ummah was constituted by three individuals, S.A. Basha, Ahmed Pasha and M.H. Jawahirullah. On 15 August 1995, Jawahirullah left the outfit to form Tamil Nadu Muslim Munnetra Kazagham (TMMK) as he was unhappy with the violent activities of the Al Ummah.

Al Ummah is a well-structured organisation with 11 member groups, and each group is under an amir (chief). S.A. Basha, who is at present behind bars, is the amir of the Al Ummah. Some of the important leaders of the Al Ummah are: Ahmed Pasha,[2] M. Mohammed Ansari, Mujibur Rehman, Ojir, Mohammed Aslam, Siraj alias Auto Siraj, etc.

Area of Operation

One of the important hubs of the Al Ummah has been Coimbatore. It also has its strongholds in Kottaimedu and Madurai.

Network and Alliance

The Al Ummah established links with many like-minded groups within Tamil Nadu and the neighbouring states such as Kerala, Andhra Pradesh and Karnataka. The Al Ummah is also reported to have links with external forces from Pakistan and countries in the Middle East. According to the Gokulakrishnan Commission report, the Al Ummah cadres video recorded the dead bodies of the Muslims killed during communal clashes and sent the recordings to the Muslim countries for sympathy and finances for their jihad in India.[3]

In Tamil Nadu, the Al Ummah has strong ties with the All India Jihad Committee (AIJC) and Islamic Defence Force. Jihad Committee, presently a dormant militant outfit, was founded by Ahmed Ali alias Palani Baba in 1986. The Islamic Sevak Sangh (ISS) from Kerala, founded by Abdul Nasser Madani, is one of the key allies of the Al Ummah.

Finance Sources and Weapons in Possession

S.A. Basha, the founder of the Al Ummah, was a timber merchant before he founded the outfit. In the beginning, Basha himself funded the organisation which, later on, got funding from the Muslim businessmen in Tamil Nadu. One of the sources indicates that the cadres of the Al Ummah went on an extortion spree for fighting for the Islamic cause.[4] Apart from local sources and extortion, the Al Ummah is also believed to have received funding from foreign sources, especially from the Middle East countries.

So far the possession of weapons is concerned, Al Ummah has access to sophisticated weapons and explosive devices. In the terror attacks[5] the outfit has carried out from 1984 to 2013, it has been found to have used improvised explosive devices (IED).

Current Status

The Al Ummah was banned on 15 February 1998, following a serial blast engineered by the outfit targeting BJP leader, Lal Krishna Advani, in Coimbatore. This serial blast killed 60 people and injured more than 150. Once the outfit was banned, it remained relatively silent. In the recent past, once again, the Al Ummah has been suspected to re-emerge as some of its cadres have been arrested in connection to the Bengaluru blast in April 2013. S.A. Basha is still behind bars. Also, many of the former Al Ummah cadres responsible for various terror attacks are in jail. Though the Al Ummah's role in the Bengaluru blast of 2013 has not been proved, yet given its past record, it is capable of such terror attacks.

NOTES

1. See T.S. Subramanian, "A Time of Troubles", *Frontline*, Vol. 15, No. 5, 7–20 March 1998, available at http://www.frontline.in/navigation/?type=static&page=flonnet&rdurl=fl1505/15050170.htm, accessed on 20 March 2013.
2. Ahmed Pasha is reported to have disassociated himself from the Al Ummah.
3. See the "Gokulakrishnan Commission", cited in P.G. Raja Mohan, "Tamil Nadu: The Rise of Islamist Fundamentalism", *Faultlines*, No. 16, January 2005, pp. 117–39.
4. See Subramanian, "A Time of Troubles".
5. For example: (a) attack on BJP leader, Jana Krishnamurthy, at Coimbatore in 1984; (b) attack on Hindu Munnani leader, Ram Gopalan, at Madurai railway station in 1987; (c) killing of Hindu Munnani leader, Veera Ganesh, in August 1989; (d) killing of Hindu Munnani leader, Veera Sivakumar, in September 1991; (e) killing of Hindu Munnani activists in Melapalayam in August 1997; and (f) serial bomb blast on 14 February 1998 targeting BJP leader, L.K. Advani. This serial blast killed 60 individuals and injured more than 150.

PART-C
PAKISTAN

22

Al Qaeda
(The Base)

Introduction

Al Qaeda (AQ) comes from the Arabic root "*qafiyan dal*", which means the base. AQ which was set up by Osama bin Laden 25 years ago (in 1988) at the tail end of the Afghan war in the 1980s, threatens a scenario of uncontrolled global terror in the next quarter century. In the past 25 years, it has become a wide spread terror outfit the like of which never existed in history. It operates in Afghanistan, Pakistan and Middle East Sunni countries overtly and covertly in the west where weakening Christianity and culture are helping it dig its deep. In the Middle East countries, lack of modernism is its great asset. Here local Sunni terrorist organisations have become its natural affiliates.

Bin Laden was born in 1957. He was son of one of the richest construction contractor in Saudi Arabia. After completing his degree in civil engineering at King Abdul University in 1979, bin Laden, along with thousands of volunteers from the Middle East, moved to Afghanistan to fight against the Soviet occupation of Afghanistan and defend fellow Muslims during 1979–88. The AQ grew out of Maktab-al-Khidmat, that is, Afghanistan Services Offices, a support network that recruited, trained and financed thousands of youths from almost all over the world. Maktab-al-Khidmat was set up in Peshawar in 1984 by bin Laden and the Palestinian Muslim Brotherhood leader, Abdullah Azam. Although both of them set up a number of training camps for Mujahideen, there were differences of opinions on the objectives of the Maktab. Little is known about the real differences between the two leaders. It is believed that while the Palestinian leader wanted to concentrate on jihad in Afghanistan, bin Laden wanted the outfit to have its tentacles all over the world.[1] In 1989, Azam was assassinated, following which bin Laden emerged as the leader of the network.

Bin Laden's initiatives to attract Muslim youths from across the countries to join the fight in Afghanistan received overwhelming support. Following the Soviet forces withdrawal from Afghanistan in 1988–89, the mujahideen went back to their countries directly or joined conflicts in Somalia, the Balkans and Chechnya.

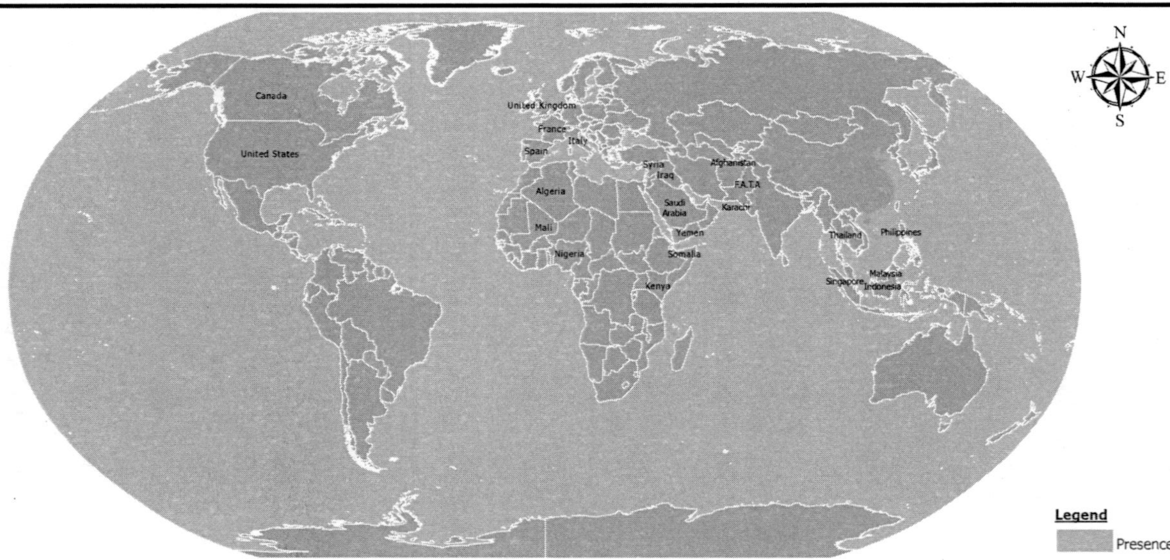

Formation: Formed by Osama Bin Laden in 1988. Involved in armed jihad against Soviet forces in Afghanistan. Responsible for the 9/11 attack on US.
Leadership: Ayman al-Zawahiri, Nasser Abdul Karim al-Wuhayshi, Adnan el-Shukrijumah, Hamza al-Jawfi, Abou Mossab Abdel Wadoud, Farman Shinwari.
Presence: Afghanistan, FATA and Karachi in Pakistan, Yemen, Saudi Arabia Iraq, Syria, Somalia, Kenya, Nigeria, Mali, Algeria, Thailand, Malaysia, Singapore, Indonesia, Philippines, Canada, France, Spain, US, UK and Italy.
Links: Al Qaeda has its links with militant groups such as: TTP, LeT, HuM, HuJI, JeM, Haqqani Network and Taliban in South Asia, Jemmah Islamiyah, Kumpulan Mujahideen Malaysia, Abu Sayyaf Group of Philippines and the Moro Islamic Liberation Front (MILF) in Southeast Asia, Salafist Groups for Preaching and Combat, Al Shabaab, Boko Haram in Africa.
Funding Sources: Pakistan-based Al Rashid Trust, Al Akhtar and Wafa Humanitarian Organization; the Kuwait-based Revival of Islamic Heritage Society; the Saudi-based al-Haramain organization; and the US-based Holy Land Foundation for Relief and Development, Personal Fortunes of Osama bin Laden, Private Donors, Zakat funds.
Current Status: Active

Al Qaeda

0 2,500 5,000 10,000 Kms

Bin Laden also returned to Saudi Arabia where he strongly opposed the stationing of the United States (US) troops and intensified campaign of jihad activities against the Saudi rulers whom he described as false Muslims. The main aim of the campaign was to topple the Saudi monarchy and instal an Islamic regime in the Arabian Peninsula. For his anti-regime activities, the Saudi government expelled him in 1991. His position further weakened as his family also cut off relations with him

Bin Laden moved to Sudan where he was welcomed by the regime of Hasan-al-Tarabi. In Sudan, with the covert support of the Sudanese intelligence, he was able to expand his network of jihadi activities. He suffered a setback when Sudanese government asked him to leave following a United Nations sanction for harbouring terrorists that attempted to assassinate Egyptian President, Hosni Mubarak, in June 1995.

Bin Laden returned to Afghanistan in 1996 where he rebuilt roads and was welcomed by the cash starved Taliban government. Here he made an effort to raise jihadi activities with few militants at his disposal. The network of bin Laden grew strength to strength as the Taliban captured political power in Afghanistan. The Taliban regime in Afghanistan was a major turning point so far the strength and network of the AQ is concerned.

Using Afghanistan as a base of its jihadi activities, the AQ intensified its activities by spreading its network and most importantly, declaring jihad against the US. The anti-America rhetoric of the AQ led to the formation of a coalition of International Islamic Front of Jihad against the Jews and Crusaders in 1998 (also known as the World Islamic Front). Initially, it comprised Islamic Jihad of Egypt, Gama al-Islamia, Jihad Movement in Bangladesh and Jamiat-ul-Ulema-e-Pakistan, besides AQ. Later, Markaz-e-Dawa-wal-Irshad, Harkat-ul-Mujahideen (HuM) and Sipah-e-Sahaba also joined this coalition—thus, the International Islamic Front. The Islamic Front included the militant organisations from Egypt, Bangladesh and Pakistan. The coalition called on all the Muslims to "Kill the Americans and all their allies—where ever they may be".[2] It was follow up of first Fatwa issued by bin Laden in August 1996 calling on Muslims to drive Americans out of Saudi Arabia. The AQ was involved in many of the terrorist attacks where it targeted the US establishment and offices before 9/11. The bombings of World Trade Centre, New York City in 1993, US embassies in August 1998 in Kenya and Tanzania, US Navy destroyer in October 2000 in Yemen and suicide attacks on 11 September 2001 in US are some of the important attacks of AQ against US.'

Objectives and Agenda

The AQ aims at the unity of the Muslims across the countries to fight the hegemony of the US. By aiming so, it also targets the defeat of Jews and Israel as a country. It calls on the Muslims to unite to expel the non-believers of Islam and the Westerners, and it opposes all the things it considers "non-Islamic". The final goal of the AQ is to establish a pan-Islamic Caliphate. As bin Laden stated, the AQ aims to establish the desired caliphate by use of force. According to Ayman al-Zawahiri, the present AQ chief, the use of force/jihad to establish an Islamic state in Arab world was most needed. He said in his book, *Knights Under the banner of the Prophet*:

> Just as victory is not achieved for an army unless its foot soldiers occupy land, the Mujahid Islamic Movement will not achieve victory against the global infidel alliance unless it possesses a base in the heart of the Islamic world. Every plan and method we consider to rally and mobilize the Ummah will be hanging in the air with no concrete result or tangible return unless it leads to the establishment of the Caliphate state in the heart of the Islamic world.[3]

Speaking on the movement to establish the pan-Islamic caliphate, al-Zawahiri further stated:

> It is not possible to incite a conflict for the establishment of a Muslim state if it is a regional conflict...The international Jewish–Crusader alliance, led by America, will not allow any Muslim force to obtain power in any of the Muslim lands...it will impose sanctions on whomever helps it, even if it does not declare war against them altogether. Therefore, to adjust to this new reality, we must prepare ourselves for a battle that is not confined to a single region but rather includes the apostate domestic enemy and Jewish–Crusader external enemy.[4]

Organisation, Structure and Leadership

The organisational structure and leadership of the AQ seems to be complex. According to one source, the organisational structure of the AQ is a blend of centralised hierarchical and decentralised flat network.[5] According to the same report, the organisational structure of the AQ could have three levels: (a) central AQ in Pakistan; (b) the second-tier leadership; and (c) cells (or micro-cells) and individuals.

At the central leadership level, the leaders do not necessarily control the movement worldwide but they do give symbolic representation and mobilise the Mujahideens to carry out the activities. At the second level, the AQ have the middlemen who help to organise, mobilise, train and radicalise the youth to carry the movement forward. This level is extremely important as the middlemen tie up with local groups and leaders with their own interest in specific conflict zones. Terrorist groups like the Lashkar-e-Taiba (LeT), Al Qaeda in Islamic Magherb (AQIM), the Moroccan Islamic Combatant Group, the revived Al Qaeda in the Arabian Peninsula (AQAP) and Al Shabaab in Somalia are considered to be either branches of the central AQ or associates who have adopted AQ brand or level.[6] In the third level, the AQ takes advantage of the cells or micro-cells or individuals who believe in the ideological orientation of the AQ.

According to another source, the organisational structure of the AQ could have five tiers. These are: central AQ, affiliated groups, allied groups, allied networks and inspired individuals.[7] This source talks of two new tiers: allied groups and allied networks. The allied groups are such that have established relationship with the AQ but have not been a formal member of the same. They act independently but ally with the AQ for specific operations, trainings, etc. The allied networks are mostly small and dispersed militant organisations with some direct connection with the AQ but are mostly independent in networking, radicalising and planning attacks.[8]

The AQ has spread into many countries and continents. Since 9/11, with Pakistan as its main operating base, it has tied up with more global network and allied groups.

Some of the important leaders of the AQ who have been killed are: Osama bin Laden (former chief of the AQ); Shaykh Sa'aid al-Masri (former chief financial officer); Abu 'Abd al-Rahman al-Najdi (former external operations chief), Anwar al-Awlaki, chief external operations of AQAP, Said al Shihri, deputy leader of AQAP, Abu Yahya al-Libi *alias* Hasan Qayid *alias* Yunis al-Sahra, leader of Libyan Islamic Fighting Group and main theologian of the AQ Sheikh Yasin al Kuwaiti (paramilitary commander), Ubaidah Abdullah al Alam (intelligence and security chief), Mullah Akhtar Zadran (military commander of Lashkar-e-zil – AQ shadow army based in Datta Khel in North Wazirstan) and Mustafa Abu Yazid (chief operational commander. At present, the chief of the AQ is Ayman al-Zawahiri. Al-Zawahiri was named as the new chief of the AQ on 16 June 2011, after the killing of Osama bin Laden. According to one source,[9] the following are some of the important leaders of the AQ:

1. Khalid al-Habib is the military commander of the AQ. According to the US military officials, he oversees the military operations in Afghanistan and northern Pakistan.
2. Adnan el-Shukrijumah is the chief of the AQ's "external operations council". He took over the charge in August 2010. An American citizen of Saudi origin, he is reportedly the first leader intimately familiar with American society to have been placed in charge of planning attacks for the groups outside Afghanistan.
3. Saif al-Adel, an Egyptian, was once the security chief of bin Laden. He is suspected to have taken over the duties of the military commander after Mohammad Atef's death in November 2001.
4. Mustafa Hamid acted as an instructor in tactics for AQ in its training camp near Jalalabad. He was arrested by the Iranian government in 2003.
5. Saad bin Laden, one of the sons of the bin Laden, is believed to have been killed by the US security forces in Abbottabad in May 2011. However, the killing has not been confirmed.

6. Hamza al-Jawfi is believed to be the AQ's external operations chief after the death of Abu Ubaidah al-Masri in December 2007.
7. Matiur Rahman, a Pakistan national, is believed to be the planning chief of the AQ.
8. Abu Khalil al-Madani, a Saudi, is believed to be a member of the AQ's shura council.
9. Midhat Mursi, an Egyptian, is responsible for overseeing the development of chemical and biological weapons of the AQ.
10. Adam Gadahn, a US citizen, is one of the main propagandists of the AQ.
11. Nasser Abdul Karim al-Wuhayshi, a former aide of bin Laden, is the chief of the AQAP. He replaced Abu Yahya al-Libi. He now holds number two position in the AQ.
2. Abou Mossab Abdel Wadoud is the chief of the AQIM. Formerly, he was the head of the Algerian Islamist militant organisation, the Salafist Group for Preaching and Combat (SGPC) which joined forces with AQ in September 2006-his real name is Abdulmalek Droukdel.[10]
13. Farman Shinwari is the AQ's new chief in Pakistan. According to media reports, 30 year old Shinwari was apparently chosen for his close association with Badr Mansoor and his background of Federally Administered Tribal Areas (FATA) in Pakistan and his family connection to Kashmir and Central Asia. After obtaining his B.Sc. degree, he did his post-graduation in international relations from Peshawar University. All his five brothers are affiliated with Tehrik-e-Taliban Pakistan (TTP) and other militant groups. Badr Mansoor was earlier de facto leader of AQ in Pakistan. In 2011, Abdul Shakoor al-Turkistani was promoted to AQ leader of FATA. There are reports that due to close rapport with other militant outfits, he was considered as a possible successor of bin Laden after his death on 1 May 2011.[11]

Cadre Strength/Recruitment/Training

It is difficult to determine the exact strength of the AQ. After the setting up of Services Office, about 20,000 recruits known as Afghan Arabs came to Afghanistan from all over the world.[12] Ayman al-Zawahiri's erstwhile organisation, Egyptian Islamic Jihad, also added strength to the AQ. For al-Zawahiri, the AQ added, or involved, "large amounts of participation in jihad, bearing the worries of ummah, and seizing the initiative in most urgent calamities confronting the ummah".[13]

By 1986, bin Laden had started setting up training camps in Afghanistan. He set up his first camp at Lion's Den (also named as al-Ansar) near Afghanistan's Shawal mountains.[14] According to one source, there were seven training camps. Zhawara was initially made the headquarters of AQ. It is located on the border region in the southern province of Khost. Seven camps include Torbuda located near Spinghar (south of Jalalabad), Khushak-i-Nakhund near Kandahar, Kargha, Rishkhor, Qala-i-Kazi, Khad-4 near Pul-i-Charkhi and Sirobi (all these five located in and around Kabul).[15] The HuM—whose central leader, Maulana Fazlur Rehman Khalil, had established close relationship with bin Laden—was given the responsibility to recruit youths from tribal areas for jihad.[16] According to another source, AQ set up number of training camps in Zhawara valley and it was from these camps that AQ declared war on the United States in the late 1990s. During 1992 to 1995, AQ initiated 'Furqan Project' which aimed at imparting training and arms to Tajik, Uzbek, Chechen and other Central Asian jihadis at these camps.[17] Bin Laden also built a fortified training camp exclusively for Arabs at Jaji in northern Paktia, which was located on the supply line between Zhawara and Ali Khel.[18] Zhawara base was funded by Saudi donors and ISI. It was built with the sophisticated machines imported by bin Laden. It had a huge complex including underground network of more than fifty caves.[19]

The training to new recruits of AQ is imparted in accordance with its training manual which, besides highlighting aims and objectives of AQ, includes specific guidelines and security precautions.[20] An English language training manual has also been issued to attract Westerners to join the AQ. Besides basic training, training is also imparted in counter-security matters, use of weapons and other technical and operational codes. According to available sources, training is now being imparted in the tribal areas in Afghanistan–Pakistan (Af-Pak) border where AQ is presently based.

Besides the traditional methods of recruitment, the AQ is also using the Internet as a means to recruit youth. This kind of recruitment first surfaced when five US nationals, who had gone to Pakistan to receive training from AQ, were arrested in the tribal areas of Pakistan in 2009. The Internet material also appeals to the youth to settle down in their own country and get trained through Internet. The text of the AQ for this purpose reads, "Oh Mujahid brother, in order to join the great training camps you don't have to travel to other lands. Alone, in your home or with a group of your brothers, you too can begin to execute the training program."[21]

AQ also started media campaign with the setting up of its media wing, 'Al Sahab' which produced state of the art footage on the Taliban and AQ attacks on NATO troops in Afghanistan and Iraqi resistance movement. Besides broadcasting speeches of its top leaders, it released documentaries based on AQs messages against both the West and its Muslim allies. Effort was also made to motivate Pakistanis particularly youths by distributing copies of articles written by several AQ ideologues.[22] By launching online jihadi magazines in English, that is, *Inspire* and *The Majestic Woman*, the outfit achieved another success by attracting native-born Americans. These included AQ's Adam Gadahn and Anwar al-Awlaki, and Al Shabaab's Omar Hamami who could attract the young American Muslims.[23]

The AQAP posted online recruitment advertisements in June 2012 to recruit and train potential suicide bombers. There are also reports that radical Islamists linked with AQ are using the United Kingdom (UK)-based website, "The hate to recruit jihadis". The website contains instructions on how to contact the Brigade 313[24] network based in the tribal areas of Af-Pak. This exercise appears to have been done as AQ is facing shortage of jihadis. If Western intelligence officials are to be believed, there are less than 200 surviving members of AQ based in Pakistan and Afghanistan.[25]

Area of Operation

The area of operation for the AQ has spread over almost 100 countries as, according to sources, it has its autonomous cells in all these countries, including the US, the UK, Italy, France, Spain, Germany, etc.[26] According to British Broadcasting Corporation (BBC), 20 July 2004, the cells in Europe are located at London, Hamburg, Milan and Madrid. These cells are engaged in recruitment, fund raising and planning operations. One of the media reports citing WikiLeaks said that Al Sunnah Al Nabawich Mosque in Montreal is suspected to be recruitment centre in Canada.[27] In South Asia, the main areas of operation for the AQ have been Pakistan and Afghanistan. Various groups from Kashmir have tied up with the AQ. One such group, HuM, which operated in Kashmir, was signatory to AQ leader Osama bin Laden's 1998 fatwa calling for jihad against the US and all Jews. However, the base area of the AQ has been the Af-Pak border. During the Taliban regime in Afghanistan, the AQ enjoyed a safe haven in Afghanistan and carried out its activities from there. In the post-9/11 period, the AQ has been operating from North Waziristan and South Waziristan, where it reportedly runs two operations centres.[28] To escape the US-led war in Afghanistan, some of the AQ leadership fanned out to urban areas in Pakistan and made Karachi their base. Karachi, according to one source[29] remained the biggest mastermind and financier of terrorism in the early 2000s. It was here that they carried out suicide bombing of French naval workers, attack on President Musharraf, the attack on the US Consulate in 2002, and also plotted to crash a small aircraft loaded with explosives into the US Consulate on 2 May 2003 with the support of local groups. And it was in Karachi where 86 AQ fighters were nabbed by Pakistan security agencies. They included Ramzi bin al-Shaibah, who once worked from AQ's Hamburg cell, and Jack Thomas, an Australian AQ fugitive; and Khalid Sheikh Mohammad (who became AQ's operational chief in 2002 and ran AQ from Karachi) was arrested in March 2003 in Rawalpindi.[30] The main agenda of the AQ in Karachi was to export the sectarian and ethnic conflicts, create a trap for the Pakistan Army and disrupt North Atlantic Treaty Organisation (NATO) supplies.

The AQ militants were also involved in the Lal Masjid operation in 2007 in Islamabad. Nearly 300 people were killed in this operation which sparked a wave of protests all over the country, giving a pretext to AQ leaders to call for popular uprising in Pakistan.[31] It may be mentioned that the two brothers who were manning the Lal Masjid—Abdul Rashid Gazi and Abdul Aziz—were in constant contact with senior AQ leaders, including Tahir Yaldochiv and Sheikh Essa, who were giving necessary instructions on operational strategy not to allow Pakistan Army to enter Lal Masjid.[32] The AQ, which had long viewed the Musharraf regime as its legitimate target owing to his joining the "war on terror", exploited people's anger by declaring war against the Pakistan state. The first declaration was made on 1 August 2007 by Abu Yahya al-Libi, a top ideologue and propagandist of the group. His call was, reportedly, repeated several times by al-Zawahiri asking Pakistanis to overthrow the state. It was further alleged that that the assassination of the former Prime Minister, Benazir Bhutto, was also part of AQ's plan to draw the various Taliban and jihadists groups into open war against the Pakistan state. Quoting the US officials, Bill Roggio said that it was bin Laden and AQ top council, Majlis al-Shura, who ordered Abu Ubaidah al-Masri, AQ former external operation chief, to assassinate Benazir Bhutto after her return to Pakistan in October 2007. Abu Ubaidah al-Masri' later fell ill and died of hepatitis in December 2007.[33] AQ strategy to bring jihadi groups under one platform worked following the formation of Punjabi Taliban in Pakistan. With the formation of Punjabi Taliban in 2010, AQ appointed Mulana Asmat Ullah Mu'awai as head of the operation command in Pakistan. Mulana Asmat was earlier associated with JeM and was given the task to recruit cadres from Punjab.

As mentioned earlier, there have been a number of cells of AQ in many of the countries worldwide. The main branches of the AQ, where these outfits are active in carrying out terrorist activities, are the AQIM, AQAP, AQ in Iraq (AQI) and its allied groups in Egypt, Syria and Pakistan. The AQ has gained prominence in Iraq in the post-US invasion period.

Network and Alliance

The AQ is supposed to be the most organised, linked and networked group in the world. As mentioned earlier, it has its branches, in some form or the other, in almost 100 countries and also, many affiliated groups.

As far as the links and network of AQ in South Asia are concerned, the links between the AQ and the Taliban regime are a well-known fact. Both have shared intelligence, military and other sources for their operations. Apart from the Taliban, many other militant groups have tied up with the AQ in the subcontinent. The most important, as perceived by many, is the Haqqani Network. The Haqqani Network has been operating in Pakistan's FATA. In all these years, especially after the 9/11, the Haqqani Network has become more important than any other militant group to the development and sustainment of AQ and the global jihad.[34]

Another important group that has close ties with the AQ is the LeT. The LeT commander Zaki-ur-Rehman Lakhvi's association with the AQ is very special as he is the brother-in-law of one of the deputies of bin Laden, Abu Abdur Rahman. In the immediate post-9/11 period, after NATO forces attacked Afghanistan, it was gathered by the intelligence agencies that new recruits of AQ were trained in the LeT training camps. Some of the other militant groups that have links with the AQ are: HuM, HuJI, JeM and TTP.

The AQ in South East Asia has been active in the recent years. Apart from its own base, the AQ has also close links with many militants groups operating in different countries in South East Asia. Jemmah Islamiyah (JI) is one of the most important groups that the AQ has close links with. The JI has its own connection with many militant organisations in this region and has been receiving grants from the AQ since the mid-1990s. Kumpulan Mujahideen Malaysia (KMM) in Malaysia, Abu Sayyaf Group of Philippines and the Moro Islamic Liberation Front (MILF) in Philippines are some of South East Asian groups that have close links with the AQ.

The AQ has its core affiliate groups operating in different countries. They are: AQIM, AQ in Yemen (AQY), AQAP, AQI and AQ Kurdish Battalions (AQKB) and Jabhat al Nusra in Syria which was established with the assistance of AQI. The AQIM is a combination of the AQ and the Salafist Groups for Preaching and Combat (GSPC). The GSPC (an Algerian-based outfit) is mainly a Salafist organisation formed in 1998 which has been trying to overthrow the Algerian government. The AQIM was formed in September 2006 with the merger of the GSPC and the central AQ. The AQY came into existence in the year 2000. It got prominence as it attacked the Western establishments in Yemen. The AQY merged with its Saudi counterpart, AQAP, in 2009.

The AQAP is considered to be one of the most active and strong affiliates of the AQ central. It is active mainly in Yemen and Saudi Arabia. Believing in the Sunni ideology, it aims at creating an Islamic caliphate. The AQI has become active after the US invasion on Iraq. Following the death of its leader, Abu Musab al-Zarqawi, the AQI adheres to the ideology and tactics of the AQ.

Finance and Funding

Like its organisational structure, the source of funding and finance for the AQ also flows from decentralised, compartmentalised and diverse sources. Apart from the personal sources of finance which bin Laden used in the initial years of the setting up of the AQ, these days, the AQ receives funds from various sources and methods. One of the major sources of finance for the AQ is donations from the common Muslims. Zakat, the religious duty for the Muslims wherein the Muslims offer some amount for charity, is most of the times misused by the intermediaries, non-governmental organisations and mosques. Such offerings of the common Muslims are hardly accounted for and audited. The AQ has been one of the most important beneficiaries of all these undocumented and unaccounted amounts.

The AQ has also been receiving huge grants from some wealthy supporters and some of the charity organisations. Some of the fund-raising organisations which have been helping the AQ in raising funds are: Afghanistan-based terrorist-financing Afghan Support Committee; the Pakistan-based Al Rashid Trust, Al Akhtar and Wafa Humanitarian Organisation; the Kuwait-based Revival of Islamic Heritage Society; the Saudi-based al-Haramain organisation; and the US-based Holy Land Foundation for Relief and Development.[35]

One of the major sources of finance for the AQ is the traditional *hundi* (hawala) system. This is a sort of underground banking system which allows money transfer without actual money movement. The AQ takes advantage of the huge amount of money that gets transferred everyday from the Middle East to the South Asian countries.

The AQ also exploits the finance sources of its affiliate and allied organisations to raise funds. There have been reports which suggest that the AQ has used commercial companies to raise funds and transfer the cash. Barakaat, a network of companies which had its presence in almost 40 countries, was one of the most important sources for the AQ.[36]

It is, however, important to mention that some of the reports indicate the weak financial strength of the AQ in the recent years. In October 2009, the Assistant Secretary for Terror Financing at the US Treasury Department, David S. Cohen, revealed that the AQ was in its weakest financial conditions in last few years.[37]

Arms Possession and Procurement

According to one report, till September 2012, the AQ and many of its alliances (AQIM, Taliban, AQ cell in Kenya) were in possession of a number of Man-Portable Air Defence System (MANPADS) that includes Strela-2M (SA-7), Stinger, HN-5, blow pipe and many other small arms.[38] There are also reports that the AQ, through its allied groups, has procured arms from Syria during the Arab Spring.[39] Some of the reports also indicate that the AQ cell in North African countries is acquiring chemical weapons.[40] It may be mentioned that senior AQ leaders including bin Laden, Abu Gheith, Sheikh Nasir al-Fahd and Abu Mus'ab al-Suri, had been telling that it was the religious duty of Muslims to acquire chemical and nuclear weapons to defend Muslims. There were also reports that two former top scientists of Pakistan Atomic Energy Commission, Sultan Bashiruddin Mahmood and Abdul Majeed, had reportedly met bin Laden twice in Kandahar in October–November 2001 on the pretext of construction of a flour mill.[41]

In the Af-Pak border, the AQ has been able to sustain whatever arms and weapons it possesses with the help its affiliated groups like the Haqqani Network, TTP and LeT.

Current Status

The killing of Osama bin Laden by the US security forces has weakened the strength of the AQ central to a considerable extent. But at the same time, the allied AQ cells in various parts of the world have been getting strengthened. The AQAP and AQIM are very active and are able to carry out major attacks. The AQ has gone few steps ahead by recruiting militants from the Western countries through its Internet propaganda. It is also using the Internet for operational and fund-raising purposes. According to a report on the AQ, it was operating approximately 5,600 websites in 2007.[42] The report added that Internet has become a major weapon in AQ's strategy. The Somalian Islamist militant group, Al Shabaab, has tied up with the AQ, further strengthening the AQ in Africa. Africa is turning to be a major strong hub for the AQ. With Islamist militant groups signing on to AQ's ideology in Somalia, Nigeria, Mali and beyond, Africa is becoming AQ's newest base. The recent attacks by Al Shabaab at West Gate Mall in Nairobi and the closure of 20 US Embassies in Middle East and North Africa due to continued potential terrorist attacks have proved that international terrorist body has been able to spread its tentacles in all over the world.

In the Indian subcontinent, the AQ is looking apparently weak. But it is not out of the scene. Militant outfits like the Haqqani Network, TTP, LeT and few others are of major help to the AQ in sustaining its strength and position. As the US prepares to withdraw its security forces from Afghanistan in 2014, one should not be surprised to see the AQ becoming more active and strong in the years to come.

NOTES

1. For details, see M. Ilyas Khan, "The Phantom Menance", *The Herald*, October 2001, pp. 39–43.
2. See "Al Qaeda", available at http://www.adl.org/terrorism/profiles/al_qaeda.asp (accessed on 7 January 2013).
3. See al-Zawahiri, as quoted in William McCants, "Al Qaeda's Challenge", *Foreign Affairs*, Vol. 90, No. 5, September–October 2011, p. 25.
4. Ibid.
5. For details, see Statement by Martha Crenshaw, Center for International Security and Cooperation, Stanford University, 19 November 2009, available at http://iis-db.stanford.edu/pubs/22749/MCrenshaw.pdf (accessed on 10 January 2013).
6. Ibid.
7. See Bruce Hoffman, "Inside Terrorism", as cited in Seth G. Jones, "The Al Qa'ida Threat in Pakistan", Testimony presented before the House Homeland Security Committee,

Subcommittee on Counterterrorism and Intelligence, 3 May 2011, available at http://www.rand.org/content/dam/rand/pubs/testimonies/2011/RAND_CT359.pdf (accessed on 11 January 2013).

8. Ibid.
9. For details, see "Al-Qaeda's Remaining Leaders", available at http://www.bbc.co.uk/news/world-south-asia-11489337 (accessed on 10 January 2013).
10. For details see "Al Qaeda's remaining leaders", The BBC News South Asia, 6 August 2013, available at http://www.bbc.co.uk/news/world-south-asia-11489337, (accessed on 2 September 2013)
11. Jacob Zenn, "Key Pakistan Area Gets New Al Qaeda Chief", 14 July 2012, available at http:www.atimes.com/South_Asia/NG14Df01.html. (accessed on 12 January 2013)
12. For details, see "The Most Wanted Face of Terrorism", *The New York Times*, 2 May 2011, available at http://www..nytimes.com/2011/05/02/world/02osama-bin-laden-obituary.html?pagewanted=all&_r=0 (accessed on 5 January 2013).
13. See McCants, "Al Qaeda's Challenge", p. 23.
14. Muhammad Amir Rana, Safdar Sial and Abdul Basit, *Dynamics of Taliban Insurgency in FATA*, Islamabad: Pakistan Institute for Peace Studies (PIPS), 2010, p. 16.
15. See Khan, "The Phantom Menance".
16. See Rana et al., *Dynamics of Taliban Insurgency in FATA*, p. 16.
17. Vahid Brown & Don Rassler, Fountainhead of Jihad: The Haqqani Nexus 1973-2012, Hachette India, 2013, p. 95.
18. Ibid, p.75
19. Ibid, p.67-68
20. See "Details of AQ Training", available at http://www.fas.org/irp/world/para/manual 1_4.pdf (accessed on 28 March 2013).
21. For details, see "Al Qaeda", available at http://www.adl.org/terrorism/profiles/al_qaeda.asp (accessed on 10 January 2013).
22. Syed Saleem Shahzad, Inside Al-Qaeda and the Taliban, Pluto Press, London. 2011, p. 81
23. For details, see Brian Michael Jenkins, "Is Al Qaeda Internet Strategy Working", Testimony presented before the House Homeland Security Committee, Subcommittee on Counterterrorism and Intelligence, 6 December 2011, available at http://www.rand.org/content/dam/rand/pubs/testimonies/2011/RAND_CT371.pdf (accessed on 10 January 2013).
24. Brigade 313 is named after 313 companions of Prophet Mohammad who fought during the Battle of Badr. It was set up by AQ in 2010 with a task to plot against South Asian countries and the West.
25. See Fawaz Gerges, "The Rise and Fall of Al Qaeda: Debunking the Terrorism Narrative", *The Huffington Post*, 3 January 2012, available at http://us.mc1617.mail.yahoo.com/mc/welcome?.Gx=1&.tm=1324747333&.rand=7d5crgp01 (accessed on 1 January 2013).
26. See Jayshree Bajoria and Greg Bruno, "Al Qaeda", 6 June 2012, available at http://www.cfr.org/terrorist-organizations/al-qaeda-k-al-qaida-al-qaida/p9126#p2 (accessed on 10 January 2013).
27. See "WikiLeaks: Montreal mosque 'is a top Al Qaeda recruiting zone", The Daily Mail, 27 April 2011, available at http://www.dailymail.co.uk/news/article-1381033/WikiLeaks-Montreal-mosque-Al-Qaeda-recruiting-zone.html, (accessed on 25 September 2013)
28. Kristina Zetterlund, *Pakistan: Consequences of Deteriorating Security*, Swedish Defence Research Agency (FOI), January 2009, cited in Qandeel Siddique, *Tehrik-e-Taliban*, Copenhagen: Danish Institute for International Studies, 2010, p. 34.
29. See Ali K Chishti, "Al Qaeda: the Karachi Connection", *The Friday Times*, Vol. XXII, No. 44, December 17-23, p. 3.

30. See Ali K. Chishti, "Taliban Gain Strength in Karachi", *The Friday Times*, Vol. XXIV, No. 39, 9–15 November 2012, available at http://www.thefridaytimes.com/beta3/tft/article.php?issue=20121109&page=6, (accessed on 4 January 2013).
31. Anne Stenersen, "Al Qaeda's Foot Soldiers: A Study of the Biographies of Foreign Fighters Killed in Afghanistan and Pakistan", *Studies in Conflict and Terrorism*, Vol. 34, No. 3, March 2011, p. 178.
32. Syed Saleem Shahzad, *Inside Al Qaida and the Taliban*, South Yarra, Victoria: Palgrave Macmillan, 2011, p. 43.
33. Bill Roggio, "Top Link between Al-Qaeda and Taliban Thought Killed in US Predator Attack in Khyber", *The Long War Journal*, 30 May 2010, available at http://www.longwarjournal.org/archives/2010/05/top_link_between_al.php (accessed on 18 November 2012).
34. See Don Rassler and Vahid Brown, "The Haqqani Network and Al-Qaeda", available at http://afpak.foreignpolicy.com/posts/2011/07/19/the_haqqani_network_and_al_qaeda (accessed on 10 January 2013).
35. For details, see *Terrorist Financing*, Task Force Report, Council on Foreign Relations, 2002, pp. 5–12.
36. For details, see Juan Miguel del Cid Gomez, "A Financial Profile of the Terrorism of Al Qaeda and its Affiliates", *Perspectives on Terrorism*, Vol. 4, No. 4, 2010, available at http://www.terrorismanalysts.com/pt/index.php/pot/article/view/113/html (accessed on 10 January 2013).
37. See David S. Chen, quoted in Greg Bruno, "Al-Qaeda's Financial Pressures", 1 February 2010, available at http://www.cfr.org/terrorist-organizations/al-qaedas-financial-pressures/p21347 (accessed on 11 January 2013).
38. For details, see "Guided Light Weapons Reportedly Held by Non-state Armed Groups 1998–2012", Small Arms Survey, available at http://www.smallarmssurvey.org/fileadmin/docs/M-files/armed-groups-guided-missiles.pdf (accessed on 11 January 2013).
39. For details, see David E. Sanger, "Rebel Arms Flow is Said to Benefit Jihadists in Syria", *The New York Times*, 14 October 2012, available at http://www.nytimes.com/2012/10/15/world/middleeast/jihadists-receiving-most-arms-sent-to-syrian-rebels.html?pagewanted=all&_r=0 (accessed on 10 January 2013).
40. See "Al Qaeda May Have Chemical Weapons, Spain's Counter-terror Chief Warns", *The Telegraph*, available at http://www.telegraph.co.uk/news/worldnews/europe/spain/9735472/Al-Qaeda-may-have-chemical-weapons-Spains-counter-terror-chief-warns.html (accessed on 11 January 2013).
41. Julian Burger, "Pakistan Nuclear Scientists Admit Meeting Terror Group", *The Guardian*, 12 November 2001, available at http://www.guardian.co.uk/world/2001/nov/12/pakistan.afganistan (accessed on 15 July 2012).
42. See Jennifer Yang Hui, "The Internet in Indonesia: Development and Impact of Radical Websites", *Studies in Conflict and Terrorism*, vol.33, 2010, pp. 171-191.

23
Haqqani Network

Introduction

The Haqqani Network (HN) is named after its leader, Jalaluddin Haqqani. He was initially a member of Hizb-e-Islami led by Gulbuddin Hikmatyar which had waged a relentless war against Sardar Daud in the 1970s who had ordered a crackdown of Islamists influenced by Muslim Brotherhood. It is believed that Haqqani was influenced by radical Islamists principles drawn from early Muslim Brotherhood in Egypt. In the late 1970s, the Hizb-e-Islami was divided into two factions: one led by Hikmatyar and the other led by Yunus Khalis. Haqqani opted to join the Yunus group, following which he became one of most important commanders in the Hizb-e-Islami (Khalis). Following the 1978 coup against Sardar Daud, and uncertainty in Afghanistan, the Soviet troops invaded Pakistan. This was widely condemned by the United States (US) and Pakistan. Haqqani, who was at that time in Pakistan, made North Waziristan his base, where he started operations against Soviet forces with the support of the Central Intelligence Agency (CIA) and Pakistan's Inter Services Intelligence (ISI) directorate. For launching deadly operations against the Russians, CIA treated him as a commander of formidable power and repute, worthy of an invitation to meet the then President Ronald Reagan at the White House.[1] In 1992, he was appointed Justice Minister in the first mujahideen government with the Taliban who gave him position in the Taliban Council of Ministers. During American attack in Afghanistan in December 2001, Haqqani was the Governor of Paktia province. He then shifted to North Waziristan, from where he is carrying out operations against the coalition forces in Afghanistan.

The US military has repeatedly blamed the HN for most of the attacks on its forces as well as the coalition forces. Major terror attacks included: January 2008 attack at the Kabul Serena Hotel; April 2008 assassination attempt against President Hamid Karzai; July 2008 and October 2009 suicide attacks against the Indian Embassy in Kabul; February 2009 assault on Afghan ministries; May 2010 suicide car bomb attack on a North Atlantic Treaty Organization (NATO) convoy in Kabul; and September 2011 truck bomb explosion outside Sayedabad in Wardak province and attack on the US Embassy nearby NATO bases in Kabul.

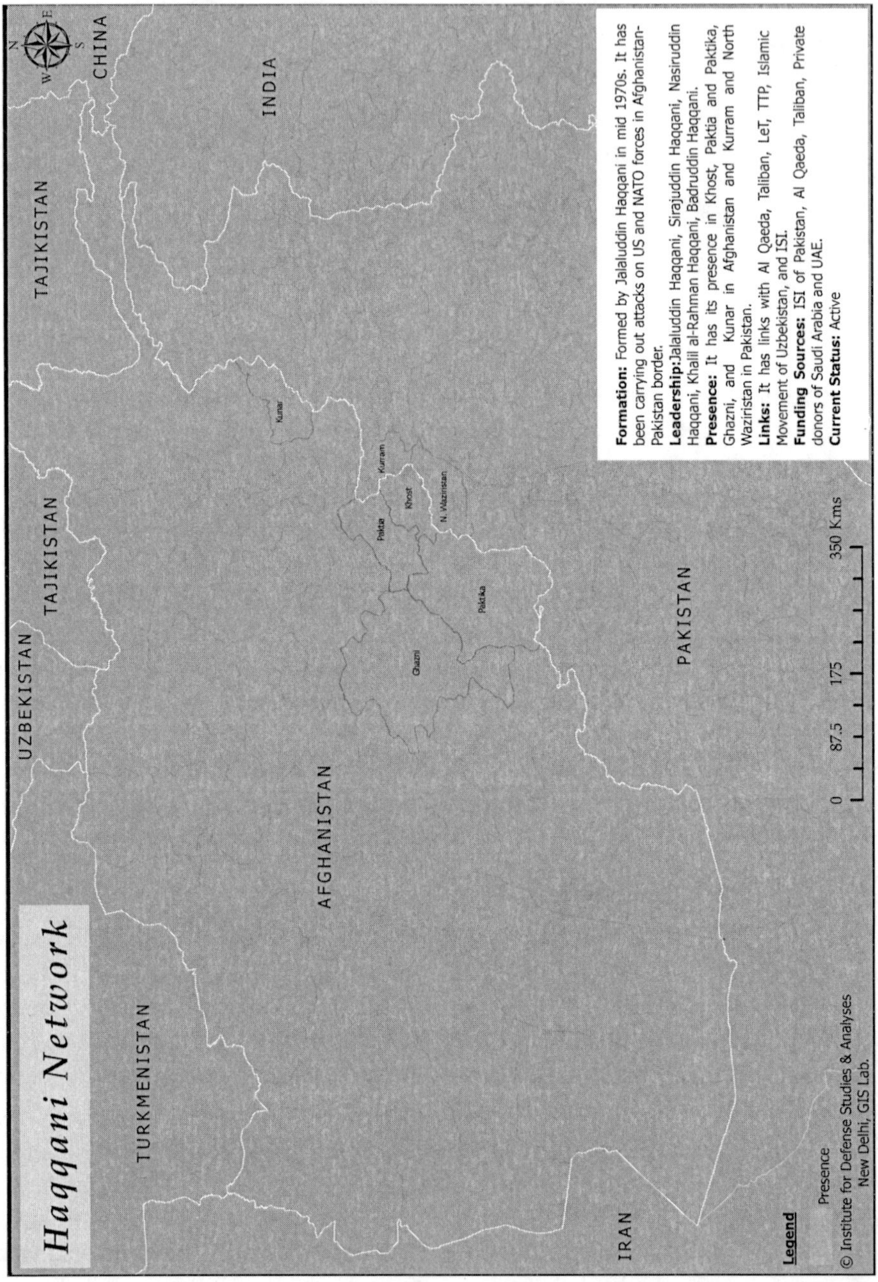
Haqqani Network
TURKMENISTAN
UZBEKISTAN
TAJIKISTAN
TAJIKISTAN
CHINA
INDIA
IRAN
AFGHANISTAN
PAKISTAN
Kunar
Kurram
Khost
Paktia
N. Waziristan
Paktika
Ghazni
0 87.5 175 350 Kms
Formation: Formed by Jalaluddin Haqqani in mid 1970s. It has been carrying out attacks on US and NATO forces in Afghanistan-Pakistan border.
Leadership: Jalaluddin Haqqani, Sirajuddin Haqqani, Nasiruddin Haqqani, Khalil al-Rahman Haqqani, Badruddin Haqqani.
Presence: It has its presence in Khost, Paktia and Paktika, Ghazni, and Kunar in Afghanistan and Kurram and North Waziristan in Pakistan.
Links: It has links with Al Qaeda, Taliban, LeT, TTP, Islamic Movement of Uzbekistan, and ISI.
Funding Sources: ISI of Pakistan, Al Qaeda, Taliban, Private donors of Saudi Arabia and UAE.
Current Status: Active
Legend
Presence
© Institute for Defense Studies & Analyses New Delhi, GIS Lab.

Although the complicity of ISI behind these attacks could not be ruled out, the US intelligence intercepted conversation which proved the ISI's direct involvement in the 2008 Indian Embassy bombing.[2] The group had captured an American sergeant in June 2009. Haqqani militants had also abducted David Rohde, a reporter of *The New York Times*, in November 2008. He was, however, released in June 2009. Admiral Mike Mullen, former Chairman of the Joint Chiefs of Staff, asserted the lethal network as "a veritable arm of the Inter-Services Intelligence which exports violent extremism to Afghanistan".[3] The US, however, backed away from such comments of Mike Mullen. In September 2012, the US State Department placed the HN on the official list of foreign terrorist organisations. In addition, 10 of its leaders have been designated by the US State Department as terrorists/supporters of terrorism. On 6 November 2012, United Nations (UN) Security Council's Taliban Committee also added HQ to a UN blacklist.[4]

Objectives/Agenda

The main objectives of HN are to force the withdrawal of all American and coalition forces from Afghanistan, and ensuring a secure Afghan state under Sharia rule and establishing a reformed, nationalist Afghan government.

Leadership

Jalaluddin Haqqani, who founded the HN, has been the undisputable leader of the group. Due to old age and illness, his son Sirajuddin has taken over the responsibility. In 2009, the US had announced $5 million bounty on Sirajuddin. Most of the leaders who are running the group are closely related or associated with Jalaluddin Haqqani. They are: Sirajuddin Haqqani, who is overall leader of HN as well as the leader of the Taliban's Miramshah Regional Military Shura, besides being a member of the Al Qaeda's top council; Nasiruddin Haqqani, one of Siraj's brother, is a key financer emissary for the network (was killed in Islamabad in November 2013); Khalil al-Rahman Haqqani, Siraj's uncle, a key fund raiser, financier and operational commander, is also assisting Al Qaeda's military called Lashkar al-Zil or Shadow Army; Badruddin Haqqani, another one of Siraj's brother, is operational commander. Fazl Rabi is a key financial fund raiser; Ahmed Jan Wazir is deputy, adviser and spokesman of Sirajuddin; Mullah Sangin Zadran was senior lieutenant to Siraj and operational commander (Sangin Zadran was killed in a US drone attack in North Wazirstan on 6 September 2013); Haji Mali Khan is senior commander; Abdul Rauf Zakir is the head of suicide operations in Afghanistan and group's operational commander in Kabul, Takhar, Kunduz and Baghlan provinces; and Bakht Gul is communication official who works directly for Badruddin as his chief of staff. All these leaders have been added to the US' list of global terrorists. The US has not, however, added Jalaluddin in the list despite his close links with both Taliban and the Al Qaeda.[5] On 5 November 2012, the UN Security Council's Sanction Committee also added HN to its blacklist.[6] The commander of the Arab fighters who are fighting along with the HN is Abdul Lais al-Jazari, a Saudi national.

Cadre Strength/Recruitment/Training

The exact strength of the group is not known but it is estimated that group has 4,000–12,000 militants. The cadre consists of Afghanis, Pakistanis and foreigners—Arabs, Uzbeks, Chechens and Turks. According to Amir Mir, the network consists of four groups: those who joined during Russian occupation; those who joined after the 9/11 from south-eastern Afghanistan; tribals from North Waziristan; and foreigners—Arabs, Chechens and Uzbeks.[7] The group has also set up madrassas, training camps and safe houses in North Waziristan. Most of the training camps are located in and around Miramshah. The militants are given training in basic small arms, heavy weapons, basic improvised device construction, suicide missions, extortion and kidnapping methods. Training is imparted under the supervision of Abdul Rauf Zakir. As mentioned earlier, in addition, he is head of the suicide operations and also in charge of all operations in Kabul, Takhar, Kunduz and Baghlan provinces in Afghanistan.

Area of Operation

The network operates on both sides of Afghanistan–Pakistan border. Its traditional base has been the provinces of Khost, Paktia and Paktika. After setting up cells in Kabul, Logar, Wardak, Ghazni, Zabul, Kandahar, Baghlan, Kunduz and Takhar, it has also expanded its operational base to distant Afghan provinces of Badakshashan, Faryab and Kunar. The ISI has also permitted the group leaders to settle down in the Kurram Agency,[8] which provides the strategic route for launching attacks on Kabul and to Orakzai Agency for escaping the drone strikes.[9] While Jalaluddin Haqqani is based in Miramshah, capital of North Wazirstan and also the headquarters of the network, Sirajuddin operates in Ghazni, Kunar, Paktia, Paktika and Khost areas.

Network/Alliances

The Haqqanis belong to Zadran tribe and have close ties with other clans. Majority of its leaders are based in Miramshah. Here, it has set up Miramshah shura—Pakistan chapter of the network to take important political decisions and discuss military strategy, that is, acquiring arms and ammunition and planning operations. The adviser of the shura is Jalaluddin. However, it is headed by Sirajuddin who, besides handling political and military activities, keeps liaison with "Quetta Shura" headed by Taliban supreme leader, Mullah Omar, Al Qaeda and Pakistan Taliban. He is assisted by Bakht Zan who remains in touch with Tehrik-e-Taliban Pakistan and other jihadi groups based in North Waziristan. Other key members of the Miramshah shura are Haji Ibrahim and Haji Khalil, the brothers of Jalaluddin Haqqani. North Waziristan is totally under the control of the network, where it has set up a mini-state with courts, tax offices and radical madrassas producing a ready supply of fighters. They also secretly run a network of front companies throughout Pakistan selling cars and real estate, and have tied to at least two factories churning out the ammonium nitrate used to build roadside bombs in Afghanistan.[10] The HN has also set up a publicity department called *Manba' al Jihad* which regularly produces magazines and videos glorifying its jihadi activities.[11] One such magazine is *Mànba' al Jihad* which is brought out in multiple languages such as Arabic, Pushto and Urdu.

The Haqqanis have established relationship with groups sharing a commitment to global jihad, such as Al Qaeda, Islamic Movement of Uzbekistan (IMU), the Taliban, Tehrik-e-Taliban and Lashkar-e-Taiba. According to reports, both the HN and IMU not only attend the meetings of Al Qaeda's shura but also carry out joint operations with other groups. Haqqanis relations with the Taliban are deep rooted as its chief pledged allegiance to Taliban supreme leader, Mullah Mohammad Omar. Jalaluddin's close relationship with Osama bin Laden goes back to 1980s when bin Laden set up a camp in Haqqani territory. The HN has been assisting the transportation of Al Qaeda and Taliban militants against NATO and coalition forces in south-eastern provinces of Afghanistan.[12] Haqqanis' connection with ISI dates back to the times of jihad against Soviet forces in Afghanistan.. The ISI continues to maintain regular contacts with the HN: allowing Haqqani operatives to run legitimate business in Pakistan, facilitates their travel to Persian Gulf states and has continued to donate money.[13] The Haqqanis, with the assistance of ISI, are alleged to have been behind many attacks in Afghanistan. The US intelligence believes that Islamabad has maintained relations with the Taliban-associated groups which support and conduct operations against the US and NATO forces in Afghanistan. It is in this context that Pakistan Army Chief, General Ashfaq Kiyani, is reported to have said in an interview that he considered the HN an "asset" for Pakistan. However, such a statement was sugarcoated by the then Pakistan Foreign Minister saying that Ashfaq Kiyani had made such statement four years back and this does not hold any value any more.[14]

Finance/Funding

The HN has never faced any financial difficulty right from its formation. During the 1980s, it was flooded with financial aid and weapons from both the CIA and the ISI. After the Soviet forces left Afghanistan, the ISI had been actively assisting the group. Similarly, its allied groups such as Al Qaeda and Taliban have also been providing financial and military support. In addition, a large chunk of the network's funding is drawn from donations and contributions from Saudi Arabia. Moreover, the wives of both Jalaluddin and his son, Nasiruddin, are Arabs and through them, they have been able to raise funds. Nasiruddin is reportedly a key fund raiser and visited Saudi Arabia and United Arab Emirates where he collected large amount for the HN, Al Qaeda and the Taliban.[15] There are reports that Haqqanis continue to receive funds from private donors in the Gulf. The funds have been coming through Saudi banks. The report was corroborated by *The Times* (London, 31 May 2010) that said over $920 million had flowed from Saudi Arabia donors to Afghan insurgents, mainly via Waziristan, over the last four years (2007–10).[16] Other funding sources include cross-border smuggling, kidnapping, extortion, recycling metal, guns and other weapons collected from battlefield, collection of donations through mosques and taxation of trade in areas under their control. As mentioned earlier, there are also reports that the group secretly operates several front companies in selling cars and real estate.

Weapons in Possession

Since its formation, the HN did not find shortage of weapons. During the Afghan jihad against the Union of Soviet Socialist Republic (USSR) in the 1980s, it got massive weaponries from the CIA and the ISI. It is not known whether they are still in possession of sophisticated arms such as anti-aircraft guns and stinger missiles that were given to them by the Americans in the 1980s. They are now getting small and heavy weapons from diverse sources, that is, the ISI, Taliban and the Al Qaeda. There are reports that TTP has been imparting suicide bomber training to HQ mujahideen at a camp near Shawal.[17] Pakistan has been supplying weapons and other logistical material from the supply base of the Haqqani Network at Miramshah in North Wazirstan to Khost. This is evident from the interviews given by the Haqqani and Taliban commanders to the press detailing how the ISI has been supplying them with weapons and other material since at least 2004.[18] Besides this, they are also purchasing weapons directly from arm smugglers in Pakistan and Afghanistan. In addition, the Haqqani militants are believed to be equipped with sophisticated US-made weapons which they have procured from Afghan soldiers who have deserted, or have snatched them from Afghan and US troops during combat. Weapons in possession included pistols, all types of rifles, including M-4 rifle, grenades, fuses, mortars and rocket-propelled grenades (RPGs), RPG boosters, anti-aircraft ammunition and explosives, roadside bomb material to target army vehicles, remote control bombs and heavy machine guns. The group owns at least two factories making ammonium nitrate used in the improvised explosive devices (IEDs). The HN is also believed to have procured sophisticated communication system and has been using, frequently, remote detonation through cellular phone signals and frequency. These days, the HN is composed of highly trained combatants who also fought against the Soviets. This was evident from their assault on heavily guarded US Embassy in Kabul in September 2011.

Current Status

In spite of the US declaring the group as a terrorist organisation and the group's addition to the UN blacklist, there is no concrete proof that the Pakistan government has taken any action against the group. The action obliges all UN members to implement an asset freeze, travel ban and arms embargo. Following UN action, a spokesman of the Pakistan government said that Pakistan is already cracking down on the group and does not need to impose extra measures.[19] Both Pakistan Army and the ISI have made no comments on the UN sanctions and the US designation of Haqqanis as a terrorist organisation, which means they continue to view the HN as a strategic asset and a possible ally in Afghanistan.

It is unlikely that the sanctions will have a major effect on the militant activities of the outfit. This is because most of the funds collected are transferred through hawala or carried by human couriers. Further, the command of the network is now in the hands of Sirajuddin, who is believed to one of the most strongly committed Islamists, unlike his father whom the US has not added to the list of terrorists. Being a steady regional partner of AQ and Afghan Taliban, Haqqanis are likely to play a significant role after the withdrawal of American forces in Afghanistan in 2014.

Among the various sections of Taliban, the HQ is known to be the most conservative and opposed to any idea of reconciliation. It is likely to retain its linkage with Pakistan ISI and splinter AQ's inspired outfits in the tribal borderland straddling Pakistan and Afghanistan. In case of any reconciliation, the Haqqanis are likely to stay out and push for military take over of Kabul depending on ground situation and if it suits, Pakistan intelligence agencies may help them in their military adventure.

NOTES

1. For details, see Amir Mir, "Haqqanis Sidestep US Terror List", *Asia Times*, 15 October 2011, available at http://www.atimes.com/atimes/South_Asia/MJ15Df01.html (accessed on 10 January 2013).
2. For details, see Bill Roggio, "US Adds Haqqani Network to List of Terror Groups", *The Long War Journal*, September 2012, available at http://www.longwarjournal.org/archives/2012/09/us_adds-haqqani_netw_1.php (accessed on 10 January 2013).
3. See Amir Mir, "Haqqanis sidestep US terror list", *Asia Times*, 15 October 2011, available at http://www.atimes.com/atimes/South_Asia/MJ15Df01.html (accessed on 10 January 2013).
4. See "UN Adds Haqqani Network to Blacklist", 6 November 2012, available at http://www.aljazeera.com/news/asia/2012/11/20121166251166331.html (accessed on 10 January 2013).
5. For details, see Roggio, "US Adds Haqqani Network to List of Terror Groups".
6. See "UN Adds Haqqani Network to Taliban's Sanction List", *BBC News*, 5 November 2012, available at http:www.bbc.co.uk/news/world-asia-2021421 (accessed on 17 January 2013).
7. See Mir, "Haqqanis Sidestep US Terror List".
8. See Roggio, "US Adds Haqqani Network to List of Terror Groups".

9. See Asim Awan, "Looking for New Havens", *The Friday Times*, vol.XXII, No.41 26 November–2 December 2010, p.7.
10. For details, see "Brutal Haqqani Crime Clan Bedevils U.S. in Afghanistan", *The New York Times*, 25 September 2011, available at http://www.nytimes.com/2011/09/25/world/asia/brutal-haqqani-clan-bedevils-united-states (accessed on 19 January 2013).
11. Vahid Brown & Don Rassler, Fountainhead of Jihad: The Haqqani Nexus 1973-2012, Hachette India, 2013, p.3.
12. See "Haqqani Network", available at http://www.stanford.edu/group/mappingmilitants/cgii-bin/groups/view/363 (accessed on 20 December 2012).
13. For details, see "Haqqani Network", *The New York Times*, 19 January 2012, available at http://topics.nytimes.com/top/reference/timestopics/organizations/h/haqqani_network/index (accessed on 19 January 2013).
14. See "Those Calling Haqqanis Asset do not Represent Pakistan Government: FM", *Dawn*, 16 January 2013, available at http://dawn.com/2013/01/16/those-who-call-haqqani-network-an-asset-do-not-represent-pakistan-govt-fm-khar/ (accessed on 20 January 2013).
15. See Animesh Roul, "Nasiruddin Haqqani (a.k.a Dr. Khan): The Haqqani Network's Emissary and Fundraiser", *Militant Leadership Monitor*, Vol. III, No. 8, August 2012, available at http://www.jamestown.org/uploads/media/Militant_Leadership_Monitor_-_Volume_III__Issue_8_02.pdf (accessed on 20 January 2013).
16. See Surender Kumar Sharma, "Action against Haqqanis—Key to Success in Afghanistan", *South Asia Tribune*, 22 July 2011, available at http://southasiantribune.com/action-against-haqqanis-key-to-success-in-afghanistan/ (accessed on 19 January 2013).
17. See Imtiaz Gul, The Most Dangerous Place: Pakistan's Lawless Frontier, New York, Viking,2010, p.86, cited in Vahid Brown & Don Rassler, p.146.
18. See Vahid Brown & Don Rassler, pp. 179-180.
19. See "Pakistan Already Cracking Down on Haqqani Network: Government", *The Express Tribune*, 6 November 2012, available at http://tribune.com.pk/story/461640/pakistan-already-cracking-down-on-haqqani-network-government/ (accessed on 20 April 2013).

24

Lashkar-e-Taiba
(Soldiers of the Pure)

Introduction

The Mumbai carnage of 26 November 2008 and subsequent designation of Lashkar-e-Taiba (LeT—soldiers of the pure) as a terrorist organisation by the United Nations (UN) and the Pakistani government promises to control the organisation have not affected the activities of the terrorist body at all. On the contrary, the activities of the organisation have been intensified and extensified, while the UN and the Pakistan government remain silent. Pakistan's former President, General Parvez Musharraf, banned LeT in January 2002, along with four other militant groups. Within few months of its ban, it reportedly renamed itself Jamaat-ud-Dawa (party of the calling).

Genesis of LeT

Jamaat-ud-Dawa or JuD—the new name of the outlawed LeT in Pakistan—has been derived from Markaz-e-Dawa-wal-Irshad (MDI), an organisation which Hafiz Mohammad Saeed and his associates established in 1986. The initiative was taken when some teachers of the Ahle Hadith, associated with the Department of Islamiat at the University of Engineering and Technology, Lahore, decided to participate in the Afghan war. Hafiz Mohammad Saeed, a former Professor in the Department of Islamic Learning at the University of Engineering and Technology, Lahore was given the responsibility to lead that organisation. One activating force behind this decision was a promise of aid from Saudi Arabia made by some teachers of Medina University.[1] The group's Afghan operations were mainly focused in the Jalalabad, Nooristan and Sarobi areas, under the leadership of Afghan Ahle Hadith commander, Sheikh Jameel-ur-Rahman. The group's presence in Afghanistan ended in1993 at the peak of the infighting between various Afghan factions. However, before the winding up of the operations in Afghanistan—in which 2,500 militants participated, of which 60 of them were killed—the organisation had already commenced its activities in Kashmir in 1989. In the initial two years, the organisation operated under the

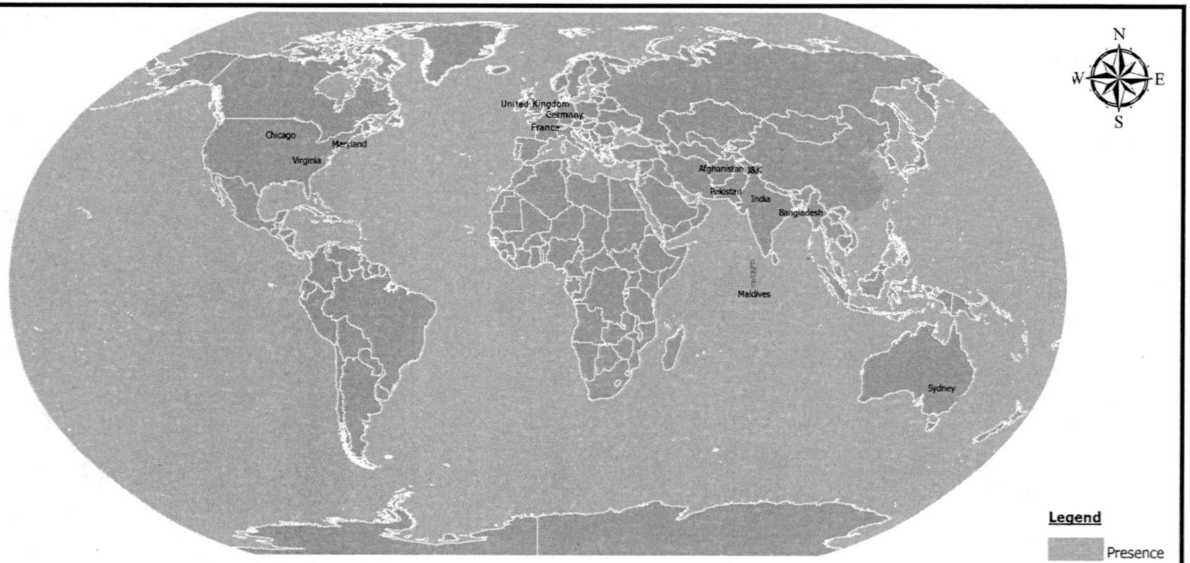

Formation: Formed in 1991 by Hafeez Mohammad Saeed and his associates. It launched its Kashmir chapter in 1993. It renamed itself as Jamaat ud Dawa after former President of Pakistan, General Parvez Musharraf, banned it in January 2002. The LeT was behind the infamous Mumbai terror attacks in November 2008.
Leadership: Hafiz Mohammad Saeed, Zaki-ur-Rehman Lakhvi, Haji Mohammad Ashraf, Mehmood Mohammad Ahmed Bahaziq, Abdul Rehman Makki, Amir Hamza, Azam Cheema, Mia Abdullah, Maulana Abdul Aziz Alvi.
Presence: Pakistan, PoK, Af-Pak Border, Bangladesh, Jammu and Kashmir, Maldives, Virginia, Maryland and Chicago in USA, UK, France, Germany and Australia (Sydney).
Links: Al Qaeda, Haqqani Network, Tehreek Taliban Pakistan, Jaish-e-Mohammad, Indian Mujahideen, Chechanya militants, Islamic Movement of Uzbekistan, Jamaat-ul-Mujahideen-Bangladesh.
Funding Sources: ISI, Charity Networks such as: Idara Khidmat-e-Khalq, Falah-e-Insaniyat Foundation and Tehreek-e-Tahafuz-e-Hurmat-e-Rasool, Private Wahabi donors from Saudi Arabia, UAE and UK.
Current Status: Active

Lashkar-e Taiba

0 2,550 5,100 10,200 Kms

cover of Al Barq. However, in 1991, Hafiz Saeed and his associates decided to form their own militant group, LeT.[2] This, obviously, happened at the behest and with the support of Inter Services Intelligence (ISI).

Militancy in Jammu and Kashmir (J&K), beginning in 1989, provided an active battleground for the LeT militants who were launched in the Valley in 1993. At the same time, Maskar-e-Aqsa was established near Baitul Mujahideen in Muzaffarabad (Pakistan-occupied Kashmir [PoK]) for imparting training to Kashmiri militants. In early 1991, Badr Post and Maskar Umm al-Qura were also formed. During this period, the first batch of MDI/LeT terrorists who got training from these "Maskars" crossed over to the Valley in August 1992, under the command of first-ever LeT Kashmir Amir, Abu Hafiz. During 1993–94, one more training centre called Maskar Abdullah bin Masood was established in Muzaffarabad. Almost immediately, the LeT shot into prominence by launching several guerilla attacks against the Indian security forces in J&K, thereby establishing itself as a deadly jihadi outfit, initially in J&K and then beyond in the hinterland.

Objectives/Agenda

The main objective of the LeT is to establish an Islamic state in South Asia by uniting all Muslim-majority regions in countries that surround Pakistan. So far its objective pertaining to Kashmir is concerned, it wants the liberation of Kashmir and the destruction of India.

As mentioned on the official website[3] of the JuD, Hafiz Saeed clearly states that the solution to all the problems faced by the Muslim ummah is jihad as all anti-Islam forces have resorted to tyranny against Muslims. Hafiz Saeed has gone on to say that "We consider Jihad as Islamic Politics. Muslims have always participated in politics on the basis of Jihad. Territories were conquered, nations were built and Muslims came into power through Jihad."[4] Addressing JuD militants at Waheri on 12 April 2002, Hafiz Saeed announced that Kashmiris would soon breathe in an atmosphere of freedom and the entire map of the region would change after liberation of Kashmir. Speaking at a gathering in Okara on 13 April 2002, Hafiz Saeed accused India and Israel of subjecting Muslims to repression at the instigation of the United States (US).

But unlike the Al Qaeda which is solely dedicated to jihad, the LeT complements "armed struggle" with education—*da'wah* and jihad—a combination which makes the LeT a "long distance runner" in the field of jihad.[5]

Organisation

The JuD owns a sprawling 200 acre centre in Muridke, which is 30 km to the south-west of Lahore, where all its organisational, jihadi and educational activities are planned and executed. It runs several educational centres, including an Islamic

University, separate boys and girl's colleges, a madrassa and hostels for students and teachers.

To manage and coordinate its various activities in Pakistan and abroad, JuD or LeT has set up various departments such as Department of Preaching and Reform, Department of Ulema and Teachers, Department of Education, Jamaat-al-Dawa al-Islamia (Construction of Mosques and Madrassas), Department of Resources (fund raising for jihad), Martyrs Department (to provide financial aid to families of martyrs), External Affairs, Dar al Andalus (Department of Press and Publication) and Department of Public Relations.

The most effective of JuDs department is the Centre of Education which runs schools and colleges where the curriculum is different from that in other educational institutions. In these institutes, Arabic, Urdu and English are taught as compulsory subjects and the rest of the syllabus is based on Islamic belief.[6]

Zafar Iqbal, who taught with Hafiz Saeed at the University of Engineering and Technology, Lahore, and was also the co-founder of MDI, said, "We will continue to work in the twin fields of education and jihad. Jihad is carried out to establish the system of Allah in the world. But this system cannot be established without education. Therefore, education is equally important."[7]

The Department of External Affairs liaises with jihadi organisations in Pakistan and as well as abroad. Through this department, LeT has established close ties with more than dozen jihadi groups in the Middle East, South East Asia, Bosnia, Chechnya and other countries. It has also established contacts with a number of foreign governments and political parties; it mailed 3,000 letters and e-mails to 130 different countries.[8]

In its efforts to spread the message of Ahle Hadith faith in Pakistan, Department of Construction of Masjid and Madrassas opened madrassas. In addition to madrassas at Muridke, two other prominent ones were Jamia Abu Bakr and Jamaat-ul Dirasat-ul Islamiyah at Karachi. The former followed the same curriculum as Medina University in Saudi Arabia and the latter educated approximately 500 students, many of whom came from South East Asia. From 1998, LeT included additional religious training. Until that time, its basic training course consisted of Daura-e-Aam (general session), which was essentially a three-week introductory course given to everyone, and Daura-e-Khasa (special session) consisting of three-months military training offered to select individuals. Additional specialised military courses were offered even on a more selective basis.[9] One such course in Daura-e-Rahat, which focuses on surveillance, counter-intelligence and recruitment, is primarily intended for members who will operate in India.

Besides lecture on Islam-ul-Jihad, trainees are put through rigorous physical training, including hand-to-hand combat, swimming and guerilla training. They are taught to assemble and use 24 different types of guns, hurl hand grenades, use anti-aircraft guns and landmines and make bombs from everyday substances such as over-the-counter medicines.[10]

Recruitment and Training

Extremist literature plays an important role in recruiting new jihadis. The JuD has organised publication network through which it promote its ideology through publications such as weekly *Jarrar* and the monthly *Zarb-e-Tayyaba* for men and *Al Saffat* for women. These periodicals generally carry stories about Indian, American and Israel conspiracies against the Muslim world, religious information and reports on the activities of so-called organisations in Pakistan, Afghanistan, Iraq, Palestine and Chechnya. The focus, however, is on J&K and several stories carry bylines of journalists stationed in that area who report on alleged actions against Muslims and the activities of LeT in the area.

Since its inception, it has managed to attract thousands of young men to its fold. Most of those who join LeT are from lower classes of Punjab. Unemployment, poverty, lack of education, social rejection, an unhappy family environment, romanticised notion of jihad and growing influence of the mosque–seminary network have all played a role in the indoctrination of young men.[11]

With over 50,000 armed cadres trained in guerilla warfare, intelligence gathering, explosives and sabotage, LeT has unique leverage vis-à-vis the Pakistan military hierarchy. For Islamabad, it has become a reliable military reserve force that can be used by the Pakistani Army, like it did during the Kargil war waged by Pakistan's former President, General Parvez Musharraf, in 1999.

The outfit has more than 3,000 offices across Pakistan and over two dozen launching camps for militants along the line of control (LoC). The LeT is believed to be the only jihadi group operating out of the PoK that still keeps a comparatively large group of activists at its Khairati Bagh camp in Lipa Valley. Another camp is said to be functional at Nala Shui in Muzaffarabad, from where young militants are indoctrinated at Muridke. Compared to other militant groups active in J&K, the LeT has commanded significant attention for two reasons: first, for its well-planned and well-executed fidayeen attacks on Indian security forces in J&K; and second, for the dramatic massacres of non-Muslim civilians.[12]

The LeT runs a number of training centres in Khyber Pakhtunkhwa, Sindh, Baluchistan, Punjab and PoK. The objective is to have an office and a centre in every district of Pakistan. Each recruit is paid \$100–\$300 per month. The three-month advanced course for Daura-e-Khasa cost \$1,700 per trainee.[13] It also has an annual training budget of \$5 millions.[14]

Some of the major training camps of the LeT are Maskar Tayyaba camp, Muzffrabad, Maskar-e-Aqsa camp at Muzaffarabad, Umm al-Qura camp, Muzaffarabad, Abdullah bin Masood camp, PoK, and Markaz Muhammad bin Qasim at Maldasi, Sanghar district in Sindh.[15]

Finance and Funding

The Herald magazine reported in June 2006 that ISI pay-offs has reached as much as $50,000–$60,000 every month. The LeT is also perhaps the only terrorist group in the world which gets grants from any government. In 2010, the Punjab government gave a grant of close to $82 million to LeT's parent body, JuD.[16] The LeT also manages to collect millions of dollars by engaging in charity and relief work in some areas where the feeble administration has not been able to deliver.[17] The LeT also maintains a website, under the name of JuD, through which it solicits funds and provides information on the group's activities. In anticipation of asset seizures by the Pakistani government, the LeT withdrew funds from bank accounts and invested in legal businesses, such as commodity trading, real estate and production of consumer goods.

The LeT also draws its money from indigenous private benefactors, private Wahabi donors and from the large and munificent coffers of the ISI of Pakistan.[18] Reports of ISI providing fake Indian currency notes (FICN) to various terrorist groups like the LeT, Harkat-ul-Mujahideen (HuM), Hizb-ul-Mujahideen (HM) and Al Badr exist. Both LeT and Jaish-e-Mohammad (JeM) were reportedly collecting almost five million pounds annually in British mosques, mostly from Kashmiri community.[19]

The other key source of LeT money is Islamic charities across the world, particularly those based in Saudi Arabia and United Arab Emirates (UAE). Inside Pakistan, LeT acts primarily as a Dawa group promoting a radical interpretation of Islam much on the lines of its Wahabi patrons in Saudi Arabia and the UAE. This alliance brings the group an enormous amount of petrodollars as donations to its madrassas and mosques in Punjab.

The JuD also uses its charity networks (both social and political), like Idara Khidmat-e-Khalq, Falah-e-Insaniyat Foundation and Tehrik-e-Tahafuz-e-Hurmat-e-Rasool, to collect funds.[20]

Leadership

The chief of the LeT is Hafiz Saeed. The chief of operations of the outfit is Zaki-ur-Rehman Lakhvi. Lakhvi has directed a number of military operations, including in Chechnya, Bosnia, Iraq and South East Asia. He was also one of the handlers of the terrorist group which attacked Mumbai in 2008 and was later arrested by the Pakistani authorities. Lakhvi became close to the Al Qaeda leadership after his sister married Abu Abdur Rahman Sareehi, a Saudi national close to Osama bin Laden. Apart from thousands of recruits from Punjab and other provinces in Pakistan, he has also recruited several Indians and Bangladeshis into the LeT.

Haji Mohammad Ashraf, who has been LeT's chief of finance, reportedly travelled to the Middle East in 2003 and 2004, where he personally collected donations on behalf of the LeT.

Mahmoud Mohammad Ahmed Bahaziq is a Saudi national who has coordinated LeT fund raising with Saudi non-governmental organisations and Saudi businessmen, and encouraged LeT operations to continue and accelerate fund raising and organising activities. Bahaziq has also played a key role in LeT's propaganda and media operations. Some of the other important leaders of the LeT are given next.

Abdul Rehman Makki, a cousin and brother-in-law of Hafiz Saeed, is the head of the Department of External Affairs. He is one of the ideologues and second only to Hafiz Saeed in the hierarchy. He was once a teacher in Medina University in Saudi Arabia. In 2004, he wrote a book on fidayeen missions wherein he dispelled the common misconception that fidayeen missions were suicide missions. Yahya Mujahid is one of the general secretaries and spokespersons of JuD. He is one of the closest persons to Hafiz Saeed.

Amir Hamza is the head of external wing and publication division. Amir Hamza, who now runs a proxy organisation, Tehrik Hurmat Rasool, is at the forefront of reviving the fortunes of the terrorist group which has come under close scrutiny following the 2008 Mumbai attacks. He is an old Afghan jihad veteran. He wrote extensively on jihad in Kashmir and elsewhere, and gave extensive accounts of the LeT training infrastructure in various publications. According to some LeT publications, it was Zaki-ur-Rehman Lakhvi and Amir Hamza who laid the foundation of the MDI in the early 1990s.

Azam Cheema is the intelligence chief of LeT. He is an expert map reader. Azam Cheema, popularly known among LeT cadres as Babaji, is considered as Lakhvi's second in command. He operates from his house in Bahawalpur, Punjab, where he runs a small weapon laboratory and trains the new recruits in explosives. Cheema is the main accused in July 2006 serial train bombings in Mumbai which killed 200 people. Cheema had launched on intense recruitment drive in Mumbai after the 2002 riots in Gujarat.

Mian Abdullah is the chief of training camps and trader's wing. A close associate of Hafiz Saeed, Abdullah has worked as a trainer under Lakhvi at an LeT camp in Afghanistan. Later, he was commander of LeT in Peshawar and director of finance in 2008 when Ashraf was proscribed by the US Treasury. In 2009, after Lakhvi was arrested for Mumbai attacks, Saeed appointed Abdullah as the overall in-charge of training camps.

Maulana Abdul Aziz Alvi is the head of Kashmir unit. Maulana Alvi is originally from Ganderbal near Srinagar, where he was a religious leader. Alvi heads the LeT's Kashmir unit, although it is Lakhvi who planned and carried out terrorist attacks in Kashmir and other places in India.

Nasir Javaid is the head of Punjab division. He is originally from Gujranwala (Punjab). He was also an operational commander from 2001 to 2008 and was commander of training centres at Mansehra, Abu Hurera and in Khyber Pakhtunkhwa. Besides this, he was also in charge of the "basic course" or Daura-e-Aam at the LeT camp, Ummer bin Khattab, located behind Karakoram Highway.

Muzamil alias Yousuf is the head of the LeT training camp at Dulai, in the PoK. He is an expert in tactical training and pre-assault reconnaissance. Muzamil crossed over to Kashmir in 1999, where he was appointed as divisional commander for Pulwama till 2003. After he returned to Pakistan, he was made launching commander in Muzaffarabad. While Lakhvi and Abu Quhafa remained in touch with the terrorists from Karachi during 2008 Mumbai terrorist attacks, it was Muzamil who was coordinating the attack from Lahore.

Sajid Mir is the secretary to Abdul Rehman Makki and in charge of LeT's external operations. Number of times, he has accompanied Makki to the Middle East to look for potential recruits and funders. It was Mir who recruited, trained and handled David Coleman Headley, a key accused in the Mumbai attacks, who was responsible for scouting potential targets. Mir also visited India as a part of group which came to see India–Pakistan cricket match in 2005. Mir is also one of the LeT's key contacts with the Pakistani Army and the ISI.

Zarar Shah is the in-charge of the communication department. Shah is believed to have set up the network that allowed the 26 November 2008 Mumbai attackers to communicate with their handlers in Pakistan. He is suspected to be a key liaison between the LeT and the ISI.

Network and Support

The LeT and its parent body, the JuD, get massive popular support from many parts of Pakistan and PoK. During the earthquake in October 2005 that hit PoK and the northern parts of Pakistan, the JuD was among the first to start rescue and relief operations. The relief activity it carried out in the PoK not only bolstered its image but also won the group the gratitude and support of the general public. The PoK Prime Minister, Sardar Sikandar Hayat, met Hafiz Saeed and thanked him on behalf of the PoK government. The PoK President, Lieutenant General (retd) Sardar Mohammad Khan, even visited the JuD's medical camps in Muzaffarabad. Admitting that some external outfits placed on the government's watch list are engaged in relief work, President Musharraf, in an interview with CNN on 20 October 2005, said that their activities are being watched closely. Musharraf's statement was followed by a statement by the Interior Minister, Aftab Khan Sherpao, who while acknowledging the role of Islamist groups, declared that "they (the jihadis) are the life line of our rescue, and relief work in Azad Kashmir now". The JuD described its relief and rescue efforts in PoK as a new jihad or Holy war.[21]

The LeT has worldwide connections with number of militant groups such as Taliban, Pakistani Taliban, Al Qaeda and the Haqqani Network. In Central Asia, LeT has cooperated with both with Islamic Movement of Uzbekistan and local Islamist rebels in the Caucasus. The LeT's links with the Chechen militants are worth highlighting. Shamil Basayev, the Chechen rebel leader, was trained at the Khost camps in 1994 and later, stayed with LeT's parent organisation, MDI, at Muridke.[22] Also, LeT is actively involved in supporting the Muslim resistance in Bosnia, while raising funds and building sleeper cells in countries such as Spain and Germany.[23]

In addition to series of terrorist attacks in the Indian subcontinent, the LeT has also been involved in terrorism in the US, the United Kingdom (UK), European countries, Central Asia, Russia, Africa, West Asia, South East Asia and Australia.

The US

Available reports indicate that a number of recruits from America have received training in terrorists travel camps in Pakistan and Afghanistan since 1989. At least a dozen of them—Afro-Americans—went to Jamia Abu Bakr madrassa in Karachi run by the LeT. One of them was Abu Adam Zabreel, a convict from a rich Atlantic family who, after training at Muridke in 1997, was killed in Kashmir by Indian security forces. The US authorities also arrested three Maryland citizens—Tarik Ibn Osman Shah, Rafiz Sabir and Mahmud Faruq Brent—in 2006, who worked for LeT in raising funds and materials and facilitating travel in Pakistan.

In August 2006, Ali Asad Chandia, who migrated to the US in 1994 and was teacher at the Muslim School in Maryland, was charged with assisting an LeT operative and weapons procurement agent in acquiring military purpose equipment for use against India in future terror attacks. He was also held guilty of helping the Virginia jihad network ideologue, Ali-al-Tamimi, and sentenced to 15 years of imprisonment.

The UK

It was the Global Jihad Fund (GJF), established in London during the mid-1990s by two Saudis, which facilitated LeT's expansion in the UK. The GJF had marshalled substantial resources to raise funds for jihad in Bosnia, Afganistan, Kashmir, Kosovo and Chechnya. A case involving a British terrorist with LeT links became public after series of bomb attacks on 7 July 2007, in which 50 persons were killed and 700 injured. It may be noted that one of the suspects, Shaheed Tanweer, had visited the LeT headquarters in Muridke for a few days.[24]

Europe

The LeT has made its presence felt in France. The security agencies of France revealed that a British national, Richard Colvin Reid, was indoctrinated and tasked by the local group's head, Ghulam Mustafa Rama, to blow up an American

Airlines Boeing 767, flying from Paris to Miami, using plastic explosives. In June 2005, three Muslims of Pakistan descent were sentenced in Paris for providing logistical assistance to Reid—two of them had been trained in LeT camps in Afghanistan.

The LeT's network in Germany was run by Aleen Nasir, who began raising funds for jihad in Kashmir and Afghanistan in 1999. Nasir, a Pakistani, was a mechanical engineer who immigrated to Germany in 1987. The LeT also threatened to launch suicide mission against Germany after Amir Cheema's murder. Cheema, a textile student, was found dead in cell in Berlin after he was arrested on charge of plotting the killing of editor-in-chief of the German newspaper, *Die Welt*.

Australia

One of the significant Australian connections to the LeT was David Hicks who was arrested in Afghanistan. In 2000, David Hicks was trained at LeT's al-Aqsa camp in Muzaffarabad. Another important LeT man in Australia was Willie Virgile Brigitte. In 2003, he moved to Australia, where he was arrested for allegedly being a member of the LeT terrorist organisation, forming secret cells and planning to perpetrate terrorist attacks against targets in Australia: the nuclear research reactor in Sydney; the American–Australian intelligence facility; and military bases across the country. Brigette was extradited to France where he was sentenced to nine years in prison.

Bangladesh

In Bangladesh, Abdul Karim alias Tunda handled LeT operations during the 1990s and became a conduit for recruits transiting from or through Bangladesh to its camps. Tunda was one of the first LeT recruits in India to launch terrorist attacks in 1993, and later fled to Bangladesh where he sent Sheikh Abdul Rehman, who founded the Jammat-ul-Mujahideen Bangladesh (JMB), to Pakistan.

It was revealed that LeT has been able to establish an extensive network in Bangladesh when, in July 2009, two LeT managers in Bangladesh, Maulana Mohammad Mansoor Ali alias Maulana Habibullah and Mufti Sheikh Abdullah, were arrested. They came to Bangladesh in June 1995 and were trained in usual weapons and explosions at Harkat-ul-Jihad-al-Islami (HuJI) training camp in Afghanistan.

Maldives

The emergence of Salafi groups in the Maldives has considerably helped the LeT to expand its recruitment drive in the Maldives. One of the first reported incidents of a Maldivian link to global jihadi movement was the arrest of a Maldivian national, Fauzee, in May 2002 from Al Qaeda safe house in Karachi. This was further confirmed by the confession made by a Maldivian national, Ali Jaleel, who was part of the suicide attack on Pakistan military on 27 May 2009. The Maldivian President, Mohammad Nasheed, said that hundreds of Maldivians Muslims were recruited by terrorist groups like the LeT.

Current Status

The LeT is today one of the most dangerous terrorist groups—its operational reach and capability is transnational and it continues to enjoy patronage of the powerful Pakistan Army and the ISI, and Saudi Arabia. The top leadership of LeT remains free and are engaged in raising funds, recruiting new cadres and expanding its network of influence through charity work. Its link with other terrorist and extremist groups like Lashkar-e-Jhangvi (LeJ) and the Taliban has given the group additional edge and scope. Besides actively recruiting agents and cadres in Western countries, the LeT remains focused on strengthening its network in India, Bangladesh, Nepal, Pakistan, Sri Lanka, Maldives and Myanmar.

There are reports of LeT reclaiming some of the Taliban training camps in Kunar and Paktia after the International Security Assistance Force (ISAF) withdrawal in December 2014. The LeT has had both training and operating bases in Kunar, Paktia and Nooristan during and after the Afghan jihad where it worked closely with Afghan mujahideen leaders, many of whom went on to lead Al Qaida. The possibility of ISI helping LeT in occupying these training camps in Afghanistan remains high. In 2006, it was ISI which helped the group in setting up training camps in Dir and Upper Dir districts in the erstwhile North-West Frontier Province (NWFP; renamed as Khyber Pakhtunkhwa) to train new cadres for the Taliban. Stephen Tankel predicts that whatever the outcome in Afghanistan after the withdrawal of the US and *North Atlantic Treaty Organisation* (NATO) forces, "LeT is likely to keep a small presence in the Northeast where its members have worked to carve out territory".[25] In a paper, Tankel warned that the group is also likely "to agitate for regenerating the jihad directly against India, both in the form of terrorist attacks against the mainland and increases activity in Kashmir".[26] Similar views have also been expressed in another report.[27]

The May 2013 killing of LeT chief Hafiz Saeed's chief security officer, Khalid Bashir, in Lahore has, however, put a question mark on the terrorist group's internal dynamics. There have been reports about dissension within the group about Saeed's decision to lie low after the November 2008 Mumbai attacks and divert the group's focus on charity and religious activities. The younger cadres and leaders were unhappy about the senior leadership's "abandonment" of Kashmir jihad. Similar dissensions were noted when Saeed changed the name of the terrorist group to JuD in December 2001 and declared that he would be focusing more on charity and religious matters. Several of his senior colleagues revolted openly, accusing Saeed of usurping the money collected for "Kashmir jihad". The key accused in the Mumbai attacks, Zaki-ur-Rahman Lakhvi, led the revolt and set up a rival group, naming it Khair-un-Naas (KuN). The group's members took an oath to kill Hafiz Saeed. Although ISI brought Lakhvi and Saeed together, both remained wary of each other and operated independently—Saeed in Lahore and Lakhvi in Muzaffarabad, where he ran the main training campus at Baitul Mujahideen. Several others have also parted ways since 2001 because of Saeed's refusal to take on the Pakistan military for helping the US. Bashir's abduction, torture and killing could be a spillover of another round of internal struggle within the terrorist group. Saeed and his family's tight control over the group and the growing dissension among the younger cadres and leaders might, in the near future, prove to be the undoing of the group as such.

NOTES

1. See Muhammad Amir Rana, *A to Z of Jihadi Organisations in Pakistan*, Lahore: Mashal Publication, 2004, p. 317.
2. See Amir Zia, "Out in the Cold", *Newsline*, Karachi, January 2009, p. 45.
3. For details, see the official website of JuD, available at www.jamatdawa.org.
4. See Wilson John, *The Caliphate Soldiers—The Lashkar-e-Tayyeba's Long War*, New Delhi: Amaryllis, p. 18.
5. Ibid., p. 20.
6. For details, see Muhammad Amir Rana, *Gateway to Terrorism*, London: New Millennium Publication, 2003, pp. 337–45.
7. See Zaigham Khan, "Allah's Army Waging Jihad in Kashmir", *The Herald*, Karachi, January 1998, p.125.
8. See Rana, *Gateway to Terrorism*, p. 327.
9. See Stephen Tankel, *Storming the World Stage—The Story of Lashkar-e-Toiba*, UK: C. Hurst & Co., 2011, pp. 74–75.
10. See Kaleem Moosa, "Militancy", *The Herald*, Karachi, 2010.
11. See Azmat Abbas, "Making of a Militant", *The Herald*, Karachi, July 2003, p. 58 A recent study by West Point has also concluded that the majority of recruits of LeT are from Pakistan's Punjab province, which is also the recruiting ground for Pakistan Army, See *The Times of India*, New Delhi, 6 April 2013.
12. See Amir Mir, "Lashkar-e-Toiba in the Dock", *Asia Times*, 14 September 2011, available at http://www.atimes.com/atimes/South_Asia/MI14Df03.html (accessed on 16 October 2012).
13. See Wilson John, *The Caliphate Soldiers*, pp. 219–20.
14. See S.K. Sharma, "The Tangled Web they Weave", *The Times of India*, New Delhi, 27 May 2011, available at http://articles.timesofindia.indiatimes.com/2011-05-27/edit-page/29586591_1_qaida-terror-attacks-madrassas (accessed on 27 May 2011).
15. See Rana, *Gateway to Terrorism*, p. 352.
16. See "Punjab Govt gave Rs 82 m to JD: Papers", *Dawn*, 16 June 2010, available at http://archives.dawn.com/archives/35861 (accessed on 16 October 2012).
17. See Sharma, "The Tangled Web they Weave".
18. See Brian M. Downing, "Lashkar-e-Toiba—Safe at Home", *Asia Times*, 17 September 2011, available at http://www.atimes.com/ atimes/South_Asia M11 7D fo2.Htmt (accessed on 21 December 2011).
19. See "Pakistan Madrasas, Extremism and the Military", International Crises Group, 29 July 2002, available at http://www.crisisgroup.org/~/media/Files/asia/south-asia/pakistan/Pakistan%20Madrasas%20Extremism%20And%20The%20Military.pdf (accessed on 16 October 2012).

20. See Wilson John, *The Caliphate Soldiers*, pp. 241–42.
21. See Amir Mir, “Militant Philanthropy”, *Newsline*, Karachi, 15 November 2005, available at http://www.newslinemagazine.com/2005/11/militant-philanthropy/ (accessed on January 12, 2013).
22. For details see Ilyas M. Khan, “Between Jihad and Terror”, *The Herald*, Karachi, January 2002, pp. 50-52.
23. For details, see Ashley J. Tellis, “The Menace that is Lashkar-e-Taiba”, Policy Outlook, Carnegie Endowment for International Peace, March 2012, available at http://carnegieendowment.org/files/LeT_menace.pdf (accessed on 16 October 2012).
24. See Wilson John, *The Caliphate Soldiers*, p. 50.
25. Tankel, *Storming the World Stage*, pp.74-75.
26. Stephen Tankel, “The Militant Groups Next Door”, *Foreign Policy*, 24 April 2013, available at http://afpak.foreignpolicy.com/posts/2013/04/24/the_militant_groups_next_door (accessed on 1 June 2013).
27. See Don Rassler, C. Christine Fair, Anirban Ghosh, Arif Jamal and Nadia Shoeb, “The Fighters of Lashkar-e-Taiba: Recruitment, Training, Deployment and Death”, April 2013, available at http://home.comcast.net/~christine_fair/pubs/Fighters-of-LeT_Final.pdf (accessed on 22 June 2013).

25

Harkat-ul-Mujahideen

(The Movement of Islamic Holy Warriors)

The Harkat-ul-Mujahideen (HuM), the movement of the holy warriors, also known as the Harkat-ul-Ansar (HuA), the Jamait-ul-Ansar (JuA) and Al Faran, is a Sunni (closer to Deoband school of thought and Wahabism) organisation which was formed in 1985. It was formed as a breakaway faction of the Harkat-ul-Jihad-al-Islami (HuJI), with the patronage of Inter Services Intelligence (ISI), to fight the Soviet military in Afghanistan. The activities of the HuJI started when its founder and amir (chief), Maulana Irshad Ahmed, along with Qari Saifullah and Maulana Abdus Samad Siyal, went to Afghanistan on 25 February 1980 and fought in the Afghan jihad against Soviet troops along with Ahmed Shah Masood and Rabbani's forces. However, on 25 July 1985, Irshad Ahmed was killed and Maulana Saifullah succeeded him as the amir. His leadership was resented by the cadres, which ultimately led to the creation of HuM. Following this, Maulana Fazlur Rehman Khalil became the first amir and Maulana Masood Alvi the first centre commander of the HuM. However, Alvi was killed in a landmine blast.

The HuM was reorganised and commenced its jihadi activities immediately after its formation. It also established contacts with Maulvi Yunus Khalis of Hizb-e-Islami. With its manpower resources, HuM played a major role in the victory of Khost, although it lost most of its commanders. After the withdrawal of the Soviet forces from Afghanistan in 1989, the main focus of the HuM was to join the jihad against Indian security forces in Jammu and Kashmir (J&K) with the active support of the Pakistan government. In 1993, under the guidance of the ISI, the HuM reunited with the HuJI to form a new organisation, HuA. Available reports indicate that the HuM militants are fanatic Sunni Muslims and distinguish themselves from other Sunni Muslims by describing themselves as Ansar, the term given to actual Muslim residents of Madina by Prophet Mohammad. With the creation of the HuA, there was increase in jihadi activities, like kidnapping of two British tourists in 1994, kidnapping of few Americans and British citizens in Delhi in the same year and kidnapping of some Europeans in Kashmir in 1995 for the release of Maulana Masood Azhar and Commander Sajjad Afghani.

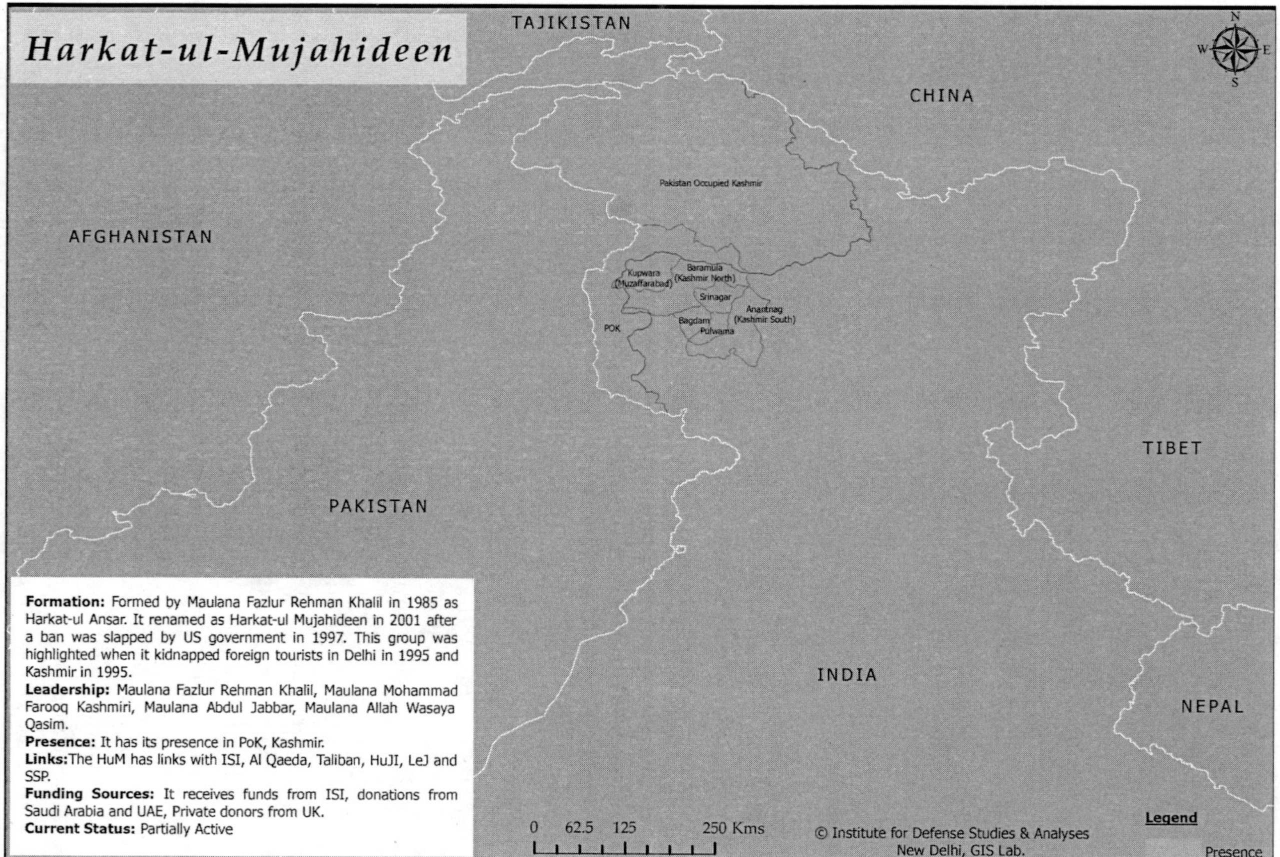
Harkat-ul-Mujahideen
TAJIKISTAN
CHINA
AFGHANISTAN
Pakistan Occupied Kashmir
Kupwara (Muzaffarabad)
Baramula (Kashmir North)
Srinagar
Anantnag (Kashmir South)
Bagdam
Pulwama
POK
PAKISTAN
TIBET
INDIA
NEPAL
Formation: Formed by Maulana Fazlur Rehman Khalil in 1985 as Harkat-ul Ansar. It renamed as Harkat-ul Mujahideen in 2001 after a ban was slapped by US government in 1997. This group was highlighted when it kidnapped foreign tourists in Delhi in 1995 and Kashmir in 1995.
Leadership: Maulana Fazlur Rehman Khalil, Maulana Mohammad Farooq Kashmiri, Maulana Abdul Jabbar, Maulana Allah Wasaya Qasim.
Presence: It has its presence in PoK, Kashmir.
Links: The HuM has links with ISI, Al Qaeda, Taliban, HuJI, LeJ and SSP.
Funding Sources: It receives funds from ISI, donations from Saudi Arabia and UAE, Private donors from UK.
Current Status: Partially Active
0 62.5 125 250 Kms
© Institute for Defense Studies & Analyses New Delhi, GIS Lab.
Legend
Presence

After abductions of foreigners in Kashmir by the Al Faran, the United States (US) designated it as a foreign terrorist organisation in 1997 due to its association with Osama bin Laden, and HuA changed its name to HuM. In 2001, HuM too was designated as a terrorist organisation by the US. Following this, the then President of Pakistan, Parvez Musharraf, while announcing crackdown on extremist outfits, outlawed HuM along with several other groups. This led to the emergence of JuA but, in 2003, the Pakistan government slapped a ban on it also.

Earlier (January 2000), HuM was shocked when Maulana Masood Azhar announced the formation of its own group, Jaish-e-Mohammad (JeM), in Karachi following his release from India. It may be mentioned that Azhar and two other extremist leaders—Mushtaq Zarger and Ahmed Omar Saeed Sheikh—were freed by the Indian government in exchange for the release of Indian passengers taken hostage by the terrorist group in December 1999.

Objectives

Initially, the objective of the HuM was to organise humanitarian relief for the Afghan refugees who had taken shelter in Khyber Pakhtunkhwa (KP) of Pakistan. It then became part of Afghan jihad which called for driving Soviet troops out of Afghanistan. Since then, HuM has been involved in waging jihad against secular Muslim governments, India and the Western countries. After the Soviet troops left Afghanistan, the HuM shifted its focus to Kashmir, where the organisation seeks Kashmir's secession from India and its accession to Pakistan to create pan-Islamic entity.

According to HuM's website:[1]

- The prime objective of HuM is to provide awareness with regard to jihad. The HuM is determined to clear all doubts and ambiguities.
- The Muslim ummah has lost its glory, dignity and respect all over the globe. Jews, *Qadiani*'s and Hindu's have joined hands to establish jihad as an act of terrorism and horror. The HuM appraises the world to differentiate between terrorism and jihad. In terrorism, indiscriminate killing is justified, jihad bans it. Jihad permits arms against arms only. Jihad prohibits indiscriminate killing. Jihad guarantees safety of unarmed women, children and elderly people irrespective of religion, race or cast. Jihad assures personal or religious rights of non-Muslims until aggressed.
- Jihad is not terrorism; it strongly condemns terrorism. In fact, terrorists condemn jihad because jihad is the biggest obstacle in achieving terrorists' ulterior motives.
- Jihad is a symbol of peace, prosperity, equity, progress and strong tool for propagation of Islam as laid down very clearly in the Holy Quran.
- To achieve above-mentioned objectives, jihad strongly advocates adherence of latest technology, preparation of arms, provide help to suppressed, etc., under guidance from Quran.

- Let the world not be misguided by the propaganda against Islam and mujahideen. History of Europe, Africa and South East Asia should remain a guiding factor and an eye opener for anti-mujahideen propagandist that non-Muslims preferred living under Muslim laws when Muslim mujahideen conquered their territories. Therefore, HuM is determined to liberate suppressed humanity throughout the world and eliminate discrimination, injustice, terrorism and *kufr* no matter what comes their way.

Organisation and Leadership

The HuM has a well-formed organisational structure. In Pakistan and Pakistan-occupied Kashmir (PoK), it is headed by an amir who has *naib* amirs (deputy chiefs), a secretary, publicity chief and in-charge training under him. Some of the important leaders of the HuM are as follows.

Maulana Fazlur Rehman Khalil is the general secretary; although Khalil is now the general secretary of the HuM, he is practically the amir of the outfit. He is a veteran of the Afghan war and was also a founding member of Osama bin Laden's International Islamic Front for Jihad against Jews and Crusaders, formed in 1998. Khalil worked closely with Pakistan intelligence and continued to lead jihadi groups. Khalil did his studies from the famous Binori madrassa in Karachi where Taliban leader, Mullah Omar, had studied. This is the reason that Khalil continues to maintain strong ties with the Al Qaeda and Taliban. Khalil was arrested by the Pakistan government in May 2004 after the Karzai government complained to Pakistan that the terrorists of Taliban and Hizb-e-Islami (HI) were being trained in secret training camps run by Jamiat-ul-Ansar (JuA) in Baluchistan and Federally Administered Tribal Areas (FATA) under the supervision of Khalil.[2] Available reports indicate that Khalil was given special treatment during detention and kept in an ISI safe house for eight months before being released in December 2004. Khalil's name also cropped up during the interrogation of two residents of California—Hamid Hayat and Umar Hayat—who were arrested for the suspected involvement in an Al Qaeda plot against the US in June 2005. Both the men revealed to the Federal Bureau of Investigation (FBI) that they had received extensive training in a HuM camp run by Khalil.

Maulana Mohammad Farooq Kashmiri became the centre amir after Khalil stepped down as an amir in February 2002. Maulana Abdul Jabbar is a centre leader looking after military affairs. He is also a veteran of the Afghan war. Maulana Allah Wasaya Qasim is a central *nazim* looking after propaganda and is in-charge martyr's wing. Maulana Mohammad Sajid is central secretary (Dawat and Irshad). Qari Mohammed Sadiq is the secretary of Department of Resources.

Other prominent leaders include Maulana Sadad Atullah Khan, Maulana Masood Azhar, Saeed Omar Sheikh, Sajjad Afghani (who was killed in jail break attempt in 1999) and Nasrullah Mansoor Langrial *alias* Darwesh (who was arrested in Kashmir along with Pakistan commando turned terrorist, Ilyas Kashmiri, in 2000).

Cadre Strength and Training

According to a report, HuM has several hundred armed cadres located in Pakistan, PoK, south Kashmir and Doda district. Cadres are mostly Pakistanis and Kashmiris but also include Afghans and veterans of Afghan war.[3] As mentioned in the same report, the core strength of the HuM may be around 300. However, the organisation structure of HuM has grown to considerably weaker after the formation of JeM.

The HuM recruits the youth from all the provinces of Pakistan, PoK and Kashmir. Earlier, it had a strong network in Afghanistan that included Afghans as well. It draws its cadres from madrassas and Tabligh-e-Jammat.

The main training camps of the HuM were located in Afghanistan which were closed after the end of Taliban regime. The training camps include Khalid Bin Walid camp in Zhawara in Khost province; Liza camp at Tania in Khost province; Salman Farsi camp in Jawash, 2 km inside Afghanistan territory from Pakistan border post of Saidgai; and another camp close to Darwanta hydropower station near Jalalabad.[4]

So far the training of the HuM cadres is concerned, it involves training in the use of small arms, rocket launchers and grenades, ambush, unarmed combat, handling wireless set, etc.

Area of Operation and Influence

In Pakistan, the HuM is based in Muzaffarabad, Rawalpindi and several other cities. As mentioned earlier, until the end of Taliban regime, the HuM used to have its active presence in the border areas of Pakistan and Afghanistan. Also, as the militant group primarily carries out its militant activities in Kashmir, it has its influence in several places in Kashmir as well. The areas in Kashmir where it has its influence include Srinagar, Budgam, Pulwama, Baramullah, Rajouri, Poonch, etc.

According to the available sources, some of its training camps were temporarily closed in the PoK and FATA region with an apprehension of the US attack in 2001.[5] However, these training camps are suspected to be now switching to an active mode.

Weapons

According to the available sources, it is believed that the HuM is equipped with sophisticated weapons and arms. As mentioned earlier, the HuM militants are trained to handle small arms and rocket launchers. This is an indication of the fact that the HuM cadres use both light and heavy machine guns, assault rifles, mortars, explosives and rockets. The HuM's strong links with other militant groups like the Al Qaeda and the ISI are the main sources of arms procurement.

Finance and Funding

The HuM collects donations from supporters in Saudi Arabia and other Gulf and Islamic states. It also collects funds from the Pakistanis and the Kashmiri Muslims settled in the UK and the US. It also receives considerable help from the ISI. Apart from donations, the HuM publishes appeals for donations in its monthly magazine *Sada-e-Mujahid*, and weekly magazine *Al-Hilal*, both in Urdu.

Besides collecting funds for jihadi activities, HuM militants visit farmers at the time of harvest to collect donations in kind and cash. Irrespective of the ban imposed by the Pakistan government, the HuM cadres continue to collect hides of sacrificed animals from which substantial amount of money earned. There are also reports that the HuM has also invested in legal businesses.

The modus operandi of sending funds to Kashmir is either through militants posing as couriers or hawala transactions. The Pakistan government froze the assets in 2001 following the inclusion of HuM in the list of US terrorist organisations. However, despite a ban imposed on the HuM, it is believed that the outfit is active in generating funds for its jihadi activities.

Networks—Local, Regional and Global

As it has been already mentioned, the HuM is believed to have strong relations with the ISI of Pakistan and with the Pakistan government. It has maintained a special relationship with the Taliban, TTP and Haqqani Network also. This is evident from the fact that a number of HuM militants were killed in a US military attack on a camp in Khost province.

The HuM leadership, especially Khalil, had maintained strong links with Osama bin Laden. The HuM is a part of Laden's International Islamic Front for Jihad against Jews and Crusaders.

As a report reveals, it is believed that the HuM provided refuge to the Lashkar-e-Jhangvi (LeJ) militants in Afghanistan who tried to kill the former Prime Minister of Pakistan, Nawaz Sharif, in Lahore.[6] The HuM also has links with Jamiat-ul-Ulama-i-Islam (JUI) and Sipah-e-Sahaba Pakistan (SSP).

Current Status

The HuM continues to be a banned militant outfit in Pakistan, India and the US. The media reports suggest that several hundred HuM militants are active in the PoK and J&K. According to a media report, it is revealed that the HuM has resurfaced in Karachi in the recent past under a different name—Al-Hilal Trust.[7] According to this report, the Al-Hilal Trust's main office is working inside a mosque and is run by Muhammad Yar Rabbani in the Sher Shah area of

Karachi. It is important to note that the Al-Hilal Trust has been instrumental in sending cadres to Kashmir and Afghanistan.

According to another report, Fazlur Rehman Khalil, continues to enjoy the hospitality of the Pakistan state. As the report claims, the Pakistani authorities are well aware of the whereabouts of Khalil.[8] The report claims the presence of Khalil in an Islamabad suburb.

NOTES

1. For details of HuM's objective and ideological orientation, visit http://www.harkatul mujahideen.org/.
2. See B. Raman, "Links between Harkat-ul-Mujahideen (HuM) & Bin Laden/Al Qaeda", *Indian Defence Review*, 24 June 2011, available at http://www.indiandefencereview.com/ spotlights/links-between-harkut-ul-mujahideen-hum-and-bin-laden-al-qaeda/ (accessed on 3 June 2012).
3. See "Harkat-ul-Mujahideen", Country Report on Terrorism, US Department of State, 2011, chapter 6, available at http://www.state.gov/j/ct/crt/2011/195553.htm (accessed on 3 June 2012).
4. See B. Raman, "Harkat-ul-Mujahideen: An Update", available at http://www. southasiaanalysis.org/%5Cpapers%5Cpaper42.html (accessed on 5 June 2012).
5. See "Militant Training Camps Closed in PoK", *The Times of India*, 15 September 2001, available at http://articles.timesofindia.indiatimes.com/2001-09-15/india/27224937_1_ training-camps-pok-militants (accessed on 5 June 2012).
6. See S.V.R. Nasr, "Islam, the State and the Rise of Sectarian Militancy in Pakistan", in Christopher Jaffrelot (ed.), *Pakistan: Nationalism without a Nation?* New York: Zed Books, 2002, p. 99.
7. See "Harkat-ul-Mujahideen Resurfaces in Karachi", *The Indian Express*, available at http: //www.expressindia.com/latest-news/harkat-ul-mujahideen-resurfaces-in-karachi/3540 (accessed on 5 June 2012).
8. See "Terror Leader Lives Freely Near Pakistani Capital".

26

Jaish-e-Mohammad
(Army of the Prophet)

Introduction

Jaish-e-Mohammed (JeM), which literally means the Army of Mohammad, was founded by Maulana Masood Azhar at Binori mosque in Karachi on 31 January 2000. Azhar was one of the three terrorists released by the Indian government in exchange for 155 passengers of Indian Airlines flight, IC-814, that had been hijacked and flown to Kandahar in Afghanistan a month earlier in December 1999. Azhar was associated with Harkat-ul-Ansar (HuA), which changed its name to Harkat-ul-Mujahideen (HuM) after it was put under the list of terrorist organisations by the United States (US). After he formed the new outfit, Azhar was backed by majority of HuM leaders and travelled to Afghanistan where he met Osama bin Laden. His association with bin Laden was quite old as he had fought along with Al Qaeda against the US troops in Somalia and participated in the training of Al Qaeda supporters in Yemen. The HuA kidnapping in 1994, by Omar Sheikh, of the US and the British nationals in New Delhi and the HuA/Al Faran kidnapping in July 1995 of Westerners in Kashmir were two of the several previous HuA efforts to free Azhar. In fact, Azhar was on an important mission to India when he was arrested in Anantnag (Jammu and Kashmir [J&K]) on 11 February 1994. He arrived in India with a Portuguese passport he had obtained in London.

According to a leading Pakistani journalist, Amir Mir, the formation of JeM had the backing of top Islamic Deobandi[1] scholars, specially Mufti Nizamuddin Shamzai of the Jamia Binori mosque[2] of Karachi, who was known for his pro-Taliban stand, and Maulana Yousuf Ludhianvi, who was the chief commander of the Sipah-e-Sahaba Pakistan at that time.[3] These two scholars emerged as the chief ideologue and the chief commander of the JeM respectively. Three important leaders representing respective religious school of thoughts supported the formation of JeM. They were: Mufti Nizamuddin Shamzai of the Majlis-e-Tawan-e-Islami, Maulana Mufti Rashid Ahmed of the Dar-ul Ifta-e-wal-Irshad and Maulana Sher Ali of the Sheikh-ul-Hadith Dar-ul Haqqania. The JeM got into prominence

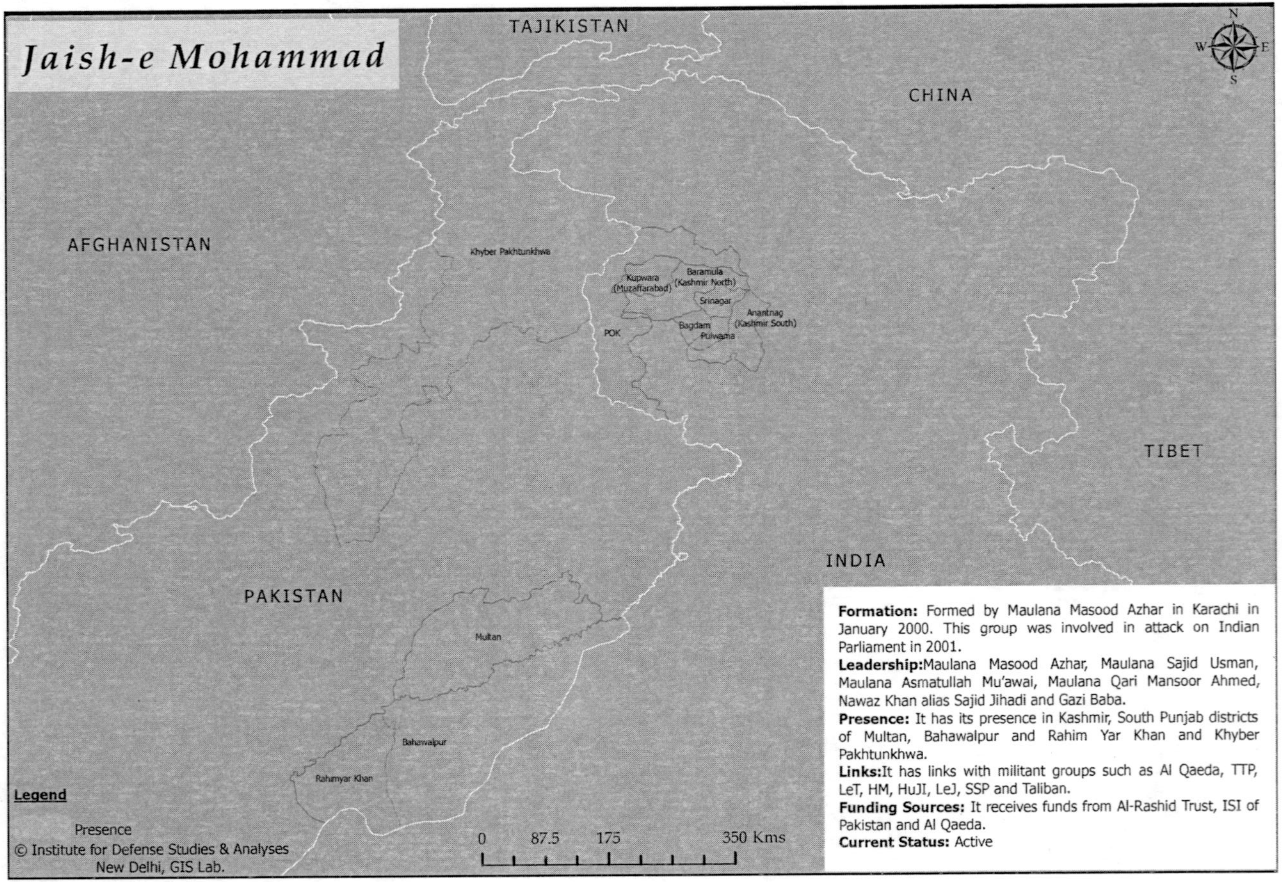
Jaish-e Mohammad
TAJIKISTAN
CHINA
AFGHANISTAN
Khyber Pakhtunkhwa
Kupwara (Muzaffarabad)
Baramula (Kashmir North)
Srinagar
Anantnag (Kashmir South)
POK
Bagdam
Pulwama
TIBET
INDIA
PAKISTAN
Multan
Bahawalpur
Rahimyar Khan
Legend
Presence
© Institute for Defense Studies & Analyses New Delhi, GIS Lab.
0 87.5 175 350 Kms
Formation: Formed by Maulana Masood Azhar in Karachi in January 2000. This group was involved in attack on Indian Parliament in 2001.
Leadership: Maulana Masood Azhar, Maulana Sajid Usman, Maulana Asmatullah Mu'awai, Maulana Qari Mansoor Ahmed, Nawaz Khan alias Sajid Jihadi and Gazi Baba.
Presence: It has its presence in Kashmir, South Punjab districts of Multan, Bahawalpur and Rahim Yar Khan and Khyber Pakhtunkhwa.
Links: It has links with militant groups such as Al Qaeda, TTP, LeT, HM, HuJI, LeJ, SSP and Taliban.
Funding Sources: It receives funds from Al-Rashid Trust, ISI of Pakistan and Al Qaeda.
Current Status: Active

when it carried out a suicide attack at an army base in Badamibag, Srinagar in April 2000 attack on the J&K Assembly in 2001 and Indian Parliament in December 2001.

Objectives

The main aims of the JeM are: to overthrow Indian rule in Kashmir and unite Kashmir with Pakistan; and expel the US troops from Afghanistan.

While launching of the JeM in Karachi, Azhar said, "I have come here (Karachi) because this is my duty to tell you that the Muslims should not rest in peace until they destroy India and the US".[4] According to the assessment of Amir Mir, the sole objective of the launching of the JeM was to become the undisputable leader of the Deobandi pan-Islamic militants in J&K.[5] During his speeches in various places in Pakistan after the launching of his group, Azhar said that he would eliminate (the then) Indian Prime Minister, Atal Bihari Vajpayee, whom he taunted as "Abu Jahl"—father of ignorance. He added that in its fight against India, JeM would not only liberate J&K but also take control of the Babri mosque in Ayodhya, Amritsar and Delhi.

The JeM also believes that each of its offices in Pakistan would serve as centres of jihad. Most JeM leaders endorsed the idea of establishing an Islamic caliphate in South Asia and expelling Hindus from Indian subcontinent. It indicates that the JeM is opposed to all other religions, including the Shia Islam. Till December 1999, Azhar was also an office bearer of Siph-e-Sahaba (in addition to being an office bearer of the HuM) and was known for his strong anti-Shia views,[6] as stated in reports in Pakistan's Shia media. The JeM as an organisation is politically aligned with radical pro-Taliban political bloc, Jamiat Ulema-e-Islam of Fazlur Rahman (JUI-F).

Organisation and Leadership

Ever since the formation of the JeM in 2000, Azhar remains the amir (chief) of the organisation. There was a split in the outfit in 2003. One faction, Khuddam-ul-Islam (KuI), is headed by Azhar himself and the other, Jammat-ul-Furqan (JuF), is led by Abdul Jabbar who was arrested in December 2003 by Pakistan security forces and was released in August 2004. The Pakistan government banned both the groups in the year 2003. Yet, JeM continues to be one of the major terrorist groups in Pakistan.

The structure of the JeM is based on military and missionary groups administered through various departments; the Department of Dawat and Irshad organises preaching, publicity and jihadi activities. The military department trains mujahideens and launches them into target areas. The martyrs department is in the charge of maintaining records of the jihadis killed in various operations in places like Afghanistan and Kashmir. The Department of Matrimonial arranges alliances for mujahideens. The JeM has a grievances and redressal mechanism. It also has an exclusive department for broadcasting and publications.[7]

Prominent leaders of the JeM are Maulana Asmatullah Mu'awai, who is the amir of the JeM Kashmir. He is a former militant of the Sipah-e-Sahaba. Maulana Sajid Usman heads the finance branch of the JeM. He was the deputy chief of the Harkat-ul-Jihad-al-Islami (HuJI).

As mentioned earlier, Maulana Masood Azhar continues to be the amir (chief) of the JeM, whereas Maulana Qari Mansoor Ahmed heads the propaganda wing and Shah Nawaz Khan alias Sajid Jihadi and Gazi Baba are the chief commanders in charge of J&K.

A JeM leader who was close to Azhar was Sheikh Omar Saeed who was charged with the murder of Daniel Pearl, South Asia Bureau Chief of *The Wall Street Journal*. Pearl was abducted in January 2002. It may be noted that British-born Saeed was arrested by the Indian security agencies in 1994 on charges of kidnapping an American and three British citizens; he was also freed along with Azhar in December of 1999.

Cadre Strength and Training

The JeM's cadre strength is reported to run into several thousands: 300–400 of them are active militants who are trained to carry out terrorist activities. The militants of the JeM are generally recruited from various parts of Pakistan and Kashmir. A few of them hail from Arab countries and Afghanistan.

According to an expert, JeM's catchment area is primarily south Punjab districts (such as Multan, Bahawalpur and Rahim Yar Khan) and Khyber Pakhtunkhwa (KP) districts (Peshawar, Nowshera and Kohat).[8] The JeM recruits from educational institutes, mainly from madrassas. The important madrassas from where the JeM recruits its cadres are educational institutions that have units of Jamia-e-Tulba-e-Islam and Wafaq ul Madaris ul Arabia. Also, the Sipah-e-Sahaba students constitute a large portion in the JeM's strength.[9]

Other madrassas from where the JeM recruits its cadres are: Jamia-ul-Ulum-e-Islamia, Darul Ulum Farooqia and Darul-Ulum-Hamadia in Karachi; Jamia Ashrafia and Jamia-Manzurul-Islamia of Lahore; Jamia Farroqia in Baluchistan; Darul-Ulum-Islamia in Muzaffarabad and Azad Kashmir; Jamia-Nomania-Salehia in Dera Ismail Khan; Darul-Ulum-Azazil and Jamia-Haqqania in Nowshera; Jamia-Farooqia in Shujabad; Jamia-Rahimia-Tarteelul Quran in Rahim Yar Khan; Jamia-Usmania in Shorkot; Madrassa Khalidia in Chichawatni; Jamia Islamia in Kashmir Road, Rawalpindi; Jamia-Imdadia Babul-Ulum in Kehror Pakka; Jamia-Mohzinul-Ulum in Khanpur; Madrassa Jaishe Mohammed in Shikarpur; Jamia-Muftahul-Ulum in Hyderabad; Madrassa Bonistan in Baluchistan; Jamia Islamia in Dera Ghazi Khan; and Khairul-Madaris in Multan.[10]

Until 2001, JeM had its training camps in Afghanistan, which were closed after the collapse of the Taliban regime. Its military department then relocated its trainees to Balakote and Muzaffarabad in Pakistan-occupied Kashmir (PoK) and Camp Hajera and Camp Mansehra in KP, where they were given both religious and military training. The military training includes armed assault, guerilla training, use of small and sophisticated weapons and fidayeen attacks.

At JeM camps, training and support are also provided not only to JeM cadres from Kashmir and Pakistan but also to individual jihadists from other parts of the world. Available reports also indicate that the JeM may be helping to facilitate the activities of the international jihadists intending to conduct terrorist operations outside Kashmir and also in the United Kingdom (UK) and the US.[11] The JeM also trains militants in Bangladesh, Nepal and the Middle East. Many JeM militants are believed to be veterans of war in Afghanistan.

Area of Operation and Network

The JeM's presence is spread over most part of Pakistan. In India, its activities are mostly confined to Kashmir.

The JeM is closely associated with the Taliban and Al Qaeda. For carrying out its military operation in Kashmir, the JeM sometimes conducts joint operations with Lashkar-e-Taiba (LeT) and Hizb-ul-Mujahideen (HM). In Pakistan, it is closely associated with HuJI, Lashkar-e-Jhangvi (LeJ) and Sipah-e-Shahaba Pakistan and TTP.

The JeM is a member of the United Jihad Council which was formed in 1990 to bring all Kashmir-focused militant groups under a single banner. According to a report, since 2008, the JeM joined the Taliban in militant attacks against the government and coalition forces in Afghanistan,[12] under a decision taken at a joint meeting of various militant outfits in June 2008.

Pakistani security agencies suspect that the JeM is working in tandem with the Al Qaeda, Taliban and the Haqqani Network in North Waziristan.[13]

Funding

The JeM usually raises its finance through donations from its supporters and sympathisers across Pakistan and Kashmir. The finance wing of the JeM is active throughout the year in collecting funds. There are also two funding agencies that support the JeM. One of them is the Al-Rashid Trust, which was a major contributor to the Taliban regime in Afghanistan. The US has banned the Al-Rashid Trust and its bank account has been frozen by the Pakistan government.

Al-Rashid Trust coordinator, Asfaq Ahmed, indicated that trust was very active in the Punjab and KP provinces in 2011.[14] The trust uses Masood Azhar's name for garnering support from the people as it had once enjoyed during the conflict in Afghanistan. What is a matter of concern, however, is the indifference of Pakistan government to obstruct Al-Rashid Trust's fund-raising drive. The second important source of funding is the income from the publications of the JeM, such as *Al-Qalam* and *Muslim Ummah*, that flaunt the certificates issued by Audit Bureau of Circulation (ABC) which enables them to solicit advertisement.[15] The sale of the magazine is an important source of fund raising by the JeM.

A report by the British Broadcasting Corporation (BBC) Urdu reveals that the JeM and many other proscribed militant groups have been opening new bank accounts under pseudonyms to receive funds from local as well as foreign sources.[16]

Osama Bin Laden is said to have supported JeM with money and weapons in its formative period.

Pakistan's ban did not adversely affect its financial position. Reports suggest that the Inter Services Intelligence (ISI) had alerted the outfit about the action to be taken by the Pakistan government. In anticipation of assets seizure by the Pakistani government, JeM withdrew its funds from the bank accounts and invested in legal business such as commodity trading, real estate and production of consumer goods.[17]

Arms and Weapons in Possession

The JeM uses light and heavy machine guns, assault rifles, mortars, improvised explosive devices and rocket-propelled grenades.[18] A report said that a large quantity of small and light weapons from Afghanistan which were siphoned off by Pakistan had been smuggled to Kashmir by the JeM along with the LeT and HuM.[19] It indicates that the JeM is in the possession of both small and sophisticated weapons.

The JeM is the first Pakistan-based terrorist outfit to introduce suicide attacks in Kashmir. With the aim to kill maximum number of security personnel and civilians, JeM uses rocket grenades, bombings and indiscriminate firings. It has also been observed that during suicide attacks, the JeM militants target military bases, security camps and petrol parties. The JeM also indulges in kidnappings.

Current Status

According to a Pakistani media report, the JeM and many other proscribed militant organisations have resumed full-scale public activities.[20] In order to revive the terrorist activities, the JeM is on a full-scale fund-raising drive. In this connection, the younger brother of Masood Azhar, Amar Azhar, visited Saudi Arabia to seek donations.[21]

Reports also suggest that JeM has started its recruitment drive in Punjab to send its militants to J&K. A major factor that has forced a number of *pancha*s and *sarpanche*s to resign from their posts is diktats from the JeM.

The ISI has been given the task to train the terrorist outfits like the JeM to use cyber and computer technology for their terrorist activities, revealed the security review at the meeting of the *director generals of police* (DGPs)/inspector-generals of *police (*IGPs) held in New Delhi on 8 September 2012.[22] The meeting also revealed that there is a possibility that the ISI might train the Indian Mujahideen (IM) cadres along with JeM, LeT and other terrorist groups. The Indian security agencies have intercepted a communication between the IM and the JeM in this regard. According to a media report, such an interception had also taken place some time in October 2011.[23] The same report revealed that the JeM has started its terror training with sophisticated facilities in Bahawalpur; Masood Azhar's brother, Mufti Asghar, is in charge of the training. Masood Azhar has since come back to Bahawalpur to resume his activities, it is reported.

The JeM continues to be one of the major terrorist groups in South Asia despite the ban imposed on in by India and Pakistan and by the US and many other countries. Though the past record of the JeM's terror activities in India has been mostly confined to Kashmir, its spread to other parts of India cannot be ruled out. It might carry out spectacular attacks like it did in 2001, when it attacked the Parliament of India, and in July 2005, when it staged an attack in Ayodhya.

NOTES

1. Derived from Deoband, India, where Darul Uloom Deoband is situated, Deobandi stands for revivalist movement in Sunni Islam (Ahlus-Sunnah wal-Jama'ah) under the Hanafi school. It has its roots across India, Pakistan, Afghanistan and Bangladesh.
2. The Binori mosque is one of the most influential centres of hardline Sunni ideology. This mosque has indoctrinated some of the important leaders of Taliban as well as militants like Maulana Azim Tariq of Sipah-e-Sahaba of Pakistan.
3. See Amir Mir, "More Power to Pakistan's Jihadis", *Asia Times*, 2 September 2011, available at http://www.atimes.com/atimes/South_Asia/MI02Df02.html (accessed on 29 May 2012).
4. Ibid.
5. Ibid.
6. See B. Raman, "The Jaish-e-Mohammad", South Asia Analysis Group, Paper No. 376, 16 December 2001, available at http://www.southasiaanalysis.org/%5Cpaper376.html (accessed on 28 May 2012).
7. For details, see Muhammad Amir Rana, *Gateway to Terrorism*, London: New Millennium Publication, 2003, pp. 214–22.
8. See Muhammad Amir Rana, *A to Z of Jehadi Organisations in Pakistan*, Lahore: Mashal Publication, 2004, pp. 230–31.
9. Ibid.
10. Ibid., p. 232.
11. See "Jaish-e-Mohammad", available at http://www.national security.gov.au/agd/WWW/nationalsecurity.nsf/page/what_Government (accessed on 29 May 2012).
12. Ibid.
13. See Mir, "More Power to Pakistan's Jihadis".
14. See Zia Khan, "Militant Group's Resurgence: Dreaded Jaish Looks to Rise Again", *The*

Express Tribune, 19 August 2011, available at http://tribune.com.pk/story/234738/militant-groups-resurgence-dreaded-jaish-looks-to-rise-again/ (accessed on 1 June 2012).
15. See Animesh Roul, "Jaish-e-Muhammad's Charity Wing Revitalizes Banned Group in Pakistan", *Terrorism Monitor*, Vol. 9, No. 41, 11 November 2011, available at http://www.jamestown.org/single/?no_cache=1&tx_ttnews%5Btt_news%5D=38664 (accessed on 1 June 2012).
16. See "Banned Jihadi Groups like Jaish-e-Mohammad Get their Money-trains Back Online: Report", available at http://pakistan.onepakistan.com/news/breaking/46873-banned-jihadi-groups-like-jaish-e-mohammad-get-their-money-trai%E2%80%8Bns-back-online-report.html (accessed on 1 June 2012).
17. See "Jaish-e-Mohammed (JEM)", Country Report, US Department of State, available at http://www.state.gov/j/ct/rls/crt/2011/195553.htm#jem (accessed on 1 May 2013).
18. See *Country Reports on Terrorism 2005*, United States Department of State, Office of the Coordinator for Counterterrorism, April 2006, p. 202.
19. See Gurmeet Kanwal and Monika Chansoria, "Small Arms Proliferation in South Asia: A Major Challenge for National Security", Issue Brief, Centre for Land Warfare Studies, New Delhi, available at www.claws.in/download.php?action=1274853671IB-18.pdf (accessed on 30 May 2012).
20. See Khan, "Militant Group's Resurgence".
21. Ibid.
22. See Rajnish Sharma, "LeT, JeM get ISI Cyber Training", *Deccan Chronicle*, 10 September 2012, available at http://www.deccanchronicle.com/channels/nation/north/let-jem-get-isi-cyber-training-885 (accessed on 10 September 2012).
23. See Shishir Gupta, "JeM is Back, India on its Radar Again: Intel Report", *Hindustan Times*, 13 December 2011, available at http://www.hindustantimes.com/India-news/NewDelhi/JeM-is-back-India-on-its-radar-again-Intel-report/Article1-782044.aspx (accessed on 1 June 2012).

27

Harkat-ul-Jihad-al-Islami

(Movement of Islamic Holy War)

Introduction

The Harkat-ul-Jihad-al-Islami (HuJI) is one of the most active jihadi outfits in South Asia whose main aim is the secession of Jammu and Kashmir (J&K) from India and its accession with Pakistan. It was formed in 1980 as a part of Pakistan-based jihadi network fighting Soviet troops deployed in Afghanistan. This Deobandi militant organisation was formed by Qari Saifullah Akhtar and two of his associates—Maulana Irshad Ahmed and Maulana Abdus Samad Sial—all products of Binori mosque of Karachi. Its original name was Jamiat Ansarul Afghanistan—the party of friends of Afghanistan people—which was later changed to HuJI and afterwards, it started operating as a Kashmir separatist group towards the end of Soviet occupation.

The HuJI first participated during Soviet–Afghan war and sent its jihadis to Chechnya, Uzbekistan and Tajikistan. Following the Soviet withdrawal, it shifted its focus from Afghanistan to Kashmir with the active support of Pakistan government and Inter Services Intelligence (ISI). Having lost its base in Afghanistan after the United States (US) intervention in 2001, most of its important leaders, including its amir, Qari Saifullah Akhtar, took refuge in Federally Administered Tribal Areas (FATA) region, while majority of its cadres fanned out and settled down in Pasthun region. Some of the foreign militants who were part of HuJI fled to Central Asia to avoid captured by the Americans. In 1992, HuJI expanded its network in Bangladesh, where it set up an independent unit known as HuJI-Bangladesh with the direct assistance from Osama bin Laden and the ISI.[1]

The HuJI has been banned in many countries because of its terror activities. It is a banned terrorist organisation in India under the Unlawful Activities (Prevention) Act 2004. Bangladesh government banned the militant outfit in October 2005. On 6 August 2010, the US in conjunction with the United Nations (UN) designated HuJI as a foreign terrorist organisation (FTO).

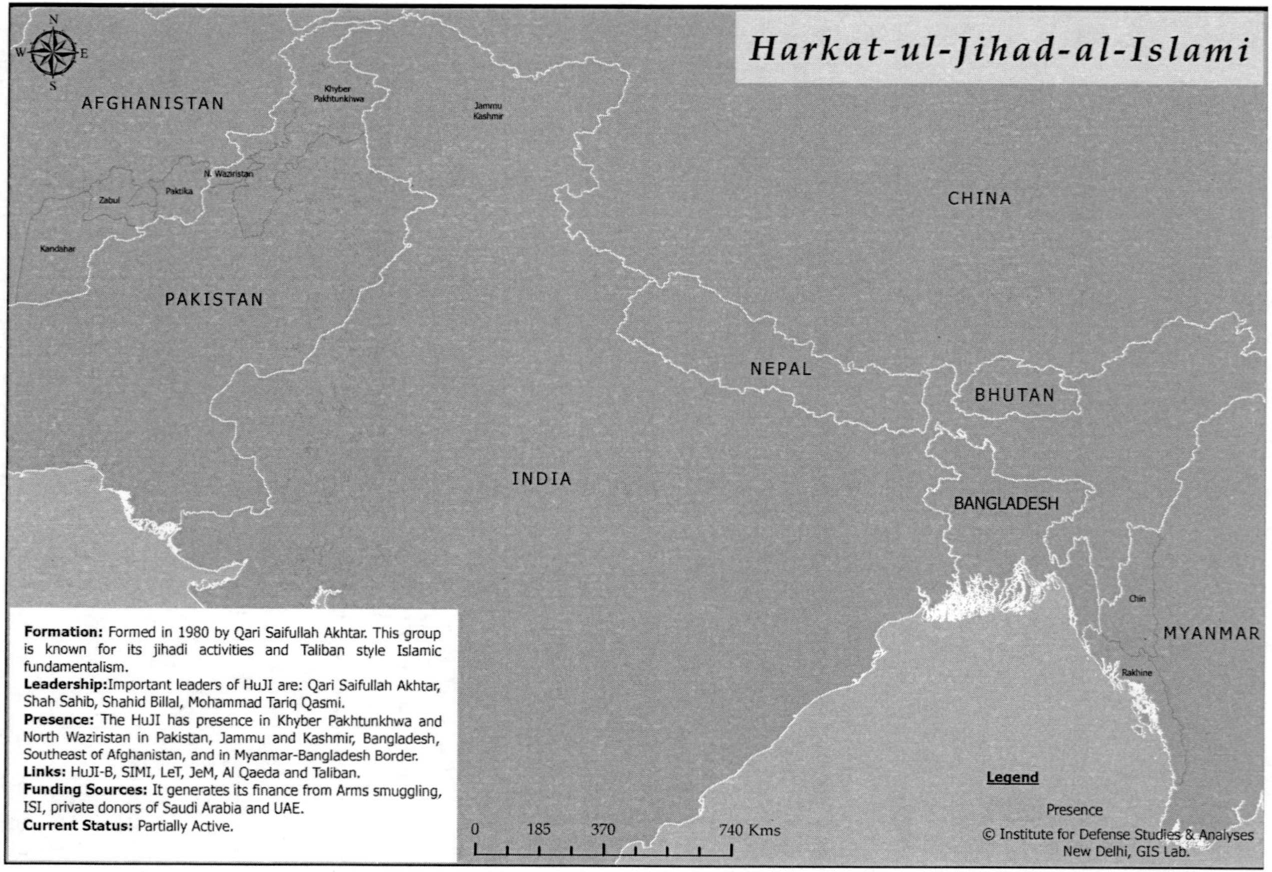
Harkat-ul-Jihad-al-Islami
N
W
E
S
AFGHANISTAN
Khyber Pakhtunkhwa
Jammu Kashmir
N. Waziristan
Paktika
Zabul
Kandahar
PAKISTAN
CHINA
NEPAL
BHUTAN
INDIA
BANGLADESH
Chin
MYANMAR
Rakhine
Formation: Formed in 1980 by Qari Saifullah Akhtar. This group is known for its jihadi activities and Taliban style Islamic fundamentalism.
Leadership: Important leaders of HuJI are: Qari Saifullah Akhtar, Shah Sahib, Shahid Billal, Mohammad Tariq Qasmi.
Presence: The HuJI has presence in Khyber Pakhtunkhwa and North Waziristan in Pakistan, Jammu and Kashmir, Bangladesh, Southeast of Afghanistan, and in Myanmar-Bangladesh Border.
Links: HuJI-B, SIMI, LeT, JeM, Al Qaeda and Taliban.
Funding Sources: It generates its finance from Arms smuggling, ISI, private donors of Saudi Arabia and UAE.
Current Status: Partially Active.
0 185 370 740 Kms
Legend
Presence
© Institute for Defense Studies & Analyses New Delhi, GIS Lab.

Objectives and Agenda

The HuJI aims at the annexation of J&K and expulsion of the US and coalition forces from Afghanistan. It believes in violent means to liberate Kashmir and make it a part of Pakistan. It also aims to establish Islamic rules in Pakistan by waging war and targeting intellectuals and Muslims with progressive outlook. Similarly, it also propagates the idea of Islamic rule in India. Since HuJI maintains strong links with the Taliban and the Al Qaeda, the group professes Taliban-style Islamic fundamentalism.

Leadership

Qari Saifullah Akhtar is the founder and amir of HuJI. He is also the commander of Al Qaeda military branch, Brigade 313. Akhtar took over the reins of the HuJI after the group leader, Maulana Irshad, was killed fighting the Soviets in 1985. A Pasthun hailing from Waziristan, Akhtar took lot of interest to expand HuJI's infrastructure in Pakistan and Afghanistan. Akhtar played an important role in bringing together Mullah Omar and Osama bin Laden.

Another important leader of the HuJI is Maulana Abdus Samad Sial. He is the patron-in-charge of J&K. Mohammad Ilyas Kashmiri was the operations commander of the HuJI and head of Brigade 313.[2] He was reportedly killed in the US drone strike in South Waziristan on 4 June 2011. His successor is Shah Sahib, a Taliban commander. Maulana Mohammad Ahmed Mansoor is the deputy amir of the HuJI. Shahid Billal is the operation chief of the HuJI. Unconfirmed reports say that he was killed by unidentified elements in Karachi in August 2007. He was reportedly involved in number of blasts in India. According to a source, he was succeeded by Mohammed Amjad in 2008.[3]

Some of the important leaders of the HuJI are: Mohammad Tariq Qasmi,head of the operation cells in Hyderabad, India. He is also area commander of HuJI in Uttar Pradesh (UP) and was allegedly in charge of the group responsible for the serial blast in Gorakhpur on 21 May 2007. He, along with his close aide Khalid Mujahid, was arrested by the security forces on 22 December 2007. However, the case against him has been taken off by the government of Uttar Pradesh in April 2013.[4]

Bashir Ahmed Mir was the commander-in-chief for the operations across India and was killed by the Indian security forces on 24 January 2008. Syed Anwar Hussain Nafees Shah is the chief patron of HuJI. Dr Usman is the tactical commander of the assault group of Brigade 313. Abu Humza is spokesman of Brigade 313.

Cadre Strength, Recruitment and Training

The exact strength of HuJI is not known. According to the US State Department, HuJI has an estimated strength of several hundred members. The HuJI is the only Deobandi outfit that gets majority of its cadres from madrassas in Punjab, Khyber Pakhtunkhwa (KP) and Pakistan-occupied Kashmir (PoK). The HuJI has a good rapport with Tablighi Jamaat, which gave it an opportunity to attract youth to join jihad at its headquarters in Raiwind during various gatherings.[5]

So far the training of the HuJI cadres is concerned, according to one source, the HuJI does not emphasise much on the religious training of its cadres; rather, it directly proceeds for military training in the camps in Afghanistan and PoK.[6] During the Taliban regime, the HuJI had six training camps in Kabul, Kandahar and Khost. It is important to note that Taliban military and police forces were also trained at these HuJI camps.[7]

The HuJI had also one of the largest camps in Kotli in PoK where 800 militants could be trained at one time. Kotli camp was later shifted to Razmek area of North Waziristan which was set up by Ilyas Kashmiri.

Area of Operation and Influence

HuJI claims to be the largest jihadi outfit in terms of its network, with the motto which says, "Harkat-ul-Jihad—the second defence line of every Muslim country".[8] According to the same source, the network of HuJI is believed to have spread over 24 countries in the world.

The HuJI area of operation extends throughout South Asia and South East Asian countries such as Pakistan, Afghanistan, India, Bangladesh, Myanmar, the Philippines and Malaysia. Another source claims that the HuJI maintained and organised seminaries in Karachi, Chechnya, Uzbekistan and Kajikistan. Its militants were believed to have participated in attacks in Afghanistan, Pakistan, Bangladesh, India, Chechnya, Uzbekistan and Tajikistan.[9]

In Pakistan, it has its offices mainly in Punjab and KP. The districts having the HuJI presence are Sargodha, Dera Ghazi Khan, Multan, Gujranwala, Gujarat, Bhakhar Mianwali, Bannu, Kohat, Dera Ismail Khan, Swat, Peshawar and Waziristan in FATA.

The HuJI started its operations in Pakistan, Bangladesh and J&K in the early 1990s. Ilyas Kashmiri headed Brigade 313 that was responsible for the initiation of HuJI operations in 1991. The HuJI's activities were at their highest in 2002, when 650 militants of HuJI were killed in a battle with the Indian security forces.

Network

The HuJI Pakistan has a very close and intense link with the HuJI-B. Support of the ISI to the HuJI has been consistent since 1993. The HuJI's links with Al Qaeda and Taliban are very strong. Its amir, Qari Saifullah Akhtar, was a close confidant and adviser to Taliban supremo, Mullah Omar. Three members of the Taliban cabinet and 22 judges were members of the HuJI. Its chief, Saifullah Akhtar, has been described a crucial figure in the efforts to unite Mullah Omar and Osama bin Laden.[10]

In India, the HuJI is believed to have established links with Students Islamic Movement of India (SIMI) and many Salafi Islamist groups. The HuJI is also linked to Lashkar-e-Taiba (LeT) and Jaish-e-Mohammad (JeM) operating in India.

Finance and Funding

Besides collecting funds from donors, the HuJI is also involved in sale of arms to smaller jihadi organisations. Its cadres are also active in various countries and regularly send collections. Besides this, it is also getting financial aid from the Pakistani intelligence agencies.

Weapons and Arms

Various attacks carried out by the HuJI are indicative of the fact that it has the possession of modern and sophisticated weapons. The improvised explosive device (IED) can well be in the possession of the HuJI.

Current Status

With the killing of its operational commander Ilyas Kashmiri in a drone attack in South Wazirstan on June 4, 2011, the militant activities of the HuJI have slowed down. Besides extending support to al Qaida, Ilyas Kashmiri used to actively participate in attacks against Pakistan government and its institutions, including the 2009 attack against the offices of the Pakistan ISI and Police Lines in Lahore. It is likely that HuJI may turn its focus in Kashmir and India if at all the Taliban are back to power in Afghanistan after the withdrawal of American forces. It may be mentioned that HuJI Amir Qari Saifullah Akhtar has closely been associated with Taliban and al Qaida for more than one decade. It was Qari Akhtar who accompanied Taliban supremo Mullah Omer when he fled to Pakistan after US stared Operation Enduring Freedom.

NOTES

1. For detailed note on HuJI-B, see the chapter on HuJI-B in this book.
2. Brigade 313 has been responsible for many high-profile attacks and terror strikes in Pakistan. It was also responsible for the assassination attempts against former President, Parvez Musharraf, and Prime Minister Gillani. Brigade 313 is one of the six known units in the Lashkar al-Zil, Al Qaeda's paramilitary Shadow Army.
3. See "Harkat-ul-Jihad-al-Islami", available at http://www.globaljihad.net/view_page.asp?id=991 (accessed on 2 June 2012).
4. See "UP Frees Serial Blasts 'Mastermind'", *The Daily News and Analysis*, 25 April 2013, available at http://www.dnaindia.com/india/1826636/report-up-frees-serial-blasts-mastermind

(accessed on 29 May 2013).
5. See Muhammad Amir Rana, *A to Z of Jehadi Organisations in Pakistan*, Lahore: Mashal Publication, 2004, pp. 266–67.
6. See Zahid Hussain, *Frontline Pakistan: The Struggle with Militant Islam*, Columbia: Columbia University Press, 2007, p. 71.
7. See Bill Roggio, "Top Al Qaeda Leaders Linked to Five Americans on Trail in Pakistan", *The Long War Journal*, 17 April 2010, available at http://www.longwarjournal.org/archives/2010/04/top_al_qaeda_leader.php (accessed on 2 June 2012).
8. See Rana, *A to Z of Jehadi Organisations in Pakistan*, p. 268.
9. See Roggio, "Top Al Qaeda Leaders Linked to Five Americans on Trail in Pakistan".
10. Ibid.

28

Tehrik-e-Taliban Pakistan
(Movement of Pakistani Taliban)

Introduction

The story of Pakistan Taliban will remain incomplete without tracing three key developments that ultimately contributed to the emergence of Tehrik-e-Taliban Pakistan (TTP) in December 2007.

Most members of the Afghan Taliban, who ruled Kabul from 1996 to 2001, went to the madrassas run by Deobandi Jamiat Ulema-e-Islam (JUI) as their families became refugees in Pakistan in the 1980s during the United States (US)-led Afghan war against the Soviet Red Army. The Islamic indoctrination they received was based on the syllabus prepared and supplied by the Americans. No Islamic religious body of theologians has ever approved this interpretation of Islam that Taliban has come to believe in and implement vigorously.

The JUI chief, Maulana Fazlur Rahman, had launched a Talibanisation movement in Pakistan before 2001. His movement was cold-shouldered across the country, except a few areas of Baluchistan. In the North-West Frontier Province (NWFP), now renamed as Khyber Pakhtunkhwa (KP), some Christian groups had set up an organisation styling it as the Christian Taliban. It disappeared without a trace soon after its launch. Clearly, therefore, Taliban's militant Islam had few takers initially. Success came their way when people of southern Punjab found their manna in the Taliban's rein of terror. These people had moved into the area in 1947 when British India was divided into Pakistan and India, but could not assimilate into Sufism-oriented local milieu. They turned to Taliban to be one-up on the fellow Punjabi Pakistanis, joined Taliban's training camps in the tribal areas and became the Punjabi Taliban, though the Punjab provincial government denied there was Punjabi Taliban.

The Federally Administered Tribal Areas (FATA)—that borders Afghanistan and where the writ of Islamabad does not run generally—had enmeshed itself in Talibanism as a reaction to Pakistan government joining the US-led war against global terrorism. This war meant a war against Al Qaeda and Afghan Taliban

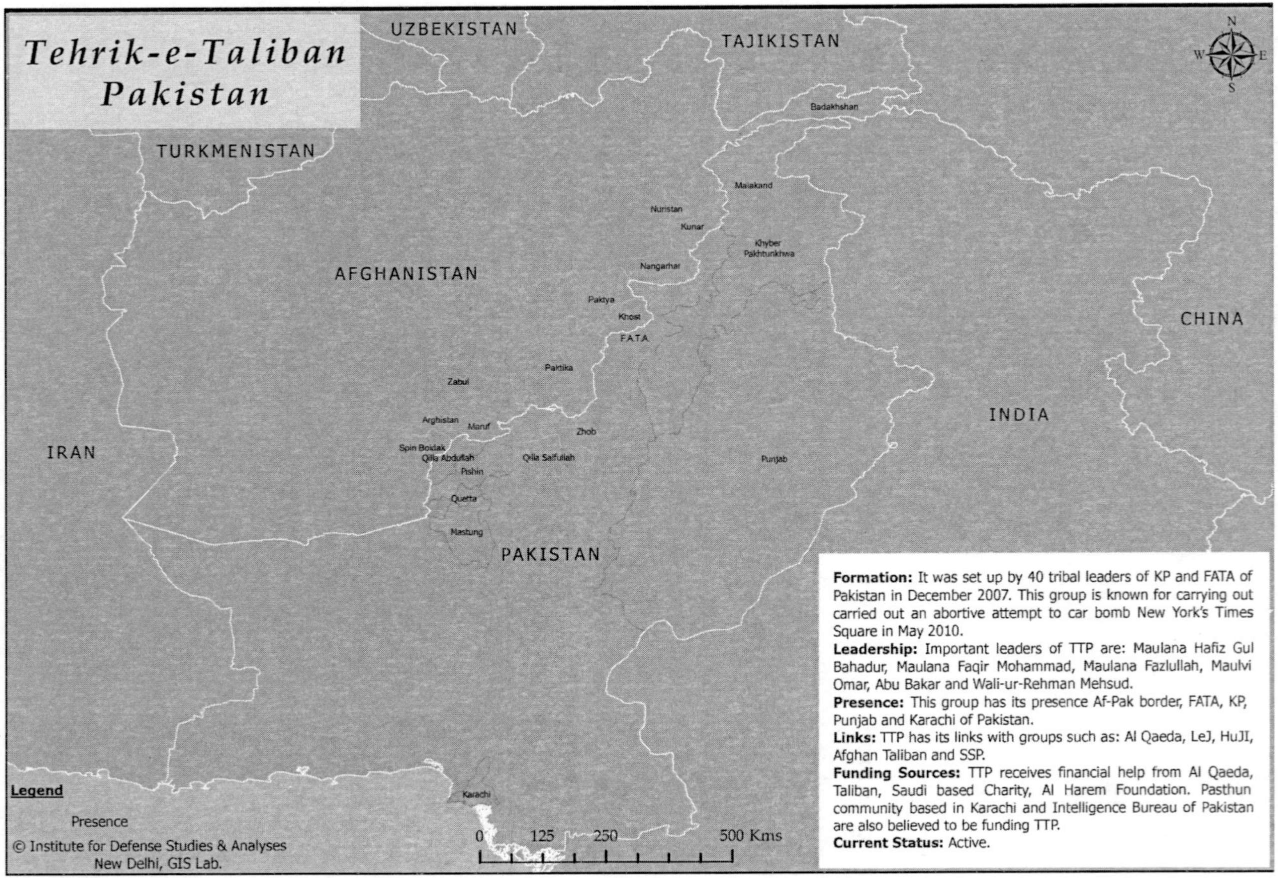
Tehrik-e-Taliban Pakistan
UZBEKISTAN
TAJIKISTAN
TURKMENISTAN
AFGHANISTAN
IRAN
PAKISTAN
INDIA
CHINA
Badakhshan
Malakand
Nuristan
Kunar
Khyber Pakhtunkhwa
Nangarhar
Paktya
Khost
FATA
Paktika
Zabul
Arghistan
Maruf
Zhob
Spin Boldak
Qilla Abdullah
Qila Saifullah
Pishin
Quetta
Mastung
Punjab
Karachi
Legend
Presence
© Institute for Defense Studies & Analyses New Delhi, GIS Lab.
0 125 250 500 Kms
Formation: It was set up by 40 tribal leaders of KP and FATA of Pakistan in December 2007. This group is known for carrying out carried out an abortive attempt to car bomb New York's Times Square in May 2010.
Leadership: Important leaders of TTP are: Maulana Hafiz Gul Bahadur, Maulana Faqir Mohammad, Maulana Fazlullah, Maulvi Omar, Abu Bakar and Wali-ur-Rehman Mehsud.
Presence: This group has its presence Af-Pak border, FATA, KP, Punjab and Karachi of Pakistan.
Links: TTP has its links with groups such as: Al Qaeda, LeJ, HuJI, Afghan Taliban and SSP.
Funding Sources: TTP receives financial help from Al Qaeda, Taliban, Saudi based Charity, Al Harem Foundation. Pasthun community based in Karachi and Intelligence Bureau of Pakistan are also believed to be funding TTP.
Current Status: Active.

based in the area with the patronage of Pakistan Army. Suspicion of the army was fuelled as a consequence, and people of FATA and KP began to see Pakistan Army as mercenaries of the US.

This suspicion turned into contempt for the army and became the third-most important factor to fuel the spread and reach of Taliban. A young warrior, by the name of Nek Mohammad Wazir, vociferously articulated this contempt towards the Pakistan Army and his campaign prepared the ground for the launch of TTP. He did not live to see his dream come true though. He was killed in an American drone attack in 2004. Three years later, in 2007, TTP became a reality. It took shape in three formations: Afghan Taliban, Pakistani Taliban and Punjabi Taliban. The Pakistan Army further divided them into good and bad Taliban, to sub-serve its geostrategic interests and to further its concept of negotiations with the Taliban.

Genesis

The TTP, which is also known as Pakistani Taliban, is one of the most active and dangerous terrorist alliances operating out of Pakistan today. This umbrella group was formed on 13 December 2007 by a shura (consultative council) of 40 senior leaders of 13 militant groups active in KP and FATA. Taliban leaders from seven tribal agencies, six frontier regions of FATA and NWFP districts of Swat, Kohistan, Buner, Dir, Malakand, Kulachi, Bannu, Lakki Marwat, Tank and Dera Ismail Khan attended the meeting and chose Baitullah Mehsud (34 years) as the chief of the alliance, who, in turn, pledged TTP's allegiance to Taliban supremo, Mullah Omar, as the Amir-ul-Momineen (Leader of the Faithful).

Since its formation, till October 2012, the TTP had carried out nearly 200 attacks killing 561 security personnel and 2,403 civilians. It targeted General Headquarters (GHQ), Manawan Police Training Centre in Lahore, key naval and air force bases, Marriot Hotel in Islamabad, scores of police stations, office of the intelligence agencies, school buses, mosques, shrines and even funerals. In addition, it carried out 1,300 improvised explosive device (IED) attacks, killing 2,060 security personnel and 2,073 civilians, and injuring 1,532 troops and 2,309 civilians.[1]

The TTP did not spare educational institutions. It burnt down 400 schools in KP and FATA. It banned administering polio drops to the children in the tribal areas as well as many settled areas of Pakistan.[2] In late 2009, the group had threatened to unleash a chemical warfare against Pakistan and planned to mix a poisonous chemical substance in the drinking water supply systems of Multan, Karachi and Rawalpindi. The TTP had reportedly stockpiled some 200 liters of a poisonous material that could be used to contaminate water sources and reservoirs in Rawalpindi and Chaklala cantonments, and perhaps in the port city of Karachi.[3]

The TTP did not confine itself to attacks within Pakistan. On 1 May 2010, the group made headlines when a US citizen of Pakistan origin, Faisal Shahzad, carried out an abortive attempt to car bomb New York's iconic Times Square.[4] Shahzad said he was trained in Pakistan by Qari Hussain, commander of TTP, who used to train suicide bombers. The TTP was quick to claim responsibility for the "attack" saying that it was intended to be in revenge for the killing of its leader, Baitullah Mehsud, and killing of two Al Qaeda leaders in Iraq.

The TTP chief, Hakimullah Mehsud, claimed that his operatives have infiltrated the US and would carry out more attacks in future. "Our fidayeen have penetrated the terrorist America. We will give extremely painful blows to the fanatic America,"[5] he was quoted as warning Washington. The New York attempt was preceded by several TTP attacks against American interests in Pakistan and Afghanistan, like suicide bombing at the US Consulate in Peshawar in April 2010, suicide bombing at a US base in Afghanistan in December 2009 and the killing in November 2008 of United States Agency for International Development (USAID) worker stationed in Peshawar. On 1 September 2010, the US State Department proscribed TTP. A year later, the United Nations (UN) listed the group as a terrorist organisation. Pakistan banned the group and froze its bank accounts on 25 August 2008.[6]

The US issued an arrest warrant against Hakimullah and TTP for "conspiracy to murder American citizens abroad and conspiracy to use a weapon of mass destruction". The US and Pakistan have announced a bounty of $5 million and $650,000 on his head respectively.[7]

However, death of other key Al Qaeda and TTP leaders in drone attacks slowed the TTP's expansion and its attacks. Baitullah's killing was followed by the death of Qari Hussain, known as TTP's *ustadul* fidayeen (master of suicide bombers), in January 2011;[8] Ilyas Kashmiri, head of Brigade 313, an Al Qaeda affiliate which worked closely with TTP, in June 2011;[9] and Badar Mansoor, Al Qaeda's operational commander in Pakistan, in February 2012.[10]

The TTP was frequently rocked by serious differences and infighting over the target of attacks, and this resulted in some heavyweights going their own way to set up their own outfits. One commander, Gul Bahadur, parted ways in 2008 and allied himself with the like-minded Mullah Nazir, as he was opposed to attacks on Pakistan Army. There were differences between Hakimullah Mehsud and Wali-ur-Rehman, who led TTP unit of South Waziristan, as both staked claim to succeed Baitullah on his death. Reportedly, the head of the TTP chapter in Bajaur, Maulana Faqir, also staked his claim.[11] This led to a clash between the supporters of these groups. In December 2011, the Taliban and Al Qaeda leadership set up a *shura-i-murakeba*, a five-member council, to resolve differences, and brokered peace among feuding elements of TTP.[12]

The council brought together the Haqqanis, TTP and other groups led by Gul Bahadur and Mullah Nazir. The shura also resolved differences between TTP head, Hakimullah Mehsud, and his deputy, Wali-ur-Rehman. Members of the *shura-i-murakeba* agreed to cease attacks on Pakistani security forces and focus attention on North Atlantic Treaty Organization (NATO) forces in Afghanistan.[13]

The TTP's August 2012 attack on the Kamra Aeronautical Complex in Punjab and on the young girl from Swat, Malala Yousfzai, in October 2012, are clear indications of the terrorist group's attempts to regain its position among jihadi networks operating in Pakistan. Notwithstanding setbacks, the group remains as serious an adversary to the security forces in Pakistan and Afghanistan as in the past. The group, working in close alliance with other extremist and terrorist groups like Al Qaeda and Lashkar-e-Taiba (LeT) is adept at carrying out attacks deep inside Pakistan and poses a serious challenge to Pakistan Army in Waziristan.

Objectives

The TTP stands for enforcement of Sharia in Pakistan. Its other key objectives—as announced by Baitullah's spokesman, Maulvi Omar, upon its formation—are: unite the Taliban against NATO forces in Afghanistan and to wage "defensive jihad" against Pakistani forces; and "freedom" to Lal Masjid Imam Abdul Aziz and other Taliban jailed across the country. It wants the government to call off military operations in Swat and North Waziristan, and abolish all military checkpoints within 10 days.[14] But the deadline was extended as the government declared mourning of former Prime Minister Benazir Bhutto's death on 27 December 2007.

In his first press conference, Hakimullah reaffirmed TTP's founding objectives, claiming that "we were primarily formed to fight NATO and the US. The Pakistan Army forced us to fight them. Our aim is to expel Americans from Afghanistan."[15]

Reiterating TTP objective in October 2009, Hakimullah said, "We want an Islamic state. If we get that (in Pakistan), then we will go to the borders and help fight the Indians."[16]

The TTP spokesman, Azim Tariq, even claimed in July 2010 that his group was training suicide bombers to attack targets in India. He further stated that TTP would fight a "decisive battle" in India once Pakistan and Afghanistan were under the control of the Taliban, adding, "Soon we will teach India a lesson as India's defeat at the hands of the Mujahideen is written in our religious books".[17]

In one of the videotapes, Hakimullah described democracy as a "system of infidels" and said, "We want the implementation of Shariah, which can only be enforced through waging Jihad. A time will come when the Muslims will establish Caliphate on the surface of the earth." Another senior TTP leader, Wali-ur-Rehman, said in the videotape, "We are fighting against the Pakistani government because it is toeing the US line. We will adopt softer approach if Pakistan abandons US slavery and pursues an independent and sovereign policy."[18]

Senior TTP leaders are often quoted saying that the TTP was formed:

> to pool the resources and manpower of Pakistan's Taliban to fight in self-defence if the security forces of Pakistan attacked their areas and also to extend help to the Afghan Taliban taking part in the "jihad", against US and International Security Assistance Force (ISAF) troops in neighbouring Afghanistan.[19]

Some reports say many men, particularly youth, wanted to join the TTP to take revenge on the Americans because of the killing of their family members by an American bomb or drone strike.

Organisational Structure and Leadership

The structure of the group is based on 40-member shura, which was set up by 13 militant organisations when they came together to form TTP. Heading the shura is an amir. Next in the line are - senior deputy amir, deputy amir and a general secretary who oversees organisational affairs. Majority of shura members are products of Deobandi madrassas and as such, their objective is to turn Pakistan into an Islamic state.[20]

For smooth functioning of TTP, the tribal areas have been divided into various administrative zones. Each zone is headed by a military commander who reports directly to the supreme commander of the local Taliban and shura. Administrative zone is further divided into various departments like intelligence collection, identification and elimination of spies, revenue collection and maintenance of law and order. Majority of the TTP leaders have been trained and fought in Afghanistan.

At the time of its inception, TTP announced a set of office bearers, including its Amir. A prominent fighter from Mehsud tribe, Baitullah Mehsud, was appointed as the leader of the group.[21] Maulana Hafiz Gul Bahadur of North Waziristan was made his deputy; third-in-command was Maulana Faqir Mohammad of Bajaur Agency (the smallest agency in FATA). Maulana Fazlullah was declared the secretary general and head of the Swat chapter of TTP.[22] Maulvi Omar was named the spokesperson. Twenty-seven smaller groups pledged their support to Mehsud. When Baitullah Mehsud was killed in a drone attack in 2009, the leadership passed on to his cousin, Hakimullah. He was assisted by Wali-ur-Rehman Mehsud (deputy chief), Mangal Bagh (chief of Lashkar-e-Islam), Maulana Fazullah (TTP Swat chief), Akhunzada Aslam Farooqi (chief in Orakzai Agency), Abu Bakar (Bajaur Agency) and Noor Jamal (Kurram Agency).[23]

Other prominent commanders are: Maulvi Saeed Khan and Maulvi Zia-ur-Rehman, Orakzai Agency; Hafiz Daulat Khan, Kurram; Commander Khalid, Mohmand Agency; and Maulana Faqir Mohammad, Bajaur. The TTP (Mohmand) has affiliation with Hakimullah group led in the area by Commander Khalid. It has also stationed its commanders in other provinces of Pakistan. Its chief in Punjab is Asmatullah Muawiya. The organisation has also its own spokesman, Ehsanullah Ehsan (his given name is Sajjad Mohammad), who, besides issuing the press releases, also makes important announcements. He heads the Umar Studio, a media unit of the TTP, which regularly releases videos focusing on attacks at various places in FATA and other places in Pakistan.

North and South Waziristan are the hubs of Pakistan's militancy. Real power in South Waziristan was wielded by Baitullah of Mehsud tribe and Mullah Nazir of the Wazir tribe. Baitullah had a force of about 5,000 deadly militants, including Uzbeks and Chechens. Nazir commands a force of about 3,000 militants. He had entered into a peace pact with the Pakistani Army in 2007, but broke it a year later. In 2009, he formed Shura Ittehad-ul Mujahideen (United Council of Mujahideen) with Gul Bahadur and Baitullah Mehsud with the shared goal of fighting against the US. On his part, Baitullah was able to bring 13 militant groups under the TTP umbrella despite divisions, intrigues and conspiracies that are a characteristic feature of Pakistan's tribal belt.

The TTP supremo of North Waziristan is Hafiz Gul Bahadur (Uthmanzir Wazir tribe). He has also been a member of the local Taliban shura since 2005. In 2008, Mullah Nazir joined hands with him and they together formed Muqami Tehrik-e-Taliban (Local Taliban Movement), as a distinct group from Baitullah group, for which he reportedly got covert support from Pakistan government. But in 2008, he abandoned the peace deal he had negotiated with the Pakistan government and decided to attack Pakistani forces following continued drone attacks and escalating military offensive.[24] His force is around 4,000 cadre strong, though some experts point out the figure to be anywhere between 8,000 and 10,000 fighters. He maintains ties with Afghan Taliban, Haqqani Network and Al Qaeda.

Swat Valley in Malakand is led by Mullah Fazlullah, the Radio Mullah, who controls an armed faction of the Tehrik-e-Nifaz-e-Shariat-Mohammadi (TNSM). Prior to the military operation launched in 2009, Maulana commanded a force of 5,000 fighters.

The TTP Bajaur is headed by Faqir Mohammad, who is also deputy amir of the group. A member of Mohmand tribe, he was earlier associated with TNSM and acted as facilitator for Al Qaeda. He has since been arrested in Afghanistan. The group is now led by Maulvi Abu Bakar. After the Pakistan Army operation in 2008, its militants fled to Afghanistan from where they carry "hit and run attacks".[25]

The TTP Mohmand is led by Omar Khalid, who belongs to Safi tribe. The group, with some 600 fighters, has safe havens in the Afghan province of Nangarhar from where it launches cross-border attacks on army checkposts in Pakistan.

The TTP Darra Adam Khel, considered as the most dangerous of TTP groups, has a suicide brigade known as "Al Mansoorian". This 800-member strong force is a member of the sectarian outfit targeting Shias. Tariq Afridi, its commander, was reportedly killed in August 2012.

The TTP Dir is led by Commander Hafizullah alias Commander Kochwan and is supported by Mullah Fazlullah of Swat. He is hiding with his 500 fighters in Afghanistan from where he launches attacks on Pakistan Army checkposts from time to time.

The TTP Kurram has split into two factions: one led by Hakimullah loyalist, Commander Noor Jamal alias Mullah Toofan; and the other led by Maulana Fazle Saeed Haqqani. Their fighters number only a few hundred.

The TTP Mansehra is led by Momin Khan, while TTP Orakzai is headed by Qari Saeed. The strength of this group is around 200.

Area of Operation and Influence

The TTP has been able to establish its hold in FATA, Peshawar, Nowshera, Charsadda, Hangu, Bannu, Lakki Marwat, Dera Ismail Khan, Kohat, Tank, Swat and Dir districts of KP, and some areas of Punjab and Karachi. Its headquarters is in Ladha area in South Waziristan. After taking over the reins of TTP, Hakimullah targeted the security forces and the civilians alike. His cadres carried out assaults on the GHQ of the Pakistan Army, the Parade Lane Mosque in Rawalpindi, Manawan police training centre in Lahore and lately, on leaders and workers of Awami National Party (ANP), Pakistan Peoples' Party (PPP) and Muttahida Quami Movement (MQM).

The TTP's tools to spread fear and terror and keep its hold are brutal punishments and psychological warfare. To demoralise the army, it kidnaps soldiers and even decapitates the victims. It strikes in big cities like Lahore, Peshawar, Islamabad and Karachi are aimed at getting publicity besides embarrassing the government.[26]

Alliances—State/Non-State

The TTP has developed links with many other militant and sectarian groups in Afghanistan and Pakistan. "TTP and al Qaida have a symbolic relationship," according to the US Ambassador-at-large for Counterterrorism, Daniel Benjamin, who opines that TTP draws ideological guidance from Al Qaeda, while Al Qaeda relies on the TTP for safe haven in the Pashtun areas along the Afghan–Pakistani border. This mutual cooperation, and in a way dependence, gives TTP access to both Al Qaeda's global network and the operational experience of its members. It is this that makes TTP a force multiplier of Al Qaeda.[27]

The TTP maintains some links with the Afghan Taliban as many TTP leaders held important positions in the Taliban regime and Baitullah owed allegiance to Taliban supremo, Mullah Omar.[28]

Some experts hold the view that the Lashkar-e-Jhangvi (LeJ) and TTP are closely aligned, with LeJ supplying young and seasoned recruits who are popularly known as "Punjabi Taliban".[29] The TTP and LeJ differ in their objectives and motives but what binds them is their use of imported militants from Central Asia and the Middle East. Both have had direct and indirect operational links to the Afghan Taliban in Afghanistan and FATA in the past as also the present. Most significantly, both these Sunni outfits have operational links with Pakistan's military intelligence agencies owing to their anti-India jihadi campaign in Kashmir in the past, and the current anti-American tactical alliance with Afghan Taliban in Waziristan.[30] The TTP also has a tie up with the Haqqani Network and lends manpower for Haqqani attacks on the US-led NATO forces in Afghanistan.[31]

Other outfits having linkages with TTP are LeT, Jaish-e-Mohammad (JeM), Harkat-ul-Mujahideen (HuM) and Harkat-ul-Jihad-al-Islami (HuJI), among others. Media reports on 11 January 2011 said that five groups—LeJ, SSP, JeM, HuM and Harkat-ul-Ansar (HuA)—had decided to make TTP their umbrella because of their common aims and enemies. Calling it a merger of dreaded terrorist groups,TTP spokesman, Azam Tariq said, "We have not forced anyone to join TTP, and the leaders and activists of the banned religious organisations have united themselves under the umbrella of the TTP on their own choice".[32]

Cadre-Strength, Profile and Training

The actual strength of TTP remains shrouded in mystery, particularly the number of foreign fighters in its ranks. Some estimates put its cadres at a modest 5,000, while some others aver that TTP is 30,000 men strong. Peshawar-based, noted Pakistani journalist, Rahimullah Yusufzai, holds the view that realistic figure would be 10,000 if "reserves" were also counted.[33] Another Pakistani expert on terrorism, Muneeb Ansari, is convinced that the estimated strength of TTP is about 15,000 militants and avers that the majority of TTP cadre is based in FATA and that some of them are dispersed over KP and other regions of Pakistan.[34] But Islamabad-based FATA Research Centre says that the total strength of TTP is no more than 8,000 and that a majority of them, numbering anywhere between 3,000 and 4,000, are from the Hakimullah group.[35]

The TTP's main training bases are in South and North Waziristan. Majority of its recruits belong to poor families who are indoctrinated through Deobandi madrassas spread across Pakistan. There are roughly 2,000 madrassas in the Afghanistan–Pakistan border belt; according to one report, all these religious schools run by local mosques are involved in brainwashing and indoctrination of young minds.[36]

Taliban also forcibly pick up poor children from rural Pakistan to mould them into jihadi warriors. It has also reportedly scouted successfully in the 11 camps of internally displaced persons (IDPs) in KP since children constitute 60 per cent of these refugees in the camps.[37]

The militant leaders have also been able to radicalise the Pashtun society by spreading the "good word" through a network of FM radio stations they have set up in the tribal heartland. These are not legal radios and therefore, without any checks, they incite people to jihad, redefine role of women in the society and intimidate the general public by reading out fatwas against tribal elders, "spies" and security officials whom they decide to kill or hang until death.[38]

Qari Abdullah is the overall commander of the training programme, which covers handling assault rifles, AK-series rifles and explosive devices, ambush assaults and suicide missions. The cadres are also trained to carry out kidnappings and bank robberies.

Most of the suicide attacks claimed by the TTP are carried out by children who were trained by Qari Hussain. Around 1,200–1,500 boys in the age group of 11–18 years were picked up for training in suicide missions in Swat before the Pakistan government signed a peace deal in February 2009, and handed over control of the Swat Valley to the TTP militants, according to Pakistan Army itself.[39] On his part, Commander Qari Hussain once claimed that TTP recruits children as young as 5 years old, adding, "Children are tools to achieve God's will...".[40]

Financial Resources

The annual budget of the TTP is estimated to be about Pakistani rupee (PKR) 3.6 billion (approx. $42 million). Most of this money comes from Afghan drug trade.[41] The TTP relies heavily on extortion and kidnapping for ransom to fund its terrorist activities. The group has been involved in bank robberies, thefts and car jacking. According to one estimate, 20 per cent of TTP funds come from crimes like kidnappings and bank robberies; 50 per cent from donations and extortions; and the remaining 30 per cent from drug money.[42] Foreign terrorist groups, including Al Qaeda, as also Islamic institutes abroad regularly contribute to the TTP. For instance, in September 2009, TTP is alleged to have received $15 million from a Saudi-based charity, Al-Harem Foundation, which is said to be linked to Al Qaeda.[43]

TTP cadres often extract money by posing as government or aid workers in areas where foreign, non-governmental organisations (NGOs) are funding educational and other charity work.

Reportedly, the TTP has taken control of marble and emerald mines in Pakistan's tribal belt.[44] It closed ranks with Swat's timber ma?a, and collects commissions from the owners and managers of coal mines in Orakzai Agency. Taliban militants are reported to be plundering archaeological sites in Swat to cash in on the overseas craze for artefacts.

For the TTP, collecting ransom is also a form of jihad. Rich industrialists, businessmen, soldiers and government employees have been routinely targeted for kidnapping for ransom.[45] It operates "Commando squads" for undertaking the kidnappings.

In August 2007, for the release of 280 kidnapped soldiers, the TTP terrorists were paid PKR 60 million. On 11 February 2008, Pakistan's Ambassador to Afghanistan, Tariq Azizuddin, was kidnapped. He was released in exchange for 55 militants held by Pakistan Army, and a ransom of PKR 20 million.[46] A major source of TTP funds is the large Pashtun community in Karachi with its monopoly over transport business. A former chief of Pakistan's Intelligence Bureau (IB) terms Karachi as "TTP's cash-cow", since it stages bank robberies, extortion and even revenge killings in Pakistan's commercial capital. He says that the Taliban wanted to take over the Pashtun-dominated areas from ANP, and this is the reason why ANP leaders are being targeted by TTP militants.[47]

Another revenue source for TTP is the heroine trade, with the drug being exported to foreign countries through Karachi's air and seaports.[48]

The TTP charges smugglers for the "safe passage" of contraband shipments from Afghanistan to FATA/KP and to Baluchistan. Protection money is also extorted from non-Muslim minorities as *jiziya*. For example, in April 2009, the Sikh community in Orakzai Agency in FATA paid PKR 20 million to the militants as *jiziya* after being coerced by the Taliban, who had confiscated their homes and held a Sikh leader as hostage.[49]

Weapons

The TTP has an array of automatic assault rifles, particularly AK-series rifles, mortars and rocket-propelled grenade launchers. Its militants are increasingly using improvised explosive devices (IEDs), suicide vests and suicide vehicle-born IEDs (SVBIEDs). The seizure of weapons cache and the haul of 209 kg of explosives in Karachi in February 2013 showed that the TTP is in possession of large quantity of explosives.[50] On 1 April 2013, police raided Karachi's Jinnah Colony, where also they recovered large quantity of explosives and weapons from arrested TTP militants.[51] Some of these weapons were either looted or stolen during raids on the camps of security forces.

Networks—Local, Regional and Global

People living in Pakistan's tribal areas are Pashtuns. They are an ethnic group with an estimated 15 million population living in both sides of Durand Line, that is, south-eastern Afghanistan and north-western Pakistan. They consist of about 60 tribes who are broken into clans and sub-clans. Prominent tribes include Wazirs in North Waziristan; Mehsuds and Ahmedzais in South Waziristan; Yusufzais in Malakand and Bajaur Agency; Afridi and Shinwari in Khyber Agency, Peshawar and Kohat; Mohmands in Mohmand Agency; Turis and Bangash in Orakzai Agency; Khattaks in east and south-east of Kohat; and Bhittani in Tank and Lakki Marwat.

The tribals, their lifestyle, customs and traditions, all are guided by Pashtunwali—the code of conduct decreed to them over ages. It comprises notions such as *nang/ghairat* (honour/pride), *melmestia* (hosptality), *badal* (revenge), *khegara* (benevolence) and *panah* (sanctuary).

Traditions such as *teega* (ceasefire), *rogha* (peace making), *nanawate* (forgiveness), *swara* (marrying girl for peace making) and *meerata* (without male progeny) are honoured to this day without a murmur.

Punjabi Taliban

Both in theory and practice, Punjabi Taliban network is a loose conglomeration of banned military groups of Punjab origin which are active locally on the sectarian front and Kashmir front. It has strong linkages with TTP, Afghan Taliban and other militant groups based in the FATA and KP.

The origin of the "Punjabi Taliban" dates back to mid-1990s, when the name was used for the first time for ethnic Punjabis associated with HuJI, according to Pakistan security analyst, Hassan Abbas. These jihadis, led by Qari Saifullah Akhtar, went to Afghanistan in support of the Taliban and joined Mullah Omar regime in mid-1990s.

Recruits of the JeM and LeT getting trained at Taliban camps are also commonly referred to as Punjabi Taliban.

The third time the term Punjabi Taliban was used was in 2001–03, when the then Pakistan President, Pervez Musharraf, banned some militant and sectarian groups that had a support base in Punjab. It was again the news in 2007 when Mullah Nazir, a prominent leader from South Waziristan, recruited some Punjabi militants to oust some Uzbek militants from FATA.[52]

Going by Pakistani analyst Raheel Khan, two significant developments gave a fillip to Punjabi Taliban during this time. One was that insurgency decreased in Kashmir following ceasing of support to militants by Pakistan. Two was the military operation to cleanse Islamabad's Lal Masjid of militants in 2007. Following this, about 5,000 young Punjabis joined militant training centres in North and South Waziristan.[53] They belong to groups such as SSP, LeJ, JeM and LeT.

The Punjabi Taliban have spread their network across Lahore, Bahawalpur, Faisalabad, Gujranwala, Multan, Dera Ghazi Khan, Sargodha and Rawalpindi divisions;[54] Karachi in Sindh; and Quetta in Baluchistan. Their strength is not clearly known. At least in Punjab, their number is available with Punjab government's counter-terrorism department. It estimates that 2,487 militants trained in Afghanistan and 556 militants released from Afghan prisons have surfaced in the province and are engaged in terrorist activities.[55]

The network has deepened its ties with the Al Qaeda and the Taliban; it is a part of TTP's 40-member shura.[56] Amongst the TTP leaders who have established strong ties with Punjabi Taliban are Hakimullah Mehsud, Wali-ur-Rehman and Qari Hussain.

The network has carried out several deadly attacks. Its targets included: Marriot Hotel in Islamabad in September 2008; police training centre outside Lahore in March 2009; Sri Lanka cricket team in Lahore in March 2009; the GHQ in Rawalpindi in October 2009; ISI office in Multan in December 2009; military mosque in Rawalpindi in December 2009; two Ahmediya mosques in Lahore in May 2010; Data Ganj Bakhsh shrine in Lahore in July 2010; Shia's procession in Lahore in September 2010; Pak Naval Air Force base in Karachi in May 2011; and Pakistan's largest airbase at Kamra in August 2012.

Current Status

The TTP has grown to be a serious threat to Pakistan as it has spread its network beyond FATA. Its presence in Punjab and in Karachi has been cause of serious concern to the security forces in Pakistan. The TTP has also been systematically targeting the security forces with the sole objective of forcing them to accept the terms of negotiation which the group has kept as a pre-condition for talks. On 28 December 2012, the TTP offered to hold peace talks with the government but put a condition that it would not lay down arms until the implementation of their version of Sharia in the country.

Nawaz Sharif, while talking to newly elected members of his party, said that "we should take Taliban offer of talks seriously". The statement was welcomed by TTP spokesman, Ehsanullah Ehsan.[57]

However, the possibility of holding talks with the TTP received a big setback following the killings of Wali-ur-Rehman, second-in-command of the TTP, on 29 May 2013 and its chief Hakimullah on 1 November, 2013 in drones attacks. Before his death, Rehman like his chief had also $5 million US government bounty on his head and was involved in many attacks against the Pakistani government and military, besides the 2009 attack on Central Intelligence Agency (CIA) post in Khost in Afghanistan in which seven CIA operatives were killed. In nutshell, he was understood to be the operational head of TTP and behind much of its strategy.

Although the killing of Hakimullah Mehsud is a big blow to TTP after the death of Wali-ur-Rahman, it may not be correct to say that with his killing TTP has weakened. Following his killing, TTP spokesman announced the withdrawal of its offer of talks with the government saying that the Pakistan military are cooperating with the US on drone strikes by providing ground intelligence to the CIA and warned that TTP will avenge its chief's assassination. With the death of Hakimullah, the TTP shura announced Mullah Fazlullah as its new chief and Sheikh Khalid Haqqani as deputy chief. This is the first time, the TTP shura has appointed its leadership comprised from non-Fata region. 39-year old Fazlullah whose given name is Fazal Hayat hails from Swat in KP and is known as "Radio Mullah. He is presently in Nooristan from where he is directing operations against Pakistan. Similarly his deputy is a resident of Swabi district in KP. As Fazllulah is in Afghanistan, its deputy chief would be its operational head to provide effective leadership to TTP. Announcing this decision, TTP executive shura Asmatullah Shaheen Bhittani while blaming Prime Minister Nawaz Sharif responsible for the death of Hakeemullah, made it clear that it would not negotiate with the government "until it announces the complete enforcement of sharia." He also announced unleashing a wave of revenge attacks against the Sharif government adding,"We will also target the security forces, political leaders, the government installations and police in Punjab."[58]

Like his predecessor, Fazlullah is also hardliner and was involved in many brutal attacks including the failed suicide attack targeting the President of the Awami National Party, Asfandyar Wali Khan in Charsadda in KP on October 2008, the beheading of 17 Pakistan Army soldiers after an attack in June 2012, shooting of Malala Yousuafzai, a school girl in Mingora in October 2012 and the killings of two senior army officers - Major General Sanaullah Khan Niazi, General Officer Commanding (GOC), Swat Division and Lt. Colonel Tauseef in Upper Dir in KP in September 2013. Before Fazlullah fled to Afghanistan following Army operation in Swat in 2009, he had imposed harsh measures by destroying 400 schools, banned polio vaccinations stopped women from going to school, flogged people openly, including women and executed scores of people in public.[59]

From all accounts, Nawaz Sharif cannot afford to succumb to any of the TTP's demands. Taliban has made it clear that it does not recognise the Pakistan constitution. They also say that democracy in Pakistan is un-Islamic. Taliban also know that the government which has emerged out of democratic elections will never concede to its demands. Moreover, meaningful dialogue is only possible with the blessings of armed forces. Army Chief, General Ashfaq Parvez Kayani, said, after the May 2013 elections, that the high turnout—despite Taliban threats—showed that the people had defied the threats of an "insignificant and misguided minority".[60] Before the elections, General Kayani had made it clear that TTP should surrender before any talks, saying that negotiations were "only possible once they unconditionally submit to the state, its constitution and the rule of law".[61]

The death of Hakimullah Mehsud and the subsequent selection of fugitive Taliban Commander Mullah Fazlullah may affect the future scenario not only in Pakistan but in India and Afghanistan also. It is significant that TTP Majlis Shura against its tradition chose its chief and deputy chief from a non-FATA area. It is yet not clear what consideration forced the TTP shura to break this tradition. In the light of above facts, a few presumptions can be made about the future scenario in this region:

(i) It is clear that FATA TTP has surrendered its traditional right to the

Amir-ship to KP. According to Pakistan media reports, Fazlullah has the blessings of Taliban supremo Mulla Omar who reportedly intervened after the TTP Shura could not take a decision for three days following claim by many TTP commanders to head the TTP. The FATA TTP consideration may be: to concentrate on Afghanistan along with Afghan Taliban where the American and Coalition troops are leaving in 2014. If this presumption is correct, it will be a threat to Pakistan's integrity in the coming years. There is every possibility that Taliban will take over power in Afghanistan once the foreign troops leave that country. If that happens, the Pakistan Taliban belonging to FATA may not like to stay in Pakistan.

(ii) Nawaz Sharif's government efforts to have a negotiated peace with Taliban will not be possible with Fazlullah in command of TTP. The Pakistan Army will not be in a mood to forgive him for his role in Swat and then attacks on it from Afghanistan.

(iii) Educated unemployed people from Punjab are increasingly joining the TTP. These young people are influenced by the perpetual anti-India propaganda in Punjab. In other words, they will be injecting anti-India sentiments in the TTP and drag this organization into action in Kashmir and other parts of India.

There are reports that TTP, Punjabi Taliban or its allies may possibly attack Pakistan's nuclear facilities by detonating a small, crude nuclear bomb. Musa Khan Jalazai, the author 'Punjabi Taliban' said that this looks possible as TTP and its allies have already established network with the help of their radical elements in the Pakistan armed forces making them easy to gain access to nuclear facilities. According to him, the possibility of a nuclear attack might be of several types which include, "a commando type attack that might cause widespread dispersal of radioactivity, aircraft crash into an atomic reactor and cyber attack."[62]

NOTES

1. See Mohammad Shehzad, "Brotherhood of Bombs", *The Friday Times*, Vol. XXIV, No. 39, 9–15 November 2012, p. 4
2. See Mohammad Shehzad, "The State of Islamic Radicalism in Pakistan", *Strategic Analysis*, Vol. 37, No. 2, 2013, p. 190.
3. See Animesh Roul, "Taliban and Weapons of Mass Disruption Threat", *CBW Magazine*, Vol. 3, No. 1, January 2010, available at http://www.idsa.in/cbwmagazine/Talibanand WeaponsofMassDisprutionThreat_aroul_0110 (accessed on 15 December 2012).
4. See Benjamin Weiser and Colin Moynihan, "A Guilty Plea in Plot to Bomb Times Square", *The New York Times*, 22 June 2010, available at http://query.nytimes.com/gst/fullpage.html?res=9B05E0DA1030F931A15755C0A9669D8B63 (accessed on 12 August 2012).
5. See the profile of Tehrik-i-Taliban Pakistan, available at http://www.adl.org/NR/exeres/E8CF6B69-8289-43B6-BD56-661B60DD35,DB7611 (accessed on 17 October 2012).

6. See Ali K. Chishti, "To Talk or Not to Talk", *The Friday Times*, Vol. XXIV, No. 52, 8–14 February 2013, p. 2.
7. See Declan Walsh, "Pakistan's Top Taliban Commander Baitullah Killed in US Drone Attack", *The Guardian*, 7 August 2009, available at http://www.guardian.co.uk/world/2009/aug/07/taliban-leader-baitullah-mehsud-killedS (accessed on 15 October 2012).
8. See "Pakistan Taliban Commander Qari Hussain Killed in US Drone Attack", *Daily News and Analyses* (Mumbai, India), 2 January 2011, available at http://www.dnaindia.com/world/report_pakistan-taliban-commander-qari-hussain-killed-in-us-drone-attack_1488967 (accessed on 15 December 2012).
9. See Sailab Mehsud, "Drone Strike Kills Ilyas Kashmiri", *Dawn*, 5 June 2011, available at http://dawn.com/2011/06/05/ilyas-kashmiri-killed-in-us-drone-strike/ (accessed on 15 December 2012).
10. See "Badar Mansoor Eliminated: Pakistan Al Qaeda Chief Killed by US Drone", *The Express Tribune*, 11 February 2012, available at http://tribune.com.pk/story/334355/badar-mansoor-eliminated-pakistan-al-qaeda-chief-killed-by-us-drone/ (accessed on 22 September 2012).
11. Muhammad Amir Rana, Safdar Sial and Abdul Basit, *Dynamics of Taliban Insurgency in FATA*, Islamabad: Pakistan Institute for Peace Studies (PIPS), 2010, pp. 100–01.
12. For details, see "Shura i Muraqaba, an Assessment", Geneva Centre for Training and Analyses of Terrorism, 15 February 2012, available at http://www.gctat.org/fr/analyses-rapports-et-notes/29-ranoc/180-shura-i-muraqaba-an-update.html (accessed on 22 December 2012).
13. Ibid.
14. See "Centralised Taliban Organization Set Up", *Dawn*, 15 December 2007, available at http://archives.dawn.com/2007/12/15/top7.htm (accessed on 22 September 2012).
15. See Muneeb Ansari, "Tehrik-i-Taliban Pakistan: Reaction or Revolution?", available at http://www.academia.edu/803760/Tehrik-i-Taliban_Pakistan_Reaction_or_Revolution7 (accessed on 15 January 2013).
16. See "Taliban chief threatens to dispatch militants to fight India", Times of India, 15 October 2009, available at http://articles.timesofindia.indiatimes.com/2009-10-15/pakistan/28077089_1_taliban-chief-hakimullah-mehsud-drone-attack-pakistani-taliban, (accessed on 22 September 2012)
17. For details, see "Tehrik-e-Taliban Pakistan (TTP)", *Jane's World Insurgency and Terrorism*, available at http://articles.janes.com/articles/Janes-World-Insurgency-and-Terrorism/Tehrik-e-Taliban-, (accessed on 22 January 2013)
18. See "TTP Terms Democracy System of Infidels", *The News*, 8 April 2013, available at http://www.thenews.com.pk/Todays-News-13-22133-TTP-terms-democracy-system-of-infidels (accessed 15 April 2013).
19. For details, see Rahimullah Yusufzai, "A Who's Who of the Insurgency in Pakistan's North-West Frontier Province: Part One—North and South Waziristan", *Terrorism Monitor*, Vol. 6, No. 18, 22 September 2008, available at http://www.jamestown.org/single/?no_cache=1http://centralasiaonline.com/en_GB/articles/caii/features/pakistan/main/2011/01/11/feature-01 (accessed on 12 November 2012).
20. See Rana et al., *Dynamics of Taliban Insurgency in FATA*, p. 100.
21. See "Baitullah Mehsud's First Television Interview", *Al Jazeera*, available at http://www.youtube.com/watch?v=XAjj4XQL2_E, (accessed on 22 January 2013).
22. See Hassan Abbas, "A Profile of Tehrik-i-Taliban Pakistan", *CTC Sentinel*, Vol. 1, No. 2, January 2008, available at http://belfercenter.ksg.harvard.edu/files/CTC%20Sentinel%20-%20Profile%20of%20Tehrik-i-Taliban%20Pakistan.pdf (accessed on 25 April 2013).
23. See Chisti, "To Talk or Not to Talk".
24. See Carolone Wadhams and Colin Cookman, "Faces of Pakistan's Militant Leaders", Centre for American Progress, 22 July 2009, available at http://www.americanprogress.org/issues/

security/news/2009/07/22/6316/faces-of-pakistan (accessed on 2 November 2012).

25. Shehzad, "Brotherhood of Bombs".
26. See Qandeel Siddique, "Tehrik-e-Taliban Pakistan", DIIS Report 2010-12, November 2010, p. 50.
27. See "Pakistani Taliban a Force Multiplier for Al Qaida: US", *Hindustan Times*, 2 September 2010, available at www.hindustantimes.com/world-news/Pakistan/Pakistani-Taliban-a-force-multiplier-for-al-Qaeda-US/A (accessed on 12 April 2013).
28. See Rana et al., *Dynamics of Taliban Insurgency in FATA*, p. 103.
29. See Shahzad Raza, "Stalemate", *The Friday Times*, Vol. XXV, No. 2, 22–28 February 2013, p.2 .
30. See Najam Sethi, "Terrorism: Problems and Solutions", *The Friday Times*, Vol. XXV, No. 2, 22–28 February 2013, available at http://www.thefridaytimes.com/beta3/tft/article.php?issue=20130222&page=1 (accessed on 29 May 2013).
31. Shehzad, "Brotherhood of Bombs".
32. See Javed Mahmood, "TTP, Other Militants Merge", *Central Asia Online*, 11 January 2011, available at http://centralasiaonline.com/en_GB/articles/caii/features/pakistan/main/2011/01/11/feature-01 (accessed on 21 September 2012).
33. See Yusufzai, "A Who's Who of the Insurgency in Pakistan's North-West Frontier Province".
34. See Ansari, "Tehrik-i-Taliban Pakistan: Reaction or Revolution?"
35. Shehzad, "Brotherhood of Bombs".
36. For details, see "Pakistani Taliban's Indoctrinated Child Bombers", *Al Jazeera*, 17 October 2012, available at http://www.aljazeera.com/indepth/opinion/2012/10/20121014102539659862.html (accessed on 16 April 2013).
37. See Syed Irfan Ashraf, "Will They Grow Up to be Militants?", *Dawn*, 2 May 2009, available at http://www.archives.dawn.com/archives/25801 (accessed on 29 December 2012).
38. See Mukhtar A. Khan, "FM Mullahs Spread the Taliban's Word", *Asia Times*, 4 June 2009, available at http://www.atimes.com/atimes/South_Asia/KF04Df02.html (accessed on 15 December 2012). The FM radios are very popular in the tribal areas. According to Pakistan Electronic Media Regulatory Authority (PEMRA), there are about 300 pirated radio stations in the tribal areas which are owned by influential persons.
39. See "Teenage Bombers are Rescued from Taliban Suicide Training Camps: Report", *The Nation*, 27 July 2009, available at http://www.nation.com.pk/pakistan-news-newspaper-daily-english-online/Politics/27-July-2 (accessed on 15 December 2012).
40. See *Al Jazeera*, n.36.
41. See Ansari, "Tehrik-i-Taliban Pakistan: Reaction or Revolution?"
42. See "Taliban's Income All Termed Illegal", Central Asian Online, 16 April 2010, available at http://centralasiaonline.com/en_GB/articles/caii/features/pakistan/2010/04/16/feature-02 (accessed on 12 April 2013).
43. See Siddique, "Tehrik-e-Taliban Pakistan", p. 52.
44. See "Taliban Take Over Swat's Emerald Mines", *Dawn*, 25 March 2009, available at http://archives.dawn.com/archives/123764 (accessed on 2 May 2013).
45. See Asad Kharal, "TTP Plans Kidnappings, Robberies to Generate Funds", *The Express Tribune*, 24 August 2012, available at http://tribune.com.pk/story/425001/ttp-plans-kidnappings-robberies-to-generate-funds/ (accessed on 12 September 2012).
46. Shehzad, "Brotherhood of Bombs".
47. See Ali K. Chishti, "Taliban Gain Strength in Karachi", *The Friday Times*, Vol. XXIV, No. 39, 9–15 November 2012, p. 6.
48. See Eric Schmitt, "Many Sources Feed Taliban's War Chest", *The New York Times*, 19 October 2009, available at http://www.nytimes.com/2009/10/19/world/asia/19taliban.html (accessed on 12 September 2012).

49. See Siddique, n.43.
50. See "TTP Blamed for Karachi Violence", 26 February 2013, available at http://tacstrat.com/content/index.php/2013/02/26/ttp-blamed-for-karachi-violence/ (accessed on 15 April 2013).
51. See "Eleven Pakistani Taliban Militants Arrested in Karachi", *Dawn*, 2 April 2013, available at http://dawn.com/2013/04/02/eleven-pakistani-taliban-militants-arrested-in-karachi/ (accessed on 15 April 2013).
52. See Hassan Abbas, "Defining the Punjabi Taliban Network", *CTC Sentinel*, Vol. 2, No. 4, April 2009, available at http://www.belfercenter.hks.harvard.edu/publication/18978/defining_the_punjabi_taliban_network.html (accessed on 23 November 2012).
53. Raheel Khan, "Untangling the Punjabi Taliban Network", 3 March 2010, available at http://www.ctc.usma.edu/posts/untangling-the-punjabi-taliban-network (accessed on 17 October 2012).
54. See Mujahid Hussain, *Punjabi Taliban—Driving Extremism in Pakistan*, New Delhi: Pentagon Press, 2012, pp. 35–93.
55. Zia ur Rehman, "Punjabi Taliban in Crosshairs of Karachi Officials", *Central Asia Online*, 15 December 2012, available at http://centralasiaonline.com/en_GB/articles/caii/features/pakistan/main/2011/12/15/feature-01 (accessed on 17 July 2012).
56. Khan, "Untangling the Punjabi Taliban Network".
57. See Tahir Khan, "Dialogue offer: Taliban offer ceasefire to new government", *The Express Tribune*, 16 May 2013, available at http://tribune.com.pk/story/550034/dialogue-offer-taliban-offer-ceasefire-to-new-government/, (accessed on 20 September 2013)
58. See Amir Mir, "TTP Fidayeen dispatched to Lahore, PM warned", *The News*, 11 November, 3013, available at http://www.thenews.com.pk/Todays-News-13-26587-TTP-Fidayeen-dispatched-to-Lahore-PM-warned; (accessed on 12 November 2013)
59. See Aoun Sahi and Mark Magnier, "Pakistani Taliban's choice of leader signals an ominous turn", *L A Times*, 10 November 2013, available at http://www.latimes.com/world/la-fg-pakistan-taliban-20131110,1495234,5490165.print.story (accessed on 12 November 2013)
60. See Kamran Yousaf, "Kayani praises nation for defying 'misguided minority", *The Express Tribune*, 21 May 2013, available at http://tribune.com.pk/story/552237/kayani-praises-nation-for-defying-misguided-minority/, (accessed on 20 September 2013)
61. See "Take Taliban talks offer seriously: Sharif to MPs", *The Telegraph*, 21 May 2013, available at http://www.telegraphindia.com/1130521/jsp/foreign/story_16920813.jsp#.UkQGSNJHJBk, (accessed on 20 September 2013)
62. Musa Khan Jalzai, "The prospect of jihad in South Asia", *Daily Times*, 3 October, 2013, available at http://dailytimes.com.pk/default.asp?page+2013/10/03story_3-10-2013_pg3_5, (accessed on 3 Oct 2013).

29

Tehrik-e-Nifaz-e-Shariat-e-Mohammadi
(Movement for the Enforcement of Islamic Law)

Tehrik-e-Nifaz-e-Shariat-e-Mohammadi (TNSM), or the Movement for the Enforcement of Islamic Law, is an extremist group set up by Sufi Mohammad, an active member of Jamaat-e-Islami (JeI) and a cleric, on 28 June 1989 at his native Lal Qila, a small town in the Lower Dir district of Khyber Pakhtunkhwa (KP) province. He had won his jihadi spurs by supporting Gulbuddin Hekmatyr's Hizb-e-Islami (HeI) with men and material during the United States (US)-led Afghan war against the Soviet forces. Sufi Mohammad was influenced by the Wahabi school of Islamic thought and associated himself with Saudi-sponsored groups both during and after his action in the Afghan theatre.

Initially, Sufi Mohammad's goal was to establish rule of Sharia in Pakistan. But he chose to confine TNSM activities to Malakand division comprising the districts of Upper Dir, Lower Dir, Chitral, Swat, Buner, Shangla and Malakand. In 1969, the former princely state of Swat was included in the Malakand division. He came into prominence when he took on the state in 1991. Along with hundreds of his supporters, Sufi laid siege of Temergarh (the district headquarters of Lower Dir) demanding implementation of Sharia.[1] He declared that those opposing Sharia in Pakistan were *wajib-ul-qatl* (worthy of death).

The TNSM leader had strong support from the district administration and this enabled him to mobilise considerable public funds. The provincial government of Pakistan Peoples' Party (PPP) capitulated and fulfilled his wish by promulgating the Sharia Regulation 1994 in November of 1994. The ordinance did not stand the scrutiny of judiciary and it was declared as against the constitution.

Sufi Mohammad and his group re-emerged in 2001 when he sent a few thousand of his cadres to fight with the Taliban against the Western forces.[2] The then President, General Pervez Musharraf, imprisoned him after slapping various criminal charges on him. His ambitious son-in-law, Maulana Fazlullah, took over the TNSM reins and struck a deal with Musharraf, promising to avoid a bloody confrontation in the area. This "good" deed did not last long. In 2002, Pakistan government banned the TNSM under Anti-Terrorism Act. Popularly

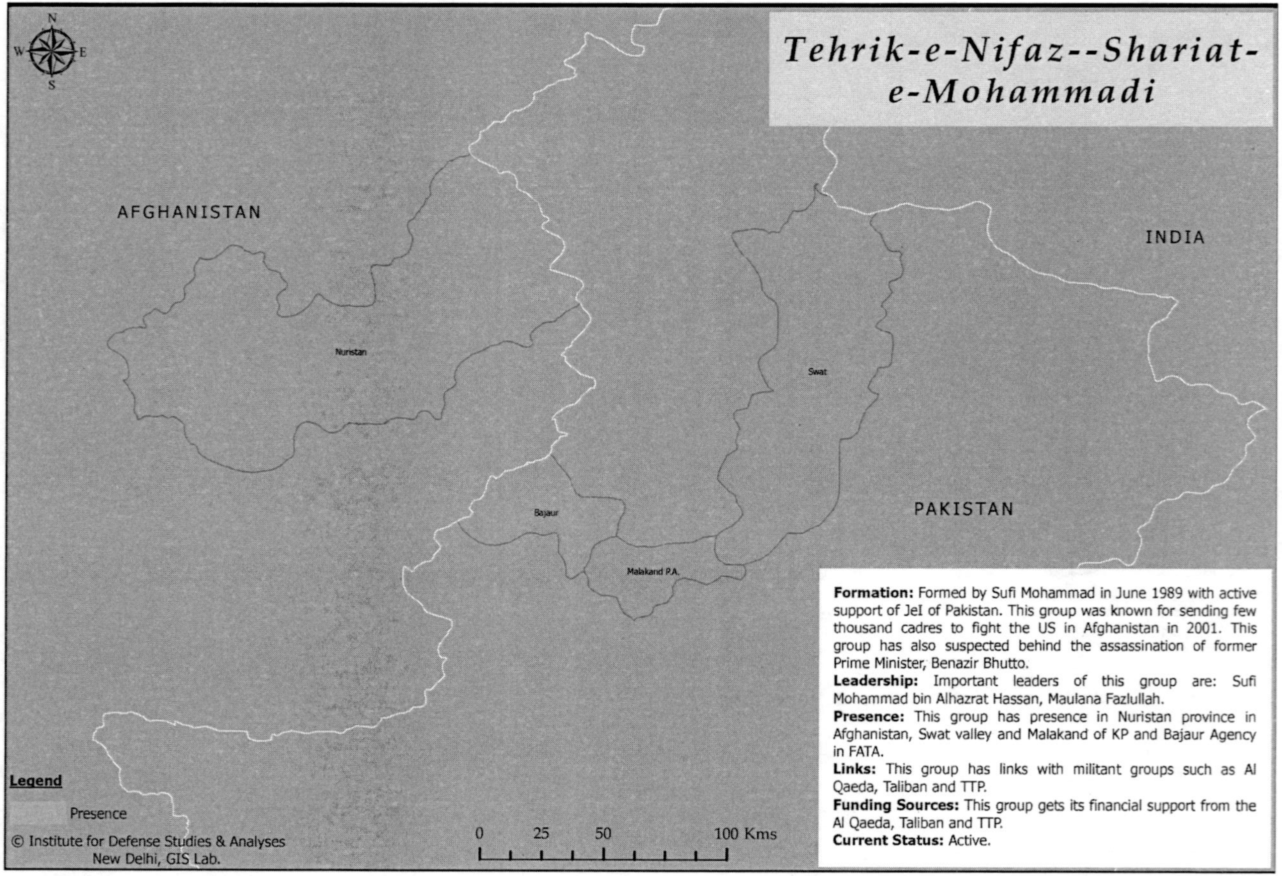
Tehrik-e-Nifaz--Shariat-e-Mohammadi
N
S
E
W
AFGHANISTAN
INDIA
PAKISTAN
Nuristan
Swat
Bajaur
Malakand P.A.
Legend
Presence
0 25 50 100 Kms
© Institute for Defense Studies & Analyses New Delhi, GIS Lab.
Formation: Formed by Sufi Mohammad in June 1989 with active support of JeI of Pakistan. This group was known for sending few thousand cadres to fight the US in Afghanistan in 2001. This group has also suspected behind the assassination of former Prime Minister, Benazir Bhutto.
Leadership: Important leaders of this group are: Sufi Mohammad bin Alhazrat Hassan, Maulana Fazlullah.
Presence: This group has presence in Nuristan province in Afghanistan, Swat valley and Malakand of KP and Bajaur Agency in FATA.
Links: This group has links with militant groups such as Al Qaeda, Taliban and TTP.
Funding Sources: This group gets its financial support from the Al Qaeda, Taliban and TTP.
Current Status: Active.

known as "Mullah Radio", Fazlullah used the pirated FM radio stations to spread his brand of Islamist ideology. The radio became his platform to incite people to attack the security forces.[3] Not only this, he started a campaign opposing polio vaccine and girl's education, and worked to establish a parallel government in parts of Swat.[4]

After lying low for four years, TNSM reared its head once again with its humanitarian work in the aftermath of the October 2005 earthquake in Pakistan-occupied Kashmir (PoK). As relief work progressed, its ranks swelled and so did its resources.

Alarm bells rang in Islamabad when Maulana Fazlullah managed to seize Swat, imposed Sharia and began meting out harsh punishments. Pakistan government used the services of Sufi Mohammad by releasing him from prison, to broker a peace deal between the provincial government and the Taliban in Swat, forcing Pakistan government to promulgate Nizam-i-Adl Regulation 2009[5] with the objective of enforcing Sharia in Malakand. Fazlullah agreed to a ceasefire. Sufi Mohammad took advantage of the weakness of the Pakistan government and demanded that he may be given authority to appoint Qazis (religious judges) for Sharia courts as part of the deal, which he said would be subject to appeal at the civil Peshawar High Court or Supreme Court of Pakistan.[6] On 4 March 2009, the North-West Frontier Province (NWFP; now KP) government gave additional concessions by announcing 17-point plan to enforce Sharia in Swat, which included measures against obscenity and corruption, closing down music shops and expelling prostitutes and pimps from Swat.[7]

As the situation worsened in Swat and nearby areas, the Pakistan Army decided to launch a military offensive that lasted several months. Maulana Fazlullah ran away to Afghanistan. He is today one of the most wanted terrorists of Pakistan.

On 16 February 2009, the Pakistani government announced that it would allow Sharia in the Malakand region. In return, Fazlullah's followers agreed to observe a ceasefire negotiated by Sufi Muhammad. Seven days later, on 24 February, Muslim Khan publicly announced that Swati Taliban would observe an indefinite ceasefire. There were strong reactions to the agreement, largely from the international community. North Atlantic Treaty Organisation (NATO) feared that the agreement would only serve to allow militants to regroup and to create a safe haven for cross-border attacks into Afghanistan.

The fears were not misplaced. In the past few years, the group has managed to regroup in Nuristan province in Afghanistan and has been launching attacks on the security forces in Pakistan, either independently or in collusion with Tehrik-e-Taliban Pakistan (TTP).[8] The TNSM cadres are easily identified by their black turban, and as mentioned earlier, Fazlullah is one of the most wanted terrorists in Pakistan today.

Objectives

The TNSM in its formative years had the following objectives:[9]

1. The implementation of Shariat-e-Mohammadi in Malakand division.
2. The Islamisation of judiciary and judicial procedures.
3. The separation of the judiciary and executive.
4. The establishment of Qazi courts.
5. The availability of free and speedy justice to everyone.
6. The Islamisation of society through judiciary
7. The eradication of un-Islamic laws and practices.
8. The establishment of a true Islamic society.

The group adopted a three-point strategy to achieve its objectives. These are: *itifaq* (unite the people); *bara't* (boycott and oppose all un-Islamic systems and institutions); and jihad (physical or financial war).

Organisation

The TNSM's organisational structure took shape in 1994 with the launch of its campaign against the state in Malakand. The main headquarters was established at Amandara in Malakand where a council of clerics and council of tribals were formed. The two councils backed its plans of instituting a Sharia-based legal system and enforcing a moral and social code of Islamic behaviour. District-level offices were created in each of the districts in KP. The members of district units were selected locally but appointed to the job with the approval of amir (the central leader). The district was subdivided into *tehsil* and mohalla units,[10] which clearly meant that he TNSM leadership was keen on spreading the outfit to the grassroots level. The functions of each unit were clearly spelt out. Following this, Maulana Fazlullah set up a Sharia court in his native village, Imam Dheri, and on 9 October 2006, formed Shaheen Commandos, a volunteer force, to control law and order and traffic problems in Matta *tehsil* of Swat district.[11]

Leadership

Sufi Mohammad bin Alhazrat Hassan remains the amir of TNSM but for all practical purposes, it is his son-in-law, Maulana Fazlullah, who is running the group today. Sufi Mohammad was a member of JeI for long, till he decided to form his own group. He was active during the Afghan jihad, helping HeI and other groups to fight against the Northern Alliance. After this jihad ended, he returned to Malakand to set up TNSM and launched an armed agitation to impose Sharia in the region. He was first arrested in 2002 and remained in jail till 2008, when he agreed for peace talks with the government. He was locked up again in 2009, and has been charged with sedition, conspiracy and aiding terrorism.

Maulana Fazlullah is, in effect, the leader of TNSM at present. He is operating out of Afghanistan and has vowed to take revenge on Pakistan Army for pushing him out of Swat in 2009. Fazlullah is known as the "FM Radio Mullah" for the illegal radio stations he used to run to propagate Sharia and spew venom against Pakistan Army.

In October 2007, the Maulana declared Swat as his emirate and began his rule of the district with the help of his 4,500-strong armed cadre. He was pushed out by the army subsequently. Fazlullah has been trying hard to return to Swat. He, today, operates out of Nuristan province in Afghanistan, where, media reports say, he effectively controls a 20 sq km area.

There are reports that Maulana Fazlullah had aligned with the TTP. It is also said that he was behind the assassination of former Prime Minister, Benazir Bhutto.

Maulana Faqir Mohammad is a confidant of Sufi Mohammad and had been his right-hand man during the early years of TNSM. It was Sufi Mohammad who trained and introduced Faqir Mohammad to jihad and sent him to Afghanistan. He comes from Bajaur Agency and belongs to the Mohmand tribe. His two sons, Maulvi Mohammad Karim and Maulvi Jan Mohammad, are members of TNSM and have had a stint in Afghanistan. They were arrested when they returned home after the fall of the Taliban in 2001. Both are languishing in a Dera Ismail Khan jail. Maulana Mohammad is an expert in small arms, rocket launchers and anti-aircraft weapons. He is known to be a facilitator for Al Qaeda and Taliban elements sheltered in the tribal areas and KP. He is wanted by the police.

Maulana Liaqatullah Hussain, another key TNSM leader, was killed in an aerial bombing of his madrassa in Bajaur in October 2006. He was targeted on information that he was sheltering some key leaders of Al Qaeda, including Ayman al-Zawahiri. A revenge attack in November 2006, carried out by a suicide bomber, killed 42 Pakistani soldiers in Dargai, about 100 km short off Islamabad. Hussain was deputy to Maulana Mohammad.

Cadre Strength/Camps/Area of Operation

The TNSM's traditional operational space was Malakand division in KP and Bajaur Agency in Federally Administered Tribal Areas (FATA), where it ran camps to train its volunteers.[12] Its cadre strength, before the Pakistan Army started operation against them, was approximately 5,000. After 2001, the group consolidated its control over Swat till it was forced out by the military when it launched Operation Rah-e-Rast in the region. The operation continued for four months during which TNSM lost many of its cadres. The army also got a major success by arresting TNSM chief, Sufi Muhammad, TTP Swat chapter spokesman, Muslim Khan, and head of beheading squad, Sher Qasib, who later succumbed to his injuries in military hospital.[13] The TNSM chief, Maulana

Fazlullah, today operates in the Nuristan province in Afghanistan. His alignment with TTP gives his group operational and training leverage in the tribal areas, especially in North Waziristan. In recent days, the group has made efforts to regain control or influence in Swat but not with much success. The sporadic attacks in Swat and Buner by some TNSM militants who still remain in the area are an indication of the group's efforts to recapture its past glory.

Funding Sources

The TNSM depends largely on drugs and extortion for running its operations. The TTP also supports Fazlullah's group financially.[14] There is speculation that both TNSM and Fazlullah have had support from Al Qaeda and the Taliban for facilitating safe transit and custody.

Weapons

The group has in its possession, different types of Kalashnikovs, rocket launchers, hand grenades, swords and improvised explosive devices (IEDs).

Current Status

The TNSM, based in Malakand, does not pose any significant threat to Pakistan or any other country. It is today much weakened and relies on local support to sustain its operations and campaign for Sharia. With the arrest of Sufi Mohammad, most of TNSM militants have gone underground. Its headquarters have also a deserted look and most of the cadres have stopped wearing the characteristic black turban and cut their hair short.[15] However, Fazlullah poses a serious threat to Pakistan and Afghanistan. Fazlullah's association with TTP and other terrorist groups operating in Afghanistan and Pakistan presents a major challenge for the Pakistan Army.

NOTES

1. See Hassan Abbas, "The Black-turbaned Brigade: The Rise of TNSM in Pakistan", *Terrorism Monitor*, Vol. 4, No. 23, 30 November 2006, pp. 1–4.
2. See Anwarullah and Haleem Asad, "TNSM Supporters Head for Kabul', *Dawn*, 28 October 2001, available at http://archives.dawn.com/2001/10/28/top6.htm (accessed on 15 September 2012).
3. See Arif Jamal, "Islamist Militants of the TNSM Plan Return to Pakistan's Swat Valley", *Terrorism Monitor*, Vol. 9, No. 3, 20 January 2011, pp 4–5.
4. See Caroline Wadhams and Colin Cookman, "Faces of Pakistan's Militant Leaders", Center for American Progress, 22 July 2009, available at http://www.americanprogress.org/issues/security/news/2009/07/22/6316/faces-of-pakistans-militant-leaders/ (accessed on 2 November 2012).
5. See Noor ul Haq, "Swat Peace Accord", Islamabad Policy Research Institute, April 2009, available at http://www.ipripak.org/factfiles/ff109.pdf (accessed on 25 May 2013).
6. Wadhams and Cookman, "Faces of Pakistan's Militant Leaders".

7. See "Pakistan: The Militant Jihadi Challenge", International Crisis Group, Asia Report No. 164, 13 March 2009, p. 14.
8. See Anne Stenersen, "Al-Qaeda's Allies", New America Foundation, April 2010, available http://www.newamerica.net/publications/policy/al_qaeda_s_allies, (accessed on 15 September 2013)
9. See "TNSM Demands Sharia", *Daily Times*, 24 April 2007, available at http://www.dailytimes.com.pk/default.asp?page=2007%5C10%5C07%5Cstory_7-10-2007_pg7_2 (accessed on 15 September 2012).
10. See Fazal-ur-Rahim Khan Marwat and Parvez Khan Toru, *Talibanization of Pakistan: A Case Study of TNSM*, Peshawar: Pakistan Study Centre, University of Peshawar, 2005.
11. See Muhammad Amir Rana, Safdar Sial and Abdul Basit, *Dynamics of Islamic Insurgency*, Islamabad: Pakistan Institute for Peace Studies (PIPS), 2010, p. 104.
12 See B. Raman, "TNSM's Jihadi Shadow over London", *International Terrorism Monitor*, South Asia Analysis Group, Paper No. 232, 11 May 2007.
13. See Rana et al., *Dynamics of Islamic Insurgency*, p. 107.
14. See Abbas, "The Black-turbaned Brigade".
15. See Manzoor Ali Shah, "TNSM a Thing in the Past, Analysts Argue", *The Express Tribune*, 12 June 2010, available at http://tribune.com.pk/story/20623/tnsm-a-thing-of-the-past-analysts-argue/ (accessed on 15 October 2012).

30

Lashkar-e-Islam
(Army of Islam)

History/Genesis

Lashkar-e-Islam (LeI) is a Deobandi group based in Khyber Agency of Federally Administered Tribal Area (FATA) in Pakistan. Khyber is strategically located as it borders Peshawar as also Nangarhar province in Afghanistan. The valley is hotbed of militancy from where the Al Qaeda militants escaped into Pakistan after the United States (US)-led intervention in Afghanistan in 2001. It was set up in 2004 by Mufti Munir Shakir, a local Deobandi cleric, with an aim to fight criminals. Gradually, the group followed a formula, somewhat similar to that of the Taliban, and took initiatives to punish those who did not offer *namaz*, forced closure of shops and markets during prayer time and punished those found involved in "immoral activities". Alarmed by the growing popularity of Mufti Shakir with these steps, Pir Saif-ur-Rahman, a Barelvi cleric who headed Ansar-ul-Islam (AuI), challenged his authority. Private local radio stations were set up by both groups to propagate their vices amongst local population. This led to violence between these groups. Later, Mangal Bagh, who happened to be a student of Mufti Shakir and belonged to Afridi tribe, took over the reins of LeI. The LeI became an organised militant group under the leadership Mangal Bagh, a former bus driver. He imposed a strict moral code and carried out public executions which created a wave of terror among the local population of Khyber Agency. Pakistan government banned the LeI in 2007, but it continued to operate as Bagh had established links with Pakistani military and intelligence services by forming the Muqami Tehrik-e-Taliban (Local Taliban Movement). This group was formed together with Haji Namdar, head of the Tanzim Amir bil Maroof wa Nehi Anil Munkir (Suppression of Vice and Suppression of Virtue), and Hafiz Gul Bahadur to resist the Tehrik-e-Taliban Pakistan (TTP) and the founder of TTP, Baitullah Mehsud.

Objectives/Agenda

The main aims of the LeI are: to implement Sharia in the Khyber Agency;

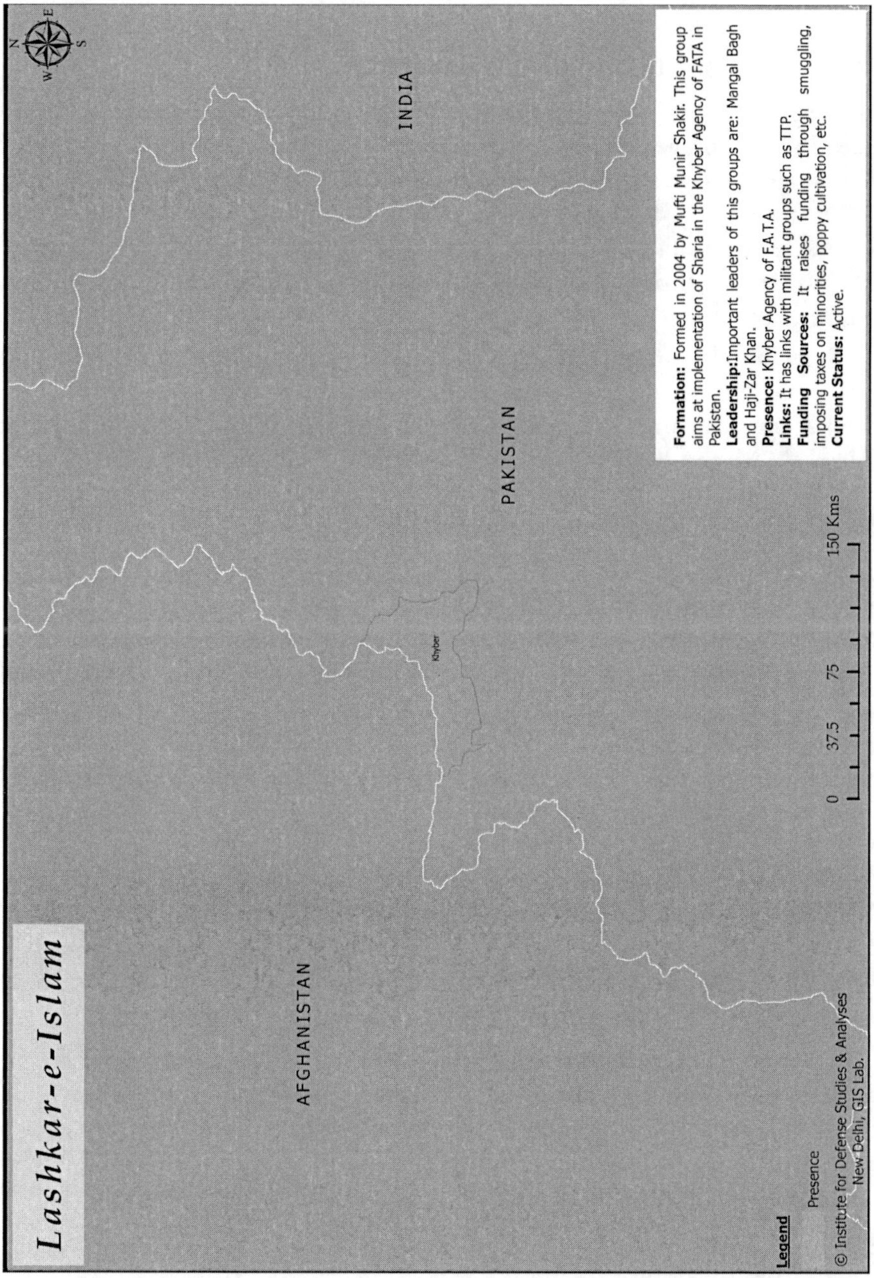
Lashkar-e-Islam
TAJIKISTAN
AFGHANISTAN
PAKISTAN
INDIA
Khyber
N
E
S
W
0 37.5 75 150 Kms
Legend
Presence
© Institute for Defense Studies & Analyses
New Delhi, GIS Lab.
Formation: Formed in 2004 by Mufti Munir Shakir. This group aims at implementation of Sharia in the Khyber Agency of FATA in Pakistan.
Leadership:Important leaders of this groups are: Mangal Bagh and Haji-Zar Khan.
Presence: Khyber Agency of F.A.T.A.
Links: It has links with militant groups such as TTP.
Funding Sources: It raises funding through smuggling, imposing taxes on minorities, poppy cultivation, etc.
Current Status: Active.

eliminate "social vices" from the society; and justify use of force for religious ends.

Organisational Structure and Leadership

The organisation of the LeI is headed by the shura (supreme body). This body takes decisions on important matters and makes appointments for heads of various departments such as administration, fatwa, finance and military. The group is headed by Mangal Bagh who is more violent than Mufti Shakir and who stepped up attacks on AuI and even engaged in clashes against Pakistan Frontier Corps after its personnel destroyed LeI headquarters in Bara which is a subdistrict of Khyber Agency.

It has about 18 commanders who have been assigned their area of operation. Prominent commanders with their areas of operation include: Safoor Afridi (Naray Baba Ziarat), Rehmat Shah (Shah Dheri), Mutabar Khan (Galooch), Qandhar (Akakhel), Misre-i-Khan (Akakhel), Dr Akhhtiar (Malikdinkhel) and Mohammad Hussain (Sholabar). Besides this, Maulana Siraj heads the fatwa wing, while Haji Zar Afridi is the spokesman of the group.[1]

Cadre Strength/Recruitment/Camps

While Mangal claims that LeI has 10,000 men at arms, another report estimates its strength to be around 5,000. According to one report, both the groups—LeI and AuI—run competing Sharia courts and have engaged in violent intra-sect conflict, with hundreds of followers of both groups killed since 2006.[2] It was made compulsory for each local family to enrol at least one member to join LeI in its war against AuI in the remote Tirah Valley.[3] Reportedly, LeI pays recruits a monthly salary and also offers free meals as an incentive for them joining the group. The LeI's headquarter is located in Bara. It has also operational bases at Akakhel, Nala-Malikdinkheland Shalobar areas of Bara.

Area of Operation/Network

According to reports, until 2008, Mangal Bagh portrayed LeI as a religious, reformist social organisation against vices in the Bara area. It was able to spread its network in Peshawar also, where it forced shopkeepers to shut down music shops and was even involved in targeting minorities. In June 2008, it kidnapped a group of 16 Christians from Peshawar who were subsequently released following negotiations with local administration.[4] There was also a report that the group was linked to a suicide attack on the US Consulate in Peshawar in April 2010.[5] The Pakistan security forces launched four operations against the Mangal Bagh forces in July 2008, September 2009, March 2010 and October 2010. Before the launch of September 2009 operation, Mangal Bagh militants were in control of almost all of Khyber Agency, except parts of Jamrud *tehsil* and a 2 km stretch in Maidan area of Tirah Valley. There are also reports that some militants have taken refuge in Sipah, Tirah Valley. In its efforts to crush the militancy in the Khyber Agency, the government also announced a reward for information leading to the capture of Mangal Bagh.[6] As Tirah Valley has become hotbed of militancy, where TTP militants are also entrenched, Pakistan security forces launched an operation again in April 2013.

Alliances

Since Amar-bil-Maroof wa Nahi-Anil-Munkar (Promotion of Virtue and Prevention of Vice or PVPV) considered AuI its ideological enemy, it sided with the LeI to counter its influence in the Khyber Agency. While the group has sympathised with the mission of TTP, they deny affiliation with the larger terrorist group.

Finance/Funding

The main source of income is fines recovered from the people who stay away from the *siraat-e-mustakeen* or the path of righteousness. Heavy penalties are imposed on the people who do not cover their head with a cap or those who drink liquor.[7] According to another report, the group is also engaged in raising funds by levying taxes on vehicles plying through Khyber or by smuggling goods. Another source is protection money which is being collected from embattled minorities groups, including Sikhs.[8] The group also makes money from narcotic drugs as the Tirah Valley, where it has partial control, is famous for poppy cultivation.[9]

Weapons

The group is possession of machine guns, rocket-propelled grenades, mortars and improvised explosive devices (IEDs). The PVPV, with which it has an alliance, also supplies weapons, ammunition and other support to LeI.

Current Status

The situation is tense in Tarah Valley in Khyber Agency where the Pakistan security forces launched an operation against LeI militants (who have sneaked into the valley following military operations), as also TTP which captured the area dominated by Kuki Khel and AuI, in May 2012 and March 2013. While the army launched a ground offensive against the LeI, Pakistan Airforce fighters conducted several sorties over the area under the control of the TTP. Still, the valley has not been cleared of the militants. If the security forces, jet fighters and helicopter gunship continue to pound militants' positions, the militants are likely to sneak into the other tribal regions near the Afghan border. It may be mentioned that the Pakistan Army made an unsuccessful attempt to curb infiltration of Al

Qaeda militants into Pakistan after the Tora Bora debacle in 2002. Meanwhile, TTP has denied a report published in the Pakistan media that Mangal Bagh has become the supreme leader of both LeI and TTP for the tribal region of Khyber. Reacting to reports, TTP spokesperson, Ehsanullah Ehsan, said that that TTP had "cordial relations" with LeI and the group as a whole, but refuted report that decision to elevate Mangal Dam was taken at a joint shura of the Taliban and LeI commanders.[10]

NOTES

1. Muhammad Amir Rana, Safda Sial and Abdul Bist, "*Dynamics of Taliban Insurgency in FATA*" Pakistan Institute of Peace Studies (PIPS), Islamabad, 2010, p. 108.
2. See " Pakistan: The Militant Jihad Challenge", Asia Report No. 164, International Crisis Group, 13 March 2009, available at http://www.crisisgroup.org/~/media/Files/asia/south-asia/pakistan/164_pakistan___the_militant_jihadi_challenge (accessed on 20 October 2012).
3. *The News*, 21 July 2008, cited in Rana et al., "*Dynamics of Taliban Insurgency in FATA*" Islamabad: PIPS, 2010, p. 109.
4. Zahid Hussain, "Are We Losing the War against Militancy", *Newsline*, 15 July 2008, available at http://www.newslinemagazine.com/2008/07/are-we-losing-the-war-against-militancy/ (accessed on 21 September 2012).
5. See Syed Manzar Abbas Zaidi, "The Role of Lashkar-e-Islam in Pakistan's Khyber Agency, Combating Terrorism Center at West Point", 1 October 2010, available at http://www.ctc.usma.edu/posts/the-role-of-lashkar-i-islam-in-pakistan%E2%80%99s-khyber-agency (accessed on 12 August 2012).
6. Rana et al., "*Dynamics of Taliban Insurgency in FATA*" p. 111.
7. Ibid., p. 109.
8. Zaidi, "The Role of Lashkar-e-Islam in Pakistan's Khyber Agency".
9. See Ibrahim Shinwari, "Mangal Bagh becomes LI, Taliban Supremo in Khyber", *Dawn*, 10 April 2013, available at http://dawn.com/2013/04/10/mangal-bagh-becomes-Li-taliban-supremo-in-khyber/ (accessed on 20 April 2013).
10. See "TTP Denies Mangal Bagh Appointed Khyber Militant Chief", *TheDawn*, 11 April 2013, available at http://dawn.com/2013/04/11/ttp-denies-mangal-bagh-appointed-khyber-militant-chief/ (accessed on 20 April 2013).

31

Lashkar-e-Omar
(Army of Omar)

Introduction/History

The Lashkar-e-Omar (LeO) as a militant outfit first came to notice when it sent messages to newspapers in Islamabad and Rawalpindi declaring Pakistan a theocratic state (*darul mukaffar*), and also that jihad against President Parvez Musharraf was the foremost duty of each Muslim. Its name surfaced again on 28 October 2001, when it claimed responsibility for the attack on Catholic Church in Bahawalpur killing 16 Christians and one Muslim. The message said, "We accept the challenge of the crusade declared by the American President, George W. Bush. This is our first fight to Bush. If he does not stop raids in Afghanistan, we will continue to do this."[1] On 17 March 2002, the outfit was suspected to have carried out another attack at a church in Islamabad in which five people, including wife of a United States' (US) diplomat in Pakistan and daughter, were killed. However, the origin of LeO is not clear. According to one report, it is named after Mullah Mohammad Omar, Taliban supremo, and consists of the dregs of Taliban, Al Qaeda and Pakistani jihadi outfits allied with Osama bin Laden's International Islamic Front who crossed over into Pakistan. According to some other reports, it is named after Saeed Ahmed Omar Sheikh and consists of hand-picked cadres of Harkat-ul-Jihad-e-Islami (HuJI), Jaish-e-Mohammad (JeM) and Lashkar-e-Jhangvi (LeJ).[2] According to one source,[3] in addition to these outfits, the coalition also includes several like-minded freelance terrorists.

Objectives/Agenda

The LeO vehemently opposes the Western culture. It aims at targeting the Western interests, establishments, the Christians and what they call, American campaign against the Muslims across the world. This was evident from an attack that was plotted by the LeO on the US Consulate in June 2002, killing 11 people and injuring 45. The statement by the LeO followed the attack, which said, "America, its allies and its slave Pakistani rulers should be prepared for more attacks".[4]

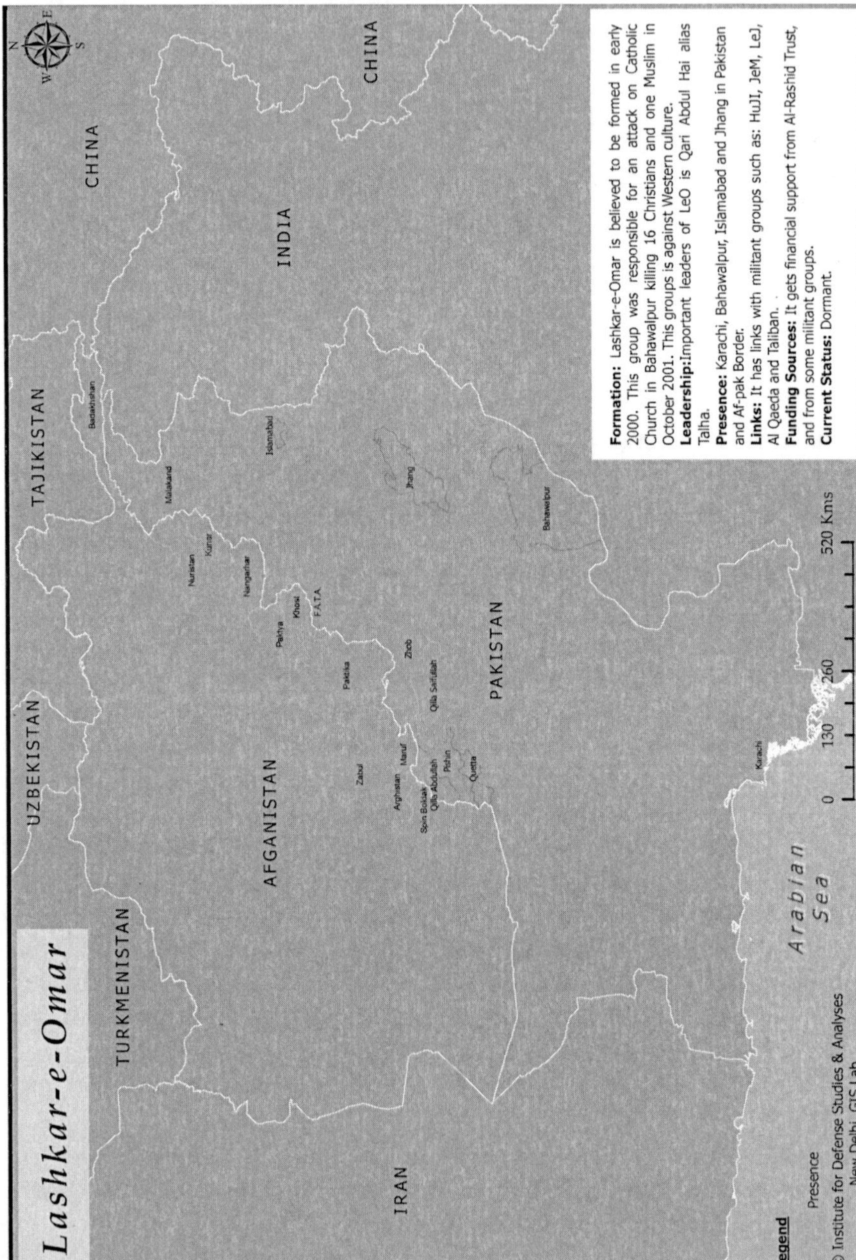
Lashkar-e-Omar
TURKMENISTAN
UZBEKISTAN
TAJIKISTAN
CHINA
CHINA
INDIA
AFGANISTAN
PAKISTAN
IRAN
Arabian Sea
Badakhshan
Malakand
Islamabad
Nuristan
Kunar
Nangarhar
Paktya
Khosi
FATA
Paktika
Zhob
Qilla Saifullah
Zabul
Maruf
Arghistan
Spin Boldak
Qilla Abdullah
Pishin
Quetta
Jhang
Bahawalpur
Karachi
0 130 260 520 Kms
Formation: Lashkar-e-Omar is believed to be formed in early 2000. This group was responsible for an attack on Catholic Church in Bahawalpur killing 16 Christians and one Muslim in October 2001. This groups is against Western culture.
Leadership:Important leaders of LeO is Qari Abdul Hai alias Talha.
Presence: Karachi, Bahawalpur, Islamabad and Jhang in Pakistan and Af-pak Border.
Links: It has links with militant groups such as: HuJI, JeM, LeJ, Al Qaeda and Taliban.
Funding Sources: It gets financial support from Al-Rashid Trust, and from some militant groups.
Current Status: Dormant.
Legend
Presence
© Institute for Defense Studies & Analyses New Delhi, GIS Lab.

Cadre Strength, Profile and Training

It is difficult to estimate the exact strength of the outfit as LeO is primarily a convenient cover adopted by JeM, HuJI and LeJ to avoid scrutiny and prosecution. Majority of its members are of the same class—extremist in religious orientation, with criminal background—and have been trained by Amjad Faruqui and Omar Sheikh in Afghanistan. Currently, this group is headed by Qari Abdul Hai alias Talha, who is also the chief of LeJ's Majlis al-Shura.

Area of Operation and Influence

The outfit had been operating in Afghanistan and Pakistan. Its operational base is in Karachi. It also has its network in Bahawalpur, Jhang and Islamabad.

Alliance/Funding

Besides being the front for JeM, LeJ and HuJI, LeO is closely associated with Al Qaeda and Taliban. It is getting funds from the Karachi-based Al-Rashid Trust and parent organisations. According to one source Al-Rashid Trust first came into limelight when it was banned by the US in the wake of 9/11, with the Pakistan government subsequently followed suit, as it was allegedly financing and supporting international jihadi organisations. It is worth noting that Daniel Pearl's body was found near the trust's compound, off the super highway in Ahsanabad area in Karachi's Gulzar-e-Hijri Scheme 33.[5]

Current Status

No major militant activities by the LeO have been reported for last few years. The outfit, as mentioned earlier, is a convenient camouflage for the organisations like the HuJI, LeJ and JeM. Though the group seems to be silent these days, the possibility of being used by the above-mentioned outfits cannot be ruled out.

NOTES

1. See Muhammad Amir Rana, *Gateway to Terrorism*, London: New Millennium Publication, 2003, p. 291.
2. For details, see B. Raman, "Kaluchak and After", available at http://www.rediff.co.in/news/2002/may/17guest.htm (accessed on 15 October 2012).
3. Available at www.start.umd.edu.
4. See Anton La Guardia, "Karachi car bomb kills 11 outside US consulate", The Telegraph, 15 June 2002, available at http://www.telegraph.co.uk/news/worldnews/asia/india/1397397/Karachi-car-bomb-kills-11-outside-US-consulate.html (accessed on 15 October 2012).
5. For details see Mubashir Zaidi, "Second Wave", The Herald, Vol.33, No.6, June 2002, pp. 32-33.

32

United Jihad Council
(Muttahida Jihad Council)

The United Jihad Council (UJC) is an umbrella organisation of some 16 jihadi outfits engaged in terrorist activities in Jammu and Kashmir (J&K). In the early 1990s, a number of terrorist outfits mushroomed in the state with the active support of Pakistan's intelligence agency, Inter Services Intelligence (ISI). In its efforts to ensure complete control on their jihadi activities, Pakistan created an alliance of 13 leading jihadi outfits called the Muttahida Jihad Council (MJC) in November 1994 under Commander Manzur Shah, leader of the Jamaat-ul-Mujahideen.[1] By 1999, three Pakistan-based outfits—Lashkar-e-Taiba (LeT), Jaish-e-Mohammad (JeM) and Al Badr—were also roped in, taking the total number to 16. According to one media report, the Jammu and Kashmir Liberation Front (JKLF), Yasin group, left the UJC in April 2004 accusing its chief, Syed Salahuddin, of preparing to announce an unconditional ceasefire in J&K.[2]

Following is the list of the jihadi outfits who are members of the UJC: Hizb-ul-Mujahideen (HM), JKLF, Harkat-ul-Ansar, Tehrik-e-Jihad, Tehrik-ul-Mujahideen, Jamaat-ul-Mujahideen, Al Jihad, Al Umar Mujahideen, Jammu Kashmir Islamic Front, Muslim Janbaz Force, Hizbullah, Al Fatah, Hizb-ul-Momineen, LeT, JeM and Al Badr Mujahideen.

At a meeting in October 2003, the MJC was restructured into two groups which represented various outfits that would no longer use the words jihad, lashkar, jaish or mujahideen as part of their names, and thus appear political rather than militant. However, the exception was HM as it was the main group.[3] The two groups are known as Kashmir Resistance Forum (KRF) and Kashmir Freedom Forum (KFF).

Objectives

The UJC stands for merger of J&K with Pakistan. Its commander, Manzur Shah, declared in 1994 that the sole objective of the escalating jihad in Kashmir was to incorporate it into Pakistan, adding that "all Kashmir militant organisations have announced that Pakistan is their ideal end goal...the freedom fighters will surrender (Kashmir) to the Pakistani military and government". He added: "Jihad has been getting stronger...the Mujahideens are getting organised now and attacking the Indian military strategically".[4]

In an interview with Baba Umar of *Tehlka*, the UJC chairman, Syed Salahuddin, said that he formally believed that it is in the interest of the subcontinent that Kashmir goes to Pakistan as he felt that majority of the people suggest this stance.[5] The UJC also aims to bring unity among all the constituents of the conglomerate, plan a collective military strategy and formulate a common stand on national and international issues.[6]

Leadership

The first chairman of the UJC was Azam Inqilabi who is now the chief patron of J&K Mahaz-e-Azadi. He proved to be ineffective in handling the activities of the outfit. He was replaced by Tanvir-ul-Islam, who headed the organisation till 1995. In December 1995, a meeting of all the outfits was called, which elected Syed Salahuddin, the supreme commander of HM, as chairman. The meeting also elected Sheikh Jamil-ur-Rehmanof Tehrik-ul-Mujahideen as general secretary and Liaquat al-Azhari of Lashkar-e-Islam as deputy chairman.

Other prominent office bearers are: Mohammad Usman, amir of Muslim Janbaz Force; Mohammad Ashfaq, amir of Harkat-ul-Mujahideen (HuM, PoK); Jan Mohammad, amir of Harkat-ul-Jihad-al-Islami, PoK; and Suja Abbas, amir of Hizb-ul-Momineen. The spokesman of the MJC is Ehsan Elhai, a senior functionary of the HM.

At times, MJC has witnessed disagreements and confusions over the leadership issue. In fact, it suffered a big setback when its main constituent, HM, declared ceasefire in Kashmir on 24 July 2000 that was initially endorsed by Syed Salahuddin. Following this, the MJC leadership unanimously expelled the HM from the alliance and dismissed Salahuddin as its chief. Mohammad Usman, amir of Muslim Janbaz Force, was made the chief. Salahuddin withdrew support to ceasefire under pressure from UJC. Announcing this, he said that he kept this condition that the ceasefire will remain if India calls back its troops from Kashmir, continues trilateral talks and accepts Kashmir dispute.

Interestingly, MJC chief also revealed that Pakistan-origin United States (US) citizen, Mansoor Ijaz, who was involved in the memo controversy, had offered an economic package to MJC over ceasefire in Kashmir.[7]

Salahuddin has been regularly organising conferences, media meets and issuing press releases, wherein he has been raising the issue of self-determination, asking India to vacate Kashmir and declaring, "if India accepts the reality of the Kashmir issue there will be no need for an armed struggle, but if India continues to use its military against the people of Kashmir there will be no alternative to the gun".[8] He even claimed that jihad has entered the final stage in "Indian held Kashmir" which would soon be freed.

Salahuddin vehemently criticised former President Pervez Musharraf's offer for the resolution of India–Pakistan dispute. For him, it was a "unilateral concession" and he averred that the people of Kashmir cannot compromise on their right to self-determination.

Area of Operation

The headquarters of the MJC are located at Muzaffarabad (PoK). Since the prime objective of all the 16 groups is to liberate Kashmir from India, the area of operation of the MJC is mainly Kashmir.

Network and Alliances

The MJC was created by the ISI to have tight grip on its constituents as some of them became difficult to handle. Besides its members from J&K and Pakistan, there is a report that the United Liberation Front of Asom (ULFA) has taken up formal membership with MJC. It is suspected that such an alliance between the ULFA and the MJC might have been done by the director general of field intelligence (DGFI) of Bangladesh.[9]

It has also been reported that the UJC has links with the underworld criminal groups like Don Dawood Ibrahim.

Infrastructure

Under the leadership of Syed Salahuddin, the MJC has played the role of an instructor. Although it did not have its own armed men, it prepared a secret "war strategic plan" in case of threat on borders. All jihadi outfits operating in Kashmir were asked to deposit maps and battle plans seized from Indian Army camps to prepare counter action plan. Accordingly, 35 hit squads were set up for emergency duty.[10]

Four constituents of the UJC played an active part in the Kargil war. Militants belonging to LeT, HuM, Al Badr and Teherik-e-Jihad said the guerrillas will not leave the area because it their homeland.

Finance and Funding

The ISI is believed to be the major financer for UJC. It is for this reason that it has gained considerable support from official state machinery. Funds are also collected from donors in Punjab and PoK.

Current Status

Recently, the UJC chief has created fear in Kashmir by issuing threats to thousands of *panch*s and *sarpanche*s that "militants would kill sarpanchas and panchs as they are being used as tools by Indian agencies".[11] Earlier, he had called for limiting the number of pilgrims on the annual Amarnath Yatra. He alleged that "increasing number of Amarnath Yatris, setting up permanent Yatra infrastructure and increasing interference of non-local laborers in private and public sector is an indication of the governments plan to change the Muslim character of the J&K state".[12]

Like other militant outfits, the UJC has also opposed Pakistan's move to grant Most Favoured Nation (MFN) status to India. In this connection, Salahuddin joined a rally organised by various jihadi groups in Islamabad on 29 December 2011. The UJC, led by Syed Salahuddin, continues to operate as one of the most anti-India forums with an aim to liberate Kashmir from India. Media reports indicate that the UJC/MJC was involved in the Hyderabad blasts in February 2013.

NOTES

1. See Yossef Bodansky, "Pakistan, Kashmir and the Trans-Asian Axis", available at http://www. Kanshmir-information.com/Bodansky/Bodansky4.html (accessed on 10 September 2012).
2. See "JKLF leaves Jihad Council", *Daily Times*, 22 April 2004, available at http://www.dailytimes.com.pk/default.asp?page=story_22-4-2004_pg7_47 (accessed on 10 September 2012).
3. See Muhammad Amir Rana, *The Seeds of Terrorism*, London: New Millennium Publication, 2005, p. 304.
4. See Bodansky, "Pakistan, Kashmir and the Trans-Asian Axis".
5. See Baba Umar, "We aren't Fighting from Pakistan, We are Fighting from Liberated Kashmir", *Tehelka*, 11 February 2012, available at http://www.tehelka.com/story_main49.asp?filename=Ne020411We_are.asp (accessed on 10 September 2012).
6. See Muhammad Amir Rana, *Gateway to Terrorism*, London: New Millennium, 2003, p. 545.
7. See "Mansoor Ijaz Offered Package to MJC over Ceasefire in Occupied Kashmir: Salahuddin", available at http://www.kashmirglobal.com/2011/11/27/mansoor-ijaz-offered-package-to-mjc-over-ceasefire-in-occupied-kashmir-salahuddin.html (accessed on 10 September 2012).
8. See "United Jihad Council Chairman Says Dialogue is Useless, Armed Struggle will Continue", available at http://www.thefortress.com.pk/dialogue-is-useless-armed-struggle-will-continue-united-jihad-council/ (accessed on 10 September 2012).
9. See Sultan Shahin, "A New Dimension in India's Northeast Woes", *Asia Times*, 23 October 2004, available at http://www.atimes.com/atimes/South_Asia/Fj23Df02.html (accessed on 10 September 2012).
10. See Rana, *Gateway to Terrorism*, pp. 545–46.
11. See "Threat Divides Panchas, Sarpanchas", available at http://www.greaterkashmir.com/news/2012/Nov/6/threat-divides-panchs-sarpanchs-48.asp (accessed on 10 November 2012).
12. See "Jihad Council Calls for Limiting Number of Amarnath Pilgrims", *Deccan Herald*, 2 September 2012, available at http://www.deccanherald.com/content/276082/jihad-council-calls-limiting-number.html (accessed on 7 November 2012).

33

Tehrik-e-Jihad
(Movement for Struggle)

Introduction

The Tehrik-e-Jihad (TeJ) was formed on 19 April 1997, by the Inter Services Intelligence (ISI), out of the merger of small groups such as Al Baraq (Farooq Qureshi faction), Hizbullah, Muslim Mujahideen (Salim Wani group), Ansar-ul-Islam and a section of Harkat-ul-Ansar (HuA) militants. The decision to form the TeJ was reportedly taken by the ISI as it started loosing its grip on the Kshmiri militants and its failure to intensify violence in Kashmir. The formation of the TeJ was supported by Sardar Abdul Qayuum Khan, former Prime Minister of Pakistan-occupied Kashmir (PoK). In the initial years, the TeJ had the potent of increasing the ISI's grip over the jihadi movement on one hand, and weakening the emotive demand of *azadi* (independence) on the other.

Objective

The TeJ aimed at pursuing the Pakistani agenda to liberate Kashmir through armed movement and merge it with Pakistan. As mentioned earlier, after realising that locals of Jammu and Kashmir (J&K) were not following the Pakistan agenda of merger of this region with Pakistan, the ISI decided to intensify jihad in Kashmir by inducting foreign militants into the outfit.

Organisational Structure and Leadership

The organisation of the TeJ is divided into Department of Management and military wing. Department of Management looks after political, finance, media, jihadi preaching matters and induction of youth. The amir (chief) heads the department supported by a *naib* amir and central Amir. The amir of the TeJ is Farooq Qureshi, who is a leader of the Gujjar community and was earlier amir of Al Barq. Other prominent leaders of the TeJ are Mohammad Aftab Wani, *naib* amir; Major (retd) Tariq Zul-Qarnain, central amir; Ashfaq Ahmed Bharwal, supreme commander; Sanaulllah Khan, Chief commander; and Shah Nawaz, launching commander.

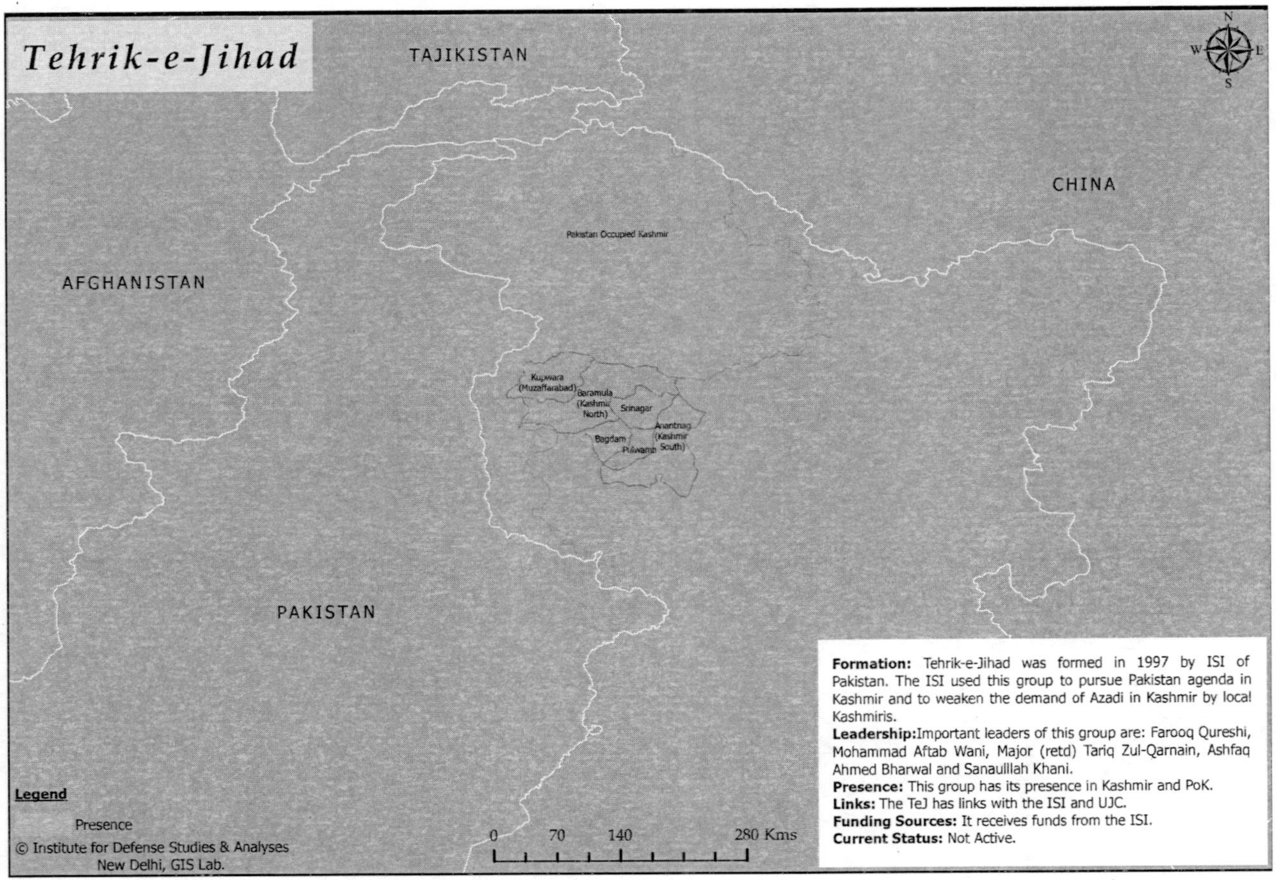
Tehrik-e-Jihad
TAJIKISTAN
CHINA
AFGHANISTAN
PAKISTAN
Pakistan Occupied Kashmir
Kupwara (Muzaffarabad)
Baramula (Kashmir North)
Srinagar
Anantnag (Kashmir South)
Bagdam
Pulwama
N
W
E
S
0 70 140 280 Kms
Legend
Presence
© Institute for Defense Studies & Analyses New Delhi, GIS Lab.
Formation: Tehrik-e-Jihad was formed in 1997 by ISI of Pakistan. The ISI used this group to pursue Pakistan agenda in Kashmir and to weaken the demand of Azadi in Kashmir by local Kashmiris.
Leadership: Important leaders of this group are: Farooq Qureshi, Mohammad Aftab Wani, Major (retd) Tariq Zul-Qarnain, Ashfaq Ahmed Bharwal and Sanaulllah Khani.
Presence: This group has its presence in Kashmir and PoK.
Links: The TeJ has links with the ISI and UJC.
Funding Sources: It receives funds from the ISI.
Current Status: Not Active.

Although all these leaders were appointed on the recommendation of the ISI, it was Major Tariq who was closely associated with ISI to organise the various activities of the outfit.[1]

Cadre Strength

Although the outfit claims that its 1,000 militants have been killed in Kashmir, it appears that the outfit did not have more than 500 militants on its roll. With the aim of facilitating infiltration/exfiltration across the line of control (LoC) and supply of arms to the militants in the J&K, the ISI had engaged some retired Pakistan Army personnel and mercenaries and posted them near the LoC with the TeJ militants.[2] At present, the strength of the TeJ is believed to very less as the organisation is inactive in carrying out its activities.

Area of Operation

The main area of operation of the TeJ includes Kupwara, Baramulla, Rajouri, Surankot and Poonch. The outfit earned prominence during Kargil conflict when it claimed in Islamabad that its militants had captured 500 sq km of area of Kargil and taken up positions on the heights of Kargil and Dras sectors.[3]

The headquarters of the TeJ are located at Muzaffarabad where operations are planned under the supervision of ex-Major General Nayeem Akhtar of Pakistan Army. The training for the TeJ militants was believed to be given at Nissar camp, Chela Bandi near Muzaffarabad. The TeJ has also branches in Sialkot in Punjab from where military operations in Jammu were launched. The TeJ was also active in parts of Surankot, Mendhar, Naushehra and Badhal as the Brigade 111 of the outfit was assigned to carry out activities in these areas.[4]

Alliances and Network

Besides its association with the ISI, the TeJ has established links with Muslim conferences of PoK and Muslim conference of J&K headed by Abdul Gani Bhat. It is also a member of the United Jihad Council (UJC).

Funding and Finance

The outfit is totally financed by the ISI.

Weapons in Possession

The outfit is in possession of both small and sophisticated weapons, including pistol, revolvers, AK-series rifles, light machine guns (LMGs), grenades and rocket launchers and modern communication systems. So far the procurement of the weapons of the TeJ is concerned, the outfit was able to procure large quantities of weapon from across the border through Gujjar guides.

Current Status

The outfit was under the full control of the ISI, but still it made no headway in intensify its militant activities in J&K as it lacked the support of the local Kashmiri militants. The outfit seems to be not very active for the last few years.

NOTES

1. See Muhammad Amir Rana, *Gateway to Terrorism*, Landon: New Millennium Publication, 2003, p. 424.
2. See K. Santhanam (ed.), *Jihadis in Jammu and Kashmir*, New Delhi: Sage Publications, 2003, p. 260.
3. See "Tehrik-e-Jihad", available at http://www.globalsecurity.org/military/world/para/tej.htm (accessed on 4 October 2012).
4. See Rana, *Gateway to Terrorism*, p. 424.

34

Sipah-e-Sahaba Pakistan
(Corps of the Prophet's Companions)

Introduction

Initially known as Anjuman-e-Sipah-Sahaba, Sipah-e-Sahaba Pakistan (SSP) is a Sunni Deobandi militant organisation. It was formed in September 1985 by four prominent anti-Shia clerics: Maulana Haq Nawaz Jhangvi; Maulana Zia ur Rehman Farooqi; Maulana Esar ul Haq Qasmi; and Maulana Azim Tariq. The main aim of forming the SSP was to counter the activities of the Shia sect which had formed Tehriq-e-Nifaz-Fiqah-Jafaria under the leadership of Mufti Jafar Hussain and had organised a large-scale demonstration. The move resulted in the Islamabad agreement in which Pakistan government agreed to separate Islamiat course for Shia sect who were given exemption from collection of zakat and other demands.

The Islamic revolution in Iran and the subsequent assistance from the Iranian government was also a source of encouragement for the Shia outfit. This provoked the Sunnis, who were already feeling weak in front of the Shia feudal landlords holding political and economic power in Jhang and the adjoining areas

This led to great resentment among the Sunnis who decided to hit back by forming Anjuman-e-Sipah-Sahaba, which later became the SSP. It is reported that the SSP as a militant outfit had the support of General Zia-ul-Haq's regime which wanted to neutralise Tehriq-e-Nifaz-Fiqah-Jafaria which enjoyed the support of the Iranian government.[1] This marked the beginning of sectarian terrorism in Pakistan, resulting in increasing violence in Punjab, and eventually taking entire country in its grip. More than 300 people from both the sides were killed in these violent clashes during the period 1986–89.

The militant activities of the SSP were fuelled by the ever-present sectarian violence between the Shias and the Sunnis. Especially, there was a major escalation of violent activities from the SSP side during the 1986 anti-Shia riots. The SSP was involved in the killing of the Tehriq-e-Nifaz-Fiqah-Jafaria leader, Arif Hussain, in 1988. Similarly, the assassination of Maulana Haq Nawaz Jhangvi of SSP in February 1990 further escalated the violent activities of the SSP. The SSP retaliated by killing many Shia scholars and political leaders.

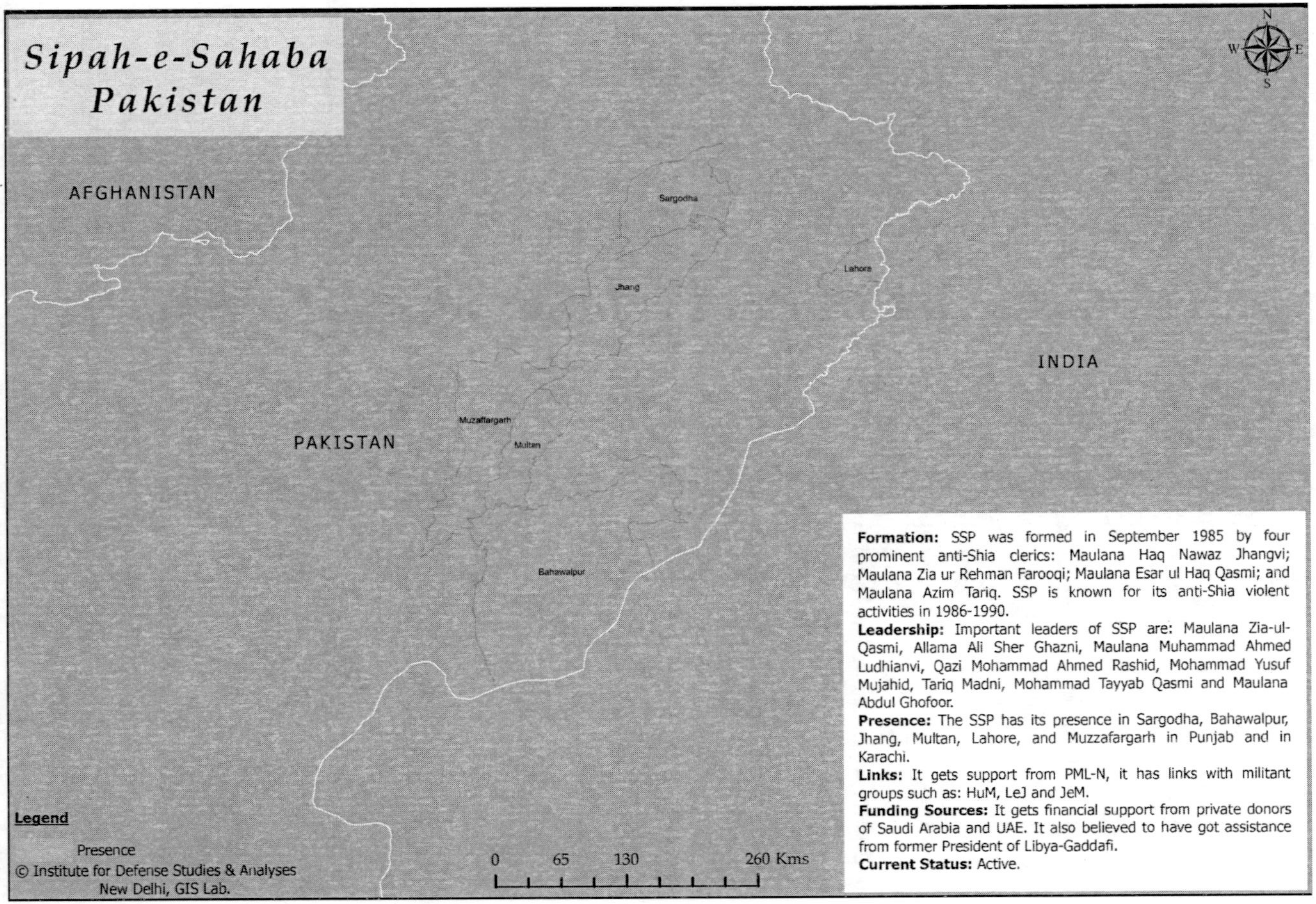
Sipah-e-Sahaba Pakistan
AFGHANISTAN
PAKISTAN
INDIA
Sargodha
Jhang
Lahore
Muzaffargarh
Multan
Bahawalpur
N
W
E
S
Legend
Presence
© Institute for Defense Studies & Analyses New Delhi, GIS Lab.
0 65 130 260 Kms
Formation: SSP was formed in September 1985 by four prominent anti-Shia clerics: Maulana Haq Nawaz Jhangvi; Maulana Zia ur Rehman Farooqi; Maulana Esar ul Haq Qasmi; and Maulana Azim Tariq. SSP is known for its anti-Shia violent activities in 1986-1990.
Leadership: Important leaders of SSP are: Maulana Zia-ul-Qasmi, Allama Ali Sher Ghazni, Maulana Muhammad Ahmed Ludhianvi, Qazi Mohammad Ahmed Rashid, Mohammad Yusuf Mujahid, Tariq Madni, Mohammad Tayyab Qasmi and Maulana Abdul Ghofoor.
Presence: The SSP has its presence in Sargodha, Bahawalpur, Jhang, Multan, Lahore, and Muzzafargarh in Punjab and in Karachi.
Links: It gets support from PML-N, it has links with militant groups such as: HuM, LeJ and JeM.
Funding Sources: It gets financial support from private donors of Saudi Arabia and UAE. It also believed to have got assistance from former President of Libya-Gaddafi.
Current Status: Active.

The group was proscribed as a terrorist organisation by President Musharraf on 12 January 2002. Following the ban, the group was renamed as Millat-e-Islamia Pakistan. This name was also included in the list of terrorist groups by Musharraf in September 2003. In April 2005, the United States (US) listed the SSP as a foreign terrorist organisation (FTO). In spite of the ban, the SSP continues its sectarian violent activities under a new name, "Ahle-Sunnat-Wal-Jamaat" (ASWJ).

Objectives

The SSP belongs to Deobandi school of thought and its primary objective is to establish the country as a Sunni state and see that the Shia Muslims be declared as the infidels. It wants that the books that insult the companions of the Prophet should be banned. It also demands that those Shia speakers and scholars who insult the companions of the Prophet should be punished. The SSP also operated as a political party and its leaders, Maulana Esar Qasmi and Maulana Azim Tariq, held seats in Pakistan National Assembly. The group's main aim was to counter Shia's influence in Pakistan's political, social and economic structures. Although in its objectives, the SSP is overtly sectarian and is opposed to all other forms of Islamic beliefs, in its website,[2] the outfit claims that its movement is "non-violent and non-aggressive towards its opponents (the non-Muslims who abuse Sahaba)".

Leadership

The SSP is managed by a supreme council headed by Maulana Zia-ul-Qasmi. Allama Ali Sher Ghazni is the chief patron of the SSP. The president of the SSP is Maulana Muhammad Ahmed Ludhianvi. Ludhianvi is also an important leader of the Difa-i-Pakistan (Defence of Pakistan Council), a coalition of around 40 religious and ultra-nationalist parties. The other important leaders of the SSP holding positions in the supreme council are Qazi Mohammad Ahmed Rashid, Mohammad Yusuf Mujahid, Tariq Madni, Mohammad Tayyab Qasmi, Maulana Abdul Ghofoor Nadeem and Maulana Muhammad Balakoti.

As cited in SSP's website, some of the important leaders of the outfit killed in the sectarian violence are Sheikh-ul-Hadith, Maulana Muhammad Amin, Mufti Saud-ur-Rehman, Maulana Ahsaanullah Farooqui, Maulana Abdul Ghafoor Nadeem, Engineer Ilyas Zubair, Qari Shafeeq-ur-Rehman, Hafiz Ahmed Buksh, Maulana Haroon Qasmi, Maulana Izhar-ul-Haq Jhangvi, Haji Muhammad Waris, Allama Shoaib Nadeem, Maulana Abdus Samad Azad, Maulana Syyed Sadiq Hussain Shah, Maulana Rasheed Ahmed Madni, Bhae Habib-ur-Rehman, Haji Aziz-ur-Rehman, Qari Muhammad Huzaifa, Maulana Muhktar Ahmed Sial and Mian Iqbal Hussain.[3]

Cadre—Strength, Profile and Training

The SSP is believed to have approximately 3,000–6,000 trained militants, mostly from Punjab. Majority of them have been picked up from various Deobandi madrassas in Punjab and Karachi. The SSP has also set up its own madrassas in various towns of Punjab/Khyber Pakhtunkhwa (KP) and Sindh. Its centres in Lahore, Jhang, Faisalabad and Samundri are engaged in organisational activities, and also serve as secretariats. Its centre in Lahore is Jamia Farooqi, where all organisational activities in whole of Pakistan are monitored.[4]

Similarly, activities of its centres in foreign countries are controlled by Madrassa Jamia Mahmudia in Jhang.[5] According to one report, the SSP militants were believed to have undergone training in Afghanistan while fighting with the Talibans.[6] Complementing this report, another report revealed that the militants of the SSP had long-standing links with militant groups across Pakistan and Afghanistan. The SSP militants were believed to have frequently travelled to Kabul and Kandahar in Afghanistan to consult with Mullah Omar and his companions.[7]

The important training camps of the SSP are currently located in Punjab, Karachi and the adjoining areas of Pakistan, and also in parts of Kabul and Kandahar.

Area of Operation and Influence

The SSP is considered to be the most powerful sectarian outfit in Pakistan. It is active in the areas of Sargodha, Bahawalpur, Jhang, Multan and Muzaffargarh in Punjab and various parts of Karachi.

The outfit claims to have its presence in 74 districts, and also had 225 *tehsil*-level units before it was banned in 2002. It is also believed to have 17 branches in foreign countries, including Saudi Arabia, Bangladesh, Canada and the United Kingdom (UK). Its office in the UK is located at Mufti Mustafa madrassa in London. The outfit has also tried to spread its network through its monthly mouthpiece, *Khilafat-e-Rista*.

Some reports suggest that the SSP has both of its headquarters inside two of the largest Deobandi madrassas of Punjab. They are: Jamiat-ul-Uloom Eidgah in Bahawalnagar and Darul Uloom Deoband Faqirwali in Fort Abbas.[8] However, there are other reports which indicate that the SSP is controlled through its regional headquarters, Jamia Farooqi, Jia Moosa, Shahdara near Lahore, and the international units are controlled by Madrasa Mahmudia in Jhang.[9]

Network

The SSP enjoys support from some of the political parties like the Nawaz Sharif faction of the Pakistan Muslim League (PML (N)). The former Governor of Punjab, Salma Taseer, in an interview said that the PML (N) has links with militant organisations like the SSP and the Lashkar-e-Jhangvi (LeJ).[10] The LeJ is supposed to be a natural ally of the SSP. Both SSP and the LeJ are suspected in helping the Taliban in its activities in Pakistan. The SSP also maintains a close network with militant groups like the Harkat-ul-Mujahideen and the Jaish-e-Mohammad.

Finance and Funding

During the initial years of the formation of the SSP, the financial support came from the Saudi coffers. The support from Saudi Arabia and the United Arab Emirates (UAE) continues to flow. A report revealed by the WikiLeaks stated that the SSP, along with the LeJ, got substantial financial support from the ex-President of Libya, Gaddafi.[11] The SSP is also suspected to have got financial support from the Pakistani diaspora in the Arab countries.

Weapons in Possession

The SSP procured most of its weapons from the LeJ. The weapons that the SSP possesses are believed to have come from Afghanistan and were distributed to many militant groups like the SSP through the Inter Services Intelligence (ISI). The weapons include rocket launchers, assault rifles, mines and different small-caliber arms. The assault rifles have been used to carry out indiscriminate firings at Shia processions and religious places.

Current Status

Currently, the SSP is working under the label of ASWJ. The ASWJ has come out openly in support of the political party, PML (N), during the elections. With the support from the ruling party, the ASWJ and the SSP are intensifying their activities. The SSP, with well-established network with many militant groups, will continue to be one of the most important militant outfits in Pakistan.

NOTES

1. See Muhammad Amir Rana, *A to Z of Jehadi Organisations in Pakistan*, Lahore: Mashal Publication, 2004, pp. 194–95.
2. For details of SSP's official position, see its website, available at http://www.sipah-e-sahaba.webs.com/.
3. Details available at http://www.sipah-e-sahaba.webs.com/.
4. See Rana, *A to Z of Jehadi Organisations in Pakistan*, p. 199.
5. Ibid.
6. See Animesh Roul, "Sipah-e-Sahaba: Fomenting Sectarian Violence in Pakistan", *Terrorism Monitor*, Vol. 3, No. 2, 5 May 2005, available at http://www.jamestown.org/single/?no_cache=1&tx_ttnews%5Btt_news%5D=323 (accessed on 18 July 2012).
7. See Nicholas Schmidle, "Talibanistan: The Talibs at Home", *World Affairs*, Fall 2009, available at http://www.worldaffairsjournal.org/article/talibanistan-talibs-home (accessed on 19 July 2012).
8. See Roul, "Sipah-e-Sahaba: Fomenting Sectarian Violence in Pakistan".
9. Ibid.
10. For details, see Ali Salman Alvi, "Tintinnabulations of a Vandalised Future", *Daily Times*, 17 December 2012, available at http://www.dailytimes.com.pk/default.asp?page=2012%5C12%5C17%5Cstory_17-12-2012_pg3_5 (accessed on 17 December 2012).
11. See "SSP–LeJ–JuI and the Lybian Connection: In the Lights of Wikileaks", available at www. Criticalppp.com/archive/60652 (accessed on 20 October 2012).

35

Sunni Tehrik

Genesis

Sunni Tehrik (ST), a group that claims to represent the Barelvi school of thought, is an aggressive sectarian organisation. It was formed in Karachi in 1990 by Mohammad Saleem Qadri. Its main aim was to promote the interests of Barelvi Muslims in conflicts against competing Deobandi and Wahabi sects. Soon after its formation, ST took on the form of an aggressive sectarian organisation, with Sipah-e-Sahaba Pakistan (SSP) and Lashkar-e-Taiba (LeT) as its main targets.[1] This led to violent sectarian clashes among the outfits. The ST focused on the Ahle Hadees and Deobandi mosques that it thought to have been taken away from their original Ahle Sunnat affiliation.

Objective/Agenda

The main aim behind the creation of the ST was to counter the growing influence of Ahle Hadith and Deobandi organisations. These organisations had allegedly taken control of all government religious institutions, departments and positions. The main objective of the ST is to protect the beliefs of Ahle Sunnat. In the process of protecting the Ahle Sunnat, it aims at protection of Ahle Sunnat mosques, maintenance of these mosques, etc. Contrary to the official objective, the chairman, Sarwat Izaz Qadri, of the ST has gone on the record to say that "only in Sufism lay Pakistan's survival". He added that inter-faith harmony was imperative to save the nation from destruction.[2]

Leadership/Network

Soon after its inception, ST showed its strength by holding rallies in Karachi and capturing of mosques in 1992. The ST workers fanned out in Sindh and Punjab and in the next 10 years, they had liberated 62 mosques. The group also established a good rapport with Muttahida Quami Movement (MQM) as many MQM activists joined the ST. It has 20 Barelvi organisations.

So far the leadership of the ST goes, its present amir (chief) is Sarwat Izaz Qadri, who is assisted by a number of central leaders. It does not have a provincial structure; instead, conveners at divisional level are answerable directly to the amir

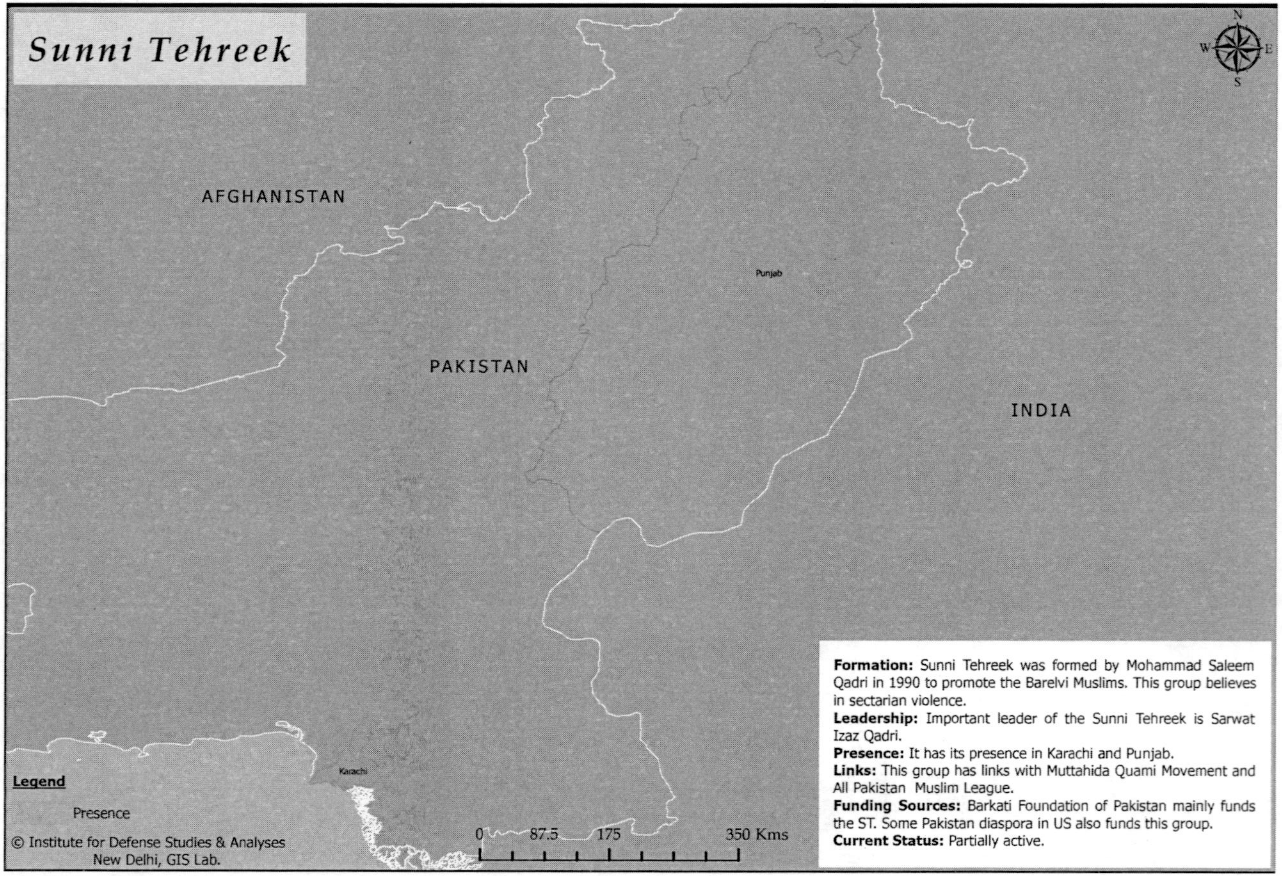
Sunni Tehreek
AFGHANISTAN
PAKISTAN
INDIA
Punjab
Karachi
Legend
Presence
© Institute for Defense Studies & Analyses
New Delhi, GIS Lab.
0 87.5 175 350 Kms
N
W
E
S
Formation: Sunni Tehreek was formed by Mohammad Saleem Qadri in 1990 to promote the Barelvi Muslims. This group believes in sectarian violence.
Leadership: Important leader of the Sunni Tehreek is Sarwat Izaz Qadri.
Presence: It has its presence in Karachi and Punjab.
Links: This group has links with Muttahida Quami Movement and All Pakistan Muslim League.
Funding Sources: Barkati Foundation of Pakistan mainly funds the ST. Some Pakistan diaspora in US also funds this group.
Current Status: Partially active.

at the centre. The ST has its main secretariat on Baba-e-Urdu Road in Karachi. It has a network of 14 divisions and districts in the country. Many of the ST members, including Sarwat Izaz Qadri, are the members of Sunni Ittehad Council whose declared agenda is to tackle extremist ideology. According to a media report, the ST has been planning to join some political parties. In early 2012, the chief of the ST, Izaz Qadri, declared that the ST was thinking seriously to join the Pakistan Tehrik-i-Insaf (PTI). But a week's later, it was reported that the ST was also warming up with the Pervez Musharraf-led All Pakistan Muslim League (APML).[3]

Finance and Funding

The ST has no shortage of funds as Barkati Foundation leads its funding. Its members also give monthly donations and donation is also collected from various charities. It is to be noted that Markaz Ahle Sunnat and the hospital in Saidabad in Karachi have been constructed with Barkati Foundation funds. Some media reports suggest that the ST also received a substantial amount of funds from the United States (US) to protest against the Taliban in Pakistan.[4]

Weapons

The exact kind weapons possessed by ST are not known. But the group is suspected to have some small weapons with it.

Current Status

In January 2012, the ST announced that it would convert itself into a political party called as the Pakistan Sunni Tehrik (PST). The outfit, even after being banned by the state of Pakistan, is involved with sectarian clashes. Along with the Sunni Ittehad Council and Sunni Force, the ST engaged in violent clashes with some other groups on 29 February 2012 in Karachi. The ST, even as a political party, will go on polarising the society which will result in violent clashes among the various sects of Islam in Pakistan.

NOTES

1. See Muhammad Amir Rana, *Gateway to Terrorism*, London: New Millennium Publication, 2003, p. 201.
2. See Owais Jafri, "Swept by Tsunami: Sunni Tehrik Contemplates Joining PTI", *The Express Tribune*, 17 January 2012, available at http://tribune.com.pk/story/322918/swept-by-tsunami-sunni-ittehad-council-contemplates-joining-pti/ (accessed on 13 October 2012).
3. See Owais Jafri, "After Thinking about Joining PTI, Pakistan Sunni Tehrik Swings towards APML", 15 February 2012, *The Express Tribune*, available at http://tribune.com.pk/story/336916/after-thinking-about-joining-pti-pakistan-sunni-Tehrik-swings-towards-apml/ (accessed on 13 October 2012).
4. See Huma Imtiaz, "US Aid to Sunni Ittehad Council Backfired", *The Express Tribune*, 12 January 2012, available at http://tribune.com.pk/story/320193/one-off-grant-us-aid-to-sunni-ittehad-council-backfired (accessed on 13 October 2012).

36

Sipah-e-Mohammad Pakistan (Soldiers of Prophet)

Introduction/History

Sipah-e-Mohammad (SMP), a group of Tehrik-e-Jafariya (TJP), emerged as a prominent Shia terrorist outfit in 1993. It was formed by Maulana Mureed Abbas Yazdani, president of TJP, Jhang district, to counter Wahabi militancy led by Sipah-e-Sahaba Pakistan (SSP) and Lashkar-e-Jhangvi (LeJ). The decision to form the SMP was reportedly taken as the Shia youth had been pressurising the TJP to counter Sunni militancy, some of whose outfits were engaged in targeting some of Shia beliefs.

Asif Zardari (now President of Pakistan) was reportedly behind the formation of SMP after SSP threatened to kill him. He even gave financial assistance and arms to SMP to neutralise SSPs terrorist activities.[1] Maulana Yazdani got a good response as many youth belonging to Imamiya Students Organisation and Imamiya Organisation joined the outfit. As a show of strength, SMP called a meeting in Lahore and also addressed a press conference where its leaders declared, "We are weary of carrying corpses. God willing, we will settle all the scores now. We will wipe out the name of Sipah-e-Sahaba from history."[2] The security agencies did not take them seriously. However, they were alarmed when SMP claimed the responsibility of the attack on SSP chief, Azim Tariq, in Sargodha. Following this, the Shia outfit intensified its activities and was involved in 250 attacks between 1993 and 2001. The outfit was banned on 14 August 2001.

Objective/Agenda

The main aim of the outfit is to protect the Shia community by training its young cadre to physically counter the Sunni militant groups. Its main rivals are SSP, LeJ and their allied organisations and cells. In order to protect its community, the group attempts to terrorise these Sunni outfits by organising rallies and targeting mosques, religious institutions and their cadres and sympathisers.

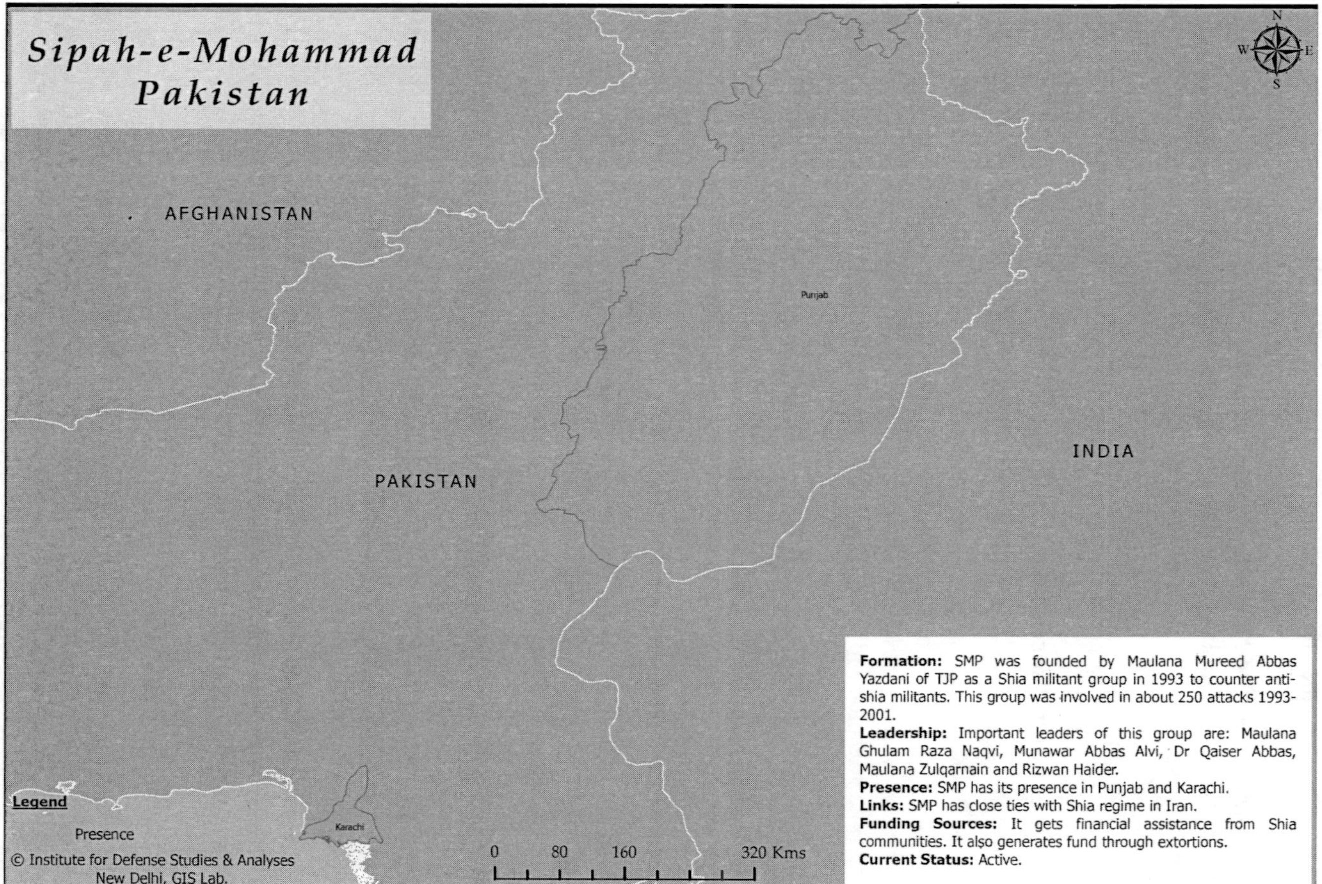
Sipah-e-Mohammad Pakistan
CHINA
AFGHANISTAN
PAKISTAN
INDIA
Punjab
Karachi
Legend
Presence
© Institute for Defense Studies & Analyses New Delhi, GIS Lab.
0 80 160 320 Kms
N E S W
Formation: SMP was founded by Maulana Mureed Abbas Yazdani of TJP as a Shia militant group in 1993 to counter anti-shia militants. This group was involved in about 250 attacks 1993-2001.
Leadership: Important leaders of this group are: Maulana Ghulam Raza Naqvi, Munawar Abbas Alvi, Dr Qaiser Abbas, Maulana Zulqarnain and Rizwan Haider.
Presence: SMP has its presence in Punjab and Karachi.
Links: SMP has close ties with Shia regime in Iran.
Funding Sources: It gets financial assistance from Shia communities. It also generates fund through extortions.
Current Status: Active.

Leadership

With the killing of Maulana Yazdani due to internal rivalry, Maulana Ghulam Raza Naqvi became the president of SMP in 1996. Naqvi was arrested in the same year for his involvement in about 30 cases of murder and looting. Other senior leaders of SMP include: Munawar Abbas Alvi, who is behind bars; Dr Qaiser Abbas, an explosive specialist; and Muhammad Ali, right-hand man of Maulana Naqvi, who was arrested with him but escaped from prison, but was recaptured later. Other prominent leaders who fled the country after crackdown on SMP include Maulana Zulqarnain and Rizwan Haider.

Cadre Strength/Recruitment/Training

The SMP, at one stage, was believed to have a cadre strength of 30000 which also included cadres of TJP. Majority of them were from Faisalabad, Jhang, Multan, Bhakkar Lahore and Toba Tek Singh in Punjab and Karachi in Sindh. Its headquarters is located at Thokar Niaz Beg, a village in the suburb of Lahore, which had become a fortress for the Shia community. The cadres are given training in handling all types of weapons and explosives. According to a confession made by some arrested activists, SMP cadres are also imparted training in Iran. Majority of the cadres have criminal background for their involvement in robberies and *dacoties*.

Area of Operation/Network

With the setting up of its strong base at Thokar Niaz Beg in 1994, the SMP under Maulana Naqvi intensified its activities by targeting SSP and LeJ cadres and leaders and their religious places. According to a confession made by an arrested terrorist, more than 200 terrorist, after getting training from Iran, have fanned out in various cities to target SSP and LeJ militants. Some of them are also deployed in Karachi University where they enjoy the patronage of some influential teachers and through them, are fanning sectarianism on campus.[3]

Alliances/Funding

There are allegations that SMP is maintaining its links with Shia regime in Iran where its cadres were being trained. Main source of income is collection from Shia community, businessmen and through extortion.

Weapons in Possession

According to a report, SMP fortress in Thokar Niaz Beg is in possession of 2,300 weapons which include pistols, Kalashnikovs, G-3s (Iran made) and other rifles, machine guns, rocket-propelled grenades, bombs, etc.[4] The outfit has also the capability to use remotely triggered devices. This kind of device was used during the bombing of the Lahore Sessions Court in 1997, killing SSP leader Maulana

Zia ur Rehman Farooqi. The security agencies also suspect the involvement of SMP militants in throwing hand grenades at the Saudi Consulate at Karachi on 11 May 2011 and the killing of Saudi diplomat on 16 May 2011.

With the killing of Maulana Naqvi and the arrest of its senior leaders and subsequent crackdown by the Punjab government, the terrorist activities of the SMP have gone down considerably.

NOTES

1. See Muhammad Amir Rana, *Gateway to Terrorism*, London: New Millennium Publication, 2003, p. 455.
2. Ibid., p. 456.
3. See Tariq Habib, "200 Iranian-trained Sipah-e-Muhammad Activists Hunting Down ASWJ Workers", 25 May 2011, *Pakistan Today*, available at http://www.pakistantoday.com.pk/2011/05/26/city/karachi/%E2%80%98200-iranian-trained-sipah-e-muhammad-activists-hunting-down-aswj-workers%E2%80%99/ (accessed on 18 December 2012).
4. See "Shia Militancy", available at http://www.kr-hcy.com/articles/militancy.shtml (accessed on 20 December 2012).

37

Lashkar-e-Jhangvi

(Army of Jhangvi)

History/Genesis

Lashkar-e-Jhangvi (LeJ), also known as Army of Jhangvi, is a Sunni Deobandi terrorist outfit. Formed in 1996, it takes its name from Maulana Haq Nawaz Jhangvi, the founder of anti-Shiite organisation, Sipah-e-Sahaba Pakistan (SSP), who was reportedly assassinated by Shia terrorists on 23 February 1990.

Akram Lahori, Malik Ishaq and Riaz Basra had carved out LeJ from SSP. Their differences with the SSP leadership were primarily centred on means to achieve the goal of enforcing Sharia rule. The trio advocated the path of violence and accused the SSP leadership of deviating from the ideals of Maulana Jhangvi.

The split did not make much difference to the threat posed by the SSP. In fact, it has given a new dimension to Sunni Deobandis' warfare against minorities, particularly Shias, Ahmediyas and Christians in Pakistan. It is this reality check that makes the split of SSP and emergence of LeJ no more than eyewash.

The SSP and LeJ have been operating separately but there is reason to aver that, today, LeJ is the armed wing of the SSP. It is like the arrangement in the militant Shia camp.

Sipah-e-Mohammad Pakistan (SMP) and Tehriq-e-Nifaz-e-Fiqah-Jafaria (TNFJ)[1] are two separate entities amongst the Shiites. But it is no secret that TNFJ uses SMP as its armed wing even as it enjoys the denial mode and chases political mirages.

Likewise, LeJ is enabling the SSP to concentrate more on overt ground political activities.[2] On their part, the SSP leaders are taking care of LeJ interests. They are seen visiting LeJ leaders lodged in jails, and this is a giveaway that SSP and LeJ are the two sides of the same coin.

For example, Maulana Azim Tariq, former amir of the SSP, time and again, distanced himself from the terrorist activities of the LeJ. But he offered to pay *qisas* (blood money) to Iran when LeJ terrorist Sheikh Haq Nawaz was to be hanged for the killing of Iranian diplomat, Sadiq Ganji, in Lahore in March 2001.[3]

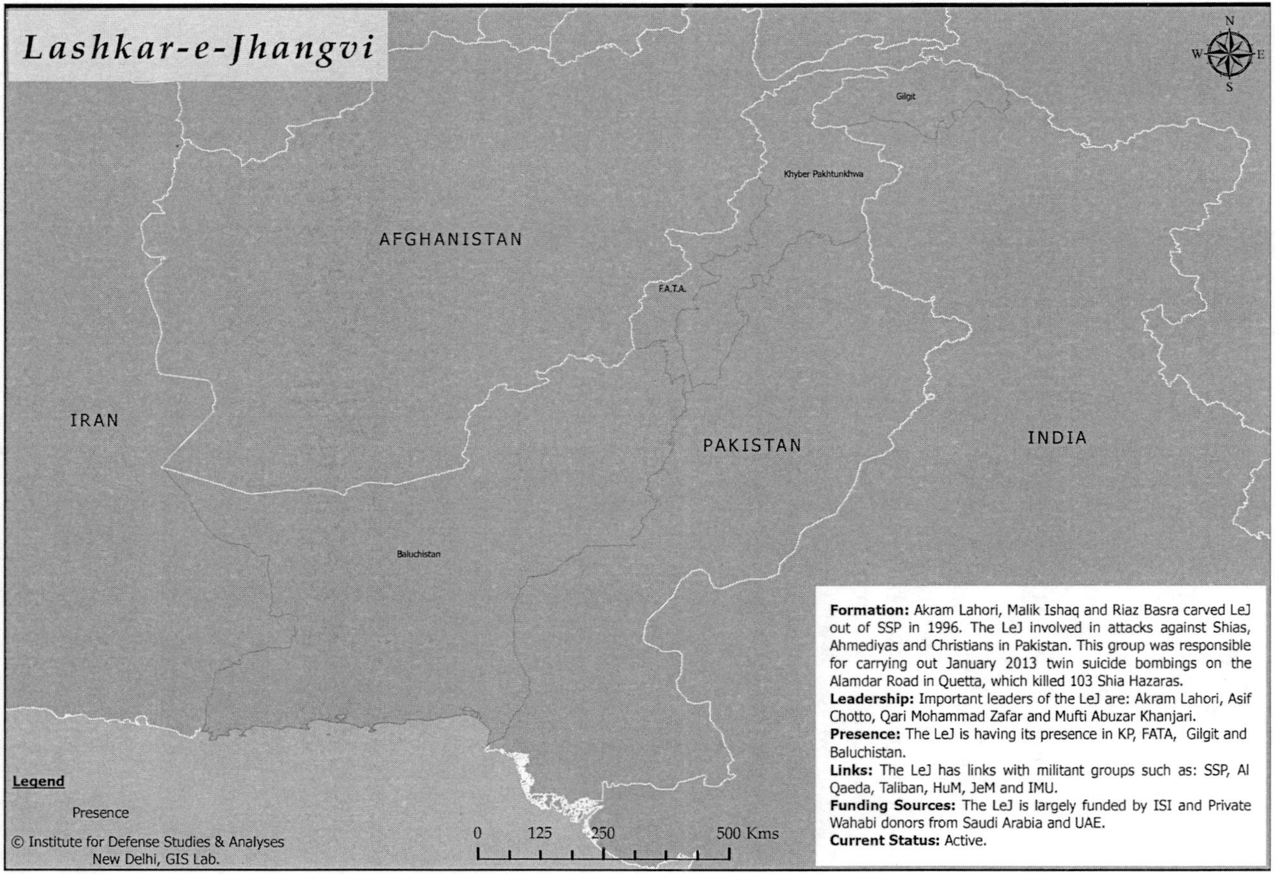
Lashkar-e-Jhangvi
N
W
E
S
AFGHANISTAN
IRAN
PAKISTAN
INDIA
Gilgit
Khyber Pakhtunkhwa
F.A.T.A.
Baluchistan
Legend
Presence
© Institute for Defense Studies & Analyses New Delhi, GIS Lab.
0 125 250 500 Kms
Formation: Akram Lahori, Malik Ishaq and Riaz Basra carved LeJ out of SSP in 1996. The LeJ involved in attacks against Shias, Ahmediyas and Christians in Pakistan. This group was responsible for carrying out January 2013 twin suicide bombings on the Alamdar Road in Quetta, which killed 103 Shia Hazaras.
Leadership: Important leaders of the LeJ are: Akram Lahori, Asif Chotto, Qari Mohammad Zafar and Mufti Abuzar Khanjari.
Presence: The LeJ is having its presence in KP, FATA, Gilgit and Baluchistan.
Links: The LeJ has links with militant groups such as: SSP, Al Qaeda, Taliban, HuM, JeM and IMU.
Funding Sources: The LeJ is largely funded by ISI and Private Wahabi donors from Saudi Arabia and UAE.
Current Status: Active.

Even the present amir of the SSP, Muhammad Ahmed Ludhianvi, has visited jailed LeJ leader Malik Ishaq a number of times. He did not hide these visits from public view. He not only acknowledged them but also stated that he had made these "courtesy calls" at the behest of Pakistan Muslim League (Nawaz) PML (N) leader, Shahbaz Sharif, who was the Chief Minister of Punjab from 2008 to 2013. Ludhianvi was outside the jail gate to receive Malik Ishaq when he was released.[4]

Evolution

From day one, the LeJ started targeting Shia politicians, professionals, doctors and scholars. It also has been targeting religious places and institutions of Christians, Ahmediyas and the Westerners.

Within five years of its formation, the LeJ became the deadliest terror outfit by carrying out 350 attacks,[5] mostly against the Shias. It also carried out a number of attacks against Iranian nationals. The 1997 attack killing four American oil workers in Karachi was an LeJ feat. Its footprint was also clearly visible in January 2002 kidnapping and murder of American journalist Daniel Pearl.

In 1998, Pakistan government ordered the first of several crackdowns as a part of its campaign to cultivate the Western capitals engaged in the war against terror. Each crackdown was followed by arrest and even killing of dozens of LeJ cadres.

The LeJ retaliated every time. It targeted the then Prime Minister, Nawaz Sharif, first, and later, the then President, Pervez Musharraf. Displaying an audacity, which has been its hallmark, the LeJ had offered a reward of Pakistan rupees (PKR) 135 million to whoever killed Nawaz Sharif, his younger brother Shahbaz Sharif and the then Punjab Information Minister, Mushahid Hussain.[6]

The offer was announced through a press release before LeJ actually made an attempt on the life of Punjab's strongman. Sharif is said to be close to the SSP–LeJ combine. It is possible to view the attack on Sharif as LeJ's way of telling the world that they were not beholden to him. More than that, it is a clear signal that the hardcore Sunni fundamentalists will go to any length to achieve their sectional goals.

Given the personality orientation of LeJ, it could not survive as a single outfit for more than four years. It split into two in October 2000—one headed by Riaz Basra and the other headed by Qari Asadullah.

Qari Asadullah's real name was Qari Abdul Haye; he was popularly known as Talha in the organisation. He was the chief of Majlis-e-Shura and headed the training camp at Sarobi in Afghanistan.

Basra and Talha fell out over an operational issue. The LeJ was on a low key after the military coup in October 1999. Basra wanted to return to the killing mode to force the authorities to release the arrested LeJ leaders and to make the government declare Shias as infidels in Pakistan.

Qari Asadullah considered the plan as suicidal for the organisation as well as for Pakistan itself. He was convinced that the military regime of General Pervez Musharraf would come down on LeJ with an iron hand.

When Basra remained adamant, supporters of Qari Asadullah took control of LeJ's training camps. This led to an armed clash between the two factions but the timely intervention of Jaish-e-Mohammad (JeM) leader, Mufti Abdul Sagheer, averted a bloodbath.

In an effort to iron out differences, the JeM leader invited the two chieftains to a joint meeting. Riaz Basra rejected the invitation and announced the expulsion of Qari Asadullah from LeJ.[7] Both were eliminated in police encounters much later, hence the dividing line between the two groups disappeared over time.

President Musharraf banned LeJ in 2001. Two years later, in January 2003, the United States (US) added the outfit to its list of foreign terrorist organisations (FTO). Neither proscription has tamed this armed Sunni group. It went on a killing and bombing spree in Islamabad, Karachi and other parts of Pakistan

Major attacks mounted by LeJ during this period included suicide attack at the International Protestant Church in Islamabad (March 2002); car bomb attack on the French civilians working on a submarine project outside the Sheraton Hotel in Karachi (May 2002); car bomb explosion outside the US Consulate in Karachi (June 2002); suicide attack at a Shiite mosque in Islamabad (May 2005); suicide bombing of Marriot Hotel in Islamabad (September 2008); twin suicide bombings in Lahore (March 2010); and suicide attacks on Ahmediyas places of worship (June 2010).

The LeJ hand is suspected in the assassination of former Prime Minister Benazir Bhutto on 27 December 2007. It is also suspected to have been behind the attack on Sri Lankan cricket team near the Gaddafi stadium in Lahore in March 2009. The LeJ demonstrated its long arm in Kabul on 6 December 2011, when a suicide bomber detonated an improvised explosive device (IED) in a crowd of Shia mourners, killing 48 people.

The LeJ has also started brutally targeting ethnic Hazara community of Shia Muslims and worshippers at Sufi shrines. According to figures released by the Baluchistan government, 700 Shias were killed in the province between 2008 and 2012.[8] The trend of killing Hazaras continued unabated in 2013 as 200 Shias, mostly Hazaras, have been killed in just two attacks in Quetta, compared with 152 Shias, who had been killed all over Baluchistan in 54 incidents in 2012.[9]

Hazaras, however, allege that since 1999, over 1,300 of its members have been killed and over 3,000 injured in targeted violence.[10] The situation is quite serious as LeJ has openly issued death threats to Shia Hazaras in Baluchistan and described them as *wajib-ul-qatl* (worthy to be killed).[11]

Objective/Agenda

The main objective of LeJ is to transform Pakistan, by violent means, into a Sunni state based on Sharia. Another objective is to have all Shias declared as infidels and to participate in the destruction of other religions, notably Judaism, Christianity and Hinduism.[12]

Elaborating the objectives of LeJ, Pakistani security analyst, Amir Mir, says:

> The LeJ stands out for its secrecy, lethality and unrelenting pursuit of its core objectives—targeting Western interests in Pakistan and the Shiite community as a way to the eventual transformation of the country into a Taliban style Islamic state. It has become the group of choice for hardcore militants who are adamant in pursuing their jihadi agenda in Pakistan.[13]

Of late, the group has intensified attacks against Shia Hazaras.[14] In an open letter addressed to the Hazara community after the 6 May 2011 attack, LeJ declared:

> All Shias are Wajib-ul-Qatl. We will rid Pakistan of (this) unclean people. Pakistan means land of the pure, and the Shias have no right to be here. We have the fatwa and signatures of the revered Ulema in which the Shias have been declared kaafir (infidel)...Like in the past, (our) successful Jihad against the Hazaras in Pakistan, and, in particular, in Quetta is ongoing and will continue (in the near future). We will make Pakistan their graveyard—their houses will be destroyed by bombs and suicide bombers. We will only rest when we fly the flag of true Islam on this land.[15]

Claiming responsibility for the 10 January 2013 twin suicide bombings on the Alamdar Road in Quetta, which killed 103 Shia Hazaras, LeJ spokesman, Abu Bakar Siddiq, said that the Hazaras have themselves invited their wrath by not heeding LeJ call to quit Baluchistan.

"Hazaras had been warned to leave Balochistan by the end of 2012 or face consequences. Many of these Hazara enemies had fled but there were those who decided to stay back as they loved their jobs and properties. God willing, the Lashkar will not allow any of these Hazaras to leave Balochistan alive",[16] he said.

Similarly, after the 16 February 2013 carnage of 90 more Shia Hazaras in Quetta, LeJ spokesman said, "The Mujahideen of the Lashkar-e-Jhangvi will continue to kill Shias regardless of the imposition of the Governor's rule or the deployment of the army". He went on to warn that

> we have 20 more vehicles which are packed with lethal explosives and ready to hit the enemy. We are only waiting for next orders from our leadership to hit our targets in Alamdar Road, Mehrabad and Hazara Town. We are neither afraid of the Governor's rule nor the Pakistan army and we will continue to kill Shias at their homes.[17]

Organisational Structure and Leadership

Majlis-e-Shura (supreme council) is the apex body that manages and guides the LeJ. Salar-e-ala (commander-in-chief) is assisted by 12 *salar*s (commanders). While Riaz Basra took over as the first chief, Qari Asadullah became the chairperson of the Majlis-e-Shura.

The entire leadership of the LeJ consists mostly of Afghan jihad veterans having strong links with the Al Qaeda and Afghan and Pakistani Taliban.

Riaz Basra (born in 1967) studied at two madrassas in Lahore and his native Sargodha. He joined the political party SSP at the age of 18 years and the first position he held was the post of Lahore district secretary. He dabbled in Punjab power politics after he became SSP's central information secretary and contested the 1998 election to Punjab assembly. He also went to Afghanistan where he received military training at camps run by Harkat-ul-Mujahideen (HuM) and took part in the jihad against the Soviet troops.

Basra was involved in 300 criminal and terrorist activities. He is credited with coordinating the killing of Iranian diplomat, Sadiq Ganji, in Lahore in December 1990, and the killing of Iranian Air Force cadets visiting Pakistan in early 1980s. He was arrested for Ganji's killing, but escaped from custody while being taken to the court in 1994. He fled to Afghanistan, and became the commander of Khalid Bin Walid training camp of the Afghan Mujahideen at Sarobi near Kabul.

Basra was killed in an encounter with police, who were assisted by banned Shia group Tehrik-e-Jafariya Pakistan (TJP), at Mailsi, Multan, in central Pakistan, on 14 May 2002.[18] Literal translation of TJP is "The Road to Victory".

Akram Lahori took over in Basra's place. His luck ran out quickly; within a month of becoming salar-e-ala of LeJ, he was arrested in Orangi Town (Karachi) on 17 June 2002, along with five accomplices. He is yet to get his "freedom".

At the time of his arrest, Lahori was carrying head money of PKR 5 million announced by the Sindh government and another PKR 5 million announced by the Punjab government. Lahori was reportedly involved in 38 cases of sectarian killings in Sindh. Three days before he landed in police custody, Lahori had carried out a car bomb blast outside the US Consulate in Karachi.[19]

Asif Chotto succeeded Lahori and he remained at the helm of the outfit till 29 September 2005 when he was nabbed by security forces in Rawalpindi. He was also involved in bomb explosions in various parts of Pakistan. Twin bombings in Karachi in May 2004, suicide bombing in Sialkot in October 2004 and 30 May 2005 attack on Shia mosque in Karachi are amongst his "major feats".[20]

In 2005, Qari Mohammad Zafar became acting chief of the LeJ but his death in a US drone strike in Miramshah on 24 February 2010 gave a lethal blow to both the LeJ and the Tehrik-e-Taliban Pakistan (TTP).

Qari Zafar was reportedly working closely with TTP's key commander, Qari Hussain Mehsud, and was involved in the attacks against former President Pervez Musharraf, Special Investigation Unit (SIU) office in Model Town, Lahore, Marriot Hotel, Islamabad, *Federal Investigation Agency* (FIA) building, Lahore, and American Consulate in Karachi.[21]

Not much is known about Mufti Abuzar Khanjari, who stepped into Zafar's shoes. Anyhow, his was a brief stint and a rather stop-gap arrangement. Following his release from Lahore jail on 14 July 2011, Malik Ishaq took over as the head of the LeJ.[22] A co-founder and group's ideologue, Malik was imprisoned for 14 years, though Pakistan Army utilised his services from time to time.

Malik Ishaq is charged with 70 murders—all sectarian killings. He stands accused in as many as 44 cases, some of them multiple killings, but he always enjoyed the benefit of doubt and walked free from jail. He was always able to communicate with his cadres on the cell phone at his disposal. One such orchestrated attack was in 2009 on the visiting Sri Lankan cricket team near the Gaddafi Stadium in Lahore. The attack did not come in the way of Sri Lanka–Pakistan ties. In fact, Colombo did not make any fuss even when it became known that Malik Ishaq was a privileged prisoner.[23]

It was shortly after this Lahore attack on Sri Lankan cricketers that the Pakistan Army utilised Malik Ishaq services at "the national level" in October 2009. He was flown to Rawalpindi in a special plane to negotiate with the TTP suicide attackers who had stormed the General Headquarters (GHQ) and had taken several people hostage, including many security personnel.[24]

Thus, Malik Ishaq established his authority in the most powerful Sunni sectarian outfit. In the words of a security expert, Khaled Ahmed, Malik Ishaq is ranked at par with the JeM chief Maulana Masood Azhar who was closely associated with Osama bin Laden and Omar Sheikh, who too was charged with planning terrorist acts from his prison cell in Sindh.[25]

Masood Azhar had his jihadi baptism in Harkat-ul-Ansar (HuA), and had won his "freedom" from an India jail in December 1999 when fellow jihadis forced India to exchange him and a few other terrorists for the passengers of an Indian plane that had been hijacked to Kandahar. Azhar has since founded his own militant group, JeM, to spread anti-India terrorist activities. His goal is pan-Islamism.

Asif Ramzi, Mati-ur-Rehman and Amanullah Afridi are amongst the other important LeJ leaders. Ramzi served as assistant to Riaz Basra, who was instrumental in establishing linkage between local militants and Al Qaeda before he was killed in 2002. Mati-ur-Rehman did a stint on behalf of Al Qaeda. This helped him to become planning director and, later on, chief operational commander of the Sunni militia.

Amanullah Afridi has been through the terrorist grind for several years. Similarly, Motiur Rehman has alo been termed as Chief operational commander of the LeJ by the US Treasury Department. Both of them were designated as global terrorists by the US Treasury Department.[26]

Recruitment/Training/Strength

While most reports say that the strength of the LeJ is about 300, Pakistan security analyst, Hassan Abbas, puts the figure at around 1,000.[27] Majority of its cadre are drawn from numerous Sunni madrassas in Pakistan.

When the LeJ was banned by the Pakistan government in 2001, most of its members sought refuge in Afghanistan. A 4 March 1999 report in a leading Pakistani daily, *The News International*, said that 800 Pakistanis were getting training at Khalid Bin Walid camp run by HuA in Afghanistan and majority of them belonged to SSP and LeJ.[28] The camp gave military training for four to eight weeks in activities that ranged from handling of sophisticated small arms to preparation and handling of explosives and hit-and-run tactics.[29] The trainees were made tough jihadis imbued with Islamist ideology before they were assigned terror mission. "Die rather than get caught (by security forces)"—was the message drilled into their ears.[30] Suicide attacks remain one of the most favoured weapons in the LeJ armoury.

The LeJ has a considerable number of women cadres. They are trained as human bombs. Islamic Movement of Uzbekistan (IMU) has deputed a woman instructor to train these women jihadis.[31]

The LeJ cadres generally wear police or military uniform while going out for a strike. The "uniform" helps them to gain easy access to mosques and places under security blanket.

Following the ouster of Taliban from Afghanistan, LeJ set up its base in North Waziristan. In 2005, it shifted its leadership and operations base from North Waziristan to Muride (Sheikhupura) and Kabirwal in Khanewal district of Punjab.[32] In addition, the group has also set up several residential and training camps in the remote Mastung area of Baluchistan, from where they have been targeting Hazara community and buses carrying Shia pilgrims to holy sites in Iran.[33]

Area of Operations

The LeJ has spread its tentacles in Punjab, Sindh, Baluchistan, Khyber Pakhtunkhwa (KP) and Gilgit–Baltistan. Jhang, Bahawalpur, Khanewal, Multan, Gujranawala, Sahiwal, Sargodha, Bhakkar, Rahim Yar Khan, Layyah, Rawalpindi, Islamabad and Lahore in Punjab. In neighbouring Sindh, it has brought Karachi, Hyderabad and Sukkur under its sway. Quetta and Mastung have become LeJ turf in Baluchistan, while Dera Ismail Khan, Bannu, Kohat, Hangu and Chitral in KP, Kurram, Parachinar, Bajaur, South Waziristan and North Waziristan in Federally Administered Tribal Area (FATA) and Gilgit in Gilgit–Baltistan are experiencing the brunt of LeJ's brand of terrorism.

Pakistan's commercial capital, Karachi, tasted LeJ's muscle power in December 2012, when it forced the closure of the entire city in protest against the killing of its activist by a rival sect. It did not acquire this grip over Karachi overnight.

The LeT deepened its roots in the city with state patronage during the regimes of General Zia-ul-Haq and General Pervez Musharraf. There was a design behind letting LeJ spread its wings in Karachi, which is traditionally the home turf of Mohajirs, who are led by London-based Altaf Hussain. While LeJ became an instrument to checkmate the Mohajir party, Muttahida Quami Movement (MQM), and the Pakhtuns, who migrated to the city to escape Taliban, most political parties cashed in on its vote bank in many areas of central and south Punjab to win parliamentary seats.[34]

Network—Local, Regional and Global

The LeJ consists of eight loosely coordinated cells spread across Pakistan with "independent" chiefs heading each cell. No one member is aware of 'full picture' and information is shared on a need-to-know basis as every operation is carried out in strict secrecy. The LeJ's biggest cell is in Karachi. It is named "Jundullah". North Waziristan cell is called Asian Tigers. It is dominated by Punjabi cadres, though cadres some from Mehsud tribe have also been welcomed into its fold.

After troops stormed the Lal Masjid (Red Mosque) and its affiliated seminary, Jamia Hafsa, in Islamabad in July 2007, the LeJ formed Jundul Hafsa with the aim to take revenge against the Musharraf regime. It is led by a former Lal Masjid student, Maulana Niaz Rahim. This group works in close coordination with Ghazi Force, a network named after one of the two clerics of Lal Masjid, Maulana Abdul Rasheed Ghazi, who was killed in the operation. It operates in the Ghaljo area of the Orakzai Agency and the adjacent Hangu district and targets military installations and personnel in parts of KP and north Punjab, especially Islamabad.

Another cell is Punjabi Taliban under which small cells operate, including those belonging to Usman Punjabi, Qari Imran, Amjad Farooqi and Qari Zafar. These cells generally pick targets in Punjab.[35]

In Baluchistan, Usman Kurd and his deputy, Dawood Badni, have created a reign of terror amongst the Shia Hazaras. Both of them were sentenced to death on 8 November 2003 for masterminding two terrorist attacks in Quetta that killed 65 people, but they managed to escape from the Quetta prison in 2008.[36]

Dawood Badni is the nephew of Al Qaeda's former number three, Khalid Sheikh Mohammad, and the brother-in-law of Ramzi Yousuf, the mastermind of the 1993 terror attack on the World Trade Center in New York. Ramzi was arrested from a guest house in Islamabad in 1995. He is believed to have been extradited to the US,[37] though both Islamabad and Washington are tight-lipped.

Baluchistan also has a local LeJ group. It consists of Baluchis and is known as Baloch Musalah Difaa Tanzeem. This group is now regarded as the de facto cell of the LeJ in Baluchistan as it targets both Baluch nationalists and Shias.[38]

The LeJ has an international wing too. Known as Lashkar-e-Jhangvi al-Almi, it is headed by Maulana Abdul Khalil, a fugitive from central Punjab. Its focus is mostly central Punjab and the tribal areas as its activists are used by Al Qaeda as foot soldiers for Arab-dominated terror group's plots inside Pakistan.[39] It is this outfit which had carried out the massacre of more than 50 Shia worshippers in the Afghan capital on 6 December 2011. The group has also claimed responsibility for killing 29 Shia on a pilgrimage to Iran from Baluchistan and also, the 2009 attack on Ashura procession in Karachi.

Lashkar-e-Jhangvi al-Almi's hand was visible in the kidnapping of two former Inter Services Intelligence (ISI) sleuths, Colonel Imam and Khalid Khwaja, along with a British journalist, Asad Qureshi, who had gone to North Waziristan to produce a film for Channel 4.[40] Most of its cadres are also involved in Pakistan's proxy war in Kashmir.[41] Operation Kashmir fits into its objective, so it embarked on this journey "by starting to murder Kashmiri Shia leaders before targeting the Indian security forces".[42]

The LeJ has an active spokesperson who is always ready with a byte. He gets in touch with the media with lightening speed after every mission of abduction or kidnapping. He reaches journalists on phone and through fax.

The LeJ has a presence on social networking sites like Twitter, Facebook and YouTube. It has dedicated websites and print magazines to carry forward its mission and to incite violence against the Shia Muslims and non-Muslims.

The LeJ's actions and justification for such actions regularly appear in its Urdu language magazine, *Inteqame Haq* (Rightful Revenge). Another Urdu magazine, *Mahnama Ablaghe Haq*, has an Internet presence at www.ableghehaq.co.cc and www.ablghehaq.com. In its special issue of September–October 2011, LeJ carried an article against Ahmediya Muslims, accusing India, Israel, Britain and the US of propping up them.[43]

The LeJ magazines and Internet portals are promoted through the Jhangvi Media Movement (JMM) website. There is also another website which contains audio–video speeches and writings against the Shiite practices. The LeJ's anti-Shia outpourings are further circulated by its Lahore-based agency, Reality Media Centre.[44]

Alliances—State and Non-State Actors

The LeJ and its parent, SSP, appeared on the scene with the blessings of the Pakistan government and its patrons to counter the growing influence of the Iranian revolution in 1979. While Pakistan intelligence and law enforcement agencies supported it as a matter of state policy, the Punjab government made a deal with it after watching its growing network.

As Punjab's Law Minister, Rana Sanaullah Khan, an associate of PML (N) supremo Nawaz Sharif, established close rapport with both SSP and LeJ. He visited Jhang where he not only paid respects at the tomb of the founder of SSP, Maulana Haq Nawaz Jhangvi, but also at the tombs of other LeJ martyrs.[45]

The LeJ was the first Punjab-based militant group to shift its members to Afghanistan during the Taliban rule to fight alongside Taliban and also, establish close ties with Al Qaeda and the IMU. As a trade-off, LeJ helped Al Qaeda leadership to sneak into Pakistan and provided them with false passports, tickets and money when needed. Because of LeJ backup, Sheikh Ahmed Saleem (who was involved in planning the East Africa bombings) was able to smuggle Al Qaeda gold out of Afghanistan.[46]

The LeJ is also closely associated with Afghan Taliban. Its members have joined the fighting against the Northern Alliance; they were also active in the brutal murder of Shias during the Taliban rule in Afghanistan.[47]

The LeJ seems to be backbone of the TTP; its militants are involved with TTP operations targeting Pakistani authorities. In one such suicide operation led by Dr Aqeel alias Mohammad Usman, they stormed the GHQ building in Rawalpindi on 10 October 2009 and made hostage 42 people, including military officials.[48]

Significantly, many senior TTP leaders, including the late head of lethal suicide training squad and a cousin of Hakimullah Mehsud, Qari Hussain Mehsud, and the TTP's current spokesman, Ehsanullah Ehsan, were once members of LeJ.[49] The LeJ has also come to maintain linkages with Harkat-ul-Jihad-al-Islami (HuJI), HuA (and its later avatar, HuM), Lashkar-e-Taiba (LeT) and JeM.[50]

The LeJ and its affiliates are said to be providing crucial technical help and manpower to the dreaded Haqqani Network and other terrorist groups operating out of Pakistan's tribal belt.[51] However, there is no independent corroboration of LeJ's links with Haqqani Network.

Funding Sources

A primary source of financial support to LeJ and SSP is Pakistan government. Gulf Arab states, particularly Saudi Arabia, fund it liberally in order to counter the rising influence of Iran's revolutionary Shiism. To keep a check on the LeJ, these funds are routed through Pakistan military and the ISI.[52]

There is also some private funding from the Gulf region. Extortion and protection money, as also narcotics trade, are the other key sources of money flow into the LeJ war chest.

According to terrorism experts, the state financing is used to build and open Wahabi and Deobandi madrassas from where its cadres are drawn.[53]

Weapons in Possession

The LeJ has specialised in suicide attacks. It has an array of assault rifles, Kalashnikovs, rocket launchers, hand grenades, light machine guns, revolvers, landmines and other explosives. According to an expert in its initial days, LeJ squads used to fire from motorcycles. Later, they adapted to timer devices. Soon, they graduated to throwing hand grenades and targeted machine gun fire. Their new tactics combined the use of hand grenades to create panic and automatic fire to eliminate those who tried to escape.[54]

Another terrorist expert, Daud Khattak, observes that the release of Malik Ishaq in July 2011 gave an unprecedented spurt to LeJ attacks on Shias in Pakistan. In some of these attacks, the LeJ employed new tactics like stopping passenger buses, screening them for Shia passengers and killing all those identified as Shias. One such targeted Shia killing took place in Baluchistan in September 2011 when 26 Shia pilgrims travelling to religious places in Iran were killed. Likewise, in August of 2002, LeJ shot dead 25 Shia bus passengers in Gilgit–Baltistan.[55]

In August 2002, Pakistan law enforcement agencies raided three safe heavens of LeJ in Karachi and seized chemicals and equipments stored for preparing poisonous vapours.[56] Initial suspicion centred on LeJ but focus soon shifted to Al Qaeda, which is closely associated with the Sunni outfit and had moved its chemical stores and shipments of gold from Afghanistan to re-establish operations in Pakistan.[57] Pakistan investigators concluded that LeJ members were not yet expert enough to have maintained cyanide and other toxic chemicals found in the laboratories.

Current Status

The LeJ remains one of the deadliest sectarian organisations in Pakistan. Right from its formation, it has carried out high-profile terrorist attacks. In addition to attacking the Shias, Ahmediyas and Barelvis, bureaucrats and policemen, the group is reportedly behind a number of attacks on Western targets in Pakistan. As mentioned earlier, the group is also linked to 2009 attack on Sri Lankan cricket team in Lahore and also, its militants have been involved with TTP operation targeting Pakistan Army GHQ building in Rawalpindi. Early this year, the LeJ militants carried out two deadly attacks in Quetta, killing nearly 200 people, a majority of them Hazara Shias. The LeJ wants to expel Shias who make up 20 per cent of Pakistan population and call them the "greatest infidels on earth".

The organisation has spread its network to all major towns of Pakistan and even in some regions of FATA and Gilgit in Gilgit–Baltistan. This has been due to blessings of the regimes of General Zia-ul-Haq and General Pervez Musharraf. Apart from the support of intelligence agencies, the courts too have failed to award sentences to LeJ leaders as judges face threats and cases became weak following the threatening calls to or even murders of witnesses and their relatives. Its chief, Malik Ishaq, spent 14 years in jail after being charged with 34 counts of culpable homicide and terrorism. However, he was released in July 2011. Interestingly, he had been issuing instructions from jail to his cadres. Even the state government has been giving financial help to Ishaq during the period he was in jail with the aim to ensure peace in the state. This is the reason that most of the political parties were depended on its vote bank in central and south Punjab. During the recent elections to the national and provincial assemblies, PML (N) tied up with its parent organisaion, SSP, which is now called Ahle-Sunnat-Wal-Jamaat (ASWJ).

There is no doubt that PML (N), led by Prime Minister Nawaz Sharif, has so far not openly condemned the LeJ. It is likely that for some time, LeJ will keep a low profile. But if the LeJ tries to disturb peace, Nawaz Sharif is likely to curb the activities of this sectarian outfit as he has the support of the masses.

NOTES

1. See Daud Khattak, "A Profile of Lashkar-e-Jhangvi Leader Malik Ishaque", 14 January 2013, available at http://www.ctc.usma.edu/posts/a-profile-of-lashkar-i-jhangvi-leader-malik-ishaq (accessed on 15 January 2013).
2. See B. Raman, "Sectarian Roots Branching Out", *Outlook*, 2 July 2002, available at http://www.outlookindia.com/article.aspx?216325 (accessed on 2 July 2012).
3. See Muhammad Amir Rana, *A to Z of Jihadi Organisations in Pakistan*, Lahore: Mashal Publication, 2004, p. 204.
4. See Nasir Jamal, "Jhang: The War Diaries", *The Herald*, May 2012, p. 52.
5. See Rana, *A to Z of Jihadi Organisations in Pakistan*, p. 205.
6. See Raman, "Sectarian Roots Branching Out".
7. See Azmat Abbas, "Lashkar's Big Split", *The Herald*, August 2001, pp. 60–61.
8. See M. Ilyas Khan, "Formidable Power of Pakistan's Anti-Shia Militants", *BBC News*, 12 January 2013, available at http://www.bbc.co.uk/news/world-asia-20983153 (accessed on 15 January 2013).
9. See Amir Mir, "Quetta Carnage was Avoidable had Kurd been Nabbed", *The News*, 19 February 2013, available at http://www.thenews.com.pk/Todays-News-13-21062-Quetta-carnage-was-avoidable-had-Kurd-been-nabbed (accessed on 20 February 2013).
10. See Niamatullah Ibrahimi, "Blood in the Streets: Quetta's Hazara Massacres", *Foreign Policy*, 5 March 2013, available at http://afpak.foreignpolicy.com/posts/2013/02/22/blood_in_the_streets_quettas_hazara_massacres (accessed on 10 May 2013).
11. Ibid.
12. For details, see the United Kingdom (UK) Home Office, "List of Proscribed International Terrorist Groups", available at http://www.homeoffice.gov.uk/publications/../terror-groups_proscribed.
13. See Amir Mir, "Pakistan Taliban Shift Focus to Afghanistan", *Asia Times*, 13 December 2011, http://www.atimes.com/atimes/South_Asia/ML13Df01.html (accessed on 12 November 2012).
14. Hazaras, who make up about a half-million strong community in Quetta, originally migrated to Pakistan from Afghanistan. They speak Persian and can easily be recognised because of their similar facial structure to the Mongols.
15. See "What an Open Letter from a Terrorist Group Looks Like", *Asia Times*, 10 June 2010, available at http://www.atimes.com/atimes/South_Asia/ML13Df01.htmlhttp://www.hazarapeople.com/2011/06/11/what-an-open-letter-from-a-terrorist-group-looks-like/ (accessed on 18 October 2012).
16. See Amir Mir, "Lashkar-e-Jhangvi Warns of Attack on Quetta Jail", *The News*, 20 February

2013, available at http://www.thenews.com.pk/Todays-News-13-21083 (accessed on 20 February 2013).

17. Ibid. Alamdar Road, Mehrabad and Hazara Town are the Hazara enclaves in Quetta in Baluchistan.
18. See "Lashkar-e-Jhangvi", *Global Jihad*, available at http:www.globaljihad.net/view_page.asp?id=1436 (accessed on 29 January 2013).
19. See Animesh Roul, "Lashkar-e-Jhangvi: Sectarian Violence in Pakistan and Ties to International Terrorism", *Terrorism Monitor*, Vol. 3, No. 11, June 2005, available at http://www.jamestown.org/single/?no_cache=1&tx_ttnews%5Btt_news%5D=497 (accessed on 12 December 2012).
20. See Shahzad Malik, "Asif Chotto Arrested", *Daily Times*, 29 September 2005, available at http://www.dailytimes.com.pk/default.asp?page=story_29-9-2005_pg1_4 (accessed on 25 December 2012).
21. See Asad Kharal, "Qari Zafar's Death a Lethal Blow to TTP, Qaeda", *Daily Times*, 3 March 2010, available at http://www.dailytimes.com.pk/default.asp?page=2010%5C03%5C03%5Cstory_3-3-2010_pg7_40 (accessed on 27 November 2012).
22. See Amir Mir, "Punjab Govt May Not Act against LeJ", *The News*, 22 February 2013, available at http://www.thenews.com.pk/Todays-News-13-21114-Punjab-govt-may-not-act-against-LeJ-PML-N-has-seat-adjustments-with-defunct-SSP (accessed on 12 July 2013).
23. See "Pakistan Arrests Banned LeJ Leader Malik Ishaq", *Dawn*, 30 August 2012, available at http://dawn.com/2012/08/30/lej-chief-malik-ishaq-arrested-in-lahore/ (accessed on 28 September 2012).
24. See "Lashkar-e-Jhangvi Chief Wielded Clout in jail; Helped Pak Army", *Hindustan Times*, 16 July 2011, available at http://www.hindustantimes.com/world-news/Pakistan/Lashkar-e-Jhangvi-chief-wielded-clout-in-jail-helped-Pak-army/Article1-721920.aspx (accessed on 2 November 2012).
25. See Khaled Ahmed, "A Most Dangerous Man", *Newsweek*, 29 July 2011, available at http://newsweekpakistan.com/the-take/365 (accessed on 22 December 2012).
26. For details see Bill Roggio, "US Designates Pakistan Based Leaders of Lashkar-e-Jhangvi, Jaish-e-Mohammad as Terrorists", *Long War Journal*, 2 December 2010, available at http://www.longwarjournal.org/archives/2010/12/us_designates_pakist.php (accessed on 22 October 2012).
27. See Hassan Abbas, "Defining the Punjabi Taliban Network", *CTC Sentinel*, 15 April 2009, available at http://www.ctc.usma.edu/posts/defining-the-punjabi-taliban-network, (accessed on 22 October 2012).
28. See The News International, 4 March, 1999 as cited in Ashok Behuria, "Many Pakistans within Pakistan: The Case of Sectarian Conflicts in a Talibanised Context", Omprakash Mishra and Sucheta Ghosh, editors, Terrorism and Low Intensity Conflict in South Asian Region, Manak Publications, New Delhi, 2003
29. For details, see http:/www.unhcr.org/refworld/country,,IRBC,COUNTRYREP,PAK,,PAK,,3ae6a8248,html.
30. See Zahid Hussain, *Frontline Pakistan: The Struggle with Militant Islam*, New York: Columbia University Press, 2007, p. 95.
31. See Roul, "Lashkar-e-Jhangvi: Sectarian Violence in Pakistan and Ties to International Terrorism".
32. See Raman, "Sectarian Roots Branching Out".
33. See Khan, "Formidable Power of Pakistan's Anti-Shia Militants".
34. Ibid.
35. See Zia Khan, "The Fision of Lashkar-e-Jhangvi", *The Express Tribune*, 17 November 2010, available at http://tribune.com.pk/story/78500/the-fission-of-lashkar-e-jhangvi (accessed on

14 November 2012).

36. See Mir, "Quetta Carnage was Avoidable had Kurd been Nabbed".
37. Ibid.
38. See Syed Shoaib Hasan, "Nationaslism, Religion a Deadly Mix in Balochistan", *Dawn*, 15 January 2013, available at http://dawn.com/2013/01/15/nationalism-religion-a-deadly-mix-in-balochistan/ (accessed on 28 January 2013).
39. See Khan, "The Fision of Lashkar-e-Jhangvi".
40. See Roggio, "US Designates Pakistan Based Leaders of Lashkar-e-Jhangvi, Jaish-e-Mohammad as Terrorists".
41. See Hussain, *Frontline Pakistan.*
42. See Hassan Abbas, *Pakistan's Drift into Extremism: Allah, the Army and the America's War on Terror*, New York: M.E. Sharpe, 2005, p. 208.
43. Tufail Ahmed, "Using Twitter, YouTube, Facebook and other Internet Tools, Pakistani Terrorist Group Lashkar-e-Jhangvi Incites Violence against Shi'ite Muslims and Engenders Antisemitism", 21 March 2012, available at http://www.memri.org/report/en/print6208.htm (accessed on 19 December 2012).
44. Ibid.
45. See Ahmed, "A Most Dangerous Man".
46. See Ahmed Rashid, *Descent into Chaos*, cited in Mapping Military Organisations, available at http://www.stanford.edu/group/mappinhmilitants/cgi-bin/groups/view/215 (accessed on 15 November 2012).
47. See "Lashkar-e-Jhangvi", available at http://www.nationalsecurity.gov.au/agd/WWW/nationalsecurity.nsf/Page/What_Governments_are_doing_Listing_of_Terrorism_Organisations_Lashkar_I_Jhangvi (accessed on 12 September 2012).
48. See Amir Mir, "Blood Flows Freely in Pakistan", *Asia Times*, 5 October 2011, available at http://www.atimes.com/atimes/South_Asia/MJ05Df01.html (accessed on 23 November 2012).
49. See Khan, "Formidable Power of Pakistan's Anti-Shia Militants".
50. See "Lashkar-e-Jhangvi" (Note 45).
51. See Khan, "Formidable Power of Pakistan's Anti-Shia Militants".
52. See S.V.R. Nasr, "Islam, the State and the Rise of Sectarian Militancy", in Christophe Jaffrelot (ed.), *Pakistan: Nationalism without a Nation?*, New York: Zed Books Ltd, 2002, p. 92.
53. For details, see http://www.stanford.edu/group/mappingmilitants/cgi-bin/groups/view/215 (accessed on 29 November 2012).
54. See Amir Mir, *The True Face Jihadis*, Lahore: Mashal Books, 2004, p. 197.
55. See Khattak, "A Profile of Lashkar-e-Jhangvi Leader Malik Ishaque".
56. See Azmat Abbas, "Trail of Terror", *The Herald*, August 2002, p. 47.
57. See "Terrorist Organisation Profile—Lashkar-e-Jhangvi (LeJ)", available at http: //www.start.umd.edu/start/data_collections/tops/terrorist_organization_profile.asp?id=65 (accessed on 25 November 2012).

38

Jundullah of Karachi

(Army of God)

Introduction

The Jundullah, also known as Army of God, was formed in March 2003 by Sheikh Atta-ur-Rahman alias Umer alias Ebrahim alias Zubair. Atta-ur-Rahman was a prominent activist of Islami Jamiat-e-Taliba, students' wing of Jamaat-e-Islami and post graduate student of statistics in the Karachi University. One of the major reasons, as stated by Atta-ur-rahman, to form this outfit was taken after the arrest of several Al Qaeda leaders including Khalid Sheikh Mohammad-the master mind of 9/11-in March 2003.[1] The Jundullah of Karachi came to notice when it carried out an ambush on Lieutenant General Ahsan Saleem Hayat in June 2004. The attack killed 11 people, including a colonel, six soldiers and three policemen, as well as injuring many. It also carried out bomb explosion near the United States' (US) consulate in Karachi, the blast at the Pakistan-American cultural Centre, the blast outside a concert hall during Indian singer Sonu Nigam's show, the blast at Bible Society, the attack on a Police station at Gulistan-e-Jauhar and an attack on a ranger's van in Karachi. Following these attacks, law enforcement agencies swung into action and nabbed many militants but some managed to flee to Wazirstan. But they came back to Karachi in 2007–08 and resumed their terrorist activities.[2]

Objectives

This small group has not come out with a definite agenda, although its sole mission during the initial years was to target anti-state and anti-American institutions. But its main objectives appear to be: strict imposition of Sharia in Pakistan; and to wage jihad to recapture areas now occupied by the non-Muslims or what it regards as apostate Muslim regimes.

Leadership

The government came down heavily on the group after the attack on corps commander and Atta-ur-Rahman, alias Umar alias Ibrahim alias Zuber, and

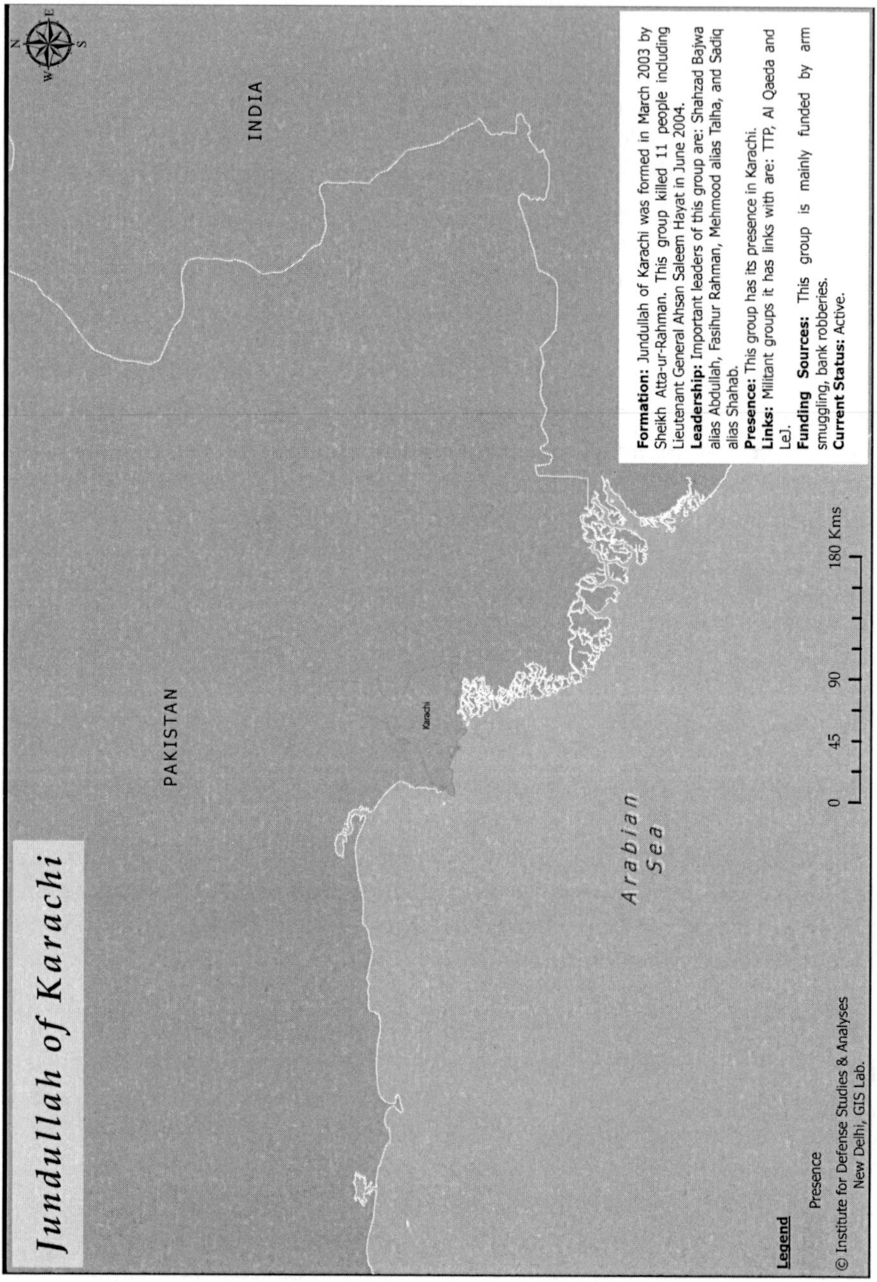
Jundullah of Karachi
INDIA
PAKISTAN
Karachi
Arabian Sea
0 45 90 180 Kms
Formation: Jundullah of Karachi was formed in March 2003 by Sheikh Atta-ur-Rahman. This group killed 11 people including Lieutenant General Ahsan Saleem Hayat in June 2004.
Leadership: Important leaders of this group are: Shahzad Bajwa alias Abdullah, Fasihur Rahman, Mehmood alias Talha, and Sadiq alias Shahab.
Presence: This group has its presence in Karachi.
Links: Militant groups it has links with are: TTP, Al Qaeda and LeJ.
Funding Sources: This group is mainly funded by arm smuggling, bank robberies.
Current Status: Active.
Legend
Presence
© Institute for Defense Studies & Analyses New Delhi, GIS Lab.

several of his associates were arrested. Rahman, who did his Master in Statistics from Karachi University, received militant training in camps reportedly run by Harkat-ul-Mujahideen. His deputy was Shahzad Bajwa alias Abdullah who was injured on 19 March 2004 during an attack on a mobile van of Pakistan Rangers. Mohammad Qasim Toori, who took over the leadership, went underground as he was also booked by the security agencies for organising and carrying out attacks on the Karachi corps commander. He was also arrested in Karachi on 29 January 2008. Both Toori and founder of the outfit were given death sentence by the anti-terrorism court. After the arrest of Toori, Hamza Joofi alias Haji Mumtaz of Al Qaeda took over the reins of the outfit along with new amir, Arif alias Raza alias Hyder. Both of them were killed during a United States (US) drone strike in August 2011. Jundullah now operates under Fasihur Rahman alias Hamid alis Adnan. According to Karachi police, Fasihur Rahman is the brain behind the group and an expert at stuffing explosives into cement blocks, which are attached to remote cellular devices. He has also been also involved in number of militant attack in Karachi.[3] Some of the prominent leaders who are absconding include Mehmood alias Talha, Sadiq alias Shahab, Rasid Khan Pathan and Shaqeeb Farooqi alias Faizan.

Cadre Strength/Camps

At the time of formation, the group consisted of about 20 youth. They were the veterans who had fought against the Soviet forces in Afghanistan. The exact strength of Jundullah of Karachi is not known but it cannot be beyond 100. There are also some women who are engaged in assisting the operations and collection of funds. The cadre largely includes residents in areas like Shah Faisal Colony, Model Colony, Landhi and Korangi in Karachi, who, inspired by Al Qaeda, decided to take to terrorist activities.[4]

The training was imparted to Hizbullah's youth after a rapport was established by Qasim Toori with Al Qaeda commander of Egyptian descent, Hamza Joofi alias Haji Mumtaz, at a training camp in Wana in South Wazirastan. The camp is being run by Syed Kashif Ali Shah alias Shaheen. Most of them are trained in small firearms and assault rifles. Some are adept at using more sophisticated weapons. It is the Waheed brothers—Dr Akmal Waheed and Dr Harshad Waheed—who have been treating the injured Jundullah militants, who were the link between Qasim Toori and Hamza Joofi. Both doctors were reportedly active Jamaat-e-Islami members and were associated with its medical wing, the Pakistan Islamic Medical Association and providing necessary treatment and shelter to Al Qaeda militants. They have been suspected of treating Osama bin Laden's kidney ailment also.[5]

Area of Operation

The Jundullah started its militant operations in Karachi immediately after its formation in 2004 by targeting law enforcers and killing several police officials. Even more, the main area of operation of this group remains certain areas of Karachi.

Alliances

The organisation has links with Tehrik-e-Taliban Pakistan (TTP) and Al Qaeda. The TTP, however, has denied its links with the Jundullah of Karachi. There is another faction of Jundullah which is headed by Shakaib Farooqi and has links with Karachi-based Lashkar-e-Jhangvi group led by Naeem Bokhari. It has, however, no connection with Jundullah which is fighting against the Iranian regime.

Funding/Weapons in Possession

The Jundullah of Karachi, initially, raised its funds mainly through bank robberies and kidnapping for ransom. Part of the looted amount was sent to Al Qaeda commander, Hamza Joofi, who was procuring arms for the outfit through a smuggler, Yaqoob Khan, based in Wana in South Wazirstan. The first consignment of arms was procured through the head of Landhi unit in Karachi of Muttahida Qaumi Movement–Haqqani group. It is in possession of pistols, all types of rifles, grenades, explosives and modern communication system.

Current Status

There is no doubt that activities of the group have gone down considerably. It could be due to the arrest of number of its leaders and cadres. Moreover, the group has not been able to generate funds through bank robberies due to constant surveillance by the security agencies. It is likely that the group may surface again and carry out surprise attacks as the security agencies have not been able to arrest any of the senior leaders in the new cadre due to lack of details about their current operations and nexus with other militant groups such as Al Qaeda, TTP and local criminal groups.

NOTES

1. See Ali K Chisti, "Jundullah, the new al Qaeda", *The Daily Times*, 7 September, 2010, available at http://www.dailytimes.com.pk/default.asp?page=2010%5C09%5C07%5Cstory_7-9-2010_pg7_25, (accessed on 22 December 2012)
2. See Salis bin Perwaiz, "Five Jundullah Suspects Held", *The News*, 30 November 2011, available at http://www.thenews.com.pk/Todays-News-4-80006-Five-Jundullah-suspects-held (accessed on 22 December 2012).
3. Ibid.
4. Ibid
5. See Ali K. Chishti, *op. cit.*, n 1.

39

Jundullah

(Allah's Soldiers or Army)

Introduction

Jundullah (Soldiers of Allah or Allah's Army) was formed in the mid-1990s, by Nek Mohammad Wazir, as a reaction to the Iranian government's execution of some Baluch activists. However, it came into prominence in 2003 under the leadership of Abdolmalek Rigi.

Abdolmalek Rigi studied at Binori madrassa in Karachi and a madrassa in Mashkel, Baluchistan, and had been living in Quetta and Karachi for many years. He was believed to have developed links with Afghan and Pakistani militants, and also Baluchis living near the border.

Jundullah, which also calls itself People's Resistance Movement of Iran (PRMI), is accused of killing over 400 Iranian soldiers since its formation. The group has been designated a terrorist organisation by Iran, Pakistan and the United States (US). It may be noted that Jundullah is a Baluch insurgent group and should not be confused with Jundullah operating in Karachi which has links with Tehrik-e-Taliban Pakistan (TTP) and Al Qaeda.

The Iranian authorities have accused Jundullah of carrying out numerous bombings, assassination attempts, kidnappings and terrorist attacks against high-profile Iranian targets, especially government and security officials.

Objective

Jundullah claims to be fighting for the rights of Iran's roughly 4 million Baluchis in Iranian-controlled Baluchistan, known as Sistan–Baluchistan, who are subjected to economic and cultural discrimination. Iran accuses it of being a US proxy, an allegation denied by the US and the group. The Iranian government has accused the outfit of attempting to separate Sistan–Baluchistan from Iran and has also alleged that it is operating from Pakistan area of Baluchistan.

Cadre—Strength, Profile and Training

The first batch of Jundullah militants comprised of 20–30 Pakistani and Iranian

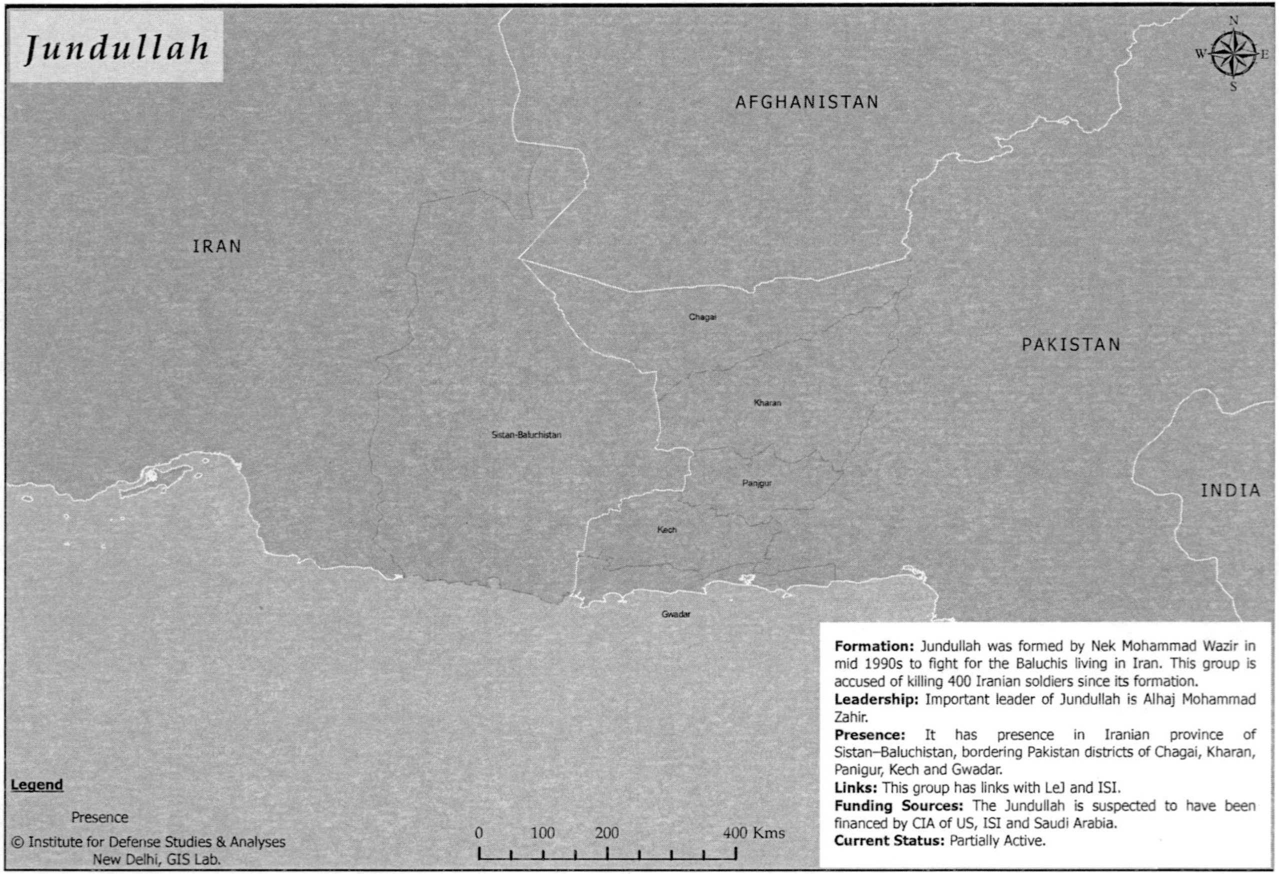
Jundullah
AFGHANISTAN
IRAN
PAKISTAN
INDIA
Chagai
Kharan
Sistan-Baluchistan
Panjgur
Kech
Gwadar
N
W
E
S
Legend
Presence
© Institute for Defense Studies & Analyses
New Delhi, GIS Lab.
0 100 200 400 Kms
Formation: Jundullah was formed by Nek Mohammad Wazir in mid 1990s to fight for the Baluchis living in Iran. This group is accused of killing 400 Iranian soldiers since its formation.
Leadership: Important leader of Jundullah is Alhaj Mohammad Zahir.
Presence: It has presence in Iranian province of Sistan–Baluchistan, bordering Pakistan districts of Chagai, Kharan, Panigur, Kech and Gwadar.
Links: This group has links with LeJ and ISI.
Funding Sources: The Jundullah is suspected to have been financed by CIA of US, ISI and Saudi Arabia.
Current Status: Partially Active.

Sunni youth. Jundullah was funded by Iranian drug traffickers. Its private strength is more than 1,000, out of which 200 are positioned on the Iran–Pakistan border. Jundullah also enjoys the support of anti-Shia Pakistani outfits such as Lashkar-e-Jhangvi (LeJ). A report claimed that the US had struck a deal with Jundullah leaders and the group's newly inducted recruits were allowed to receive training in camps located on Afghanistan–Pakistan border.[1]

Area of Operation/Influence

In the initial years of its formation, Jundullah operated in the Iranian province of Sistan–Baluchistan, bordering Pakistan districts of Chagai, Kharan, Panigur, Kech and Gwadar. The group started by targeting important state presence in Sistan–Baluchistan province, particularly the elite Iranian Revolutionary Guards, and later carried out suicide attacks against the civilian targets. Jundullah was also suspected to be involved in the kidnapping of an Iranian diplomat in Peshawar in November 2008. On 10 August 2007, the group had abducted 21 Iranian doctors and taken them to Pakistan, where they were set free by Pakistani security forces. It may be mentioned that the Jundullah had threatened that it would not allow the gas pipelines if built from Iran to Pakistan.

Leadership

The arrest of Jundullah's leader, Abdolmalek Rigi, in a covert operation by Iranian intelligence on 23 February 2010 and the earlier (2009) capture of his brother, Abdolhamid Rigi, and several Jundullah operatives dealt a serious blow to the outfit. After the arrest of Abdolmalek Rigi on 23 February 2010, his brother, Abdul Rauf Rigi, took over the command, but he was also arrested along with eight Jundullah militants in the bordering Turbat region. Some experts also claim Alhaj Mohammad Zahir as the new leader of the outfit. Zahir is unknown figure outside Jundullah and there is no available information about his background and whereabouts. There is no further information on other important leaders of the outfit.

Finance and Funding

There have been numerous reports[2] in the world media, particularly in the US, that Rigi was being financed by the Central Intelligence Agency (CIA) to destablise Iranian regime as a counterweight to Iran's interference in Iraq. During the Bush administration, there were allegation by the investigative journalist, Seymour Hresh, that CIA was supporting Iran's Baluchis, Kurdish and Arab minorities, and that some of the $400 million funds allegedly earmarked by Washington to help bring a regional change in Iran were going to Jundullah. As cited by *The Herald*, a documentary released by the ABC News also disclosed that the US encourages, supports and perhaps even finances the group to conduct terror raids inside Iran.[3] One of the media reports disclosed that some tribal leaders close to Jundullah leaders also admit that the outfit enjoyed good relations with the US and receives funds for new recruitments and logistical support.[4] They also said that US officials had made secret visits to border areas to monitor Jundullah's activities. ABC News added that funds were funnelled to Abdolmalek Rigi through Iranian expatriates settled in Europe and the Gulf states. According to the BBC, besides the US, the United Kingdom (UK), Pakistan, Saudi Arabia and militant groups such as Taliban and Al Qaeda are reportedly supporting the outfit.[5]

Alliances

The list of powers alleged to be supporting Jundullah includes the US, the UK, Saudi Arabia and militant groups such as Taliban, Al Qaeda and Mujahideen-e-Khalq. According the BBC report, the Iranians also suspect that covert support for the Jundullah is coming from Inter Services Intelligence (ISI). There are also unconfirmed reports that Abdolmalek Rigi had developed links with Afghan and Pakistani militants. This was revealed when Pakistan police conducted a raid on a safe house in January 2008 in its efforts to search for the Iranian diplomat who was kidnapped from Peshawar. During the course of search operation, the police captured several cadres of TTP and LeJ. Jundullah is also reportedly involved in narcotics smuggling across the border.

Weapons in Possession

Jundullah is in possession of AK-47 assault rifles, hand grenades, anti-aircraft guns and large quantity of explosives and sophisticated equipment to carry out attacks.

Current Status

Jundullah as a militant group has been weak as many of its front-line leaders have either been killed or have been arrested. At the same time, it will be wrong to say that Jundullah has perished as a militant group.

NOTES

1. See Shahzada Zulfiqar, "New Pawn, Old Game", *The Herald*, Karachi, May 2007, p. 59.
2. For details see "Rigi planned to meet Holbrooke in Kyrgyzstan", *The Press TV*, 28 February 2010, available at http://www.presstv.ir/detail/119672.html, (accessed on 22 December 2012) Also See "Ex-CIA agent confirms US ties with Jundullah", *The Press TV*, 24 October 2009, available at http://www.presstv.com/detail/109453.html, (accessed on 22 December 2012)
3. See the *ABC News*, cited in ibid., p. 59.
4. Ibid., p. 58.
5. See Roger Hardy, "Profile: Iran's Jundullah Militants", available at http://news.bbc.co.uk/2/hi/middle_east/8314431.stm (accessed on 5 February 2012).

PART-D
SOUTH ASIA

40

Hizb-ut-Tahrir
(Party of Liberation)

Introduction

Hizb-ut-Tahrir (HuT) (Party of Liberation) is a radical Islamist group. It calls for the return of Caliphate in the Muslim world with a view to uniting the Muslim ummah. The HuT was founded in Jerusalem in 1953 by Sheikh Taquiddin al-Nabhani, a Palestinian radical activist. Some important leaders of the HuT who were associated with the setting up of the organisation were Khalid Hassan and Asad Tahmimi.

It has a presence in 50 countries, including the United Kingdom (UK), Germany, the Middle East countries, Central Asia, Pakistan, Bangladesh and some South East countries. The party is, however, banned by more than 20 countries of the Middle East, Central Asia, Pakistan and Bangladesh. In South Asia, the HuT is active mainly in Pakistan and Bangladesh. The HuT spread into other countries after the death of al-Nabhani in Beirut in 1977.

Objectives

The HuT basically aims at the establishment of an Islamic state where all aspects of the human life would be guided by Sharia. The establishment of the Islamic state, according to the HuT, would be through three stages. In the first stage, the organisation would educate and indoctrinate its ideology to common people; in the second stage, it would focus on spreading its ideas among the people who hold power in the government, military and civil services; and in the third stage, it would proceed to establish the Islamic state. The Islamic state, according to the HuT, would be ruled by a Caliph or Khalifah. The caliph would appoint the amir and the military head who would lead the jihad activities against the non-Muslims. Although HuT advocates a strict interpretation of Islam, it does not oppose modern technology and makes extensive use of Internet to spread the message.

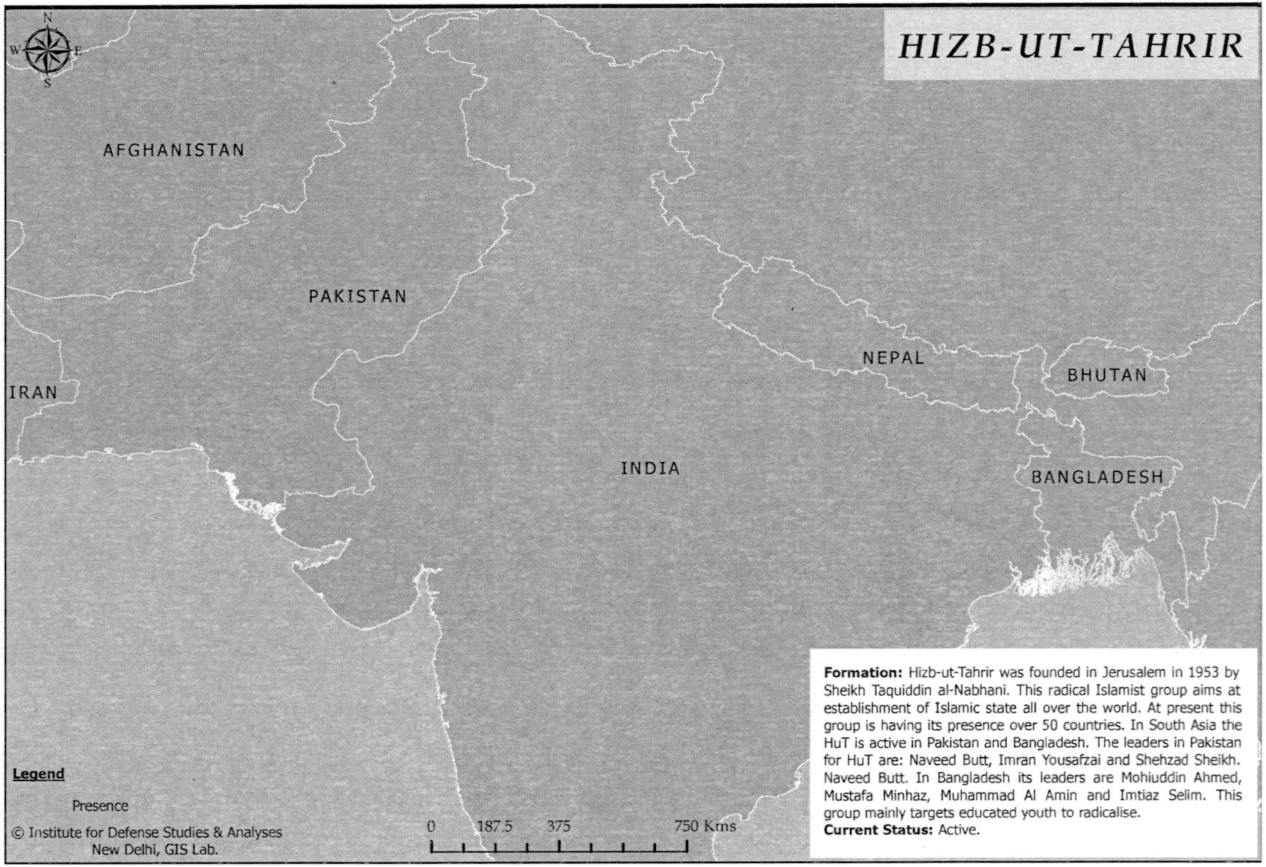
HIZB-UT-TAHRIR
N
W
E
S
AFGHANISTAN
PAKISTAN
IRAN
INDIA
NEPAL
BHUTAN
BANGLADESH
Formation: Hizb-ut-Tahrir was founded in Jerusalem in 1953 by Sheikh Taquiddin al-Nabhani. This radical Islamist group aims at establishment of Islamic state all over the world. At present this group is having its presence over 50 countries. In South Asia the HuT is active in Pakistan and Bangladesh. The leaders in Pakistan for HuT are: Naveed Butt, Imran Yousafzai and Shehzad Sheikh. Naveed Butt. In Bangladesh its leaders are Mohiuddin Ahmed, Mustafa Minhaz, Muhammad Al Amin and Imtiaz Selim. This group mainly targets educated youth to radicalise.
Current Status: Active.
Legend
Presence
© Institute for Defense Studies & Analyses
New Delhi, GIS Lab.
0 187.5 375 750 Kms

Leadership

Not all the leaders are allowed to reveal their identity. Hence, the group is organised in small cells of five to six members. Following the death of HuT's founder, al-Nabhani, in Beirut in 1977, HuT spread to many countries: first, under the leadership of Abdul Qadri Zallum till 2003; and then, under Ata Khalil Abu Rishta,[1] the present global leader.

In the UK, which is the hub of its activities, the HuT is led by Imran Waheed who remains active in organising seminars/conferences on the return of Islamic Khilafat in the Muslim world.

Prominent leaders of the Pakistan chapter are Naveed Butt, Imran Yousafzai and Shehzad Sheikh. Naveed Butt, who hails from Islamabad, did his degree in electrical and computer science from University of Illinois at Chicago and has been the media spokesman for HuT in Pakistan.

In Bangladesh, it is headed by Mohiuddin Ahmed, a lecturer at the Institute of Business Administration, Dhaka. Other prominent leaders are Mustafa Minhaz, media and promotion secretary and a lecturer at the University of Asia Pacific; Muhammad Al Amin, student's representative at Dhaka University; and Imtiaz Selim, who heads HuT's activities in the private universities.

The Indonesian chapter is headed by Muhammad Al Khaththath. The group's spokesperson is Muhammad Ismail Yusanto.

Cadre—Strength, Profile and Training

The structure of HuT makes it more difficult to estimate the real number of its members and its sympathisers. In each cell, there are three to seven people headed by a leader. The structure makes impossible for state officials to reveal the followers, leaders and activities of the organisation. It is said that HuT has a wide base with one million members worldwide. It has a strong base in the UK. In Central Asia, HuT is numerically strongest in Uzbekistan with estimates ranging from 7,000 to 60,000. There are approximate 3,000–5,000 members in Kyrgyzstan and Tajikstan, while Kazahkistan has about 300 members. There is hardly any member in Turkistan. Its strength in Indonesia is not known but it organised an international conference on the topic, "Reviving the Caliphate", in Jakarta on 12 August 2007, which was reportedly attended by 80,000 people.[2] In Indonesia, the HuT has penetrated into the educational institutions, mostly the universities, and has sizeable followers. The HuT has also a sizeable presence in a number of Muslim countries such as Iran, Iraq, Algeria, Sudan, Yemen, Pakistan, Bangladesh and Jordan.

The HuT is good at using modern technologies in recruiting the individuals. Distribution of CDs containing jihad and radical Islam literature is one of the methods HuT follows to reach people. The HuT has a well-maintained website which contains the message, literature and other information that would serve the purpose of attracting the educated youth to the outfit. Use of communication technology has helped the HuT to reach the educated youth. The HuT, through its literature, emphasises on just social order, equality and assistance to the poor, which helps common Muslims to believe in them.

Area of Operation and Influence

As mentioned earlier, the HuT has its presence in almost 50 countries. So far the operational methods of the HuT are concerned, it has preferred to remain out of violent activities. But it has been engaged in recruiting individuals, especially the educated youth, and radicalising them. The headquarters of the HuT is in London. The HuT has its presence in Central Asia, Europe, South Asia and South East Asia, particularly Indonesia, where it has gained most influence and attention. In South Asia, the HuT is very active in Bangladesh and Pakistan. The presence of the HuT in India has not been felt yet.

Network—Local, Regional and Global

Pakistan

The HuT was established in Pakistan during the 1990s. Initially, the party workers remained underground. However, it started operating openly in 2000. Its emergence was heralded by a sudden appearance of a large number of banners and placards as well as the distribution of leaflets near the mosques of Rawalpindi, Islamabad and Lahore explaining the basis for setting up the organisation and exhorting people to join the party. Prior to 9/11, young men associated with HuT used to hold weekly sittings in Pak Tea House. Although the party claims to be working for entire ummah, it plans to select some suitable Muslim state or a number of states as the seat of Khilafat. As such, it started operating in Pakistan by declaring Pakistan as "*Wilayah*" or place suitable for the assumption of power as it considers Pakistan to be an ideal country because of its geo-strategic location and rich natural and human resources. The outfit is convinced that as a seat of Khilafat, Pakistan has the potential to unite the Muslim ummah and extend the message of Islam to the whole world.[3]

The HuT in Pakistan was banned on 11 November 2003 on charges of its links with a number of terror plots, including a plot to kill the former President of Pakistan, Pervez Musharraf. The HuT in Pakistan has been trying to penetrate into the Pakistan Army to initiate the process of establishing Khilafat state in Pakistan and asking Americans to leave the region. According to the media report, the HuT has made three attempts to penetrate into the Pakistan Army in the past 10 years. This was made clear when Brigadier Ali Khan and four other army officers were arrested for their links with the outfit.[4]

Despite a ban slapped on the HuT, the later is active in engineering plots to destablise the government and penetrate into the military and the academia. In

July 2011, the Pakistan intelligence said that the HuT was trying to create Egypt-like uprising in Pakistan.[5] The HuT cadres were arrested distributing pamphlets against America and inciting the people against the "pro-American" generals in the army.

The activities of the HuT in Pakistan have been growing from strength to strength. A mere ban has not been able to stop the HuT cadres in carrying out their activities. According to a report, the cadres of the HuT are often seen in the garrison areas of Pakistan speaking to the military personnel.[6] The HuT's modus operandi has been to try to bring the military personnel, intellectuals and the elite under one umbrella.[7]

Bangladesh

The HuT was launched in Bangladesh in November 2001 with the support of a small segment of the Bangladeshi diaspora in the UK. It was established under the leadership of Syed Golam Maola, along with Nasimul Gani and Kawsar Shahnewaz. The headquarters of the HuT Bangladesh is at Dhanmondi in Dhaka. The head of HuT Bangladesh chapter is Mohiuddin Ahmad, a teacher in Dhaka University. It is significant to note that it has not only been able to penetrate state-run universities like Dhaka University, Rajshahi University and Chittagong University but also the private universities. There are more than 50 private universities which are affiliated with Western universities. Prominent among them are North South University, Independent University, American International University Bangladesh, City University and Southeast University. Apart from the academia, the HuT in Bangladesh has also won support of the intellectuals, including doctors, teachers and lawyers.

The HuT Bangladesh was banned on 22 October 2009: "The organisation has been banned as it has been carrying out anti-state, anti-government, anti-people and anti-democratic activities for long in the country."[8] The HuT has been involved in anti-India, anti-US activities in Bangladesh. The outfit also involves itself in mobilising the public against the Sheikh Hasina regime. The HuT is also suspected to have been linked to the Bangladesh Rifles (BDR) mutiny in 2009. The security forces arrested six HuT cadres with pamphlets on the mutiny.[9] The pamphlets read:

> Oh Muslims! You have been the victims of Indian aggression for decades. The enemy state killed your officers in Pilkhana. She built the Farakkah dam, she deprives you of all your rightful share of water from the common rivers and she kills your brothers and sisters in the border. And your current rulers have failed to stand up to the Indian aggression against you. There exists only one way of resisting the enemy—establishing the Khalifah state...And we have the action plan ready to regain India as a Muslim land, under the Islamic rule, which is the only true assured way of stopping Indian aggression permanently.[10]

According to the media reports, the HuT also planned for another mutiny in 2010. According to the report, the head of the HuT Bangladesh confessed before the law enforcement agencies that the HuT tried to capitalise on the Pilkhana mutiny and distributed leaflets and tried instigating the army to engineer another mutiny.[11] Similarly, the HuT was also suspected to be a part of the foiled army coup in 2011 against Sheikh Hasina.[12]

Such incidents are indicative of the fact that the HuT in Bangladesh has penetrated into the army and other security agencies. Though there have been no instances of violent activities by the HuT, it can well be a triggering point for violence.

India

It is not known when HuT had set up its chapter in India. But according to its website, it organised demonstration on 6 June 2010 against Israel's alleged atrocities. The demonstration, which was attended by 1,000 people, was held at Batla House, New Delhi. The protestors reportedly raised slogans, such as "Patience Patience oh Yahud, the armies of Muhammad will return" and "There is no god but Allah and the rulers are the enemies of Allah".[13] No further activity of its Indian chapter has come to notice.

Apart from South Asia, the HuT is active and involved in radicalisation activities in countries such as the UK, Jordan, Lebanon, Egypt, Russia, China, Tajikistan, Indonesia and Australia.

Financial Resources

Funding for the party activities is primarily drawn from private donations and through public campaign. Most of the funding is done by its centre in London. Private donations from sympathising local entrepreneurs benefit the regional HuT branch offices, while the HuT leadership committee receives funding mostly from the businessmen and Islamic charity. It is also reported that HuT members pay 10 per cent of their income to the outfit. Besides, the HuT is funded by wealthy sheikhs from Saudi Arabia and other Gulf nations who subscribe to the group's pan-Islamic agenda. In addition, HuT members also make collections during Haj. Besides many prominent people such as Members of Parliament, affluent businessmen, government officials and army officers in the Muslim countries have been providing financial, moral and other logistical support to the HuT.

Weapons in Possession, Use and Procurement

Though the HuT is not directly involved in the militant activities, it supports both militant and terror activities. According to one member of the HuT in Central Asia, the HuT approves of the Muslims who are fighting with guns in their hands against the American aggressors.[14]

According to one source, the HuT has an armed wing called Harkat ul Muhajirin Britaniya set up by Abdulkuddum Zaiuum, a former HuT leader. This group now trains its cadres to conduct chemical, bacteriological and biological war, besides dealing with sophisticated weapons, including bombs and landmines.[15]

Current Status

As mentioned earlier, the HuT is one of the most organised and dangerous radical groups. Its presence in more than 50 countries makes itself a matter of grave concern for many countries. As the outfit is mainly targeting the educated youth and the intellectuals, and radicalising them, it has the potential to wage uprisings against governments and regimes which it thinks un-Islamic. What makes the HuT more dangerous is the way it legitimises the cause to establish a caliphate.

NOTES

1. See the detailed profile of Ata Khalil Abu Rishta at the official website of the HuT, available at http://www.hizb-ut-tahrir.info/info/english.php/category_en/categ_485.
2. For details, see "Muslims Meet in Jakarta for Pan-Islamic State Talks", *Reuters*, 12 August 2007, available at http://www.reuters.com/article/2007/08/12/us-indonesia-muslim-idUSJAK28049220070812 (accessed on 24 December 2012).
3. For details, see "Pakistan, Khilafah and the Re-unification of the Muslim World", Manifesto of Hizb ut Tahrir for Pakistan, 2013, available at http://hizb-pakistan.com/hizb/images/books/Manifesto2013.pdf, (accessed on 10 January 2013).
4. For details, see "Banned Outfit Hizbut Tahrir Made Three Attempts to Penetrate Pakistan", 30 October 2012, available at http://zeenews.india.com/news/south-asia/banned-outfit-hizbut-tahrir-made-three-attempts-to-penetrate-pakistan_808399.html (accessed on 10 January 2013).
5. See "Hizb ut-Tahrir Wanted Egypt-like Uprising in Pakistan: Report", *Deccan Herald*, 25 July 2011, available at http://www.deccanherald.com/content/178942/hizb-ut-tahrir-wanted-egypt.html (accessed on 12 January 2013).
6. See Umer Farooq, "Islam in the garrison", *The Herald*, 16 August 2011, available at http://herald.dawn.com/tag/hizbut-tahrir (accessed on 12 January 2013).
7. See Ayasha Umar, "Hizb ut-Tahrir in Pakistan", *The Newsline*, 5 August 2011, available at http://www.newslinemagazine.com/2011/08/hizb-ut-tahrir-in-pakistan/ (accessed on 12 January 2013).
8. See "Hizb ut-Tahrir Banned", *The Daily Star*, 23 October 2009, available at http://www.thedailystar.net/newDesign/news-details.php?nid=110960 (accessed on 13 January 2013).
9. See "6 'Hizb-ut' Men Arrested with Leaflets on Mutiny", available at www.bdnews24.com/details.php?id=127794&cid=2 (accessed on 13 January 2013).
10. Ibid.
11. See Mukhlesur Rahman, "Tahrir Tried to Create Another Mutiny", *The Daily Star*, 10 July 2010, available at http://www.thedailystar.net/newDesign/news-details.php?nid=146138 (accessed on 13 January 2013).
12. See Saleem Samad, "Dhaka Conspiracy: Bangladesh: Coup Bid against Sheikh Hasina Foiled", 28 January 2012, available at http://indiatoday.intoday.in/story/bangladesh-coup-bid-against-sheikh-hasina-foiled/1/170876.html (accessed on 13 January 2013).

13 . See "Be Aware of these Mischief Makers", *The Milli Gazette*, 16–30 September 2010. Also, see Josy Joseph, "Hizb ut-Tahrir, Group behind Failed Bangla Coup Plot, Growing in Stature in India", *The Times of India*, 24 January 2012, available at http://articles.timesofindia.indiatimes.com/2012-01-24/india/30659021_1_bangladesh-coup-ht-prime-minister-sheikh-hasina (accessed on 15 October 2012).

14 . See Igor Rotar, "Hizb Ut-Tahrir in Central Asia", *Terrorism Monitor*, Vol. 2, No. 4, 26 February 2004, available at http://www.jamestown.org/programs/gta/single/?tx_ttnews%5Btt_news%5D=26314&tx_ttnews%5BbackPid%5D=179&no_cache=1 (accessed on 10 January 2013).

15. See "Hizb is Violent", 6 December 2010, available at https://thehizbuttahrirwatch.wordpress.com/category/news-about-hizb-ut-tahrir/hut-america/hizb-is-violent/ (accessed on 13 January 2013).

Sociogram

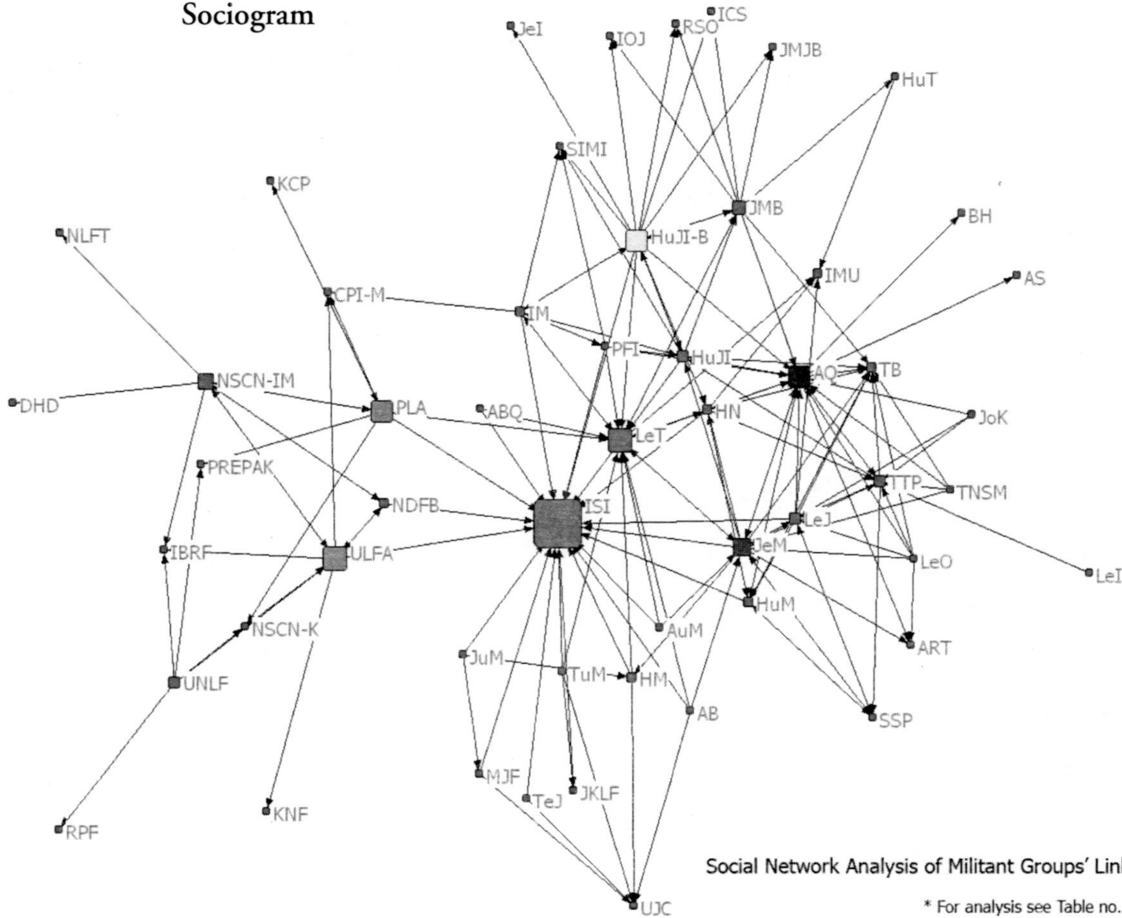

Social Network Analysis of Militant Groups' Links

* For analysis see Table no. 1.

Table 1

Multiple Centrality Measures

Node	Degree	Closeness	Betweenness	Eigenvector
LeT	27.586	14.758	14.371	43.061
AQ	29.310	14.181	11.660	47.026
JeM	25.862	14.286	8.080	45.076
ISI	36.207	14.987	35.491	43.717
TB	17.241	13.615	1.021	34.101
TTP	18.966	13.488	3.907	32.467
HuJI	18.966	14.356	3.841	38.866
HuJI-B	22.414	14.356	12.648	31.767
LeJ	17.241	14.078	4.152	30.951
HuM	10.345	13.876	1.006	22.150
HM	8.621	13.777	1.160	15.727
UJC	8.621	12.500	0.257	5.748
HN	15.517	14.251	2.273	33.850
AB	6.897	13.744	0.857	14.952
LeI	1.724	12.033	0.000	3.528
LeO	10.345	13.242	0.089	21.951
TeJ	3.448	13.272	0.266	5.375
TNSM	6.897	13.152	0.000	17.241
SSP	6.897	12.889	0.034	14.196
ST	0.000		0.000	0.000
SMP	0.000		0.000	0.000
JoK	5.172	13.034	0.000	12.001
JMB	17.241	13.876	5.418	24.245
HuT	3.448	12.473	0.091	3.955
JKLF	3.448	13.272	0.000	5.913
JuM	5.172	13.303	0.020	7.128
MJF	5.172	13.303	0.296	6.150
ABQ	3.448	13.426	0.000	9.429
TuM	6.897	13.520	0.694	10697
LJ	0.000		0.000	0.000
AuM	5.172	13.679	0.000	14.328
ULFA	13.793	13.842	13.486	6.685
NSCN-IM	10.345	12.804	6.619	2.701
UNLF	8.621	12.527	3.408	1.226
PLA	12.069	13.976	12.853	10.666
NDFB	5.172	13.615	1.543	5.770

(*Contd.*)

Node	Degree	Closeness	Betweenness	Eigenvector
CPI-M	5.172	13.063	0.466	4.205
IM	12.069	13.909	2.076	21.350
PFI	10.345	13.909	0.858	22.434
AU	0.000		0.000	-0.000
ART	5.172	13.093	0.000	12.393
IMU	6.897	13.395	1.167	12.150
AS	1.724	12.581	0.000	5.110
BH	1.724	12.581	0.000	5.110
SIMI	6.897	13.004	0.047	12.433
JoI	0.000		0.000	0.000
JeI	1.724	12.719	0.000	3.452
RSO	3.448	12.804	0.000	6.086
ICS	3.448	12.804	0.000	6.086
JMJB	3.448	12.804	0.000	6.086
IOJ	3.448	12.804	0.000	6.086
NLFT	1.724	11.485	0.000	0.294
DHD	1.724	11.485	0.000	0.294
PREPAK	3.448	12.609	0.270	1.292
KCP	1.724	12.420	0.000	1.159
RPF	1.724	11.262	0.000	0.133
NSCN-K	5.172	12.691	0.331	2.019
IBRF	5.172	12.527	0.181	1.153
KNF	1.724	12.314	0.000	0.726

* This Analysis is based on the information on Militant Groups given in the book.

Index